To Barry

Hope all is going well in the garden
but if not ... here are some words of
wisdom.

Love to You
Linda & Rally
1997

LET'S GET GROWING

A DIRT-UNDER-THE-NAILS PRIMER ON RAISING VEGETABLES, FRUITS AND FLOWERS ORGANICALLY

CROW MILLER

Rodale Press, Inc.
Emmaus, Pennsylvania

OUR MISSION

We publish books that empower people's lives.

RODALE BOOKS

Printed in the United States of America on acid-free ∞, recycled ♻ paper, containing 20 percent post-consumer waste

Library of Congress Cataloging-in-Publication Data
Miller, Crow
  Let's get growing : a dirt-under-the-nails primer on raising vegetables, fruits, and flowers organically / Crow Miller.
    p. cm.
  Includes bibliographical references and index.
  ISBN 0-87596-640-3 hardcover
  1. Organic gardening I. Title
SB453.5.M55 1995
635'.0484—dc20   94-40935
                                                    CIP

Distributed in the book trade by St. Martin's Press

2 4 6 8 10 9 7 5 3 1 hardcover

LET'S GET GROWING
EDITORIAL AND DESIGN STAFF
Editor: **Ellen Phillips**
Contributing Editor: **Warren Schultz**
Cover and Interior Designer: **Frank M. Milloni**
Interior Illustrator: **Elayne Sears**
Cover and Part Illustrator: **Len Epstein**
Back Cover Photographer: **judywhite**
Copy Editor: **Lynn McGowan**
Editorial Assistance: **Susan Nickol** and
    Stephanie Snyder
Production Coordinator: **Patrick Smith**
Indexer: **Ed Yeager**

RODALE BOOKS
Executive Editor, Home and Garden:
    Margaret Lydic Balitas
Art Director, Home and Garden:
    Michael Mandarano
Copy Manager, Home and Garden:
    Dolores Plikaitis
Office Manager, Home and Garden:
    Karen Earl-Braymer
Editor-in-Chief: **William Gottlieb**

If you have any questions or comments concerning this book, please write to:
    Rodale Press, Inc.
    Book Readers' Service
    33 East Minor Street
    Emmaus, PA 18098

This book is dedicated to Old Zeb,
the Amish farmer, and all the other
stewards of the earth.

CROW'S PRAYER

Sowing the seed,
My hand is one with the Earth;
Wanting the seed to grow,
My mind is one with the light;
Hoeing the crop,
My hands are one with the rain;
Having cared for the plants,
My mind is one with the air;
Hungry and Trusting,
My heart is one with the Earth;
Eating the fruit,
My body is one with the Earth;
When I rise up,
Let me rise up joyful like a bird (a Crow);
When I fall,
Let me fall without regret like a leaf.

Contents

How I Got Growing ———————————————— vi

Part I

Let's Get Great Soil

CHAPTER 1:   Making Sense of the Soil ——————— 1

CHAPTER 2:   Composting for Keeps ——————— 14

CHAPTER 3:   Feeding the Soil ——————— 24

CHAPTER 4:   Let's Grow Green Manures ——————— 38

CHAPTER 5:   Making the Most of Mulch ——————— 42

Part II

Let's Get Planning and Planting

CHAPTER 6:   Planning the Plot ——————— 47

CHAPTER 7:   Let's Get Sowing! ——————— 56

CHAPTER 8:   All about Planting ——————— 66

CHAPTER 9:   Let's Stretch the Season ——————— 77

Part III

Let's Grow Vegetables and Herbs

CHAPTER 10:   A Gallery of Vegetables ——————— 95

CHAPTER 11:   Herbs for Many Uses ——————— 182

Part IV

Let's Grow Fruits and Berries

CHAPTER 12:   Fruit-Growing Basics ——————— 201

CHAPTER 13:   Fruit-Growing Guide ——————— 216

CHAPTER 14:   Let's Grow Berries ——————— 240

Part V

Let's Grow Flowers, Trees and Shrubs, and Lawns

CHAPTER 15:   Let's Grow Flowers ——————— 263

CHAPTER 16:   Let's Grow Trees and Shrubs ——————— 301

CHAPTER 17:   Let's Grow a Lawn ——————— 326

Part VI

Let's Get Pests, Diseases, and Weeds under Control

CHAPTER 18:   Let's Control Pests and Diseases ——— 345

CHAPTER 19:   Let's Work on Weeds ——————— 362

USDA Plant Hardiness Zone Map ——————— 366

Sources ——————— 367

Recommended Reading ——————— 368

Index ——————— 369

How I Got Growing

A broken-down car started me on the road to this book. It was 1970. I was driving across the country, looking for some direction, as so many of us were in those days. When my old clunker of a car finally quit, I walked to the nearest farmhouse to ask for help. That was where I met Old Zeb, the man who changed my life.

Old Zeb was an Amish farmer. He offered me a place to stay and food to eat. But he surprised me when, at first, he refused my offer to help him work his land in exchange. He explained kindly that the land was sacred to him, that the methods of careful stewardship had been passed down to him from generation to generation, and that he couldn't trust an outsider to understand.

I stayed the night in the barn, and the next day he allowed me to help with other chores, tending the animals and so on. I stayed the next night, too. And worked the next day. In time, Old Zeb began to reveal his secrets of plant growing to me and allowed me to work beside him. At first I was puzzled, because everything he said and did seemed to contradict what I'd learned previously. But I soon saw that his unconventional methods worked.

Gradually, Old Zeb came to trust me. He spent the last five years of his life teaching me about farming and gardening. I've been growing crops ever since, without ever adding a speck of chemicals to the soil or the plants. In the early 1980s, I found Spring Meadow, an abandoned farm on Long Island, and I began gardening and farming it to raise food for my family. The place soon took on a life of its own. People would drive by, see the gardens, and stop. Folks started coming around on Saturdays to ask questions about gardening. Eventually, I began teaching classes.

Now, Spring Meadow Farm is a nonprofit corporation. We offer 22 different gardening and cooking workshops. We have as many as 15 student apprentices each year. We farm almost 4 acres virtually year-round. A study done by Cornell University showed that 2 acres on our farm yields as much produce as a conventional 15-acre farm.

Zeb taught me that the greatest gift a human can give to another is a good example. That's what Spring Meadow is all about: a good organic example. It's a good example because it works. It works because organic growing is very simple.

Why Organic?

People always ask me, "Why organic? Is there really a difference in organic food?" But they don't ask that after they've tasted the fruits of our labors here at Spring Meadow. Customers come back to our farm stand after buying tomatoes and ask, "What did you do to that tomato to make it taste so good?" I tell them it's no secret. You can do the same thing. What we're doing here at Spring Meadow anybody else can do.

It's simply a matter of understanding the wants and needs of the plants. And it all starts with the soil. Whatever you put into the soil—be it good or bad—will wind up in the plant eventually. Compost, mulches, ground rock powders, and manures are natural substances, so they generally contain balanced amounts of zinc, manganese, boron, and the 18 other elements known to be essential for healthy plant growth. These trace elements are essential components of plant cells. Their presence in the soil often means the difference between pallid taste and mouthwatering flavor in fruits, between sickly vegetables and sturdy, robust ones.

My theory is the opposite of conventional scientific wisdom. I believe that plants *can* tell the difference between fertilizers—plants know whether they're organic or artificial. You see, organic fertilizers break down slowly in the soil. This gradual breakdown helps plants avoid problems with nutrient overabundance followed by deficiency, the characteristic binge-and-starve syndrome of chemical feeding programs.

What is the result of flooding the plants with chemical nitrogen? Besides the possibility of forcing excess green growth (all vines and no tomatoes!), too much nitrogen can stimulate insect breeding, increasing the number of pests on the plants.

I've seen for myself the effects of organically managed soil on plants. If the soil is healthy, the plants will be healthy. A healthy soil means fewer disease and insect problems. It may even get rid of these problems altogether. The payoff for the organic gardener is healthier, more nutritious food, free from chemical contamination and full of vital elements.

There's even more to it than vegetables, fruits, and flowers. Organic gardening is an art that feeds the soul of the gardener. A garden is, by definition, a place of beauty. And an organic garden is something special, suffused with peace and beauty.

Organic gardeners are artists as well as horticulturists. And the best organic gardeners learn their art by observing. I believe this book, written over a period of more than a decade, can help you stretch your garden canvas—but it's only a start.

Pay attention to the gardens around you. Look as you've never looked before. Try to figure out what makes them succeed or fail. Ask questions. Make notes and sketches. Talk to gardeners. Join an organic gardening club.

You'll find that your garden ambition is restricted not by space or time but only by your imagination. In time, you'll be able to express your loves and aspirations through nature. I don't know of anything more satisfying.

I love "preaching" organics. It's easy to convince people because it works. All you have to do is try it and you'll soon see for yourself.

So, let's get growing!

PART I

Let's Get Great Soil

1

Making Sense of the Soil

Grow the soil first. If there's one lesson I've learned in 25 years of organic gardening and farming, that's it. Even the most callous chemical farmer recognizes the life coursing through his crops, but it takes an organic grower to understand that the soil, too, is a living, breathing organism. I've learned that, like any crop, the soil has to be attended to, nurtured, and coddled because the well-being of the soil has an impact on every plant that grows out of it.

A vibrant, robust soil helps plants get off to a quick start. It eagerly accepts the early spring rain, then allows the water to drain off, leaving a fine seedbed. Optimum amounts of nutrients in the soil help crops grow fast and get a leg up on weeds. And, most important of all, a rich, organically grown soil is teeming with beneficial organisms that keep diseases in check. Plants start healthy, stay healthy, and resist insect attacks.

You may be tempted to take shortcuts with your soil—shovel a little less muck, do without quite so much mulch. You may be impatient to get the plants in the dirt and unwilling to do the groundwork. I know how it feels when planting fever strikes. But don't shortchange the soil. The work you put into building a healthy soil pays off many times over by preventing problems that could be real time wasters and crop killers.

Cultivating Soil Sense

It doesn't pay to start building soil, though, until you understand what sort of foundation you have and know some of the building materials available. Spend some time getting to know your soil. Greet it in the spring. Let it run through your fingers. Recognize the sweet scent of organic action.

In my early farming days, my mentor Old Zeb asked me what I thought was the most important farming tool. Eager to please and show off my knowledge, I guessed item after item, starting with the draft horses, and went on through the plow, hoes, and rakes. He shook his head kindly after every answer. Only after I ran through an entire catalog of hand tools did he tell me the answer. To him, the most important tool was the power of observation. If I doubted his answer at all then, I believe it wholeheartedly now.

Stay in touch with your soil. Recognize that its makeup changes from season to season. Soil evolves. It's constantly being created. Soil is born from the physical weathering of rocks and the biological action of plants and microbes. Glacial drifts and volcanic eruptions, wind and water movements, freezing and thawing, and earthquakes break down the earth's crust until plants can gain a foothold and extract some nutrients from the fine rock particles.

Soil evolution depends on the cyclical interplay between organic matter, the mi-croorganisms (bacteria, fungi, actinomycetes, and yeasts) that decay it, and powdered rock. Deep down at bedrock, subsoil is constantly being made...slowly. It takes over 500 years for an inch of soil to form naturally.

We can do it a lot faster. Our raw material is not the earth's crust but existing soil and organic matter. Our mission, after all, is not to create soil but to improve it. In fact, all we do is prime the pump. As gardeners of the soil, we provide the best mix of ingredients—minerals and organic matter—and let nature take its course. Organic gardeners need to study nature in order to imitate it.

THE RIGHT WAY—YOUR WAY

One of the things I love most about gardening is that there is no one correct way to do things. There are as many methods of gardening as there are gardeners. The same goes for soil-building techniques.

Many organic farmers simply back the manure spreader up to the family garden and let it fly. Other gardeners, who have no ready access to manure but recognize the shortcomings of artificial fertilizers, dump on bags of crushed rock powders, natural phosphates, and other minerals.

Some swear by compost. And some follow the example of Ruth Stout and rely on massive amounts of mulch. Guess what? They're *all* right.

The Look and Feel of Soil

To make the most of your time and ingredients and to choose the soil-building style that's best for you, you should figure out what you're starting with. Take a look at your soil. I mean, **really** look at it. Turn over a spadeful. Get down on your hands and knees and take a close look at the color and texture of your soil. You'll be surprised how much you can learn.

SOIL COLOR

What's your soil's color? The darker it is, the richer it is likely to be in organic matter. A complete soil test will give you better information, but you should study the color just to become more familiar with the soil.

A close inspection of soil colors can also reveal how well drained your soil is. Light blue-gray splotches (called mottles) against the deeper red of the subsoil clay show that water is standing at that level during the spring and early summer. If mottling occurs below 18

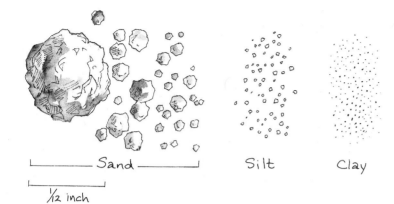

Sand — Silt — Clay

1/12 inch

All soil particles look small to us, but there's really a huge difference in their size. Clay particles are generally less than $\frac{1}{12,500}$ inch in diameter. Silt particles range in size from $\frac{1}{12,500}$ to $\frac{1}{500}$ inch. Both clay and silt are too small to really see individual particles, while sand particles can be easy to see since they may be up to $\frac{1}{12}$ inch in diameter.

inches, your soil is well drained. But mottling above 18 inches indicates that your soil tends to stay wet in the springtime. Of course, that means that you won't be able to work your soil and plant nearly as early as you might if it were well drained.

SOIL TEXTURE

After color, the most obvious soil characteristic is texture. Almost every soil is made up of different particles, which are classified as clay, silt, or sand, depending on their size. Sand particles are the largest of the three, up to 1,000 times as large as clay particles. Clay particles are extremely tiny—less than $\frac{1}{12,500}$ inch in size. Silt particles can be up to 25 times larger than clay.

Just how much of each type of particle your soil has determines the soil's texture. The texture, in turn, determines the ability of the soil to absorb nutrients and water. By knowing the mix of sand, clay, and silt in your soil, you can predict the kinds of soil problems you're likely to encounter if you grow vegetables, flowers, or trees and shrubs there.

You may be able to see a difference in color, but looking at the soil isn't enough to tell you its texture. You have to get right down and touch it. To get a feel for the texture of soil, I dig up a fresh shovelful and fill the palm of my hand with it. Then I close my eyes and run my fingers over the sample, concentrating on what I'm feeling. If the sample is dry and feels like cake flour, I can be fairly sure it's high in silt. Same thing if it's wet and feels smooth and silky. However, if it feels rough when dry or sticky and greasy when wet, then I know it's high in clay. If it feels sharp and gritty, then

there's plenty of sand there.

What kind of texture should the ideal garden soil have? Loam is what we all desire. That's a happy combination of silt, clay, and sand—just enough of each to bring out their best qualities. Silt loam soils are desirable because they have enough clay in them to store adequate amounts of water and plant nutrients, but not so much clay that it causes poor aeration or makes cultivating difficult.

As you can see from the illustration on soil texture on page 4, there are an infinite number of degrees between sand-based loam soils (sandy loams) and clay-based loam soils (clay loams). Soils high in sand are probably the simplest to work with, especially if you have a ready supply of both water and organic matter. But very sandy soil needs organic matter to give it bulk. Without improve-

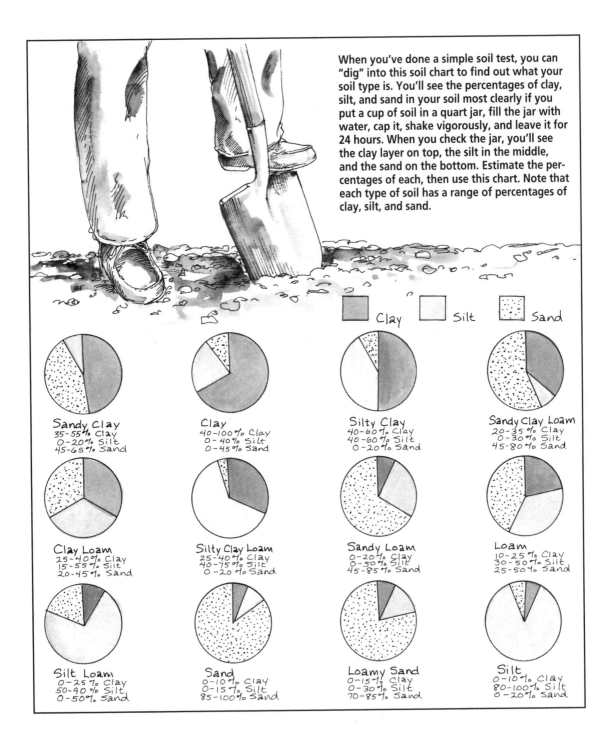

When you've done a simple soil test, you can "dig" into this soil chart to find out what your soil type is. You'll see the percentages of clay, silt, and sand in your soil most clearly if you put a cup of soil in a quart jar, fill the jar with water, cap it, shake vigorously, and leave it for 24 hours. When you check the jar, you'll see the clay layer on top, the silt in the middle, and the sand on the bottom. Estimate the percentages of each, then use this chart. Note that each type of soil has a range of percentages of clay, silt, and sand.

Clay   Silt   Sand

Sandy Clay
35-55% Clay
0-20% Silt
45-65% Sand

Clay
40-100% Clay
0-40% Silt
0-45% Sand

Silty Clay
40-60% Clay
40-60% Silt
0-20% Sand

Sandy Clay Loam
20-35% Clay
0-30% Silt
45-80% Sand

Clay Loam
25-40% Clay
15-55% Silt
20-45% Sand

Silty Clay Loam
25-40% Clay
40-75% Silt
0-20% Sand

Sandy Loam
0-20% Clay
0-50% Silt
45-85% Sand

Loam
10-25% Clay
30-50% Silt
25-50% Sand

Silt Loam
0-25% Clay
50-90% Silt
0-50% Sand

Sand
0-10% Clay
0-15% Silt
85-100% Sand

Loamy Sand
0-15% Clay
0-30% Silt
70-85% Sand

Silt
0-10% Clay
80-100% Silt
0-20% Sand

ment, it is like a sieve, letting water (and nutrients) run right through it.

Clay-based soils are generally much richer in nutrients than sandy soil. But clay dries very slowly in the spring, making it difficult to get out there and work the land early. Root crops have an especially difficult time in heavy clay soil. Although clay holds moisture once it is saturated (particularly in low-lying areas), rain often runs off before penetrating this type of soil, leaving the plants short of water in the growing season. Fortunately, no matter what type of soil you have, help is at hand in the form of organic matter.

Great Soil for Great Gardens

Organic matter is the Holy Grail of organic gardeners. The remarkable, almost miraculous thing about organic matter is that it will improve both extremes of soil—tight-textured clay and loose-textured sand—as it breaks down into humus. Organic matter makes a heavy clay soil lighter and a light sandy soil heavier. It acts like a sponge, absorbing water rather than letting it run off or sink too quickly through the soil.

Unfortunately, most of us don't start with great garden soil. We can't turn clay into silt, or sand into clay, but we can turn any type of soil into good soil, mainly by adding organic matter. We can all strive for an improved soil by following good growing practices, including regular feedings of compost, green manure, and a good organic fertilizer.

Organic Matter 101

If you're going to garden organically, you're going to get to know organic matter intimately. You have to. So what is it, exactly? For gardening purposes, organic matter consists of vegetation or animal products in various stages of decay. It could be grass clippings, manure, leaves, food scraps, even weeds. Put it all together, and in its later stages of decay, you've got compost. Add it to the soil, and it will eventually become humus. When a soil becomes rich in organic matter, either naturally or through conscientious gardening practices, fertile topsoil results.

Organic matter is a vital, versatile building block in soil making. It improves soil structure in several ways. Adding it helps to aerate the soil. The channels and pores created during the breaking down of organic matter provide the necessary habitat for microlife. More than a home for microorganisms, organic matter is the food source for all soil life. Earthworms and other life forms thrive on organic matter. They ingest it and transform it. When organic matter has been thoroughly worked by the microflora and microfauna of the soil, it becomes humus. And if organic matter is good, humus is better.

HUMUS: SPIRIT OF THE SOIL

Humus is both a cause and effect of a healthy soil. It's more than the sum of its parts. Scientists might call humus a "semi-stabilized, dark brown, amorphous soil colloid created by biochemical degradation and microbial synthesis." But from my point of view, humus is the very spirit of the soil.

Humus acts as a sponge in the soil, both holding water and allowing for aeration. It is the glue that binds minerals and organic matter into a crumblike soil structure. Humus holds nutrients and makes them readily available to plant roots. It also stabilizes and buffers the chemistry and acidity of the soil.

In a natural system, as in the prairies and forests of the past, humus reaches a self-regulating equilibrium.

Too Mulch of a Good Thing?

If a little organic matter is good, a lot is better, right? Up to a point. There is a limit to how much organic matter your soil can use. As you build up your soil's reserves, you'll notice that your plants are healthier and more productive. But once your soil contains 5 percent organic matter, dumping on more and more organic matter won't produce significantly better results. Of course, you can add as much organic matter as you like, or have energy for, without doing any harm to the soil. But for the average soil, about 2 pounds per square foot, added annually, is about right.

Before our land was disturbed by the plow, most of the virgin soil in the United States had about 4 percent humus. Today, the average American soil contains about 1½ percent. As organic gardeners operating under somewhat artificial constraints, we have to help humus along and work to keep it at an ideal level by adding lots of organic matter to our soil.

Organic Matter at Work

As a longtime organic gardener and farmer, I've come to realize that my first job of husbandry is to ensure that soil microorganisms have a ready supply of organic matter and minerals available to use as fuel to create humus. If I do my job and "farm" these soil creatures, I know that half of all fresh organic matter is transformed to humus in just two months by the bacteria, fungi, insects, and other microflora and microfauna that teem in the top 6 inches of soil.

It's almost a self-perpetuating system. As soil fertility increases, so do the number and varieties of soil life. In a healthy, well-fed soil, the population of microscopic soil dwellers is as dizzying as the stars in a country summer sky. For example, a single gram of soil may hold 100 million bacteria. All the bacteria in an acre of topsoil would weigh as much as a small truck.

EARTHWORMS AND OTHER SOIL HEROES

There are thousands of species of soil life, each with its own special function. Earthworms, for example, feed on litter, dragging it into their burrows. Ever wonder why all that mulch you laid down disappears so fast? That's why. While worms are working at the surface, microscopic actinomycetes are working deep below the surface, freeing up carbon, nitrogen, and ammonia for plant roots. Bacteria and fungi invade both fresh and weathered organic matter to break it down. It's all similar to the process that occurs in a correctly built compost pile. (You'll find out all about making compost in Chapter 2.)

Soil minerals also play an important role in humus making. Microorganisms that bond the minerals to the organic matter during the humus-making process need certain minerals in order to function and proliferate. The greater the variety of minerals you provide, the greater the variety of microorganisms, and the faster the organic matter will become humus.

Of course, we gardeners can't see most of this teeming mass of humus builders. We don't need to see them or even understand the complexity of their life cycles. But we must strive to make our patch of soil a suitable habitat for soil life so that it, in turn, can create a

Mulch

Decomposing organic matter

Topsoil

Fungi

Roots

Protozoa

Actinomycetes

Grub

Earthworm

Bacteria

Subsoil

Root Hairs

Worms are workhorses in good organic soil. They help break down mulches, aerate the soil with their tunnels, and produce nutrient-rich castings that fertilize your plants. This cutaway view of typical garden soil shows that there's more at work here than earthworms, though. Microorganisms like bacteria, fungi, actinomycetes, and protozoa are busy decomposing crop residues and other organic matter, while less welcome residents like grubs may be making meals of plant roots.

The Spring Meadow System of Organic Matter Management

At Spring Meadow Farm, we work about 4 acres nearly year-round. We don't always have as much organic matter available as we'd like to have, so we've adopted methods that conserve organic matter and humus instead of burning them up. Here are some of the rules we follow:

❧ **Keep the soil planted.** Bare soil makes me shudder. Wherever the soil is neither mulched nor planted, you can be sure organic matter is being burned without replacement. Where we're not growing food, we grow a cover crop. I don't know a way to build soil without plants.

When we are growing, we space plants to get the most from the least organic matter. Wide rows or beds let us cover more ground with plants than narrow rows. And beds or wide rows let us concentrate organic matter where the plants will grow.

❧ **Cultivate sparingly.** Cultivation—plowing, tilling, weeding, hoeing, all that fussing with the soil—dries the soil, breaks apart soil aggregates, and releases the humic acids that bind them. The plants might get a quick boost from the free humus, but you pay for the benefit with a decline in your soil's organic matter. Cultivation also speeds up the degradation of organic matter and humus,

burning up your supply faster than plants can capture and use it.

❧ **Keep the soil mulched.** Much like plants, the life in the soil needs constant feeding. If you keep the soil mulched, the organisms have a ready supply of organic matter to "snack" on. It's better to put organic matter or compost on the soil in small, regular amounts than to turn under your whole supply at the beginning of the season. Mulch also moderates soil temperature and maintains even soil moisture, both pluses for hard-working soil builders.

❧ **Put organic matter in the topsoil.** The students at our farm like this rule—it saves their backs. There's no point in burying organic matter deeply. Nature keeps humus in the top 6 inches of the soil, and so should you. Organic matter does the most good there because that's where plant roots are.

The vast majority of crop roots are in the top 6 inches of soil. The few crops that send roots deeper in search of water leave a modest amount of organic matter in the subsoil, but it turns to humus only slowly. That's because there is very little oxygen in the subsoil to support soil life. Most of the nutrients found in the subsoil are those that have leached down from the topsoil.

fertile soil. There is no one way of doing this. The differences in climate, geography, soil type, financial resources, access to material, amount of leisure time, physical ability, equipment, and especially the enthusiasm of the organic gardener dictate how each garden will develop.

As we'll see, you can improve your soil's fertility with compost, manure, cover crops, mulch, or any combination of the above. But whichever method you choose, it's important to keep the soil growing. Plant roots, cover crops, and even weeds contribute astonishing quantities of organic matter. They deposit it right where it does the most good—directly in the soil. They save us a lot of hauling, toting, and shoveling.

Soil Compaction: A Serious Enemy

You might think that once you've provided the soil microorganisms with plenty of food, nothing can stop them in their humus-building work. I'm afraid that's not so. They can be stopped in their tracks by the two Cs: chemicals and compaction.

The problem with chemicals is clear if you stop to think about it. Herbicides, insecticides, and fungicides are *designed* to kill life on and in the soil. Just as certainly as they zap bad bugs, weeds, and diseases, they'll knock off beneficial microorganisms. Use chemicals long enough and you'll sterilize your soil. It will be like an empty factory—there will be no workers there to help break down organic matter and start it on its way to becoming humus.

There's no mystery why chemically dependent lawns are plagued by thatch, which is a buildup of undecomposed organic matter. It's because lawn chemicals have stopped the breakdown system in its tracks. Even chemical fertilizers contribute to the sterilization of the soil, acidifying it and driving away earthworms as well as other organisms.

The cure is simple—cut out the chems! Then bring in a variety of vegetative material and manure to restart the "soil factory" with microorganism "workers."

COPING WITH COMPACTION

Compaction is not as easy to recognize or cure as chemical use, but it slows the soil life just as surely. To be the best that they can be, microorganisms need plenty of "elbow room" and oxygen.

Compaction is a sinister problem because it's invisible from the surface and its effects are subtle—languishing plants that just don't look right or yield as much as you expected. The fact is that soil compaction can cause poor yields.

Soil is most vulnerable to compaction when it is moist or wet. Ordinarily, the particles in dry soil (no matter what their size) have a certain rigidity. They are solid and stiff and keep their form even when pressed together. But when soil gets wet, much of its structural integrity melts away.

There are two main causes of soil compaction in the garden: tilling and foot traffic. Tilling or turning the soil dismantles its structure. Soil crumbs that were stuck together come apart. Many are shattered into smaller pieces. The more you work the soil when you till, the more you weaken it. When you break the soil into grains—especially when it's wet—your next footstep may turn it into a solid block.

Pressure from foot traffic packs the soil particles together. You end up with a tighter arrangement than the one you started with. The air spaces disappear; the pores that store air and water shrink. A soil that used to drain well stays wet. The rain runs off. That's compaction. So at Spring Meadow, we stay off the soil, especially when it's wet.

What Compaction Does

Lacking air spaces, the soil is deprived of oxygen. And oxygen is just as important to the plants' roots as water and minerals. When you compact the soil, you're suffocating the roots and the rest of the plant.

Even if the roots remain alive, they grow slowly in compacted soil. They can't reach into fresh soil fast enough to supply the leaves with water. Plants will wilt, even when the soil has plenty of moisture. Without adequate moisture, leaf pores shut down and growth slows.

But there's hope. Humus helps again, by retaining the structural integrity of the soil. A highly organic soil is not nearly as sensitive to being squeezed as clay and fine silt.

However, simply dumping on loads of organic matter won't cure compaction. Organic matter won't do any good unless it's actively decomposing. But it won't decompose unless bacteria are present, and the bacteria can't work without oxygen. Luckily, there are ways to prevent compaction before it becomes a problem.

PREVENTING SOIL COMPACTION

You can take precautions to prevent compaction in your garden. Here's what to do:

··· Add Compost

The liberal use of compost *before* the garden gets trampled will improve the structure of soils (especially soils that tend to pack down and crust over), lighten heavy clay soils, and increase the water- and nutrient-holding capacity of sandy soils.

··· Stay Out of the Beds

I've found that it's even more important to avoid all unnecessary traffic in the growing beds. And the best way to avoid traffic is to lay out your garden in beds between permanent grass walkways. The beds should be as wide as possible, but not so wide that you can't reach the middle from either side. Mine are about 5 feet wide. With grass paths, I never walk on the beds. Only the soil between the beds gets compacted.

··· Till Carefully

When tilling, vary the depth and alternate the direction from year to year. The pressure of a tiller, plow, or disk packs the soil under it in a thin layer, called a hardpan or plowpan. If you always work at the same depth or in the same direction, that layer compacts densely, shutting out roots and damming water. Double digging can help break through that hardpan. If you are preparing your garden with a tiller or shovel, cultivate only the area you will be planting.

··· Plant a Cover Crop

For Spring Meadow, I've devised a 2-acre rotation garden, so that half of the area produces vegetables while the other half is growing a green manure crop. (See Chapter 4 for more on my system.) The green manure provides the actively decaying organic matter necessary for good soil structure. If you can't bear to dedicate half of your garden space to a cover crop each year, divide it into thirds or fourths, so that the entire garden receives a green manuring every third or fourth year.

Doubtful Dust Mulch

You may have heard of dust mulch. It's based on the idea that stirring up the top of the soil during dry spells creates a dust layer that conserves the moisture in the soil beneath it. Sounds good, but does it work? Don't count on it. Once the soil surface has dried out, there's no difference in the rate of evaporation when the soil is cultivated or when it is undisturbed. Besides, breaking up the soil clumps into fine dust can damage your soil's structure. For best results, stick with a loose, fluffy organic mulch that will protect and improve the soil; don't depend on dust to do the job.

··· Mulch Heavily

Heavy mulch conserves moisture, prevents erosion, and forms a sort of cushion to lessen compaction. As it breaks down year after year, the mulch also gradually adds a layer of soft, rich organic matter that vegetables and flowers thrive in.

CORRECTING SOIL COMPACTION PROBLEMS

Perhaps you haven't taken preventive measures against compaction. Maybe you've been managing your garden like a little agribusiness: plowing or tilling the same way each year, planting in long straight rows, relying on chemical fertilizers rather than organic matter. Maybe you suspect you have a compaction problem. Here's one way to find out:

The next time you get a good, soaking rain, wait three or four days, then go into the garden with a pointed metal rod. Slowly push the rod into the soil. If your soil is compacted, you'll feel resistance at many levels before the rod finally hits the subsoil.

If you're still not sure, wait until the soil dries, then dig a soil profile. With a spade, dig a hole about 18 inches deep. Try to dig straight down so you can clearly see the soil levels in the walls of the hole. After removing all the soil from the hole, get down on your hands and knees and examine the sides of the hole. Observe the different colors of the soil. Look especially for a narrow layer of a lighter brown color about 1 foot

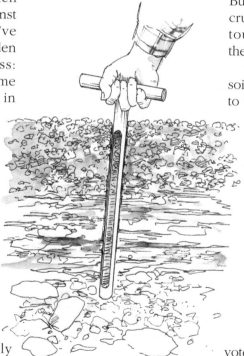

Use a soil sampling tube or any pointed rod to check for soil compaction. Push it slowly into the soil and note resistance. If you have to struggle to push it in, or if it hits a rock-hard layer (probe nearby to make sure you didn't hit a real rock!), your soil is compacted.

deep. That's what hardpan looks like.

Now, take a look at the soil you removed from the hole. Can you crumble the soil easily in your hand, or is it hard? Can you find roots penetrating more than just the top inch or two? Can you find any earthworms? You're examining the very heart of your soil. The plant food in the soil is its bloodstream. But soil that is hard and encrusted is like an arm in a tourniquet—the blood is there, but it can't circulate.

If you think you have a soil compaction problem, try to work the soil as deeply as possible. Dig it and break it up, but don't invert the soil layers too much. (You want the nutrient-rich topsoil to stay on top.)

If you find you have a hardpan, there are a few ways to handle it, depending on how much time and energy you want to devote to it. The first is the easiest, but it takes the soil out of production for several years. For this method, break up the pan in several spots with a pickax or spading fork, then sow a vigorous cover grass such as ryegrass. Let it grow without any traffic

Soil Quick Fix

Once soil has been severely damaged by compaction, chemicals, or poor culture, it takes time to recover. You can gradually "cure" it by incorporating organic matter in the form of compost, mulches, and green manures. After one year, the soil loosens up a little; after two, it gets crumbly; and after three, it will be rich and friable—perfect for growing healthy, high-yielding crops.

But what about this year? What's the best strategy to turn poor soil into good soil, so you can do some real gardening before the season runs out? Here's what I do:

❧ **Start small.** Work on the smallest scale at first. Amend just the planting holes or furrows with enriched soil or compost.

❧ **Change the texture.** If your soil is dominated by one texture, incorporate its opposite. In other words, add sand to clay and silt soils, but again, add it only to the planting holes.

❧ **Mulch, mulch, mulch.** Use mulches to introduce organic matter into your garden soil. The main point is to get lots of organic matter (compost, mulch, shredded leaves, grass clippings, straw, pine needles, well-rotted manure, or even shredded newspaper) into the top 6 inches of your soil. As the organic matter breaks down into humus, it encourages the growth of beneficial bacteria, fungi, and other microorganisms and enhances the biological activity of the soil.

❧ **Double dig.** The best way to improve soil structure and drainage and to get organic matter into the soil where it can do the most good is to use the French Intensive Method of double digging. Resolve to double dig one bed each year.

❧ **Water gently.** When you water your crops, use drip irrigation or water in a fine spray rather than a steady, heavy stream. Either technique will prevent puddling, which damages the soil structure in the top few inches.

❧ **Keep planting.** Plant a fall cover crop of rye so the soil isn't exposed to weathering (which can cause erosion) or rains (which can compact the soil and destroy beneficial microorganisms).

❧ **Test the soil.** Although green manures incorporate organic matter into the soil, a gardener usually has to correct any nutritional problems first or the crops won't grow. This is why I recommend a professional soil test, which will tell you what nutrient deficiencies your soil has and give recommendations on how to correct them.

❧ **Add organic fertilizers.** To get the best growth from your crops as quickly as possible, provide nutrients as recommended by your soil test, using natural minerals and bagged organic fertilizers. You can buy these materials pre-mixed as a general-purpose fertilizer or individually (for example, blood meal or bonemeal) from your garden center or mail-order garden supply catalogs.

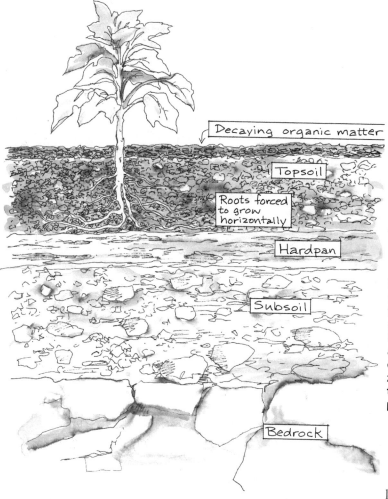

Decaying organic matter

Topsoil

Roots forced to grow horizontally

Hardpan

Subsoil

Bedrock

Hardpan (also called plowpan) is a nearly impenetrable layer of soil that's been compacted by repeated plowing or tilling until it's rock-hard. In a soil profile, it appears as a narrow band of light-colored, compressed soil. Roots grow horizontally above the hardpan since they can't get through the compacted layer.

on it for two to three years. The roots will strengthen the soil and make it less susceptible to compaction.

However, if you want to keep the garden in production, you can break up the hardpan mechanically by cultivating the soil deeply. On farms, massive chisel plow equipment is pulled through fields. But in the garden, deep cultivation must be done by hand. Instead of trying to break up all of the hardpan, you can just sink a pickax or spading fork as deeply as possible where you will be planting. For good results, you only have to pierce the hardpan in the area below each plant.

Finally, if you have a lot of time and energy, you can double dig your garden. (See "Double Dig Your Beds" on page 74 for tips on double digging.)

I hope by now you see why I think good soil matters so much! In the next few chapters, I'll show you how to make your soil the best it can be by composting, supplemental feeding, using green manures, and mulching. Then you can *really* get growing!

CHAPTER

2

Composting for Keeps

Compost is the soul of good garden soil. It's the link in the cycle of life that enables all good natural things to be returned to the earth in an economical and productive manner. Compost is recycling at its purest. When you make compost, nature returns the favor, providing an all-purpose ingredient for gardening success.

As a soil conditioner, compost improves drainage and water-holding capacity. When compost is mixed into the soil, it provides more loose, oxygen-rich growing space for plant roots. As a fertilizer, it begins releasing food for plant roots almost immediately and continues to feed the soil as it breaks down into humus.

So What Is Compost?

There's no doubt that compost has almost miraculous powers. But what is it, exactly? What makes compost? Gardeners always ask me what they can and should compost. My answer is always the same: "Anything that can be composted." In the world of computers, they have a saying: "Garbage in, garbage out." It means that worthless information creates worthless programs. But in gardening, we can say: "Garbage in, gold out." And to my mind, the more diverse the "garbage" that goes into a heap, the richer the compost that comes out. The more varied your compost recipe, the more nutrients, elements, and decomposers you're adding to the mix. Compost is ideally composed of vegetable matter and animal manure, plus some natural fertilizers such as rock phosphate, cottonseed meal, or bonemeal.

What to Put in Your Pile

My basic recipe of ingredients for a compost pile includes dry matter such as straw, leaves, and cornstalks; fresh green matter such as grass clippings, vegetables, and green manures; animal manures; rock phosphate; bonemeal or blood meal; and garden soil. But a good compost pile doesn't have to include all of these ingredients, by any means. I've made rich, steaming compost with as few as two or three of them. Composting is a lot like cooking: You can follow a recipe line by line, but often the best results come from ad-libbing with the ingredients you have on hand.

In reality, you and I don't make compost. Actinomycetes, bacteria, and fungi do. Our job is to see that these little organisms have enough of the right kind of food to live and multiply. So we need to be sure that our compost piles get all the components they need, especially nitrogen. Let's take a look at some common compost ingredients.

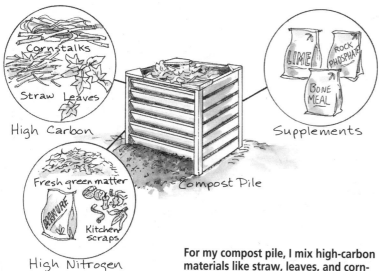

High Carbon

Cornstalks
Straw Leaves

Supplements

LIME ROCK PHOSPHATE BONE MEAL

Compost Pile

Fresh green matter
GREENURE
Kitchen scraps

High Nitrogen

For my compost pile, I mix high-carbon materials like straw, leaves, and cornstalks; high-nitrogen materials like manure, grass clippings, and kitchen scraps; and organic supplements like ground limestone, blood meal, and rock phosphate. As a rule of thumb, I use about three times as much high-carbon as high-nitrogen material, then add just a sprinkling of supplements.

GRASS CLIPPINGS

Plenty of homeowners wish that grass clippings would just stop coming! I've always found it odd that people would leave this treasure in bags by the curb. Of course, grass clippings are valuable for the lawn, too, if mulched and left in place. If you have plenty of other green sources of nitrogen, you might want to leave the clippings where they are. But in your compost, grass clippings provide lots of nitrogen—up to 2 pounds of pure nitrogen per 100 pounds of clippings. Don't just dump them on the pile, though—add them in shallow layers and mix them in thoroughly. Otherwise, they tend to clump into an impenetrable mat.

KITCHEN WASTE

Of course, kitchen waste is *not* something that's best left in place. But it's a valuable and often neglected source of nitrogen and other nutrients in the compost pile. Coffee grounds, eggshells, fruit rinds, and vegetable peelings can all be added to the pile. I try to keep bread out of the compost because it can be a breeding area for harmful mold. And I *never* add any meat or meat by-products since they attract rodents and other scavengers.

LEAVES

Pound for pound, leaves pack nearly twice as many minerals as manure does. Leaves supply the carbon part of the compost equation and may contain up to 1 percent nitrogen by weight, as well as ½ percent phosphorus and potash. But leaves are sometimes slow to break down. You can speed their decay in two ways. First, shred the leaves into small particles. Shredding speeds decomposition by increasing surface area. Then, add extra nitrogen (I use manure) to your pile. One part manure to 5 parts leaves is just about right. See "We Love Leaves" on page 20 for a *lot* more about leaves.

WEEDS

Unlike many gardeners, I welcome weeds in my garden. I know that they're a valuable addition to my compost pile. They contain just as much nitrogen, phosphorus, and potash as crop residues. Pigweed, for example, brings about 0.6 percent nitrogen and 0.2 percent phosphorus to the pile. And, fortunately or unfortunately, depending on how you look at it, weeds seem to be much more prolific than cultivated garden crops. If you like a slow-cooking pile, try to pull your weeds before they set seed. If you build hot piles, don't worry about weed seed; it will be killed by high temperatures as the compost "cooks."

SOIL

Soil is the basis of a good compost pile—and one that folks often forget. That's because soil is rich in microorganisms that work to decompose material in the pile. It also holds water well and can serve as a reservoir of moisture when added to the pile. I always build my compost pile directly on freshly dug earth.

MANURE

You *can* make compost without manure, but it's always a basic component of my compost pile. When we raised goats, chickens, and ducks, they provided plenty of compost fodder for us. Now, I rely mainly on horse manure from local stables. Manure provides the nitrogen that's essential for heating up a compost pile. The nitrogen content may vary from as high as 2 percent in hot manures such as chicken, duck, sheep, and rabbit to about ½ percent in fresh cow, horse, or goat manure.

But there's much more to fresh manure than simple elements. It also contains a large population of useful bacteria. In fact, I believe that it is the large, diverse bacterial population, rather than the nutritive elements, that makes manure so valuable in the compost pile. Those bacteria pitch right in and go to work breaking down other materials in the pile.

ROCK PHOSPHATE

I always add rock phosphate, a natural source of phosphorus, to my compost pile. It contains up to 30 percent phosphate. And acids in the compost make this mineral more readily available than if you just spread it on the soil or dig it in.

BONEMEAL

Bonemeal is another good, though expensive, source of phosphorus. Its analysis may vary considerably, from 10 to 30 percent phosphorus. I think it goes farther and that I get more for my money if I add it to the compost rather than directly to the soil. Like rock phosphate, it breaks down slowly in the soil, but the composting activity speeds the release of its active ingredients.

Bones have been used for centuries as a fertilizer. In the early days of farming in the United States, great amounts of buffalo bones were collected on the western plains for use as fertilizer. Now, the main source of bonemeal is the slaughter-house.

BLOOD MEAL

Blood meal, or dried blood, is collected from slaughterhouses. It has a high nitrogen content—11 percent. Blood meal can be used directly in the soil or added to the compost pile. Because of its high nitrogen content, a sprinkling (just enough to make a visible layer) of blood meal is enough to stimulate bacterial growth.

Piling It Up

A compost pile can be almost any shape. I like to make rectangular-shaped piles because they are easiest to handle. As for size, there is a minimum limit. There has to be a critical mass so that the pile can heat up and stay hot. Some say 3 feet high and wide is sufficient, but I like them larger. I think a pile 5 feet high and 5 feet wide is the optimum size for generating the heat necessary to thoroughly compost the material.

What about a bin? You may want to use one, especially if you have a small yard

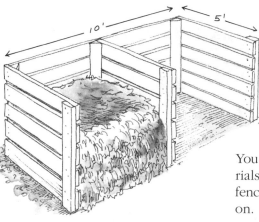

Compost bins come in all shapes and sizes. The shape doesn't matter much, but the size does. I like to make mine big enough so that I can turn the compost *inside* the bin. I use a two-part wooden compost bin, and fork the compost from one half to the other as I turn it.

and want the compost area to look as neat as possible. Bins come in all shapes and sizes, of course. There are plenty of people willing to sell you the latest plastic, *recycled* plastic, or wooden bin. I've even heard of *cardboard* bins that compost themselves!

What's most important, though, is that the bin be built in such a way that access to the compost is easy. What I like to do is build a wooden bin that's twice as big as my biggest pile. For example, if I know my materials will make a pile 5 feet high by 5 feet deep by 5 feet wide, I'll build a bin 5 feet high by 5 feet deep by

10 feet wide. That way, there's always enough space on one side to turn the material back and forth within the bin.

There are few hard-and-fast rules about bin building. You can use all kinds of materials—wooden pallets, snow fencing, wire fencing, and so on. What's important is that you can get at what's inside. Turning the compost is essential, and if you make it difficult to get to, you won't turn it as frequently as necessary, and your compost will suffer.

BUILDING THE PILE

Once you've built (or bought) the bin, it's time to build the pile. Simply stated, I pile equally thick (up to 3-inch) layers of each type of material on top of each other and repeat this procedure until I use up all the ingredients. The finer the fresh green material is crushed, chopped, or shredded, the thinner the layers must be to prevent it from compressing into a solid mat.

I start on freshly dug earth and begin to build layers, first with a "hot" layer of manure and kitchen waste about an inch or two thick. I follow that with an equally thick layer of fresh green matter—grass clippings, weeds, or crop residue. Then I sprinkle on just a dusting of rock phosphate, granite dust, and kelp meal. I top this with 1 inch of soil, then start layering the same way all over again until the pile reaches 5 feet.

A compost pile needs plenty of air. You can't allow it to suffocate. To create air spaces, you can insert 1- to 2-inch-diameter pipes into the pile during the layering, then remove them when the pile is completed.

On the other hand, you don't want the pile to be too airy. I've seen gardeners fail at composting because they pile the heap loosely with weeds and other bulky materials. Not only does it take bacteria and fungi longer to break down bulky materials, but excess air space lets the pile dry out too fast. This is why shredding and grinding help. The finer your compost material is shredded, the more surfaces will be exposed to action by microorganisms.

Water is an important ingredient of the compost pile. The pile should be moist but not soggy. If you're starting with a lot of fresh, green vegetable matter, you may not need to add water. But if any layer feels dry to the touch, moisten it until it's as damp throughout as a squeezed sponge, then check before proceeding to

Composting in Place

If you're in a hurry to enrich your soil for planting, try sheet or trench composting in place. Dig a 6- to 9-inch hole or trench in your garden and layer it with kitchen scraps, crop residues, leaves, and manure. Then cover the layers with the soil you took out of the trench. As the material decays underground, it keeps the soil loose. Nutrients from the decomposed vegetable matter will be available for plants almost immediately. This method is particularly useful in an area you plan to plant with a nitrogen-hungry crop like corn. Just plant the rows on either side of the trench.

You don't even need a pile to make compost. You can do it invisibly by sheet or trench composting. Just dig a hole or trench 6 to 9 inches deep right in your garden, fill it with kitchen scraps or other nitrogen-rich materials, then cover with a 3- to 4-inch layer of soil. The organic matter will begin breaking down almost immediately, releasing nutrients into the soil right where you want them. And you don't have to turn the compost!

the next layer. After you've piled up all the layers, give them a good watering—again, to damp-sponge consistency—then cover the pile to keep it from drying out.

WORKING THE PILE

A well-made compost pile should begin to cook almost immediately. Internal temperatures should reach 150°F within a week. If there's no heat within two weeks, you can assume that you goofed somehow when you put your pile together. If you come back a year later, you'll still have a heap of garden waste—not compost. The best thing is to start all over again.

As soon as the pile heats up, it's time to start turning it. A pile of compost, especially when wet, soon packs down and blocks out air. Since the organisms that heat up compost and break it down rapidly into humus breathe air, turning the pile is important to make sure they have an adequate supply of oxygen.

The single most important element affecting the speed at which the compost pile cooks is turning. For fast compost, turn the pile every third day for the first two weeks, then once a week for the last two weeks. This frequent turning allows air to

reach all parts of the pile and brings slower-decaying surface material to the hot center. Even in the coolness of winter or early spring, the compost pile will be ready for the garden within a month if you turn the ingredients three times a week. During the summer, turning dries out the pile, so water each time you do it.

The nose knows if you're not turning enough. With infrequent turning, ingredients will rot rather than compost. And when they rot, they stink! Odor is a sure sign that the inner pile isn't getting enough air, and it's your cue to start turning. So grab a pitchfork, hold your nose, and go to it. If you turn the smelly stuff, it will compost.

When to Compost

I can never have too much compost. All too often, the problem is the opposite—too little, too late. So in order to have generous supplies of compost on hand when I need it, especially in the spring, I've worked out a compost rotation. Although I may start compost almost any time of the year, I've found that certain times lend themselves to this task because of the materials available.

Here on Long Island, April showers bring compost

material. In May, there's plenty of young and tender green matter available. When plant material is still green, it has greater amounts of nutrients than plant matter that has dried. Because it's much easier for decay organisms to work on fresh, tender green matter, the pile will quickly break down into super compost for midsummer feeding.

Later, in midsummer, I start another pile. The summer-made compost needs less turning since I'm in no rush for it. My plan is to carry it over the winter, covered with plastic to prevent leaching of nutrients, for use in the early-spring garden. I find it's better to start in summer rather than fall because the dry, brown stuff that's available in the fall may not decompose properly when the weather turns cold.

I have no problem finding ingredients for my summer pile. I use grass clippings, weeds, refuse from the garden, yard trimmings, and waste from the kitchen, plus other green plant material.

Fresh grass clippings may contain even more nitrogen than horse manure—up to 2 percent. I try to make sure they make up at least one-third of the summer pile. Once they're thoroughly mixed in, they can get things cooking with no manure at all. I don't worry about diseased or bug-infested clippings because I know that they'll be sterilized by the heat of the pile.

Weeds make up a big part of my summer compost, too. Even if the seed has set, in they go. A compost pile that heats up to 140° to 160°F will kill all the seeds.

My summer compost pile is loaded with green matter. Since green plant matter usually contains much more nitrogen than dried material, I go easy on the manure in the pile's final mix.

Throughout spring and early summer, I dump all of our kitchen waste on the ground in the compost area. After I've collected enough other material, I start piling it up, alternating 3- or 4-inch-thick layers. I start with a few shovelfuls of garden soil to seed the pile with the right microorganisms. A 3- or 4-inch layer of manure goes over that. Then grass clippings, weeds, or kitchen wastes complete the first group of layers. I water it thoroughly with the hose, then build another group of layers, water that and add another group of layers, and on and on until the materials run out.

Because warm air increases composting activity, decomposition is faster and more foolproof in the summer. So I wait two weeks, then turn the pile, making sure the material on the outside is turned inside. By this time, the pile is hot and is using a lot of moisture, so I water it until it's moist. Then I cover it with black plastic and let it rest for the remainder of the year.

In late March, when planting time begins, I pull back the black plastic and reap the rewards of my summer work: big handfuls of rich, fluffy compost to make a soft seedbed that will nourish young vegetables.

Spreading the Wealth

You can't apply too much of this natural fertilizer and soil conditioner to your trees, gardens, and lawn. You can spread it on top of the soil, where it will decompose slowly while maintaining even moisture and coolness for plant roots. Or you can work compost into the soil to immediately improve the plant root environment for better uptake of nutrition and water. The best times to work compost into the soil are after harvest in fall and before planting in spring. Spread compost on the soil anytime. Compost can't burn plants, and the thicker you spread it, the more humus-rich, moist, and nutritious your soil will be.

We Love Leaves

Would you throw away free fertilizer? Would you work hard to throw it away? Don't be so quick to answer no. Every fall, homeowners across the country spend a lot of time, effort, and even money disposing of a very valuable fertilizer—leaves.

Leaves: Not Just for Compost

You don't have to compost leaves to use them. You can imitate nature by piling newly fallen leaves deeply around fruit trees and berry bushes each year. They'll keep roots cool in the spring and delay blooming of fruit trees, both of which help protect the plants from late-frost damage.

You can also put the leaves directly on the soil and till them into the vegetable bed as fertilizer. But do it on a calm day, since one good breeze could blow away the whole collection.

Raking, bagging, and sending them off with the trash—they don't know what they're missing. Leaves are time-release capsules of nitrogen, phosphorus, and potassium, plus calcium, magnesium, and many trace elements. Those leaves can be made into compost in as few as 14 days.

LEAVES TO COMPOST

Because I tend to make most of my compost in spring and summer, leaves are not a part of my regular mix. But it's easy to make a batch of leaf compost in the fall. Just mix 3 to 4 parts ground leaves with 1 part manure or another nitrogen-rich material, such as fresh grass clippings.

Nitrogen is the one factor that starts a compost heap heating up, and leaves alone don't contain enough nitrogen to feed bacteria. If you can't get your hands on some manure, nitrogen supplements such as dried blood, cottonseed meal, soybean meal, or fish meal will work almost as well. Add 2 cups of a natural nitrogen supplement to each wheelbarrow load of leaves.

Put the material into the heap in layers. To construct the pile, start with a 6-inch layer of leaves, then add a 2-inch layer of manure or green matter. (Or add a

The Joy of Shredding

Some leaves take up to two years to decompose. They tend to mat together, excluding air. And, of course, decomposition of organic matter requires plenty of air. The solution is to shred your leaves. Shredding will speed decay by increasing the leaves' surface area and decreasing their tendency to mat down.

If you don't have a shredder, use your lawn mower instead. Simply place the leaves in a small heap, about 5 inches deep, near a solid fence or other backdrop. Then run your lawn mower over them until you have a pile of shredded leaves against the fence.

Leaves compost more quickly when they've been shredded. But you don't need a fancy shredder to do the job. Just pile the leaves about 5 inches deep along a fence, set your rotary lawn mower at its higher setting, and mow them until they're shredded.

dusting of a nitrogen supplement as suggested above.) Keep adding the leaves and the nitrogen source, making sure you mix the leaves well with the other material. Mixing not only distributes the nitrogen for faster composting, it prevents the leaves from packing down into a dry mat.

Keep the heap moist, but not soggy. Sprinkle a dusting of dolomitic limestone over the pile once a month to help counteract the natural acidity of the leaves. Your compost pile should heat to around 160°F for about seven to ten days. When it begins to cool down, turn it over with a pitchfork and loosen any clumps of material. Rebuild the pile, putting the most decomposed material in the center, and then add a little water. Make sure the pile stays moist, but not soaking wet. Leave a depression in the middle to collect rainwater.

If you have an extended dry spell, water once a week. If the pile no longer heats up and there is still undecomposed material, add more manure. When all the leaf matter is decayed, it is ready to use.

LEAVES ALONE

If you have so many leaves on your property that you can't compost all of them, or

Easy Leaf Harvest

Don't be in such a hurry to run for the rake when the leaves start to fall this autumn. There's an easier way to "harvest" them. Let most of the leaves fall from the trees. Wait until your lawn's grass has reached at least 3 inches in height, then put the clipping catcher on your mower and mow your lawn. The long grass will hold the leaves in place, so the mower will chop them up along with the grass and discharge the mix of grass and leaves into the catcher.

Spread the chopped grass-leaf mix on your garden beds and till it into the soil. The grass will hold the leaves in place after you have spread them on the beds, so you can even work them in on windy days. And the nitrogen-rich grass clippings will hasten the decomposition of the leaves after both are tilled under. By next spring, your leaves will be completely broken down.

if you just don't have the time to make compost, you can make leaf mold. Leaf mold is not as rich a fertilizer as composted leaves, but it is easier to make and is especially useful as mulch.

To make leaf mold, you'll need a bin. I've found that a length of snow fencing fastened into a cylinder makes the best kind of enclosure. Gather the leaves in the fall, dump them into the bin, wet them thoroughly, and add a sprinkling of ground limestone. Now, stomp on them to tamp them down. Over the winter, these leaves will not break down into a

fine crumbly black compost, but they will be in a safe place, secure from the winter winds. When you pull them out next spring, they will be broken up enough to serve as a fine mulch. Some people keep leaves in cold storage like that for several years.

Why Like It Hot?

All composting, whether fast or slow, helps build soil and contributes to the overall health of your crops. So why work so hard, layering, watering, and turning your pile? The resulting hot compost offers plenty of advantages.

··· Advantage #1

All major disease organisms and insect larvae are killed. Temperatures normally reached during the hot composting process (140° to 165°F) are too high for parasites and human, animal, and plant pathogens to survive. Tests have shown that all but the most hardy strains of disease organisms die in 24 to 48 hours at 131°F. And in a well-made pile, temperatures will stay this high for weeks, ensuring complete pasteurization.

The high temperatures achieved in a well-managed compost pile aren't the only weapon against disease-causing organisms. Antibiotic substances produced by fungi and actinomycetes during the hottest stage of composting also play an important part in fighting pathogens and parasites.

··· Advantage #2

Weed seeds can't survive these high temperatures, so it's safe to include weeds in your compost pile. Their nitrogen, phosphorus, and potash content is similar to that of other plant residues, and large quantities furnish more humus for your garden. High temperatures in the middle of the heap will kill all weed seeds and, with proper turning, all seeds get their turn in the deadly middle. Regular turning keeps the biological fires burning until the decomposition process is finished.

··· Advantage #3

Although hot compost requires more attention and effort (especially during turning) than cool compost, it is odor-free. Rapid, aerobic (oxygen-rich) decomposition produces no foul smells like those associated with anaerobic (oxygen-depleted) decomposition. When cared for properly, a compost pile keeps anaerobic bacteria populations low and produces no offensive odors.

··· Advantage #4

High temperatures have a neutralizing effect on pH (acidity or alkalinity). Some compost materials may be acidic, while others may be alkaline. But put them all together and run them through a hot composting process, and the pH turns out to be neutral to very slightly alkaline—perfect for all crops and soils.

··· Advantage #5

Hot compost produces humic acids, which change plant nutrients to stable forms. (Humic acids are natural chelating compounds that absorb, then release, ions of trace elements such as iron, zinc, copper, manganese, and others essential to plant health. Without humic acids, the trace elements would be quickly fixed into forms that are unavailable to plants.) It also creates humus, which slowly releases the nutrients as plant roots need them.

··· Advantage #6

Hot compost packs more nutrients than cold compost. That's because the nutrients in hot compost aren't leached from the pile.

Whatever kind of compost you use, your soil will be healthier, your plants will thank you for it, and you'll have the very real satisfaction of knowing that you're playing a role in maintaining the natural cycle.

I guess you can tell that I'm hooked on compost. But compost isn't my only secret soil builder. Here at Spring Meadow, we use plenty of organic soil amendments, green manures, and mulch to grow our gardens. The next three chapters tell you how easy it is for you to use them, too.

3

Feeding the Soil

As miraculous as compost is, it can't provide *all* the food your garden plants need. But there's no shortage of fertilizer supplements for the organic gardener.

I know gardeners are sometimes tempted by the bags of chemical fertilizer at the garden center—they're so cheap. So available. So easy to use. (Such a waste of money. Such a sorry short-term "solution.") But organic fertilizers are available if you just look around. You can buy them by the pickup load, by the bottle, or even by the designer bag, dry and odor-free. Each type has its place in the garden.

Let's take a look at the five categories of organic fertilizer: animal manures, animal and vegetable meals, minerals, commercial granular fertilizers, and liquid organic fertilizers.

Animal Manures

There's no doubt in my mind that manure is the very best all-around fertilizer. It supplies nitrogen, phosphorus, potassium, and many trace elements. And it furnishes carbon, which is a source of energy for soil microorganisms. It adds organic matter to the soil—something no chemical fertilizer can do. Manure begins releasing its nutrients into the soil as soon as it is applied, but it releases them slowly, helping crops grow steadily throughout the season.

But the contribution of manure to your garden goes far beyond its ability to feed the soil. A rich source of organic matter, manure improves the physical character of soil as it decays. At the same time, it improves the soil's water-holding capacity

Manure as Mulch

Mulching with manure may sound like a strange idea. But we have found that manure is a valuable mulch as well as a source of plant nutrients. Crops such as corn may be top-dressed with manure after the first cultivation to conserve moisture and greatly reduce runoff. The malodorous mulch protects the soil from sun and wind, and the mulched soil will remain friable and alive with beneficial microorganisms.

and drainage. And as manure decays, it releases acids that help to dissolve minerals in the soil.

HOT AND COLD

Just like water from the tap, manure comes two different ways: hot and cold. Hot manures are the ones that contain more than 1 percent nitrogen when fresh. Duck, goose, chicken, sheep, turkey, and rabbit manure are all hot. Cold manures contain less than 1 percent nitrogen when fresh. This group includes cow, hog, goat, and horse manure.

Of course, manure manufacturing is not an exact science. Any type of manure will vary in nutrient content depending on what the animal has been fed. A first-rate manure begins with top-quality feed. So manure from animals fed with legume hay will be of higher quality than the manure of those fed with grass hay since legume hay has a higher protein content. When supplements such as soybean meal, linseed meal, oats, or barley are added to the feed, they contribute greatly to the value of the manure.

SHOPPING FOR DROPPINGS

If you have farm animals, you're lucky to have your own supply of manure. But if you don't, you may still be able to get manure free if you're prepared to do your own hauling. Check the area for horse farms or riding stables. They'll probably be glad to give you all the manure you need at no charge, as long as you haul it away. But even if you have to pay for manure, don't consider it an extravagance. It's an investment in soil fertility.

There are usually three ways manure is sold: fresh, rotted, and air-dried. Fresh is cheapest, and air-dried is the most expensive. Dried manure costs more per pound than fresh because the percentage of water is lower; therefore, the percentage of nutrients and organic matter

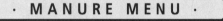

· MANURE MENU ·

Because manure quality varies, the nutrient analysis of manures is not written in stone. But here's a general idea of what you can expect from fresh manure with bedding or litter mixed in. The following are averages of actual amounts of nutrients (in pounds) per 100 pounds of fresh manure.

Type	Nitrogen (N)	Phosphorus (P)	Potassium (K)
Cow	0.6	0.1	0.5
Hog	0.6	0.3	0.5
Horse	0.6	0.2	0.5
Poultry	1.1	1.0	0.5
Rabbit	1.0	0.9	0.65
Sheep	1.0	0.75	0.4

is correspondingly higher. For example, fresh cow manure might have a NPK nutrient analysis of 0.5-0.5-0.5, whereas dried cow manure might weigh in at 2-2-2—four times as much NPK in the same amount of manure.

If you are buying manure, make sure you know something about the way it was handled or you might get burned. In fact, you might be getting burned manure. That's manure that has been piled up in a relatively dry state. The process of composting starts, but then the manure heats up so high that it actually destroys much of the nitrogen and ruins some of the value of the organic matter.

If a manure pile has mushrooms, toadstools, or fungus growing on it, you

Hen Power

Did you know that 25 hens produce about 1 ton of manure a year? That's about 20 pounds of pure nitrogen or as much N as you'll find in eight 50-pound bags of 5-10-5.

can be sure that it's gotten too wet and much of the nutrient value has been leached away. If the pile is hidden beneath a growth of weeds, it's probably chock-full of weed seeds. Either way, avoid the pile.

MIXING IT IN

I like to give my garden a generous feeding of manure every year, so I spread it at a

rate of about 2 pounds per square foot. That's enough to make a 2-inch-thick layer of fresh manure over the entire garden.

Whenever possible, I wait for damp or rainy weather before spreading manure. I know that the drying effects of sun and wind can rob manure of nutrients. I've read about tests showing that one-fourth of the nitrogen in manure may be lost within 12 hours at a temperature of 69°F with an $8\frac{1}{2}$ mile-per-hour wind. For me, that kind of information underscores the importance of storing manure properly and working it into the soil as soon as possible.

The object of manuring is not to get the manure down deep, but to mix it well into the first 5 or 6 inches of soil. A rotary tiller is my favorite piece of equipment for incorporating manure, but you can get the same results with a shovel and a lot of elbow grease.

Fall is the best time for spreading fresh manure. That way, it has time to mellow before the spring planting season. If manure is tilled under in the fall, earthworms will have all winter to "work" it. By spring, the worms' nutrient-rich castings will be available in the soil. Tilling manure under in the

Storing Manure

Manure is perishable. You must take proper care to preserve its full value. Otherwise, nutrients can leach or evaporate from the pile.

The key to storing manure is compaction, which excludes air, thus preventing loss of nitrogen. You should also protect manure from rain, which leaches out soluble nutrients (the ones most available to plants). A manure heap for storage is considerably different from a compost pile. To keep it compacted, pile it as high as possible. I use boards or hay bales to frame the heap. A plastic tarp over the top keeps the rain off.

You Won't Get Burned with Dried Manure

Dried manure won't do the same work as raw manure. It lacks bulk so it can't provide as much organic matter. But dried manure does have one big advantage: It can be used at any time during the growing season. Placed in a furrow or planting hole, it gets crops off to a good start without burning them. You can never use raw manure this way; it will burn the tender young roots. That's because the concentrated ammonia and acids in fresh manure can damage plant tissue.

without ever catching a whiff of manure. There are plenty of organic alternatives.

Animal and Vegetable Meals

In addition to dehydrated manure (usually cow or chicken), there are several other dry organic fertilizers available by the bag. They are generally either animal by-products or vegetable meals. Most are concentrated. They are high in at least one vital element, most often nitrogen. Some of their nitrogen is usually water-soluble, so it's available immediately.

These materials make good fertilizers for an early or

fall also gives the soil bacteria time to reduce the very complex protein molecules down into forms that plant roots can absorb.

TEA TIME

To give my plants an extra shot in the arm just before and after transplanting, I use manure tea. It's easy to make. I just stir 1 part manure into 3 parts water and allow the brew to steep for several days. When it's time to use it, I dilute it with water

in a watering can until it's the color of tea.

LIFE WITHOUT MANURE

But what if you didn't get fresh manure worked in last fall? What if you don't have access to manure at all? What if you just don't want to fool with it? Don't worry! You can grow a thriving, genuine, certifiable organic garden

There's no need to work manure deeply into the soil. The object is to mix it thoroughly into the first 4 to 6 inches of topsoil. I like to apply a 2-inch layer of manure and till it in with a rear-tine rotary tiller.

midsummer side-dressing. If your plants seem sluggish at any time during the growing season, place a handful of one of these organic amendments beside each plant to give them an extra boost.

Minerals for Plants

The best time to build up your soil's mineral reserves is in the late fall, after the harvest is in. Even if you've been adding manure and compost to your garden beds, you may be short-changing the soil of minerals, including phosphorus, potash (potassium), and trace elements. And the best way to replenish soil minerals is with natural rock powders.

CHOOSE THESE
FOR PHOSPHORUS

Rock phosphate includes phosphatized limestones, sandstones, shales, and other igneous rocks, as well as the fossilized remains of marine animals. Rock phosphate contains up to 30 percent phosphorus.

Colloidal or soft phosphate is a finely divided type of rock phosphate obtained from the settling ponds used in the hydraulic mining of phosphate rock. It contains from 18 to 24 percent phosphatic acid. Generally, you'll need to apply about 1½

A Method to Our Manuring

Here at Spring Meadow, our manure fertilizing program stresses these four practices:

♣ Apply plenty of raw manure several months before the new planting season.

♣ Add dehydrated manure directly into the soil when planting and transplanting.

♣ At transplanting, blooming, or fruiting time, dose individual plants with manure tea.

♣ To supplement the manuring program, use all plant debris either as mulch or in compost.

---

times more colloidal phosphate than rock phosphate when fertilizing your soil.

Superphosphate is made by mixing rock phosphate with sulfuric acid. Triple superphosphate is made by mixing rock phosphate with phosphoric acid. Organic gardeners refuse to use these artificially enhanced phosphates because the process leaves residues and leaches out phosphate.

PLENTIFUL POTASH

Potassium, or potash, is available naturally in the form of granite dust and greensand. The potash content of granite dust varies between 3 and 5 percent.

Not all granites are equal in the way they release potassium to plant roots in the soil. The best type of granite dust contains lots of small flakes of dark mica.

Help from the Henhouse

As soon as you spread rock phosphate, head to the henhouse for a truckload of manure. Acids in the manure combine with the phosphate to make the phosphorus more readily available to plants. This is a reciprocal action: The nitrogen in the manure is more readily absorbed by the plants in the presence of available phosphorus.

· WELL-BALANCED MEALS ·

These organic fertilizers may be expensive, but they're high in nutrients readily available to your plants, so a little goes a long way. Kelp, a type of seaweed, is a rich source of micronutrients, too. Here's a look at the more common fertilizer meals and their NPK analyses (in percentages).

MATERIAL	N	P	K
Alfalfa meal	2.7	0.5	2.8
Blood meal	15.0	1.0	1.0
Bonemeal	4.0	21.0	0.25
Cottonseed meal	7.0	2.5	1.5
Fish meal	10.0	5.0	0
Hoof meal	12.5	1.5	0
Kelp	1.0	0	12.0
Leather dust	8.0	0	0

Greensand contains from 6 to 7 percent potash and releases it more readily than granite dust does. Originally an undersea deposit that's now mined in New Jersey, greensand is valuable for improving the soil's physical structure. It absorbs and holds water, stimulates helpful soil organisms, and never burns plants. It is excellent for conditioning both hard and sandy soils.

USING ROCK POWDERS

When using rock powders, don't be afraid to lay them on thickly in late fall and winter. Use about 10 pounds per 100 square feet every three or four years, spreading the powder evenly on the soil surface, then tilling it in with a rotary tiller.

There are many rock fertilizers available to increase your garden's mineral reserve. Because they break down slowly, they release nutrients continuously, and each application is long-lasting.

Mixing It Up and Selling It

Put it all together—the N from manure, animal by-products, or vegetable meals and the P and K from rock dust—and what have you got? A commercial granular fertilizer. Suddenly, there are plenty of balanced, 100 percent organic fertilizers on the market. They rely on all sorts of ingredients for their natural punch, and the price varies accordingly. But most are fine for supplemental feeding. Use them as you would any 5-10-5 fertilizer: to side-dress plants during the growing season or to broadcast over beds and rows.

· ROCK ON ·

Rock powders are great soil amendments since they add phosphorus and potassium to the soil. The finer the powders are ground, the more quickly they'll release nutrients. Here are the NPK percentages.

ROCK POWDER	N	P	K
Rock phosphate	0	30.0	0
Colloidal phosphate	0	18.0	0
Greensand (glauconite)	0	1.5	6.0
Granite dust	0	0	5.0

The best way to get nutrients to your plants in a hurry is by foliar feeding. Nutrients enter the plant directly through the leaf pores rather than taking the long way around through the roots. Spray diluted manure tea, compost tea, liquid seaweed, or fish emulsion on your plants every three to five weeks during the growing season to give them a real boost. If your plants are showing deficiency symptoms, foliar-feed weekly until the symptoms are gone.

Fast, Fast Relief

There's no doubt that organic fertilizers are slower-acting than their chemical counterparts. But is there some natural way to get nutrients to our growing plants quickly during the critical season? Sure there is!

Foliar feeding is the fastest way to get the food to your plants. And the two best liquid organic materials to use for foliar feeding come from a watery environment. They're fish emulsion and seaweed.

Seaweed and fish emulsion are high in readily available, water-soluble nitrogen. When they are applied as a foliar feed in liquid form, the nutrients get to the plants almost immediately.

Plants absorb nutrients not only through their roots, but also through their leaves, stems, buds, and flowers. Foliar feeding puts those nutrients where they can be used right away. In fact, foliar feeding may be eight times more efficient than root feeding. When we apply organic fertilizers to the leaves in soluble forms, the plant may absorb as much as 95 percent of the nutrients, whereas when we apply nutrients to the soil, the plant uses perhaps only 10 percent.

Although foliar feeding should not be used as a replacement for proper soil management, it's an excellent way to correct minor mineral deficiencies and keep plants healthy when they're under stress.

WHEN TO FEED YOUR LEAVES

I like to give plants a dose of foliar spray whenever they are shifting gears: going from a slower mode of growth to a faster one, making flowers, or setting fruit. I also make a point of foliar-feeding plants whenever they're suffering from stress.

Of all the times you can use a foliar spray, I think midsummer is probably the most important. Temperatures are high then, water can be scarce, and fruiting crops like tomatoes and peppers can lose their blossoms after a few days of stress. Drought combined with a calcium deficiency in the soil can cause blossom-end rot in tomatoes and peppers. Insect and disease pressure can be high.

The trace elements and the growth-promoting hormones in diluted seaweed and the extra nitrogen and other minerals in other liquid organic fertilizers can give plants a boost when they need it most. In summer, you may want to give your growing plants a foliar feeding as often as once every two weeks to keep them in peak condition.

I also consider foliar feeding whenever there are long, hot periods without rain because I know that when the soil is dry, the plants can't get as many nutrients as they might need. In a garden's diet, manures, compost, rock fertilizers, and nitrogen-fixing legumes make up the three square meals. But foliar sprays are like vitamin supplements: They give plants an added boost during transplanting and at other stressful times.

Food from the Sea

Seaweed is very important in my total fertilizer regime. It contains traces of 70 elements from the sea, including iodine, as well as growth-stimulating hormones. Seaweed can also help unlock minerals in the soil, making them available to plants.

Seaweed is loaded with potassium. Pound for pound, it contains twice as much as barnyard manures do. Because of the high potassium content, potatoes, beets, and cabbage especially ben-

Seaweed versus Frost

If you apply seaweed to plants just before frost, it will help protect them from cold damage. Seaweed increases the sugar content in plant cells, thereby lowering the freezing point of the sap. Skeptical? Try it yourself! When a frost is expected this fall, spray one row of tomato plants with a seaweed extract and leave another row unsprayed. Then, after the frost hits, go out and see which row of tomatoes has survived better. You'll be convinced.

efit from a dose of seaweed. Seaweed is also high in iron and zinc. Zinc is in short supply in many soils, usually because the application of superphosphate fertilizers has locked it into compounds that plants can't use.

HOW TO USE SEAWEED

You can use liquid extracts of seaweed, or kelp, as a foliar feed. Mix the extract with water according to label directions and apply every five weeks during the growing season. Drench the plants with the solution until it runs off the leaves.

You can also apply seaweed meal to the soil at any time at a rate of 1 pound per 100 square feet. You can even use fresh seaweed as a mulch. Fresh seaweed has the advantage of being free of weed seeds, insect eggs and larvae, and plant diseases.

Spread seaweed on the ground while it's fresh. If you till it into the soil or add it to your compost, your garden will get the full benefit of its nutritive elements.

Seaweed is great, but it's not a complete fertilizer. Though rich in potassium and trace elements, seaweed by itself does not supply enough nitrogen or phosphorus for garden soils. These elements should be added in the form of composted manures and rock phosphate.

Perfecting pH

You can add all the manure, compost, and rock powders in the world, but if the pH of the soil is out of whack, it won't do any good. To understand why, it helps to know a little bit about what pH is.

All plants need and acquire the elements carbon,

hydrogen, and oxygen directly from nature. They get carbon by breaking down carbon dioxide from the air, and they get hydrogen and oxygen by breaking down water, a molecule made up of one hydrogen ion (a positively charged ion) and one hydroxyl ion (a negatively charged particle consisting of a hydrogen atom and an oxygen atom).

The ability of the soil to break down the hydrogen atoms is measured as pH: "potential hydrogen." Acid soil simply has more hydrogen ions than hydroxyl ions in it. The opposite is true of alkaline soil.

THE pH SCALE

The numeric value of pH designates the acidity, neutrality, or alkalinity of the soil on a scale from 1.0 to 14.0. (1.0 is the most acidic, 7.0 is neutral, and 14.0 is extremely alkaline.) Every unit of difference in pH represents 10 times more acidity or alkalinity. In other words, a soil with a pH of 5.0 is 10 times more acid than a soil with a pH of 6.0. The difference is logarithmic—a pH of 5.0 is 100 times more acid than a pH of 7.0.

Working with Wood Ash

Those of us who burn wood to heat our houses have a ready supply of valuable fertilizer—wood ashes. Wood ashes contain two of the basic components of a complete fertilizer: potassium carbonate (potash) and phosphorus (phosphorus pentoxide). They are also rich in magnesium, sulfur, and the trace elements sodium, iron, and silica. In addition, ashes are high in calcium carbonate (a form of lime), making them a speedy way to raise the pH and sweeten the soil.

How much of each element does wood ash provide? On the average, 100 pounds of wood ashes contain 20 to 25 pounds of calcium, 3 to 7 pounds of phosphorus, and 8 to 20 pounds of potassium. However, the amounts vary widely, depending on the type of tree the ash comes from. In general, the highest percentages are in hardwoods, especially young trees and twigs.

I always apply wood ashes in the spring. Because the nutrients are highly soluble, they will be leached by rain and melting snow if you apply them in the fall. I till them in so that they're mixed well with the soil. And although it might mean some extra work, it's a good idea to sift ashes before applying them. Sifting eliminates chunks of hard-to-decompose charcoal and makes uniform application easier.

Be careful when applying ashes. Throwing chunks of ashes from a soaked, caked-up pile onto a garden can do more harm than good. Too heavy a concentration of ashes can make the soil too alkaline for plant growth.

Always store ashes under cover in a fireproof container. (I keep them in a metal trash can.) Not only can the highly soluble potash leach out, but wet ashes are hard to spread, and the lye in the ashes is caustic when wet. Lye can burn seeds, stems, root hairs, and young plants (as well as your hands), so I always make sure to keep wood ashes a few inches from the stems of plants. I've found that 5 to 10 pounds of wood ashes per 100 square feet is just about right for my acid soil.

Although soils usually run from pH 4.5 to 8.5, most common vegetables, fruits, and flowers do best in soils that have a pH of 6.5 to 7.0—slightly acid to neutral. Most of the soils east of the Mississippi River and those lying immediately to the west are acid, and most of the far western soils are alkaline.

Soils in the pH range of 6.5 to 7.0 offer the most favorable conditions for microorganisms that convert atmospheric nitrogen into a form that can be absorbed by plants. They also create the best environment for the bacteria that decompose plant tissue and form humus. All of the essential mineral nutrients are available to plants in this pH range.

WHY pH MATTERS

If your soil is too acid or alkaline, it can lock up nutrients, making them unavailable to your plants. Phosphorus, for instance, becomes fixed into insoluble compounds when the pH is too low. A plant's potassium requirement rises as acidic conditions limit the amounts of available calcium and magnesium. In extremely acid soil, the yield drops due to a shortage of calcium. Because manganese and aluminum are very soluble in highly acid soils, these elements can

become toxic to plants.

In a soil that is too alkaline, the iron is tied up and the plants will turn yellow. If the pH is not corrected, these plants will become lighter and lighter yellow, reaching almost white. Then portions of the leaf margins will start to turn brown and die.

GETTING IT RIGHT

The addition of any kind of organic material to your garden beds buffers the soil. Turning in plenty of organic matter makes both acid and alkaline soils more neutral. It also makes nutrients available that were tied up by pH extremes in either direction.

Sometimes adding organic matter isn't enough. The bacteria that decompose organic matter can't live where the soil is too acid. So the humus level gradually declines, resulting in poor soil structure. At times, it's necessary to step in and adjust the soil's pH by adding lime or sulfur.

It's important to remember that soil pH can change from one season to the next, and from one place to another in your garden. If pine needles, which have a very low pH, fall on part of your garden, that section will gradually become more acid. Acid rain, which is a result of

Ashes to the Rescue

I often use wood ashes for pest protection. Early in the spring, I spread them around young radishes, onions, carrots, and cabbages and other brassicas to protect them from the egg-laying root maggot fly.

When plants are bothered by slugs, snails, or cutworms, I dig a trench 3 or 4 inches wide and a few inches deep around the plants and fill it with wood ashes. The pests will avoid crawling over them.

Old Zeb taught me another use for wood ashes. He controlled flea beetles on tomatoes and other plants by spraying them with a mixture of wood ashes and soapy water. I make this mixture much the same way I make manure tea. I fill a burlap bag and suspend it in a barrel of water. After letting it steep for a week, I strain the "tea" and mix it with soapy water to use as an insecticide.

Wood Ash Warnings

There are some cases when it's better not to use wood ashes. For example, do not use wood ashes near acid-loving plants such as blueberries, azaleas, and rhododendrons, since the ashes will raise soil pH, making the soil more alkaline. And to avoid potato scab, don't apply them to soil in which you'll be planting potatoes.

Although good wood ashes are most welcome in my garden, not all firewood makes good ashes. For instance, never use ashes from painted or chemically treated wood. And don't use ashes from coal—they contain sulfides that can be toxic to plants when wet. Some coal ashes may also contain excessive amounts of iron that can be harmful to the soil.

industrial pollution, poses a real threat to many parts of the country because it dramatically lowers the already slightly acid pH of the soil. And, of course, if you add pH-changing materials like wood ashes, limestone, or sulfur, your soil's pH will change. Test your soil's pH each season before taking corrective action.

TESTING YOUR SOIL'S pH

You can test soil pH yourself with a home soil test kit or a portable pH meter, both of which are available from garden centers and catalogs. For either method, you'll need a soil sample and distilled water to mix with the soil. By inserting a sensitive probe or strip of litmus paper in the solution, you can get a good idea of the pH of your soil.

Of course, results from home test kits or meters are less accurate than those from a soil laboratory. If your home test indicates a soil imbalance, you may want to confirm the results with a professional soil test. Adding too much of a mineral amendment can cause problems that won't be easy to correct; adding too little won't fix the problem.

Both the Cooperative Extension Service and private soil-testing laboratories perform soil analyses for home gardeners. Extension Service tests are generally inexpensive or even free in some states. (To find the Cooperative Extension Service office nearest you, look in the telephone book under

the city or county government listings.) Private labs usually charge $30 or more, but they offer a more complete test and a final report.

Exact procedures for collecting soil samples vary, so check with the lab or Extension Service first. The general steps are usually the same, however. First, remove the surface debris from the area or areas you plan to sample. Then, use a soil probe to cut a core of soil, or dig a small hole using a clean stainless steel trowel or large stainless steel spoon, and cut a slice of soil from the side of the hole. Collect the core or slice to a depth of 6 inches. Put it in a clean plastic or stainless steel container. Take 10 to 15 samples from different areas around the garden, then mix them in the container. Put the required amount of mixed soil in a plastic bag or container, then prepare it for shipment to the lab.

Before mailing your sample, don't forget to include any required information about your soil's history and your gardening plans. Be sure to ask for specific organic recommendations. The test lab will send you a report—usually in four to six weeks—on the results of their analysis, including soil pH and nutrient content.

· PLAYING WITH THE pH ·

The amount of lime or sulfur recommended to alter pH depends on soil type. Here's a guideline for how much you need, in pounds per acre, to bring soil pH to a near-neutral level of 6.5. For a smaller area, the basic rule of thumb for all soils is to add 5 pounds of calcitic limestone, 7 pounds of dolomite, or 6 pounds of wood ashes per 100 square feet to raise the pH 1 point. Add 1 pound of sulfur per 100 square feet to lower the pH 1 point. (But remember, the results won't be as accurate as they will be if you use the figures below and match them to your soil type.)

LIME NEEDED TO RAISE pH (LB./ACRE)

SOIL pH	SAND	LOAM	CLAY
4.5	50	135	195
5.0	40	105	155
5.5	30	80	110
6.0	15	40	55

SULFUR NEEDED TO LOWER pH (LB./ACRE)

SOIL pH	SAND	LOAM	CLAY
8.5	45	55	70
8.0	30	40	45
7.5	10	15	20

Signs of Trouble

There are three main groups of elements essential for healthy plant growth. The first group includes elements taken from water and air. They are oxygen, carbon, and hydrogen. The nice thing about these elements is that the plants can take as much as they need (sometimes thousands of pounds per acre), and you don't have to add them.

The second group includes the major fertilizer elements: nitrogen, phosphorus, potassium, sulfur, calcium, and magnesium. And the final group includes the trace elements: iron, manganese, copper, zinc, boron, and molybdenum. (They're called "trace" elements because the plants need only a little of each element.)

For healthy plant growth and high yields, all of these elements need to be present in the soil in sufficient quantities. But they aren't always there. The best way to detect deficiencies in the soil is through a complete soil test. But you can also learn to recognize signs of deficiency in your garden plants and nip them (the deficiencies, not your plants!) in the bud.

Here's a quick checklist of deficiency symptoms and cures. Keep in mind that application rates may vary depending on your soil type and other factors. (See "Playing with the pH" on this page for more information on applying lime and sulfur.) Also, use dolomite or wood ashes cautiously; repeated applications can cause an excess of magnesium or potassium, which in turn can harm your plants.

· · · Nitrogen Deficiency
Symptoms: Nitrogen deficiency is characterized by slow growth, slender stems, and foliage that fades to yellow. When short of nitrogen, tomatoes start to fade at the tips of the top leaves. Cucumber fruit can be pointed at the blossom end. Nitrogen-starved corn plants will be yellowish green instead of green.

Cure: Apply a nitrogen-rich fertilizer such as blood meal (up to 3 pounds

Garden plants try to tell you when they're hungry for certain elements. Here are some common signs of deficiencies on crop plants.

Nitrogen: Cucumber fruit may be pointed at the blossom end.

Phosphorus: The undersides of tomato leaves turn a dark purplish color; corn ears may be missing kernels.

Potassium: Cabbage will have parched leaves with pale, brown-spotted areas on the leaf margins.

Magnesium: Cucumbers and squash will have yellow mottling between veins on the leaves.

Boron: Tomato plants will have black-ened areas on the stems, especially at the growing tips; the terminal shoots will be yellow and curled.

Calcium: The upper leaves of tomatoes will be pale yellow, and leaves will curl backward toward the upper surface of the leaf.

per 100 square feet), cotton-seed meal (2 to 5 pounds per 100 square feet), or fish meal (up to 5 pounds per 100 square feet). You can also foliar-feed the plants with manure tea.

· · · Phosphorus Deficiency

Symptoms: A phosphorus shortage in the soil can cause purplish undersides of leaves on tomatoes or ears of corn that aren't filled out with kernels.

Cure: Apply bonemeal (up to 5 pounds per 100 square feet), fish meal (up to 5 pounds per 100 square feet), or colloidal phosphate (up to 10 pounds per 100 square feet). Wood ashes (6 pounds per 100 square feet) are also a good source of phosphorus.

· · · Potassium Deficiency

Symptoms: Potassium defi-ciencies show up in reduced plant vigor, poor growth, and low yields. In tomatoes, leaves are often ash gray, with brown edges that crinkle or curl and then become bronzed. Potassium-poor cabbage and brussels sprouts have leaves that become parched on the rim, with lighter areas that have brown spots inside. Carrot leaves curl, turning grayish green and finally bronze. Cucumber fruit de-velops an enlarged tip. Beets may develop long, tapered roots rather than round ones.

Cure: Greensand and granite dust (both up to 10 pounds per 100 square feet) are good sources of potash. Wood ashes (6 pounds per 100 square feet) are also a good source of potassium.

· · · Magnesium Deficiency

Symptoms: When lacking magnesium, plants are generally late to mature and have poor overall quality. Areas between the leaf veins turn yellow, then brown, while the veins remain green.

Tomatoes develop brittle leaves that curl up and turn yellow. Corn develops a yellow striping and white streaks on the older leaves. Light-colored spots appear on cabbage leaves, while the edges may turn white or very pale yellow. Eventually, the entire leaf becomes mottled with dead areas. If the cabbage plants are also deficient in nitrogen, the leaves turn light green, then yellow, and finally become mottled in the dead areas.

Cure: The best source of magnesium is dolomitic limestone. (To raise pH 1 point, use 7 pounds per 100 square feet on clay or sandy loam, $5\frac{1}{2}$ pounds on sand, and 10 pounds on loam soil.)

· · · Sulfur Deficiency

Symptoms: Insufficient sulfur can reduce plant growth and may cause the leaves at the tips of the branches to turn down.

Cure: Apply powdered sulfur or Sul-Po-Mag (up to 1 pound per 100 square feet).

· · · Calcium Deficiency

Symptoms: Suspect a calcium deficiency when the plant's leaves roll backward toward the upper surface and young growth is distorted.

Cure: Apply calcitic limestone (5 pounds per 100 square feet to raise pH 1 point), bonemeal (up to 5 pounds per 100 square feet), or wood ashes (6 pounds per 100 square feet).

· · · Boron Deficiency

Symptoms: Plants need only a minute amount of boron. But if this element is lacking, you'll see specific changes in different crops. Beets and turnips, for example, develop corklike areas in the roots, while a hollow stem forms in cauliflower. Celery cracks.

Blackened areas appear at the growing tips of tomato stems, while the terminal shoots curl, turn yellow, and die. The plants have a bushy appearance, and the fruit may have darkened or dried areas. In lettuce, the fastest-growing leaves are malformed and may also be spotted and burned.

Cure: Apply household borax ($\frac{1}{2}$ ounce per 100 square feet).

But don't let all these symptoms and horror stories scare you. Chances are, you won't see one of them in years of organic gardening. The beauty of organic gardening is that you generally don't have to worry about micromanagement. When you treat soils regularly with manure, compost, organic supplements, green manures, and mulch, they maintain a balance. Critical shortages rarely occur. You create a soil bank that plants can draw from during times of need.

Green manures sound mysterious and intimidating to some gardeners. Living manure? Turn to Chapter 4, and you'll find out that green manures are really just crops that feed the soil. Let's learn what they are and how to grow them.

4

Let's Grow Green Manures

Mother Nature doesn't leave the soil bare and exposed to the elements. She knows that the best way to maintain and improve the soil is to keep it covered, tie it together with roots, and add organic matter.

In the wild, good soils are never without a cover of vegetation from the earliest moment growth can begin in spring until well past killing frosts in fall. Roots spread deeply and thoroughly through the earth, opening up tight soil. When the roots die, they become food for microorganisms and earthworms, whose work improves the soil even more.

Imitating Nature

As an organic gardener, I try to emulate nature by planting cover crops, which are also called "green manures" because of the organic matter and nutrients they add to the soil. Cover cropping is the quickest, surest, most complete, and easiest method for saving the soil. Yet most gardeners I meet don't use it or even understand it. I aim to fix that, here and now.

A good cover crop keeps the soil from eroding and smothers weed seedlings. Cover crops also trap and release nitrogen, potash, and other nutrients that would otherwise be leached away from your plants.

Aside from an increase in soil fertility, you'll see the effect of cover crops on soil structure with every trowelful of earth you turn. The workability of the soil will increase tremendously the first time you plow under a cover crop. Drainage and water retention will be improved. And the

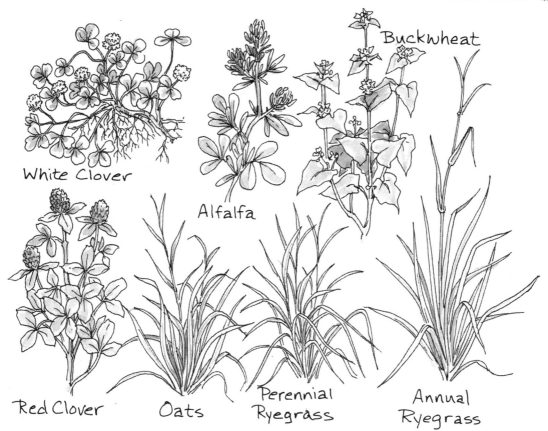

White Clover

Alfalfa

Buckwheat

Red Clover

Oats

Perennial Ryegrass

Annual Ryegrass

If you have the space, it really pays to set aside half of your garden for cover crops. Sow a crop like ryegrass or oats in half the garden one year, then plow it under the following year and plant your garden in its place. Here are some of my favorite green manures: white clover (*Trifolium repens*), alfalfa (*Medicago sativa*), buckwheat (*Fagopyrum esculentum*), red clover (*T. pratense*), oats (*Avena sativa*), perennial ryegrass (*Lolium perenne*), and annual ryegrass (*L. multiflorum*).

earthworms and beneficial bacteria will thank you.

The Great Cover-Up

We have a cardinal rule here at Spring Meadow: Don't leave the soil bare—ever! Besides adding compost, manure, and organic fertilizers, we plant a cover crop as soon as every food crop is finished. The benefits of having roots in the ground and copious green matter above are well worth the cost of the seed and the effort of planting.

There are a great number of plants that make good green manures. Buckwheat, oats, alfalfa, clovers, and annual and perennial ryegrass are some of my favorites. Some, such as oats, are best for planting in hot weather. Others, including winter rye and winter wheat, are good for sowing in fall and overwintering. Green manures, like alfalfa and clover, make (or "fix") nitrogen, while others, like buckwheat, are best at suppressing weeds.

You can spend a lot of time deciding which cover crop is best for you. But you can narrow the list fast if you first figure out when you'll have space available for a cover crop, and how long you can afford to keep that space under cover.

TRY WINTER RYE

I like winter ryegrass. I think it's the best short-term crop for any garden. Sown in the fall, it is the hardiest of all winter grains. Ryegrass has an amazing tolerance for cold weather. Seeds can germinate at soil temperatures as low as 33°F. Plants grow actively in the fall until the temperature drops below 40°F, and can survive -40°F in the dead of winter.

They resume growth when the temperature rises to 40°F in the spring.

Rye can be planted anytime from August up to mid-October here on Long Island, and even later farther south. Interplanting rye in a bed of late sweet corn is an excellent strategy. After frost kills the corn, the rye still has about a month to six weeks to grow and cover the ground.

ALFALFA FOR NITROGEN

Whenever I have an area that I can take out of production over a long period, I sow alfalfa. It's a crop that can be left in place for three years or more. During that time, it will produce a root system that

can penetrate even the heaviest soils to bring up minerals and nutrients. Alfalfa also produces a lot of nitrogen in the roots, leaves, and stems.

All the other legumes— beans, peas, vetches, and clovers—also add nitrogen to the soil. They take nitrogen from the air and store it in their roots. When you till them in, the roots break down, releasing the stored nitrogen into the soil.

Time to Take Cover

Careful timing is the key to fitting green manures into your garden plan. Some gardeners believe that the entire garden must be empty before you can plant a cover crop.

I don't wait for fallow ground to sow green manures. One of my favorite cover crop schemes is to sow oats in between rows of crops such as lettuce. The oats protect the soil from erosion, produce valuable organic matter, and shade the lettuce, which slows down bolting.

Wrong! Any empty spot, no matter how small, is a candidate for cover cropping. Pull out a 3-by-3-foot bed of carrots, and you can go right in and sow buckwheat. One of my favorite cover schemes is to sow oats in between rows of crops such as lettuce.

On the other hand, if you have space to spare, it pays to set up a cover-crop rotation. The best scenario would be to cut your garden space in two, and plant one half in regular crops and the other half in a cover crop. Then alternate the two areas each year. Trust me—you'll soon be getting just as much production from half the space with half the work because the soil will be of a much better quality.

Winter, though, is when the cover crops really earn their keep. That's when the ground is not being used for anything else, and the cover crop holds the soil against wind, water, and erosion. The roots continue to grow, even when it is too cold for plants to grow above ground. The roots sink deep into the subsoil to bring back leached nutrients that otherwise would never be available to shallow-rooted vegetables and flowers.

Winter rye, ryegrass, and winter wheat are most commonly used for overwintering. They will sprout in the fall and make enough growth to hold down erosion before winter comes. Then they will wait till the first warm days of spring to make more topgrowth.

In the North, the best time to sow legumes is in the spring. They'll grow vigorously through the summer, and many types—including alfalfa, red clover, some sweet clovers, and vetch—will live over the winter.

Sowing Green Manures

To sow grasses and grains, just till or rake the soil shallowly, broadcast the seed, rake again to cover it lightly, and pat the soil down with the back of a hoe. For large seeds, make furrows in rows, and sow in the furrows just as you would for green beans.

If the weather is dry at sowing time, you may have to water well until the seeds germinate. Where the soil is very poor, an application of compost will give the cover crop a boost, so it will grow more vigorously and produce more organic matter for the soil.

Worth Their Weight

Green manures ensure that the soil's wealth doesn't get lost or stolen, and they contribute to that wealth for as long as they're in the ground. Although they do not have the concentrated richness of animal manures, green manures are hard to beat for their convenience and organic matter production.

Think about this: A 5-pound sack of buckwheat seed planted on a 3,200-square-foot garden will produce nearly 1 ton of organic matter in only eight weeks. All you have to do is till it in! And a well-grown legume crop, plowed under at the proper stage (just before full bloom), can add 100 to 150 pounds of nitrogen per acre.

Since so much of the value of cover crops depends on their fibrous root systems, it's best to postpone working them in for as long as your planting schedule permits. The bigger the root systems get, the more organic matter your soil gets.

Perhaps the greatest benefit of using cover crops is the knowledge that you are being a steward of the soil and not a miner. You are giving back as much as you are taking away, so your soil will get better and better the longer you garden there. When I grow green manures, I feel good—and so does my soil!

CHAPTER

5

Making the Most of Mulch

Mulching is another technique we borrow from Mother Nature. We mimic nature's snowfall in winter and leaf drop in fall. No doubt about it: Applying mulch to a garden pays big dividends in terms of time, work, water use, and soil fertility.

Mulching fertilizes the soil, stops erosion, and keeps watering to a minimum. It increases the earthworm population. And mulch keeps disease-carrying soil from splashing up onto vegetables and fruits during hard rains.

Miraculous, Multipurpose Mulch

I like to think of mulching as a no-work way of improving my soil. During the course of the growing season, the mulch breaks down and releases nutrients and humic acids into the soil. The humic acids help release soil minerals, which may otherwise be in insoluble forms that are unavailable to plants.

When the summer weather turns very hot and windy, mulches protect the soil surface from rapid drying, thereby preventing plant stress. And, since the mulch is preserving your soil moisture, you won't need to water as often.

Mulch earns its keep in rainy weather, too. Many crops, such as cucumbers, squash, strawberries, and tomatoes, may rot or become moldy if left lying on the bare ground. Mulch offers a layer of protection. Produce from mulched plants is also cleaner—for example, you'll need to do a lot less washing when preparing greens for the table.

Earthworms thrive under mulch. They multiply like mad in mulched areas. And their nitrogen-rich castings make a rich addition to the soil and free up minerals that might otherwise remain locked up. Earthworm burrows also help aerate the soil.

Mulch minimizes cultivation and weeding, too. The soft soil under mulch needs little cultivation from year to year, and if any weeds do manage to peek through the mulch, they are easy to pull.

Mulching Materials

Over many years of merry mulching, I've found that the two most important factors in choosing a mulch material are whether it's easy to get and whether it's easy to handle. Here are some that meet my criteria:

Hay. I like hay. It comes conveniently packaged in bales. It's easy to spread after peeling layers from the bale.

Grass clippings and leaves. Grass clippings, of course, are free and plentiful, and so are leaves in most parts of the country. Grass clippings break down quickly and add nitrogen to the soil, while leaves break down more slowly and are a better source of organic matter. If you have a shredder, use it. Shredded leaves make a better mulch than whole leaves since they break down faster and don't mat down as much.

Pine needles. Pine needles are a good choice where they're available. A 2- to 4-inch layer is especially beneficial for acid-loving plants such as berries.

Seaweed and salt hay. Gardeners living along the East or West Coast often have easy access to seaweed and salt hay. Both are practical and effective, rich in minerals, and free of weed seeds.

Compost. Compost makes a nutritious mulch as well as an excellent soil amendment. It adds nitrogen and other nutrients to the soil. But I tend to use compost in the soil rather than on it, since it takes a lot of compost to mulch a bed, and a thin layer isn't too effective against weeds. However, you can top a thin layer of compost with a second, thicker layer of straw, hay, shredded leaves, or wood chips.

Straw. The best mulch of all, in my opinion, is straw. It holds water well. It gradually breaks down into fertilizer to feed the newly established roots of growing plants. And it's free of weed seeds.

LAYING IT ON

When it comes to most mulches, I like to lay them on thick. I use up to 1 foot for hay and straw. But I hold back on grass clippings, using only 2 to 4 inches.

I use a thinner layer of grass clippings because

The type of mulch you use determines how thickly you should spread it. I like to pile hay and straw on thick—6 inches to 1 foot. Wood chips break down slowly, so a 4-inch layer is plenty. And 3 inches of shredded leaves will keep weeds out and hold soil moisture in without matting down.

they're nitrogen-rich and basically turn into compost right where you put them. While they're "cooking," they get very hot. A thin layer breaks down fast, but a thick layer may mat down, creating an impermeable surface that lets rainwater run off rather than soak into the soil. And the heat that builds up as a thick layer breaks down can actually burn plant stems if the clippings touch them.

Wood Chips: The Way It Is

Wood chips and sawdust are good choices for permanent plantings like trees and shrubs. Since you don't have to work the soil around woodies often, you won't keep hitting chips. But these mulches may also lower the pH of the soil.

There's another potential drawback of wood chips and sawdust: Both are high in carbon and low in nitrogen, so soil microorganisms may take the nitrogen they need from the soil as they break down the mulch into humus. This may cause a temporary nitrogen shortage, resulting in a nitrogen deficiency in your plants.

To remedy this situation, you may need to mix in a mulch like grass clippings that's high in nitrogen, or add a nitrogen-rich fertilizer, such as manure, soybean meal, or blood meal. A good rate for a 1,000-square-foot garden area is 7 pounds of blood meal, 14 pounds of soybean meal, or 200 pounds of cow, hog, or horse manure. (That's 0.7 pounds of blood meal, 1.4 pounds of soybean meal, or 20 pounds of manure for each 100-foot bed.) Using aged or composted sawdust also helps prevent nitrogen deficiency, since the sawdust will already be decayed.

When I use wood chips, I try not to get carried away. A 4-inch layer is plenty for covering the soil and preventing weeds. That's because wood chips are dense and break down much more slowly than more lightweight materials like straw and hay.

Mulching Warm-Season Crops

Some vegetables, such as corn and tomatoes, need a thoroughly warmed soil for optimum growth. Since organic mulches cool the soil, they may slow down such crops if they're applied too early in the spring. Wait until it's bean-sowing time, when the soil temperature reaches about 60°F, before applying mulch to warm-weather crops.

However, for best results with warm-weather crops, you can combine mulches. For example, tomatoes will bear two weeks earlier if you use a black plastic mulch and then an organic mulch. Place a 2-foot-square piece around each plant at planting time. The plastic will absorb the warmth of the sun and heat the soil faster. Once the soil has warmed, you can replace the plastic with leaf mulch, which will allow rainwater to penetrate and will add organic matter to the soil.

Mulch, Mulch, Mulch!

Once your garden soil has warmed to at least 60°F and the plants are growing well, get out the wheelbarrow and pitchfork, and mulch, mulch, mulch! You'll be conserving water, stimulating soil organisms, protecting tender plant roots, and conditioning the soil.

Try to follow nature's plan as closely as possible. Organic mulches—both natural and applied—contribute to plant growth twice: first as mulch, and then as plant nutrients after bacteria and other organisms have worked them into the soil. You can make this system work in your garden, too. You'll be glad you did.

PART II

Let's Get Planning and Planting

6

Planning the Plot

Now let's move from the rich soil of the garden to the fertile ground of the mind. That's where every garden begins. In our minds, every garden is a perfect one: The plants spring out of the soil. They bend with abundant harvests. Pests fly by—on their way to somebody else's garden. Every day is sunny. Each evening brings thirst-quenching rain.

When you decide to get growing, a little bit of dreaming and overconfidence is allowed. What's *not* allowed is blind faith in your power of memory. There's an odd syndrome that's common to every gardener, including

me. I call it the Data Bank Brain Syndrome. We're in such a hurry to plant every spring, we don't have time for pencil and paper, note taking, and other bothersome distractions. "I'll remember which lettuce cultivar I planted and when," we say. "I'll remember when it rained, when I watered, and when the last frost came." Wrong!

Noteworthy Note Taking

In my 20-plus years of organic gardening, there's no doubt that my most important tool has been my record book. I have a complete crop

history of everything that's been planted here at Spring Meadow over the past 10 years. There are 57 beds here, and each bed does triple or even quadruple duty over the course of a year. I plant successions for spring, summer, fall, and sometimes even winter. Keeping track of the comings and goings of various crops could be a real headache. But I've devised a system that keeps it simple.

For record keeping, each bed is assigned a number. And each bed is divided by compass points. Each growing season, I keep track of every crop that grows in every part of every bed.

So, at a glance, I can see what was planted on the east side of bed 26 in the spring of 1991, for example. I also note when I fertilize or add compost or mulch.

Now I can simply pick up a notebook to "remember" that I planted lettuce on April 12 in bed 26. It's right there in black and white, along with notations that I added a 1-inch-deep layer of compost when the harvest was done in May, and then sowed a cover crop of buckwheat.

Back to the Future

The first part of planning this year's garden is looking at last year's. Ask yourself how last year's gardening season went. Were there gaps in the production of vegetables you count on? Did you manage to have lettuce early and late, and plenty of tomatoes to go with it? What insects and diseases gave you problems, and what biological controls now are ready when their cycle comes around again? Did you plant succession crops?

If you've been keeping good records, you've got the answers. If not, resolve to start—right now.

For the Record

There are as many ways to keep records as there are methods for growing tomatoes or planting a perennial bed. It's as individualistic as gardening itself. But I'd like to offer a few general guidelines to make your record keeping simpler.

No matter how sure you are that you'll remember all the details of the gardening season, somehow time can blur them into a confusing jumble. The only way to be sure you'll know what was planted where (and when) is to keep a

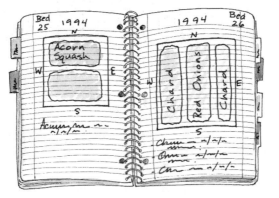

Save time and effort later by keeping good records now. By showing what you plant where and recording how each crop did, you can avoid repeating costly mistakes, prepare for pest invasions, plan crop rotations, and discover which cultivars and techniques work best for you.

garden planning and record notebook.

I like to use a thick spiral notebook with stick-on tabs to index it. When compiling information, start with the crops. Note which seeds you bought, where and when you bought them, and how much they cost. If you're experimenting with new cultivars, it might help to mark them with a star. Note sowing and transplanting dates. Keep track of how many seeds you planted in which part of the garden.

Don't forget the harvest! That's what determines success or failure of a crop. So mark down dates and amount of harvest, too. If you're canning or freezing your bounty, write down how many pints or quarts you keep.

KEEPING TRACK

That is only the beginning. Your journal won't be of much use unless you keep track of what you did to get those crops to produce. Write down all the details of soil preparation, fertilization, mulching, staking, and experimental gardening techniques.

Be specific. Was the soil tilled, double-dug, or turned

into raised beds? What types of fertilizers did you use? Did you apply lime, compost, shredded leaves, manure, wood ashes, rock phosphate, granite dust, bonemeal, or other supplements? Did you plant part of the garden in a green manure crop? If so, which green manure did you plant, and how long was the interval between planting and tilling it under? Make sure to note all of your expenses.

And don't forget the things you weren't able to control. Was the weather a real bummer this year? Make a notation of it in your record book. Did you have a late-spring frost that cut back all the tender vegetables long after the normal frost-free date had passed? The garden record book is also the place to log rainfall amounts for the various months, including, of course, details such as whether the moisture came in a deluge or at nicely spaced intervals.

SUCCESS STORIES

In the end, long after those plants fade and freeze, you'll have written proof of your successes. With a little bit of figuring, you'll be able to add up the value of your harvest.

You can even drop by the supermarket and figure out just how much you've saved. Or gloat as you com-pare your bunches of onions hanging resplendently from the basement rafters with those dull, dried-out objects being offered at an outra-geous price at the store.

Of course, there's plenty to gardening that can't be measured in dollars and cents. Stop and reflect how much inner satisfaction the garden brought you this year. How did it expand your hori-zons and keep you in touch with the foundation of life, the earth under your feet?

Make a Garden Map

All of that writing may seem overwhelming. But, of course, it doesn't have to be done all at once. The first year's record keeping starts with a map of the new garden. Make sure to divide the garden by time as well as space. No matter where you garden, there should be time for three seasons of crops.

Draw your garden map in triplicate, showing your early, midseason, and late planting patterns. Mark the number of days each crop will occupy the garden space. After you've mapped out the early garden, subsequent plans will fall into place. For example, in April you'll be able to see at a glance what room you will have in August for next winter's kale.

After you jot it all down, a pattern will begin to take shape. You'll be able to see where you want to make changes in this year's garden. You may decide to switch from bush beans to pole beans, which produce more in a limited space. You might decide that you can afford the space to put in more beets for winter use. Or there may be more room than you thought for the long-keeping winter squash.

Catalog Time

Once you've filled in your map, and only when that's done, you can yield to temp-tation and pull out the seed catalogs. You'll probably al-ready know which old fa-vorite cultivars you want to order. Look for new cultivars that tout improved flavor or growth habit. Have you over-looked some high-vitamin or disease-resistant strain?

Make a list of the culti-vars you want to order. If you're like me, you'll find that it's much too long. That's the time to pull out your garden map. With the seed list in hand, decide what to plant in each garden bed or row.

Getting plans down on paper helps you group early crops, such as radishes and lettuce; crops that remain in place all season, including peppers and tomatoes; and crops that finish with the first frost, such as kale and brussels sprouts. The plan may change as the season wears on, but it will remain a helpful guide.

CULTIVAR CHECKLIST

It's easy to be seduced by the pretty pictures in seed catalogs. And once we get past the photos, there's the hype: Bigger! Earlier! Juicier! But in most seed catalogs, there's plenty of useful information as well.

When I thumb through a catalog looking for new cultivars, I have a checklist in mind. I look first for flavor, nutritional value, good yield, and resistance to pests and diseases. I keep in mind my succession plans, and search for cultivars that will fit my spring, midsummer, and fall rotations.

DO YOU SPEAK CATALOG?

There's plenty of information in seed catalogs, but some may need a bit of decoding. Here are some of the things to look for when ordering from a catalog.

· · · Days to Maturity

Not sure about how long a certain vegetable will tie up space in your garden? Most catalogs note the days to maturity. Of course, this is only an average number, based on optimum growing conditions.

Unseasonably low temperatures, dry or wet weather, or any unusual stress factors may prolong the days to harvest. Plan accordingly, and remember to add on a few extra days for fall plantings to give crops plenty of time to mature.

· GIANTS ·

__FABULOUS FRANKIE.__ 62 days. One of our most popular tomatoes. A variety that beats any of the beefsteaks, the fruits have full, robust flavor, good flat-round shape with smooth shoulders, small blossom-end scar, and jumbo size—most of the fruits weigh almost 3 pounds. Highly resistant to fusarium and verticillium. Strong, determinate plants provide great foliage protection for fruit. *Seed sprouts at 50°F/10°C in cool soil.* **DF/HWT/GS.**

· DETERMINATE ·

__RED DAWN (F₁).__ 65 days. NEW. Early with smooth large fruit. Red Dawn's large (avg. 8-10 oz.), firm, globe-shaped fuits ripen very early. Not susceptible to cracking and blossom end defects. The plants are vigorous for an early variety for better stress and blight tolerance. This is the most interesting new, early fresh market tomato. **V/N/T.**

· PASTE ·

__BELLA.__ 70 days. Bella, a large-fruited plum type, is the best mid-early processor we have seen for home gardens and roadside stands. The red, 4-5 oz. fruits are nearly twice as large as normal plum tomatoes for easy hand harvesting and peeling. Highly rated in processing tests, especially for paste and juice. Compact plant. Determinate. **V/N/As/L.**

There's more to a seed catalog than pretty pictures. You can learn a lot if you read the fine print. Cultivar descriptions include days to maturity, insect and disease resistance, flavor, shape, size, yield, and whether the cultivar is an early-, mid-, or late-season type. The descriptions may also include details like weeks to transplanting (the indoor growing period), germination temperature, recommended spacing, and planting depth.

· DAYS TO MATURITY ·

How long does it take from the time you plant your seeds until you can expect a crop? Whether you grow your plants from seed or buy bedding plants, you can use these guidelines to find out. Some crops don't have numbers in both columns. That's because crops like beans and spinach are almost always direct-seeded rather than transplanted. Ranges are given because the maturity date varies with the cultivar. If you want a fast-maturing tomato, for example, check the catalog to find the cultivars with the shortest maturity dates.

CROP	DAYS FROM SOWING	DAYS FROM TRANSPLANTING
Beans	45–70	
Beets	50–60	
Broccoli	110–120	60–80
Cabbage	110–130	60–90
Carrots	70–80	
Cauliflower	120–130	70–90
Corn	70–90	
Cucumbers	65–85	50–70
Eggplant	130–150	70–90
Lettuce	40–70	25–50
Melons	80–100	70–90
Peas	55–90	
Peppers	130–150	60–90
Pumpkins	75–100	
Radishes	25–40	
Spinach	40–60	
Squash	85–100	50–60
Tomatoes	110–130	70–90

· · · Spacing

The amount of seed you get in a standard pack will vary, of course, from crop to crop and company to company. A ½-ounce package of summer squash seed will contain 100 to 150 seeds, for example. The same size pack of carrot seeds will contain about 9,000 seeds!

Your catalog will tell you how many seeds you should plant per row foot or

bed. So start with your garden map, decide how much space you have available, and you'll be able to figure out just how much seed you need for each crop. (Of course, for intensive gardening, you can get away with closer spacing. See Chapter 8 to find out how.)

Trust the seeds. When it comes to sowing, many gardeners think that if a few are good, then lots will be better. But "less is more" is true in the garden, too. I've seen doubtful gardeners empty a whole packet of seeds in a small space, not expecting them to germinate. But if the seed is fresh, most will germinate. In their quest for light and food, the crowded seedlings will develop tall, weak stems that never fully recover even after the surplus seedlings have been thinned out. (To say nothing of all the extra work thinning the beds!)

It's true that the seeds of some crops, such as peas and parsnips, should be sown rather thickly, but most others shouldn't be overcrowded. Read the seed packet to determine recommended seed spacing—and believe it.

· · · General Culture

General growing information is limited by catalog space, so it's usually very basic and abbreviated. However, most of the better catalogs will at least tell you the pitfalls to avoid when planting a particular vegetable. They also usually include suggested planting depths and row spacing.

··· Germination Temperatures

Seeds have very different requirements for best germination. Lettuce seed does best in cool weather, for example. Lima beans like it hot. Plants that reach maturity in warm weather usually need warm temperatures to germinate, and most of the cool-weather crops require somewhat cool temperatures even for seed germination.

Air temperatures vary from day to day and can even change drastically from minute to minute, especially during planting time. The soil temperature—how hot or cold it is around the seed itself—is more stable, so it's used as the recommended planting temperature.

Before planting seeds, test your soil temperature with a soil thermometer, available at garden supply stores and through garden catalogs. Then check "Soil Temperatures for Planting Seeds" on this page to find out what to plant.

··· Indoor Growing Period

Some vegetables, such as peppers and eggplant, must

· SOIL · TEMPERATURES FOR PLANTING SEEDS

Your seeds will just sit—or even rot—in the ground unless it's warm enough for them to germinate. Don't plant until the soil has reached the following minimum temperatures:

CROP	TEMPERATURE
Beans	60°F
Beets	50°F
Cabbage	40°F
Carrots	60°F
Lettuce	50°F
Melons	60°F
Peas	50°F
Pumpkins	60°F
Radishes	45°F
Spinach	40°F
Squash	65°F
Turnips	40°F

be started indoors so they'll have time to mature before the end of the season. That's especially true in the North, since you need a head start because of the long growing periods and heat requirements of these vegetables. Starting seeds indoors is also necessary in some parts of the South to *avoid* the hottest, most humid weather.

This period of indoor growing, from seed sowing to transplanting outdoors, is usually listed in the catalogs as "weeks to transplant." For example, peppers, which need eight weeks to transplant, should be sown in the greenhouse or under lights on April 1 for a June 1 planting-out date.

··· Disease and Pest Resistance

If hybrids have one thing in their favor, it's their improved disease resistance. There are hundreds of cultivars that are resistant to most troublesome diseases.

These resistant cultivars are marked in catalogs with letters after their name. The letters look mysterious, but they tell you which diseases the plant resists or tolerates. For help breaking the code, see "Decoding Disease Abbreviations" on page 54.

Some cultivars even resist insect pests. For instance, if your squash plants are always plagued by squash borers, you can avoid the problem by planting butternut squash. Butternut has an extra-tough stem and is rarely bothered by any kind of insect. There are also tomato cultivars that resist nematodes, and cucumber cultivars that beetles will pass by in search of tastier fare.

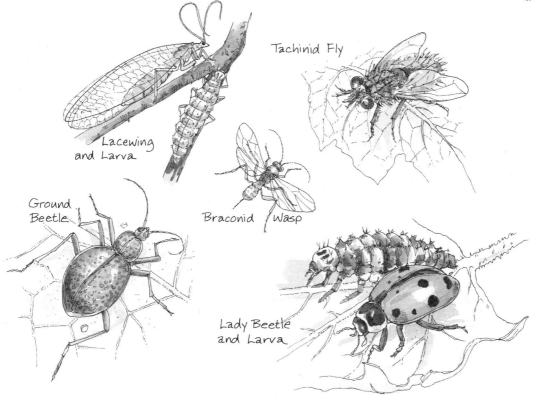

Tachinid Fly

Lacewing
and Larva

Ground
Beetle

Braconid Wasp

Lady Beetle
and Larva

Encourage these helpful insects to take over your garden's pest patrol by growing a variety of plants in your garden. Lots of different crops, planted with herbs like dill and parsley, will attract many beneficial insects. Interplanting will also confuse insect pests—they won't be able to find your crops as easily and may seek dinner elsewhere.

Diversity in the Garden

When you plan, shop for seeds, and sow, keep one thing in mind: diversity. The sheer pleasure of variety is enough to explain why gardeners enjoy growing so many kinds of plants.

But there is also security in diversifying the kinds of plants we grow. If one plant fails, another takes its place. The frost that kills a pepper plant sweetens the kale. This way, growing a variety of crops helps ensure a good harvest over a long season.

Diversity in our gardens also encourages synergism—the ability of different plants to help each other rather than compete. A deep-rooted plant such as a tomato can tap nutrients deep in the soil and bring them closer to the surface, where shallow-rooted plants such as lettuce can get at them. A garden with many different plant forms, heights, leaf shapes, and sizes uses the sun's energy more efficiently.

Your garden, by its very diversity, will encourage birds, amphibians like frogs and toads, and beneficial insects to visit or live there. These welcome visitors will, in turn, help to control many kinds of garden pests. Bees, wasps, and butterflies will

Most seed catalogs tell you which vegetable cultivars tolerate or resist certain diseases. But the cultivar descriptions often abbreviate the disease names, which can be very confusing. The next time you're paging through a seed catalog, use this handy chart to decipher the alphabet soup of disease abbreviations:

CODE	DISEASE
ALS	Angular leaf spot
Anth	Anthracnose
BLS	Bacterial leaf spot
BMV	Bean mosaic virus
CMV	Cucumber mosaic virus
DM	Downy mildew
F	Fusarium wilt
MV	Mosaic virus
PM	Powdery mildew
TB	Tipburn
TLS	Target leaf spot
TMV	Tobacco mosaic virus
V	Verticillium wilt
Y	Cabbage yellows

pollinate your plants. Earthworms will improve the soil, and millions of beneficial soil-dwelling bacteria and fungi will work hard to transform nutrients into a form that plants can use.

Diversity does not mean confusion, though. There is no reason to be hit-or-miss in planting. However eager you are to grow many different kinds of vegetables, fruit trees, berry bushes, herbs, and other useful and ornamental plants, you still need a well-focused, well-designed garden plan to make it all work.

ENSURING PLANT DIVERSITY

I like to think of heirloom cultivars as buried treasures. Most gardeners don't know about them, but when you grow a 'Moon and Stars' watermelon or 'Jacob's Cattle' beans in your garden, everybody wants some for themselves. That's because some of the most flavorful (and colorful, for that matter) vegetables we can grow are these old, nonhybrid standard cultivars.

Saving seed from honored local cultivars is the best way to preserve the diversity that is so important for the protection of our food system over the years and centuries ahead. Many of these old reliable cultivars are already disappearing, pushed out of seed catalogs by hybrids bred for size, shape, or ease of shipping rather than flavor.

You can find a delightful assortment of heirloom cultivars in catalogs like the one published by the Seed Savers Exchange (3076 North Winn Road, Decorah, IA 52101). Through these catalogs, conservation-minded home gardeners and seed companies make a dizzying array of heirloom seeds available. But the best way to ensure the availability of your favorites every year is to save the seeds yourself. It's easy! You'll find all the techniques you need in "Tips for Saving Heirloom Seed" on the opposite page.

A Last Word on Planning

When spring breaks and planting season starts, it may be hard to resist the urge to run out and sow some seed. But stop and take the time for planning season first. Planning is the first step toward gardening success.

Tips for Saving Heirloom Seed

If you'd like to save seed of heirloom cultivars, the first step is to figure out if they're self-pollinated or open-pollinated. Both types of pollination take place when pollen is transferred from the anther (male part of the flower) to the stigma (female part of the flower).

If a plant is self-pollinated, its stigma is pollinated by pollen from the same flower or from another flower on the same plant. Self-pollination is common among many of the major food crops of the world. Wheat, barley, rice, and oats are all self-pollinated; so are beans, peas, soybeans, peanuts, eggplant, lettuce, peppers, and tomatoes.

Open-pollinated crops include onions, corn, cucumbers, pumpkins, squash, broccoli, beets, carrots, cabbage, cauliflower, melons, radishes, spinach, Swiss chard, and turnips. They can't pollinate themselves. Instead, they depend on bees or other insects to transfer pollen from the anther of one flower on a certain plant to the stigma of a flower on a different plant. These plants may be pollinated by a plant of the same cultivar, a different cultivar, or a related species. (Pumpkins can pollinate squash, for example.)

To make sure your heirloom seed is true to type, isolate the plants you want to collect seed from so they can't cross with other cultivars nearby. (One way to do this is to set a tomato cage or frame around the plant and cover it with fine mesh netting to keep out bees and other pollinators.) If the plant is self-pollinated, it will take it from there. But if it's open-pollinated, you'll have to lend a hand. Lift up the netting and brush pollen from another plant of the same cultivar onto each flower's stigma with a soft artist's brush. Then replace the netting.

CHAPTER

7

Let's Get Sowing!

In that never-ending quest for variety, and in the spirit of experimentation, sooner or later you'll be starting seeds indoors. Some plants, like tomatoes and peppers, need a head start inside so they can hit the ground running as transplants. And you just won't be able to find all the newest (or oldest) cultivars as bedding plants at your local garden center.

Seed starting indoors is easy—as long as you have the right stuff. Here's a look at some of the more important ingredients and techniques for successful transplant growing.

The Right Mix

Inside or out, it all starts with the soil. There are dozens of formulas and brands of potting mix on the market. Some recipes for homemade mix include topsoil; others don't. And there's a wide array of exotic amendments and fillers, from vermiculite and perlite to water-absorbing polymers. But making a potting mix is far less complicated than you might imagine. You can do it right at home.

The goal for potting soil is the same as the goal for good garden soil: You want to create a growing medium that is bursting with life, has a good granular texture, and is rich in organic matter. It should also be spongy so it can hold enough water to keep seedlings from wilting but not so much that the roots drown.

A good soil mix only needs two basic ingredients: organic matter and a coarse aggregate, such as sand or perlite. The organic matter performs double duty in the potting mix: It absorbs and holds water, and it provides nourishment. The aggregate helps keep air spaces open. It resists packing together and maintains open pores that link up and form drainage channels. Most aggregates are inert and contribute very little in the way of nourishment.

MY SEEDLING MIX

My simple, all-purpose organic soil mix calls for equal amounts of well-made, finished compost and vermiculite or perlite. Both of these aggregates are natural products. Vermiculite is processed mica, while perlite is refined from volcanic glass. The compost supplies the necessary plant food as well as microorganisms needed for healthy root growth.

Make no mistake: When I say well-made compost, I really mean it. The compost must be cooked to temperatures of 140° to 165°F—high enough to kill disease pathogens and weed seeds. Fortunately, that heat doesn't kill off many of the beneficial soil organisms.

Why Add Compost?

Lots of homemade potting mix recipes call for sterilized garden soil instead of compost. But to my mind, there's no comparison. Sterilized garden soil comes out of the oven devoid of life. It is quickly recolonized by limited numbers of beneficial species, but these can't match the great diversity of species

Baked Soil

I like baking, but I'm not much of a fan of baked soil. Some people heat up moist garden soil in the oven to sterilize it. But sterilizing garden soil this way destroys part of its loose, crumbly structure. Sterilization also kills certain nitrogen-loving bacteria. After a few weeks, baked soil in a potting mix usually starts to emit ammonia gas, which damages seedlings. (And phew—you should smell it while it's "cooking!")

It's true that unsterilized garden soil may carry pathogens that could harm sensitive seedlings. So I don't use garden soil to start seeds. Instead, I use rich, lightweight compost, which has already been cooked in the pile. In compost, the nitrogen is firmly held as protein in the bodies of bacteria until they die. Then the nitrogen spills into the soil and is absorbed by plant roots in the form the plants prefer. So you won't get the ammonia smell—or the seedling damage.

that makes compost such a healthy medium for young plants. Packaged soilless mix is just as lifeless.

Adding Nutrients

The compost you use for potting soil should be protected from the rain, which can leach out valuable nutrients needed by young plants. Even so, because the amount of potting soil in any given pot is so small and watering is so frequent, you'll have to supplement the compost's nutrients. When you water seedlings, add biweekly feedings of a dilute solution of fish emulsion and kelp to get

fast-growing vegetables off to the best possible start.

Many potting soil recipes that are based on garden soil call for the addition of limestone or bonemeal. Not mine. My mix arrives at the pot with just the right amount of bonemeal and lime because I added them at the start of the compost pile. I always apply about 5 pounds of bonemeal and a shovelful of limestone per cubic yard of compost material when I build the pile.

Adding Aeration

The key to guaranteed success with a potting mix is

proper air penetration. The mix must be light and porous enough to allow air to reach the lower levels of the pot. Compost alone won't create enough aeration. That's where the aggregate comes in.

Vermiculite allows some aeration, though its soft, light structure is similar to that of compost. Perlite does an even better job of making space for air to penetrate.

Poor aeration causes many problems for seedlings started in pots. When you water, it compresses the mixture. The resulting lack of oxygen slows the growth of tiny rootlets and hands the advantage to pathogens that can attack and kill them. But when you mix compost with vermiculite or perlite, adequate oxygen gets into the potting soil and stays there to keep the soil-water-air system in balance.

Room for Roots

Outside in the garden, direct-seeded plants grow fast and unchecked. They germinate when the soil is properly warmed, and they grow in full sun, with plenty of soil and nothing to interfere with root growth. Indoors, the idea is to duplicate these conditions. By providing a good potting mix and moving the seedlings into a

cold frame as soon as they are up, the gardener can come close to matching Mother Nature's system.

However, there is another crucial factor related to seedling health, and that's keeping the root system growing vigorously. Although you can't see it happening, roots develop faster and spread farther than the plants' tops. In fact, a lettuce seedling can send out over 2 inches of root before its leaves break the soil surface.

Of course, pots and cell packs can never offer as much space for roots to spread as a garden bed can. But a little restriction of the root system will affect a plant

only slightly. It's when the root system is limited to the point of stunting that the early growth you're working so hard to encourage can't occur. After the roots have completely filled the soil mass in the container, the plant uses up its water and nutrient supply very quickly.

That's why you need to transplant seedlings so the roots will have enough room to spread. But the act of transplanting can be the most damaging part of the entire seed-starting process. If a plant wilts in the act, that means you've sacrificed a lot of its roots during moving. As those roots are regenerated, seedling growth slows, and

Rescuing the Rootbound

Rootbound seedlings have a tough time adjusting to the garden. Once the roots begin to circle the bottom of the pot, they seem to forget that there are other possibilities. Even after the seedlings are planted out in the garden, the roots may stay within their little ball for an entire season. Obviously, plants with roots like that are not going to stand up to the rigors of the weather. They'll be the first to succumb to drought or to topple in a strong wind. Even if they survive, they won't grow or produce well.

But it is possible to rescue rootbound plants. They just need some waking up. Before transplanting, loosen the root ball with your fingers. Then dip the entire plant—roots and all—in a mixture of liquid seaweed and water to help it get off to a good start.

some of the time gained by starting early will be lost.

So what's the answer? Here at Spring Meadow, I've worked out a system that allows me to grow seedlings with minimal root loss. The key is to keep the roots vigorous by transplanting well before a plant becomes pot-bound.

I use flats for germination only. Once the seeds have sprouted, each tiny plant gets its own individual container. That way, root loss is reduced to almost zero. Within days after the seedlings emerge, I move them from flats to either pots or cell packs. At this stage, the root system is quite undeveloped, and the plants show no signs of stress. Once they are in their pots, I water them whenever the top of the soil mix dries out and feed them biweekly with a dilute solution of fish emulsion and kelp.

I keep a close watch on the seedlings, checking the bottom of the pots to see if the roots are showing through. When they do show, I move the seedlings into larger containers within a week. If a plant can't stand a full day in direct sun without needing more water, then I know I'm late in repotting it.

From there, I get plants into the garden as soon as the soil is warm enough, covering them with hotcaps, if need be. But in the process, the plants might go through two or three pottings before the final move to the garden. It's a lot of work, but it does pay off in seedling vigor. The result is young plants that have never had any setbacks in their growth.

Getting Good Germination

Fresh seeds of most annual vegetables, herbs, and flowers require no special treatment and germinate within about 14 days of sowing. But I've picked up a few tricks and techniques that guarantee success.

BOTTOM HEAT

The ideal soil temperature for germinating most warm-season crops like corn and tomatoes is between 65° and 75°F. Cool soil temperatures can slow seedling emergence

These days, you can choose from lots of seed-starting supplies when you start sowing. Cell packs, small plastic pots, Jiffy Pots, and flats are all good seedling containers. You'll also find a dibble, a trowel, newspaper, plant labels, and a watering can useful. Make your own seed-starting mix with screened compost and vermiculite or perlite.

considerably. For example, at 60°F, tomato seed will germinate in 14 days. But raise the temperature to 68°F, and the little seedlings will pop up in just 8 days.

That's why I swear by bottom heat. Heating cables allow you to control soil temperatures accurately, and they come in a variety of sizes. But even better, in my opinion, are propagation mats. The mat I use is made of a rugged, black rubberlike material. It's about ⅜ inch thick and is 18 inches wide by 70 inches long. A thermostat allows me to set the heat at the proper level. I can place pots, flats, and even loose soil right on the mat.

BAG IT

Of course, soil tends to dry out faster when heated, so I do what I can to maintain humidity and uniform moisture. I could cover the seed trays, flats, and pots with panes of glass or sheets of rigid plastic to prevent drying. However, I've found that the best way to keep bottom-heated flats from drying out underneath is to use plastic bags.

Because the flats are heated from the bottom, that's where the soil dries out first. The mix in these flats may appear moist on top, but be completely dried out just under the surface. That won't happen when you seal the flats in a plastic bag. I like to use zipper-type food storage bags for pots and packs. You can slip large flats into clear garbage bags.

I use only new, clean, sterile plastic bags for germinating. If germination is erratic (as it will be with some types of seeds), I carefully dig out the early-sprouting seedlings and transplant them to a pot. Then I replace the seed flat and reseal the bag. Don't be in a hurry to discard the flat after just one or two seedlings appear thinking that's all that will germinate, or you could lose most of the plants.

After the majority of the seeds have sprouted, I remove the flat from the bag. I place it in a protected area, away from drafts, where it will get plenty of light, air, and warmth.

The plastic bag system is the easiest and most foolproof germination method I know of. With enough light and warmth, seeds can be started at almost any time of year.

The Seven Steps of Seed Starting

I've found that successful seed starting can be reduced to seven simple steps. Master them, and you can't fail.

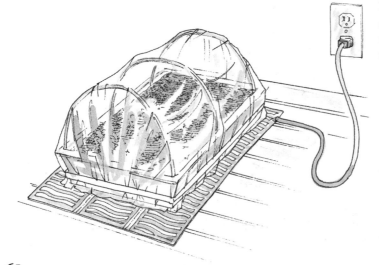

Heat or propagation mats are easy to find in garden supply catalogs and garden centers. I've found that they can really get seeds to germinate fast. But warm soil dries out quickly if you don't cover it. After watering, I wrap my flats in plastic bags to keep the soil moist longer.

··· Step 1: Germinate Your Seeds

Cover seeds lightly with organic potting soil and firm the mix gently over the seeds. Find a warm spot for them—all seeds prefer a slightly higher temperature for germinating than for growing. Don't start them on a windowsill because the temperature there can vary from hot during the day to quite cool at night. I like to use heat mats. But if you're just starting a few flats' worth of seeds, you can also place the flats on top of a refrigerator—it's surprisingly warm up there.

··· Step 2: Provide Enough Light

As soon as the sprouts start to break the soil, they need light, so move them to a sunny, south-facing window or put them under plant lights. The plant lights should hang just 3 to 6 inches above the topmost leaves. (Raise the lights higher as your seedlings grow.)

Since indoor light is not as strong as daylight outdoors, seedlings need extra light. Even if placed in a south-facing window, they may require supplementary electric light. Seedlings should be given at least 6 hours of direct sunlight or 12 hours of fluorescent light a day. New gar-

deners often complain that their seedlings grow tall and skinny. That's simply caused by a lack of light.

Ideal growing temperatures for most seedlings are in the mid-60s (65° to 68°F). I gradually expose the seedlings to more sun and cooler temperatures to strengthen them.

··· Step 3: Keep the Soil Moist

Keep the soil evenly moist. Never let it get soggy or dry. Under most conditions, a good watering every two or three days is just about right. I water early in the day so the seedlings can dry off before night—too much moisture at night will encourage damping-off.

··· Step 4: Thin Crowded Seedlings

Once your seedlings are up, they may quickly crowd each other, creating ideal conditions for damping-off. Thin them so they aren't touching and air can circulate between them.

··· Step 5: Repot as Needed

When the first true leaves appear, I transplant the seedlings into individual pots an inch or two wide. At this time, I reduce watering to encourage sturdier plant growth. Some crops, such as tomatoes, peppers, head let-

tuce, cabbage, and broccoli, seem to benefit from being repotted a few times before they go out to the garden. I repot seedlings once or twice after their first move to pots, giving them successively larger containers before setting them out. But if you're a new gardener, keep it simple: Repotting once may be enough.

··· Step 6: Harden Off Your Transplants

A week to ten days before you're ready to set out your young plants, you'll need to begin toughening them up. Stop feeding them, and cut back watering by about half. If it's above freezing outdoors, open a window to let the plants get used to a draft. A few days before planting, put them out overnight once or twice if the weather is mild.

Hardening off transplants can be tricky—you need to make sure they're tough enough to survive without killing them in the process.

··· Step 7: Set Out the Seedlings

After you've hardened off the plants, pick a mild, calm, cloudy day for setting them out in the garden. Dig all the holes first, then water each seedling thoroughly just before transplanting. Set each

Here's my foolproof system for starting seeds:

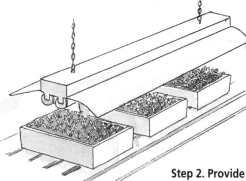

Step 1. Keep seed flats warm. Use a heat mat or put the flats in a warm place like on the top of the refrigerator.

Step 2. Provide bright light. Keep plant lights only 3 to 6 inches over the seedlings.

Step 4. Thin overcrowded seedlings by clipping them off at the base with nail scissors to avoid disturbing the roots of neighboring plants.

Step 5. Pot up seedlings regularly. Transplant seedlings into individual pots before they become rootbound.

Step 3. Water regularly but gently. Make sure the soil stays evenly moist, not soggy. Don't let it dry out.

Step 6. Harden off your transplants before planting them outside. Keep them cool, water less, and stop fertilizing them.

Step 7. To prevent transplant shock, prepare the planting holes first, water each transplant, firm the soil around the seedling, and provide shade for the first few days.

plant in a hole and firm the soil around it. Don't be afraid to pack the soil down around the plant—transplanting is the one time you don't need to worry about soil compaction. Once your transplants are in the ground, water each plant again with a dilute mixture of liquid seaweed.

Setting out your transplants begins their life in the great outdoors. Find out how to get your plants off to the best start in "Setting Out Seedlings" on page 64.

Hints for Hardening Off

Hardening off can be any process that slows down the growth of plants. Lush, fast-growing, pampered plants are tender and easily shocked by harsh outdoor conditions. (I don't know what it's like where you garden, but here on Long Island at spring planting time, the weather is unpredictable at best.)

Slowing growth before putting transplants in the ground makes them tougher. The cell walls become thicker. The percentage of dry matter within the plant increases, while the amount of freezable water decreases. There is often an increase in sugar, which acts as a natural antifreeze. Some plants even develop a protective waxy coating on their leaves.

There's more to hardening off than just moving a plant outdoors for a few days. In fact, plants can be completely hardened off indoors. The object is to subject the plant to a series of minor stresses. You can do it by working with four factors: temperature, light, moisture, and fertility.

COOL 'EM DOWN

The ideal way to harden off a plant would be to subject it to progressively lower temperatures. But that's not practical for spring transplants. Outdoors, the temperatures are usually rising from day to day. The next best method is to expose them to low temperatures for progressively longer periods of time.

For best results, you should expose plants to temperatures 5° to 10°F below their optimal growing temperatures. The best hardening temperatures for hardy crops like cabbage, brussels sprouts, and broccoli, for example, would be 50° to 60°F. The precise hardening threshold temperature varies with the species. For instance, tests have shown that cabbage can be hardened off at 54°F, while no hardening takes place at 65°F.

Downright cold temperatures—below 45°F—should

be avoided, too. When biennials like cabbage and brussels sprouts are exposed to temperatures below 45°F for a month or more, they tend to go to seed early in the season. Tender transplants, such as tomatoes and peppers, can suffer chilling injury at temperatures below 40°F. The best range for hardening them off is 60° to 70°F.

LET THERE BE LIGHT

The one stress you should never subject your plants to is lack of light. They'll be facing a lot more light once they're set out, so prepare them for it. Maintain high light levels during the hardening process. Even if you put transplants in direct sunlight during the day, make sure you place them back under lights or on the windowsill once they return indoors.

If you give your plants plenty of light, photosynthesis will continue while their growth slows, building up a food reserve to carry them through the shock of transplanting.

PUT YOUR PLANTS ON A DIET

While you're lowering temperatures and maintaining high light levels, put your plants on a starvation diet. Cut back on water, letting the soil surface dry out between waterings. And stop all fertilizing.

HOW LONG TO HARDEN OFF?

One week to ten days should be enough time to harden off a plant if it's already strong and stocky and has grown slowly. But a leggy plant may require as much as two weeks of treatment.

Weather can determine the hardening-off period, too. If your plants will be moving out to a good environment with mild temperatures and plenty of rain, then there's no great need to harden them off. But if the weather is still turning cold without warning, you can give your plants a better chance of survival by hardening them off first. Nothing's sadder than coddled seedlings killed by a cold snap.

Setting Out Seedlings

Even after transplants are hardened off, sunlight can come as a shock to them. Although sunlight is essential for plants, too much sun is as bad for them as it is for people. When you bring your plants outside in late spring or early summer, they may be subjected to double or triple the light levels they're used to.

Leaves that developed in the relatively dim light of a south-facing window can literally overheat if the plant is moved outside without some transition. Some or all of the leaves on the plant can turn pale, wither, and fall off. That's why hardening off transplants is important—it gets them used to all the conditions of the open garden.

SHADING YOUR SEEDLINGS

It's best to wait for a cloudy day to transplant. But I realize that many gardeners have only a limited window of opportunity for transplanting—often only the weekend. If you must transplant on a sunny day, wait until late afternoon, when the strength of the sun has mellowed. That way, the plants will have all night to adjust.

If the following day is going to be bright and sunny, too, give the seedlings some shade while they get established. Support a sheet of shade cloth, cheesecloth, or even window screen over the tender plants. Or prop small boards beside them to serve as sunscreens.

THE WICKED WIND

Watch out for the wind! It can be even more stressful to your transplants than sun because it dramatically increases the flow of water through the plant.

Plant roots draw water from the soil by osmosis. The water then goes up through the stem to the leaves, where most of it evaporates through the leaf pores into the air. This movement of water is essential to the plant, both because the resulting pressure helps hold the leaves upright and because water fuels photosynthesis.

Wind sucks water from the leaves faster than it can be replenished by the roots. Temporary windbreaks—fences, boards, screens, and so on—can help your transplants retain that necessary water.

KEEPING THE SOIL MOIST

Mulching with straw, grass clippings, leaves, seaweed, or hay will help retain soil moisture around your transplants by lowering the rate of evaporation of water from the soil surface. Make sure you don't completely cover the little plants with mulch, though! You can always add more as they grow larger.

A sure way to protect your young (and old) plants from drought is to use drip irrigation. Drip lines come in all lengths and configurations. You can choose a system that will allow you to place a water emitter at the base of each plant. Or you can use a soaker hose that emits a wide band of water along its length. Either way, drip lines use a minimum amount of water to provide maximum benefit.

Floating row covers are great frost protectors. They're so lightweight you can place them directly over your transplants. Make sure you bury the ends in soil so cold air can't blow inside.

FIGHTING FROST

Whenever you're rushing the season (and gardeners always do), you're bound to face frost. Frost is the great leveler. All the indoor care and outdoor hardening won't mean a thing if you leave plants out unprotected to face temperatures in the 20s.

There are ways you can thwart frost, though. You'll find a wide array of row covers and commercial frost protectors for sale at any garden center. I think the best

of all are floating row covers.

These translucent white covers are so lightweight they don't need any supports when they're draped over the plants. Yet they still provide 2° to 4°F of frost protection, maybe more. Floating row covers have been proven to protect squash seedlings down to 28°F. Since the spunbonded covers are relatively porous, they allow rain to pass through. Just make sure you bury the ends in soil, weight them with rocks, or put wire sta-

ples through them to hold down the sides and keep out blasts of cold air.

Clear plastic row covers on hoops will provide a bit more frost protection, but they also overheat during the day. If you use them, you're faced with the task of constantly opening and closing the ends of the tunnels for ventilation.

The Best Start

Starting your own plants from seed may sound like a lot of work if you're accustomed to buying seedlings at the garden center. It's not. And it's worth it.

Start your seedlings with care, and you'll be amazed at how much better they'll grow compared to those tender, greenhouse-grown, possibly stressed and rootbound plants from the store. You'll be gratified, too, by the sense of pride you can take in nurturing a plant from start to finish.

But giving your vegetables, herbs, and flowers a great start in life is only the beginning. How you plant them can make a huge difference in how well they grow and how productive they are. Turn to Chapter 8 to take the next step.

8

All about Planting

As I've planned gardens over the years, I've learned to rethink old planting techniques. When I started gardening, designing a garden entailed little more than learning the recommended distances between rows and plants.

Now, though, I think the best way to garden is with raised beds, where the plot is divided into beds that are worked and amended so they're higher than the surrounding paths.

Raised Bed Gardening

But when it comes to planning a raised bed garden, there are all sorts of variables and possible permutations. I like to divide them into three different options: one-crop bedding, interplanting and succession planting, and rows in the bed.

ONE-CROP BEDDING

Planting the entire bed with one crop is the first option. This system results in higher yields than row planting and makes it easier to rotate crops, which can just be moved from one bed to the next from year to year. For example, a bed that grew legumes like beans or peas one year could be used for tomatoes the next, followed by root crops the third year and leafy greens the fourth year.

INTERPLANTING AND SUCCESSION PLANTING

Interplanting and succession planting crops within each bed is the second option. With this method, plants are usually sown in a matrix system. There are no rows—instead, plants are spaced the same distance apart in each direction.

This method allows you to take advantage of the different nutrient, space, height, and moisture requirements of many vegetables to create a true polyculture. It takes quite a bit of forethought and some study, though. Right from the start, you have to have an idea which crops grow best together. And unless you have thought out each bed thoroughly, planting time can be a bit confusing.

ROWS IN THE BED

Planting close rows of different crops within each bed is the third option. This method has the advantage of bringing the familiar row system into the bed. The bed is easy to plant and care for, and offers many of the advantages of intercropping. Although row planting doesn't save as much space as matrix planting, it still allows you to group different plants together in one bed.

This is my pick for first-time and less-experienced gardeners. For the beginning gardener, planting rows in a bed provides the yield increases and space-saving benefits of raised bed gardening, plus the more familiar and orderly aspects of row cropping.

Saving Space

Whichever planting option you choose, you'll be planting a lot closer than you're used to. Here's why:

When you begin to plan your garden, you'll notice that the seed packets say you should leave 2 or 3 feet between each row of vegetables. Most gardening books have similar advice.

Don't believe it! That type of spacing is based on a farm scenario, where there's a need to get equipment down the rows. It has nothing to do with the actual requirements of the plants. Only a few wide-ranging vegetables like squash, pumpkins, and melons really need to be 3 feet from their neighbors. The rest can go much, much closer.

ROOM FOR ROOTS AND LEAVES

When you plan the spacing of your garden vegetables, consider both the above- and below-ground growth. The roots of the plants can range deeper and farther underground than the leaves and branches grow into the air. And the roots can intermingle freely as they snake their way through the soil.

Your crops' minute root hairs must penetrate an astounding number of soil pores in their search for nutrients and water. The leaves, by comparison, are much more limited in their spread

and their freedom to overlap without competition.

So, as you decide on plant spacings for your garden bed, think of each plant's place in the plan as a circle, as wide as the spread of its leaves near maturity. If adjacent plants begin shading each other early in the season, neither will develop fully or fruit heavily. Large, vigorous plants can totally dominate small neighbors.

If, on the other hand, you space the plants so widely that the leaves never overlap, you won't be using the space to its full potential. Where the sun can strike bare ground, water will evaporate rapidly and needlessly. Weeds will sprout. Ideally, the leaves of neighboring plants should start touching each other right around the onset of harvest.

THE BEST SPACING

French Intensive gardening—the kind I do—does not mean that plants can be crammed into a bed simply because the ground has been worked deeply and is well enriched. No matter what resources are available to the roots, when the tops crowd each other, the stems will become spindly as the plants stretch for more sun. It is that competition for sunlight that determines optimum spacing.

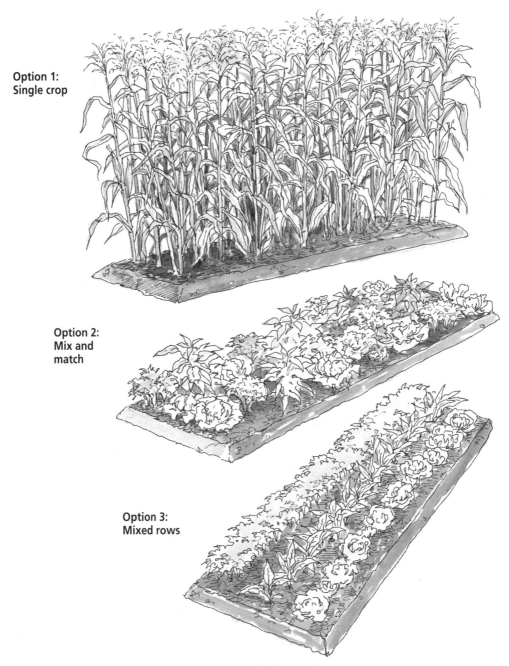

Option 1:
Single crop

Option 2:
Mix and
match

Option 3:
Mixed rows

There are three distinct styles of raised bed planting. You can plant the entire bed in a single crop, as in Option 1. You can mix and match crops throughout the bed, as in Option 2. Or you can sow and plant or- derly rows throughout the bed, as in Option 3. Whichever option you choose, you'll still get more produce from less space than if you use a traditional row system.

For best results, space plants of one kind an equal distance apart in all directions. You can start with the catalog or seed packet recommendations, but you'll find that many of them can be cut in half. Observe each plant as it grows in your bed. Take notes, and adjust the spacing the next season for maximum use of your space.

Vegetables Together

Interplanting in a bed encourages a whole new way of looking at garden plants. When plants are not segregated by rows, we begin to see how they interact with and complement each other. In the process, we use garden space to its fullest potential.

A TOOTHSOME THREESOME

For example, quick-growing radishes and slow-growing carrots and onions make a great threesome. When you plant radishes, carrots, and onions in the same row, the radishes pop up quickly. If the soil is crusted, their emergence helps to break it up. And they provide a quick, handy reminder to you where you sowed those slow-to-show carrots.

The leafy radish plants provide shade for the tiny emerging carrots, and as you pull the radishes out, you make more space for the growing carrots and onions. The onions emerge slowly, taking up little room above ground, even at maturity. And onions are said to repel the carrot rust fly.

When planting radishes and carrots together, sow them in a band 4 to 6 inches wide. That band will produce twice as much as a conventional narrow row without any more work. Plant the radish seed first—it needs to be covered with ½ inch of soil, while the diminutive carrot seed shouldn't have more than ¼ inch of soil covering it.

If you're planting onion sets in the radish-carrot band, space them at least 8

The best way to save space and increase productivity in a bed is to use matrix planting. Each plant is an equal distance apart from its neighbors on all sides. That way, you give each plant exactly the amount of space it needs, without wasting space on rows.

to 10 inches apart, or the maturing onion bulbs will crowd the carrots. You can plant the sets as close as 4 inches apart if you'll be pulling half of them early to use as scallions.

A HARD-TO-"BEET" COMBO

Another one of my favorite combinations is beets and kohlrabi. I alternate beet and kohlrabi seeds all the way down the row, then scatter a bit of radish seed over all of them. Finally, I cover everything with ½ inch of soil. The radishes will come up in a few days and mark the row. Later, as the beets and kohlrabi begin to appear and grow, I pull the radishes to make room in the row.

Beets and kohlrabi grow well together, since they feed at different root levels and don't compete with each other for soil nutrients. The shallow-rooted kohlrabi feeds near the top of the soil, while the beet roots reach farther down into the soil for food.

INTERPLANTING OPTIONS

Here are more of my favorite planting combinations:

🍃 For a fall crop of brassicas, plant seedlings of broccoli, cauliflower,

· S P A C E :   T H E   F I N A L   F R O N T I E R ·

When you grow crops in an intensive planting system, you plant them closer than you would in a conventional planting system. Here's the ideal spacing for individual plants that are grown intensively.

Crop	Inches	Crop	Inches
Asparagus	18	Lettuce, head	12
Beans, bush	6	Lettuce, leaf	9
Beans, lima	9	Mustard	9
Beets	3	Okra	18
Broccoli	18	Onions	6
Brussels sprouts	18	Parsley	6
Cabbage	18	Parsnips	6
Carrots	3	Peanuts	18
Cauliflower	18	Peas	6
Celery	9	Peppers	15
Chinese cabbage	12	Potatoes	12
Collards	15	Radishes	3
Corn	12	Rhubarb	30
Cucumbers	18	Salsify	6
Eggplant	18	Spinach	6
Endive	12	Squash	24
Garlic	6	Sweet potatoes	12
Kale	18	Swiss chard	9
Kohlrabi	9	Tomatoes	24
Leeks	6	Turnips	6

among flowers. Where space is tight, set out individual lettuce seedlings. But where there's room, set out groups of seedlings 6 to 8 inches apart, then gradually thin out and eat the half-grown plants, leaving the last plants to stand 1 foot apart.

♣ Plant leeks or sow beets or carrots between rows of bush beans. (But don't be tempted to plant bushy crops with beans. To prevent the spread of disease, sunshine must be able to reach the base of the plants, and there must be good air circulation.)

♣ Sow spinach in the same row with carrots, parsley, parsnips, or leeks.

Experiment with your own combinations, but be careful not to overcrowd. Remember that carrots and beets must be given breathing space, or they won't have enough room to make roots. And lettuce plants that are short of space won't make heads. "Space: The Final Frontier" on this page will tell you the amount of room each crop needs to mature.

NOT READY FOR BED

Salad vegetables and root crops make ideal bedfellows. But vegetables that take up a lot of ground space—like squash, pumpkins, and melons—and those

kohlrabi, or cabbage between hills of corn. After the corn has ripened and you've pulled up the stalks, the well-established cole plants will be ready to take their own place in the sun.

♣ Set lettuce seedlings in a circle around a rhubarb plant.

♣ Transplant lettuce into your asparagus bed. The ferny asparagus foliage will shield the lettuce from midsummer heat.

♣ Try lettuce under the shade of a bush summer squash.

♣ You can tuck lettuce in many places, even

Paula Piper's Plan for More Peppers

If Peter Piper planted a pack of peppers in traditional rows, he would set his plants about 18 inches apart in rows spaced 2 to 3 feet apart. A dozen pepper plants would take up two 10-foot rows, totaling about 30 square feet, including the aisles between the rows.

But in reality, a mature pepper plant needs only about 1 square foot of growing space. We also know that peppers are a long-season crop. They grow slowly, and most of that square foot isn't even occupied until late in the season. In the meantime, that space could be used by a fast, low-growing crop, such as beets, spinach, lettuce, or radishes. And, as a bonus, the shade cast by the pepper plants during midsummer could actually extend the harvest period of the spinach or lettuce by cooling it and preventing it from bolting to seed.

Let's say Paula Piper plants a pack of peppers in the same amount of space, but in the configuration of a 3-by-10-foot bed. Paula puts ten plants in a row down the center of the bed, on 12-inch centers (that is, with 12 inches between each stem). She still has plenty of room to sow a row of spinach 4 inches to the left and a row of onions 4 inches to the right of the peppers. She moves out another 4 inches and flanks those with a row of radishes on either side. There's still plenty of room in the bed, so she makes rows 6 inches out from the radishes and sows lettuce on one side and beets on the other. And there's still just enough room to squeeze in a row of bush beans along both edges of the bed.

While Peter is waiting and waiting for his peppers to mature (and working hard to keep the space in between free of weeds), Paula invites him over for plenty of homegrown salad.

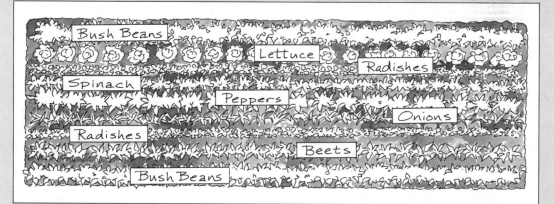

By interplanting rather than row cropping, this gardener picks just as many peppers but enjoys a bonus harvest from many other crops in the same space.

that take up a lot of vertical space—including corn, sunflowers, and pole beans—don't really make good use of a bed's advantages. I prefer to grow these crops in traditional ways, such as in hills and rows.

Succession Planting

Besides space, there's another dimension you can work with in the garden: time. In small gardens, succession planting—planting two or more crops in the same space at different times—is almost a necessity. It can have the same effect as doubling or tripling your garden space.

In most parts of the country, you can manage three crop seasons: spring, summer, and fall. The spring season starts as soon as the soil can be worked. After harvesting the fast-maturing spring crops, you replace them with summer crops, then follow those with cold-weather vegetables.

I've been planting three- and even four-season crops here at Spring Meadow for years. So I've learned a few tricks of the trade. Here's what works for me.

MIDSUMMER SOWING

Germination is a bit trickier when you're forcing the season. Few cool-season seeds will germinate well during hot, dry midsummer conditions. So, for almost all midsummer planting, I try to fool the seeds into believing they are coming up in the coolness of spring.

I've found that soaking seeds overnight before planting will help them germinate in hot weather. So will planting in the shade of other crops, keeping the rows well watered, and covering the rows lightly with mulch. I just make sure I remove the mulch as soon as young seedlings appear.

MORE TIME TO MATURE

For late crops, I always give plants more time to reach maturity than the seed packets

Don't Tuck These In Together

All is not sweetness and light in the vegetable kingdom. Some plants just don't get along and shouldn't be set in the same bed. Dill supposedly slows carrot growth. Tomatoes and kohlrabi are said to interfere with each other's growth. Crops that are subject to the same diseases or insects, such as tomatoes and potatoes or tomatoes and eggplant, should be given a wide berth from one another, or they'll be more susceptible to mass attacks.

Individual characteristics, such as deep-feeding roots, may benefit some plants while creating too much competition for others. If you plant a bed with only but shallow-rooted plants, they'll compete for a limited amount of space, water, and nutrients. But if deep- and shallow-rooted plants are grown together, there's plenty of room and food for everybody.

For example, pole beans planted with sunflowers grow poorly because of competition for light above ground and root space below. Sunflowers and potatoes are equally incompatible, and so are pole beans and beets, pole beans and members of the cabbage family, potatoes and pumpkins, onions and peas, and onions and asparagus. So think about how plants grow before you combine them.

suggest. Succession planting reverses the normal climate for cool-season crops. Warm midsummer weather accelerates growth in the early life of the plant. But the days are already getting shorter. By the time the crop begins maturing, there is much less light than in spring, and the nights are cool.

CROPS FOR SUCCESSION

When selecting brassicas for a fall crop, I always choose cultivars that take no longer than 60 to 65 days to mature. I generally sow seed in late June and transplant no later than the middle of July, keeping the young plants cool, moist, and slightly shaded.

Turnips make a wonderful fall crop. I've found I

Succession planting means sowing some crops in the heat of midsummer. They'll germinate better in the shade of neighboring crops. Here, these seeds will sprout in the shade of mature broccoli plants.

can sow them as late as September 1 here on Long Island. If I have bed space available in August, I'll sow spinach, peas, Swiss chard, mustard, and kohlrabi.

I never put my packs of carrot or beet seeds away.

These two crops can be sown in empty spaces any time up until August. I'm still harvesting beets in November. I leave the last crop of carrots in the ground under a thick blanket of mulch all winter. In the spring, I dig them up for a sweet, crunchy treat.

Greens are a mainstay of my succession plan. I sow several types in shady spots all through the season up until mid-August. Endive and kale make terrific fall crops. But they require a long growing season, so I sow seed for transplanting in early July.

Extra Nutrition

It takes a lot more than just planting vegetables close together to have a successful garden. Planting so intensively (and incessantly) calls

Remember to Rotate

Because space is at a premium and great demands are made on the soil in a raised bed garden, crop rotation is very important. In succeeding seasons, heavy feeders such as corn and tomatoes should be followed up with light feeders such as beans, carrots, beets, radishes, turnips, and rutabagas.

Keep in mind that legumes, such as beans and peas, manufacture nitrogen and even contribute some to the soil for succeeding crops to use. Leaf crops like lettuce consume a lot of nitrogen, while root crops use a great amount of potash. So you shouldn't follow turnips with carrots, for example, but with spinach or another leafy crop.

for an approach to soil fertility that's a lot different from the one required by old row gardening. Having plants so closely grouped puts a higher nutrient demand on your soil than traditional spacings.

To produce several tightly packed crops instead of one spacious one, your beds will need to be constantly replenished with organic matter like shredded leaves or straw, compost, manure, and other amendments.

FALL SOIL-FEEDING FRENZY

Every fall, I cover my beds with a thick layer of barnyard mulch—manure plus bedding. I lay it on at least 1 foot thick.

Then I till it all under in spring as soon as the soil can be worked. In addition, whenever I remove a crop from a bed, I add compost at a rate of 2 pounds per square foot.

Even so, toward the end of the growing season, some plants may begin to show stress from lack of nutrients. Give them a boost with fish emulsion or foliar feedings of liquid seaweed.

Intensive Care

Perhaps the ultimate raised bed system is the Biodynamic/French Intensive method. From soil preparation to bed making to plant spacing to harvest, everything

is pushed to extremes. As a result, yields are quadrupled. Water use is cut by at least half. Gardeners may spend years and years fine-tuning their biodynamic gardens, but basically, the system has four main components: double digging, adding organic matter, close planting, and careful watering.

DOUBLE DIG YOUR BEDS

The French Intensive method requires loose, well-worked soil. Beds are normally dug to a depth of 24 inches to encourage lush growth and deep roots. Double digging takes you down deep into the soil. It breaks up the subsoil

---

K.I.S.S

For the newcomer, raised bed gardening and intensive planting can get rather confusing. If you're just starting out, here are a few ways to "Keep It Simple (Stupid)":

♣ Plant one crop per bed. Sow one bed all in corn, for example; let winter squash stretch out in another bed. Keeping plants segregated is the simplest way to prevent overcrowding by more vigorous types.

♣ If you *do* mix plants in a bed, try to group them by maturity times. For example, if you've devoted part of a bed to early broccoli, you should fill it out with other early vegetables, such as onions, cauliflower, peas, lettuce, or spinach. That way, you'll be harvesting all the crops at approximately the same time, so you can replant the whole bed for fall crops.

♣ When you must mix vegetables, combine plants with similar growth habits. Short plants like carrots and cabbage work well next to each other in a bed. If you must mix plants, always put the taller, more vigorous ones on the side where their shade won't inhibit smaller plants. If your beds run east to west, for example, plant staked tomatoes or pole beans in a single row on the north. If the beds run north to south, place the tall plants on the west side because most smaller plants can benefit from some shade in the hot afternoon sun.

without burying the topsoil.

To double dig, first mark off your bed—let's say we'll make it 3 feet by 10 feet. Standing at one end of the bed, dig a trench across the end. It should be one spade deep by one spade wide. Throw all of the soil from the trench into a wheelbarrow or cart. Now, plunge a digging fork into the subsoil left in the trench, to the depth of the tines. Loosen the subsoil by pushing the handle of the fork back and forth.

After you've loosened the subsoil in the trench, move down and dig a second trench, right next to the first. This should also be one spade deep by one spade wide. Only this time, instead of tossing the soil into a cart, use it to fill in the first trench.

Pick up the fork again and thoroughly loosen the soil in the second trench. Then move on to dig a third trench, and so on until you reach the end of the bed. Use the soil in the wheelbarrow to fill in the last trench, and your bed will be double-dug.

ADD ORGANIC MATTER

Double digging alone improves soil structure. But if you also add organic matter, you will improve soil fertility as well. After loosening the subsoil, cover it with 3 inches

of compost or manure (you can also use old hay, leaves, straw, or crop residue). Cover that with 3 inches of topsoil, then add another layer of compost or manure. Continue layering, finishing with a 6-inch layer of topsoil.

PLANT CLOSELY

Here's where the "intensive" in French Intensive comes in. Plants are spaced closely and evenly over the entire bed, using a matrix system. This spacing creates a living mulch so when the plants mature, their leaves touch. This leaf canopy shades the ground and keeps moisture in.

Always water a French Intensive garden in the late af-

ternoon or evening. For overhead watering, wait until 2 hours before sunset so that the water can evaporate slowly and has about 16 hours to sink down to the root zone before the scorching afternoon sun appears.

Small-Space Benefits

No matter which raised bed gardening system you choose, the benefits of tending a smaller space are obvious. To get the same yield, you only need to prepare, water, and weed one-fourth of the area. This means

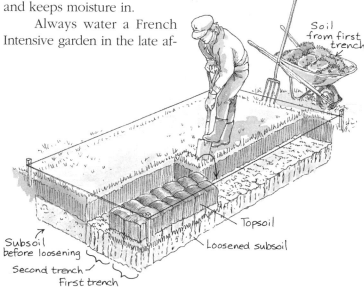

Double digging lets you work the soil very deeply. First, dig a trench, tossing the soil from it into a wheelbarrow. Then loosen the soil at the bottom of the trench. Next, dig a second trench next to the first. Toss that soil into the first trench. Loosen the soil in the second trench. Fill in the second trench with soil from a third trench, and so on. Fill in the final trench with the soil from the wheelbarrow.

· **75** ·

that less water and fertilizer are required per pound of food produced.

An additional advantage of small, high-yielding gardens is that they lend themselves to exciting innovations. For example, you can cover beds with a mini-greenhouse for late-fall, winter, and early-spring vegetables. So plant, plant, and plant again. And when it's too late for any more vegetables, plant a cover crop of winter rye to give a little back to the soil in return for a full season of good, nutritious eating.

But don't give up too soon. In Chapter 9, I'll share my secrets for getting more produce longer. It's an exciting challenge to see how long your garden will grow.

Making the Bed

To make room for the root systems of closely spaced plants, raised bed gardening requires deep soil preparation before planting. I like to work the soil to a depth of 2 feet. That way, the root systems can develop vertically instead of spreading out horizontally.

If you're in a hurry to get planting, you can just have a truckload of loamy topsoil brought in and mound it up into beds 12 inches high and 36 inches wide. But if you have time, you can save money and make your own rich topsoil the way I do. Here's my system. I call it "Crow's Customized Double Digging":

First, mark off the bed, say, 3 feet wide by 10 feet long. Starting at one end, dig up a 2-foot band of soil across the bed to a depth of about 1 foot, and toss the soil into a wheelbarrow. Work the soil in the trench you've dug with a spading fork, to the depth of the tines. Then spread a layer of old hay, leaves, manure, straw, or crop residue across the band where the soil was excavated.

Move down the bed, dig up another 2-foot-wide band of soil, and toss it over the organic matter. Work that trench, then lay another layer of organic matter where you dug out the soil. Cover *that* trench with soil dug from another 2-foot-wide band. Continue down the bed, removing soil, working the subsoil, filling in with organic matter, then covering with soil. Cover the final band with the load of soil saved at the start.

Rake the beds smooth and allow them to stand for several days. The weight of the soil will compress the buried vegetation, after which you can plant the bed without fear of settling.

I like to continue making beds this way throughout the season so they'll be ready for planting when I need them. You can do the job over a long period of several seasons, when it's most convenient for you. Whenever you have an abundance of organic matter, you can add it to a bed in progress.

Use seed-free weeds to fill in rows in midsummer, and cover them with soil. When you have them, add lawn clippings or kitchen waste and cover them up with more soil. In the fall, add shredded leaves, plus cornstalks and other garden refuse. Again, cover with soil. In the spring, the bed will be ready for planting, even if it's only a few inches higher than the surrounding area.

9

Let's Stretch the Season

The garden is, by its nature, geared for the summer. It's the midsummer crops that are the stars. We wait anxiously, saltshaker in hand, for the tomatoes, sweet corn, peppers, and cucumbers. And once these crops are planted and growing, many gardeners think their work is done. They believe that the sun rises and sets on the hot-weather crops.

But these gardeners are missing out on some of the best gardening time and some of the sweetest, most satisfying crops: crisp cab-bage, sweet brussels sprouts, buttery greens, and crunchy carrots. That's what fall gardening is all about.

The Neglected Season

Why don't more gardeners take advantage of the fall growing season? Maybe it's because squeezing in a fall crop between the July heat and the first hard fall freeze can be quite a touch-and-go proposition. For one thing, many cool-weather crops, especially lettuce and spinach, germinate poorly in the summer heat.

In summertime, the living is easy for insects, too. They seem to be every-where. And they love to feast on those tender seedlings. But if you delay planting to avoid the worst of the heat and the insects, your crops will probably wind up get-ting zapped by frost.

Does this sound hope-less to you? Well, it's not. Here at Spring Meadow, we get great fall crops every year. That's because there are simple ways to overcome all of these obstacles.

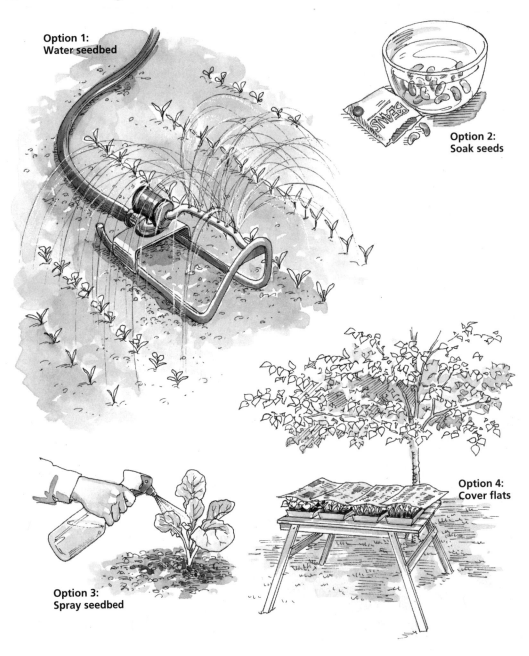

Option 1:
Water seedbed

Option 2:
Soak seeds

Option 3:
Spray seedbed

Option 4:
Cover flats

There are plenty of ways to help seeds get off to a quick start in hot weather. You can water the seedbed well, both before and after planting, soak seeds in a bowl of hot water for several hours be-fore planting, spray the seedbed with a foliar spray like liquid seaweed, or sow in flats and cover the flats with damp newspaper until the seedlings emerge.

MADE IN THE SHADE

A little bit of shade goes a long way in the summer garden. Anything you can do to block the strong sunlight so it doesn't bake newly sown seeds will help.

Stretch shade cloth or window screening over hoops to make a cool, shady bed for seedlings. Or prop up boards on the south side of planting areas. Some people even lay boards directly on seeded rows. If you do that, just make sure to check under the boards every day, and remove them as soon as the seedlings break ground.

The easiest way to block the sun, and my favorite, is to sow seeds in the shade of existing plants. Use the shadows created by tall plants such as tomatoes, corn, and pole beans for a shady sowing area.

Then there's mulch. Mulch shades the soil beneath it. It can also act as an evaporative cooler. If you can keep the mulch relatively moist with regular waterings,

it will cool the soil beneath it as the water evaporates.

Just don't pile mulch on too thickly for seedlings. In most cases, it should be less than $\frac{1}{2}$ inch thick so that seedlings can germinate through it.

If you mulch the bed, a once-weekly watering should be enough. If you leave the soil bare, you'll probably have to water every day.

DRY-WEATHER PLANTING

Back on the Pennsylvania farm, my Amish mentor, Old Zeb, always waited for rain before planting. In fact, there were many times I got soaked to my socks planting and sowing in the rain.

But, of course, it's not always possible to wait for rain. When the rain just won't

come and sowing time is passing you by, you've just got to get out there and plant anyway. Here are some tricks you can use to improve your germination and seedling survival rates:

♣ Soak hard-shelled seeds (beans, peas, corn, squash, and so on) for several hours before planting.

♣ Water the seedbed or planting hole thoroughly and slowly. Allow the water to sink deeply into the soil.

♣ After planting and watering, give transplants a micronutrient-rich foliar spray such as kelp or liquid seaweed.

♣ Sow in flats and transplant later. Put the flats on a table under a tree and cover them with damp newspaper.

A screen tent works better than any chemical to keep insects away from tender summer-sown seedlings. Fold window screening lengthwise to form a tent, set it over a row of seedlings, and block the ends with boards.

They shouldn't need much water—a pint every other day is enough for a half-dozen flats. When the seeds sprout, take off the paper, but keep the flats in the filtered shade for a week before introducing the seedlings gradually to full sun. Transplant in the evening and top the bed with mulch.

SCREEN TEST FOR BUGS

So there's plenty you can do to ensure that the seeds will sprout. But once they're up, how do you keep those darn bugs away from them?

I'm happy to say that there's one simple, chemical-free solution. I've found that window screening will keep out insects while also reducing heat and keeping the soil moist.

Here's how I do it. I cut the screening in 4-foot lengths and bend it in half the long way, making a sort of tentlike affair. After lightly tilling the bed, I make a furrow, water it well, and plant the seeds, sprinkling them widely from side to side. After covering the seeds lightly with soil, I water the row gently to settle the soil around the seeds, which ensures good germination.

Then I place the screen tents over the rows, pushing soil up around the edges to make sure that no insects crawl under them. I use scrap lumber to block the ends. For long rows, I just keep adding screen tents, making sure that the screen overlaps a couple of inches at each junction.

Under the tent, the seeds are tucked into an ideal environment: They're warm, damp, and lightly shaded. It can spell the difference between the success and failure of your fall garden.

Once you've made your screen tents, you can get double duty out of them: I've found that they also make good rabbit foilers in the spring.

Planning the Fall Garden

"Fall gardening" may be a misleading term. "Fall picking" more accurately describes what you'll be doing when cool weather arrives. You'll have to do all the sowing and planting during the summer.

So when planning your successions, you must make sure that you'll have some bare ground available 60 to 90 days before the first fall frost. That means you'll need to put your spring planting in at the first possible moment.

Love Me Tender

There are three tender crops that I routinely grow as fall crops: bush beans, peas, and summer squash. You need to sow them all in the garden about two months before the first possible frost. If you choose cultivars with the least number of days to harvest, you should get in three to four pickings of beans and four to five clusters of squash before frost hits.

Growing peas for fall reverses the natural process. Peas are meant to start in cool weather and ripen in late spring or early summer. As a fall crop, they must start in the heat of midsummer and finish up while frost threatens. Although the foliage may not be harmed by cold weather, blossoms may drop if subjected to low temperatures. Pods might not fill out if touched by frost. Timing and quick maturity are critical for fall peas. Start with an early, reliable cultivar for your area. I like 'Wando', a heat-resistant cultivar.

For example, to get respectable cabbages, broccoli, and turnips from the same ground that produced the spring spinach, you should harvest the spinach bed about 90 days before the first frost. That requires an extra-early spinach planting. I've found that if I want high production from brussels sprouts, leeks, or parsnips here on Long Island, the seeds or transplants should be in the ground by the first week in August.

A Gallery of Fall Crops

Some vegetables actually perform best as fall crops. For instance, I've found that broccoli and cauliflower are less bothered by insects when planted in summer than when set out in April.

Other members of the cabbage family, especially brussels sprouts and kale, taste better after they've been frosted. And I believe that lettuce tastes sweeter after it's been touched by a light frost. Here's a look at some of the crops you'll routinely find in my fall garden:

· · · Beets and Carrots
You can sow beets and carrots all summer, up until about two months before the first fall frost. You don't even have to worry about them maturing completely since they're edible (and delicious) at nearly any stage.

Even after a light frost, beets and carrots will continue to grow slowly through part of the fall. Mulch the row or bed with a foot of loose straw or hay after a hard frost, and they'll stay crisp in the ground until late winter.

· · · Celery
Plant celery transplants about 90 days before the first fall frost. If you protect them later with a deep mulch, almost covering the plants, you'll be able to harvest crisp, tender hearts until Thanksgiving.

· · · Curly Endive and Chinese Cabbage
I manage curly endive and Chinese cabbage the same

way. Near the end of August, I transplant young seedlings of either type directly into a cold frame. When frost threatens, I cover the frame with plastic. The plants continue to grow, snug and safe, well into the winter. They provide welcome fresh salad greens during the snowy months.

· · · Kale
Kale is a stalwart in my fall and winter garden. It's sweetest when it matures in cool weather, so I time it to mature around the first fall frost. That means I sow it about 50 days before that date.

· · · Kohlrabi
Kohlrabi is a cool-weather plant that thrives in both fall

Sprouts in the Cellar

To keep the harvest coming, you can transplant some mature plants from the fall garden into a greenhouse or well-insulated cold frame. This trick works well for brussels sprouts, cabbage, celery, and leeks. If you're not fortunate enough to have a greenhouse or cold frame, there's another trick you can try with brussels sprouts. Dig up the mature plant, retaining as much of the root ball as possible. Plop the whole thing into a large bucket or garbage can, and haul it down to your cool basement. Of course, the plant won't grow without sunlight. But you'll be surprised at how long the little sprouts stay crisp and sweet on the stem.

Transplant Time

Fall is an ideal time for transplanting some of those perennial garden crops. Transplanting is always a shock to plants, but less so when they are approaching the dormant stage. There is usually more time to do a careful job in the fall, too. And if you transplant in the fall, you'll need to do less watering than you would if you were transplanting in spring or summer. Here are a few crops that take especially well to fall transplanting:

Asparagus: Spring is normally the time for starting new beds of asparagus, but fall works as well. The problem with fall planting is that it's difficult to find roots in the garden centers at that time of the year. However, if you have an established bed, fall is a good time to dig up any tiny seedlings that have come up during the past season. Left in the old bed, they would eventually crowd it. Transplanted elsewhere, they can be used to start a new bed.

Brambles: You can plant blackberries, raspberries, and other brambles in the fall as long as you mulch them thickly to protect their roots against the oncoming winter. (Black raspberries, with their shallow roots, are more subject to winter injury.) You can also separate tip-layered blackberry plants from the mother plant in the fall, after they have firmly rooted, and set them in a new location.

Grapes: Although grapes are normally planted in the spring, the window of opportunity then—after the ground thaws and before the buds swell on the vine—can be quite limited. Fall planting allows for a much more leisurely schedule. Just make sure to protect them with a 6- to 12-inch-thick layer of straw mulch over the winter.

Perennial herbs: Chives, winter savory, tansy, rue, lemon thyme, mint, bee balm, and lemon balm all benefit from regular division in the fall. When a clump gets overgrown and its center looks bare or woody, dig it up. Discard the woody portion, then divide and reset the young outer growth.

Perennial onions: Autumn is a good time to divide perennial onions. For vigorous growth, divide big clumps every few years into smaller clusters. However, don't wait till fall to plant the little Egyptian onion bulblets that mature in July at the top of the stalks. Plant them in rows as soon as they mature, and by spring you'll have scallions to harvest.

Rhubarb: Fall is the best time to divide and transplant rhubarb. Divide clumps every six to eight years, or when stalks become thin. To divide, dig up the plant with a spade and separate the crown into divisions, making sure each has several eyes. Reset 3 to 4 feet apart, leaving one division in the original spot.

Strawberries: If you have an established bed, fall is the most convenient time to move strawberry runner plants to a new location. The following spring, these fall-set berry plants will have a head start. Mulch them well once the ground freezes. Give them another year to put on growth before fruiting by picking off all blossoms in the spring.

and spring. For a fall harvest, sow seed thickly at least 60 days before frost in rows spaced 15 inches apart. Thin plants to 5 inches apart, and harvest when the bulbs are 2 inches in diameter.

··· Lettuce

Lettuce is a mainstay of my fall garden. I sow a little bit of lettuce seed every two weeks during the summer, until about 30 days before frost. This summer succession system requires a good bolt-resistant cultivar. Loose-leaf kinds are the easiest to grow, especially when started in hot weather. Through the cool, crisp days of fall, loose-leaf lettuce keeps in better condition right in the garden than in the refrigerator. Break off leaves as needed instead of pulling up the whole plant so the plants will keep growing and producing.

··· Mustard Greens

Mustard greens can be planted in midsummer for a late fall harvest. I sow seed in rows spaced 15 inches apart, and thin seedlings to 6 inches apart. The young thinnings add a wonderful zing to salads. For cooked greens, I cut the leaves when they reach 6 inches long. If not trimmed too close, a plant will yield several cuttings.

··· Radishes

Radishes—either white or black, long or round—are hardy and should be planted after the hottest weather has passed. Most mature in about 60 days. Sow in rows spaced 12 inches apart; thin seedlings to 4 to 6 inches apart. You can leave winter radishes in the ground until after the first frost, then dig and store them in a root pit or in damp sand in a cool cellar.

··· Rutabagas

Rutabagas are usually considered a long-season crop since they take at least 90 days to mature. But you can sow them in midsummer for a fall crop. Although they won't make roots as large as spring-sown crops will, the smaller ones are finer-grained and more delicately flavored. Thinnings make good greens for early fall.

··· Spinach

Spinach is a classic cool-weather crop. Its flavor and texture are improved by fall frosts. I sow spinach seeds $\frac{3}{4}$ inch apart in rows spaced 12 to 15 inches apart, then thin seedlings to 4 to 6 inches apart. If sowing time coincides with a late hot spell, I pre-germinate seeds in the refrigerator between damp paper towels for about one week. When harvesting, I cut only the outer leaves so that the center can continue growing

··· Turnips

Turnips grow well and quickly in cool weather. Two months before the first frost, sow seed thickly in rows spaced 12 to 18 inches apart. Thin seedlings to 3 to 4 inches apart. You can leave fall turnips in the soil until after the first light frost, but be sure to dig them up before the ground freezes.

Frost Protection

Just a single night of freezing temperatures can be enough to spoil the autumn harvest you've been waiting for. Yet that first frost of fall is often followed by weeks of warm, sunny weather. It could be a time for your garden to stay productive and enjoyable.

Lots of gardeners haul out the bedsheets, blankets, and plastic when frost threatens. But I use another simple, but weird, way to fend off frost damage: I coat the plants with ice. It sounds impossible, but by sprinkling plants with water, you can actually protect them from temperatures as low as 20° to 25°F.

THE ICEMAN COMETH

This technique takes advantage of a principle of nature:

When water changes to ice, it releases heat. A pound of water gives off 144 BTUs of heat in the freezing process. It is this latent or hidden heat that can be used to guard against sudden or unseasonable frosts.

As water freezes on the plant, it creates an ice coating up to ½ inch thick. Heat trapped underneath this protective coat is enough to keep fruits, vegetables, and flowers from a frosty demise. As the ice melts, the plants emerge undamaged to continue ripening or blooming—at least until the next frost.

The amount of frost protection possible through irrigation depends on wind conditions as well as temperature. On still, clear nights, you can protect many crops from temperatures as low as 20°F. To protect the plants effectively, you'll have to continue irrigating throughout the night. To make sure the plants will be protected from freezing temperatures, turn on your sprinkler or irrigation system when the temperature drops to 34°F. Continue irrigating until the air temperature rises above 32°F and all the ice has melted off the plants.

In some cases, you can save a crop that has already been subjected to frost if you start the sprinkler before the temperature goes up, since slower thawing lessens damage to plant tissue.

ALTERNATIVES TO ICE

Of course, there are other, more conventional frost-stopping techniques available to the home gardener. Row covers and hotcaps provide 2° to 4°F of protection—in fact, up to 10°F has been documented. But actually, your frost-protection strategy should start early in the

The Killing Frost

Frost is the great dictator, ruling with an iron fist. It dictates to the gardener when to set out seedlings and sow seeds, which cultivars to plant, and even where to plant them—for example, inside a greenhouse, under cloches, or behind a protective hedgerow.

There's no bargaining with frost. Its killing power is absolute. Yet some plants are certainly better able to resist it than others. Tender plants, such as tomatoes, peppers, and petunias, shrivel at the first sign of an autumn killing frost (26° to 30°F). Plants with limited hardiness, like peas, potatoes, and marigolds, can withstand a few degrees of frost. And some crops, such as leeks and cabbage, can even survive temperatures to about 13°F.

Here's why: When the temperature drops below 32°F, the water inside plant tissues normally begins to crystallize. Ice forms inside or outside the cells. Most hardy plants survive freezing temperatures by tolerating the formation of ice around their cells. Water moves out of the plant cells, so there is less chance of cellular activity being disrupted. But tender plants can't transfer the water outside the cells. The water simply freezes inside, expands like an ice cube, and bursts the cell walls, killing the cells and the plant.

The hardier a plant is, the better it's able to tolerate water loss from its cells. As the temperature rises above freezing, water moves back into the cells of a hardy plant, and normal cellular activity resumes.

season. Make frost protection a part of your garden planning. Here's how:

♣ Choose hardy, frost-resistant cultivars whenever possible.

♣ Watch the planting location. Frost settles into valleys and other low areas. Plant late-season crops in higher areas.

♣ Plant near ponds, streams, or lakes, since these bodies of water release heat on cold nights.

♣ Plant windbreaks to protect your plantings from icy winds. Sheltered fields may be as much as 10°F warmer than exposed plots. But to prevent frost pockets, be sure to allow room for air circulation.

♣ Don't prune any frost-damaged plants until after hard frosts have passed and new growth has started below the frozen parts. Nipped or blackened plants may look neater if cut, but pruning too soon can result in greater damage from later freezes.

Benign Neglect

Fall is cleanup time in the garden, but just how you tuck the beds in for winter depends on your own style. By the time winter sets in, some gardeners have left a vegetable garden looking as polished as a plate at a junkyard dog's picnic: It's stripped clean, down to the last leaf, stake, and straw, not to mention righteously tilled, neatly raked, and well manured.

This neatnik method is highly recommended by many authorities. A thorough cleanup rids the garden of hideouts for overwintering pests and diseases. Leftover vegetable debris can be added to the compost bin, where it will be changed into valuable organic matter and later returned to the soil. What's more, plowing in the fall lets the rough clods benefit from constant thaws and freezes, which cause the earth to be more workable in the spring.

But there's another, less compulsive approach to fall chores that we use here at Spring Meadow. I call it "benign neglect." The benign neglector (that's me) may leave an army of kale in the plot. As fall progresses, the plants may be mellowed by successive frosts and they may turn a bit yellow around the edges, but they're hanging in there. I may also leave a row of Swiss chard, since the center of each plant is still fresh and green. Both the kale and the Swiss chard provide tasty greens well into winter and then again in spring. Over in the corner you might also find parsnips, with their foliage flattened against the ground. Their roots, crisp and sweet, will stay buried till spring.

And over it all, I'll have scattered a blanket of mulch. Spread thickly in the summer to battle weeds, it sinks into the earth, building the soil as it decomposes. I may even spread a fresh layer of manure over this garden after most of the crops have been removed. "Neglectful" gardeners know that this cover protects and improves the soil. They're doing their best to imitate the example offered by forest leaf mold, recognizing that, when it comes to benign neglect, Mother Nature does the best job of all.

🍂 A simple cold frame can extend the salad season a surprisingly long time. Scatter leaves among the plants in the frame to insulate their roots, and wait for sunny winter days to harvest the lettuce and other greens.

So give old Jack Frost the cold shoulder by using early frost protection. These simple techniques can add weeks of garden pleasure and plenty of vegetable harvests.

The Old-Fashioned Cold Frame

Cold frames are among the most basic plant protectors and season extenders. All it takes is a wooden frame with a plastic or glass top to bust gardening limits and break rules year-round.

When it's mid- to late winter outside, it's spring inside a cold frame. Snow might be whipping around outdoors, but as long as the soil temperature under the frame is 43°F or above, your lettuce and spinach plants will be growing, radish and parsnip seeds will be germinating, and the gardening season will be moving along. Later in the season, when the soil temperature inside the cold frame reaches 60°F, you can raise and harden off transplants of tomatoes, broccoli, and cauliflower.

STARTING UP

You can get an early start on sowing in the frame by covering the soil inside with a single layer of black plastic mulch. Leave it on for several weeks to heat the soil, then remove it at sowing time. Sow the seeds, then cover them loosely with clear plastic before closing the frame. When the seedlings emerge, remove the plastic.

You can also germinate your seedlings in the house, where temperatures are usually much warmer. Once they're up, move them to the cold frame in their cell packs or flats.

HARDENING OFF

A cold frame is ideal for hardening off, which is vital to the success of many crops. Hardening simply means slowly exposing seedlings to the harsher conditions of the outdoors.

Because cold frames can be open, partly open, or closed, they're perfect halfway points for tender plants. Once you've put seedlings out in the frame, they stay out. You don't have to shuffle them inside on cold nights because the frame provides immediate protection.

To start hardening, move your pots and flats

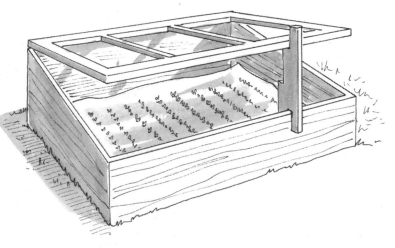

Cold frames are best for hardening off transplants. They're not usually used for starting seedlings, but later on in the spring, you can sow seeds of greens under a single layer of clear plastic in the frame. Remove the plastic as soon as the seedlings sprout.

from the house to the frame near transplanting time. Gradually expose the seedlings to more sun, cold, and wind, but less water. In one to three weeks, they'll be ready to transplant.

SUMMER IN THE FRAME

You shouldn't abandon your cold frame in summer. It's a perfect place to sow biennial and perennial flowers that need overwintering.

While you're at it, you can use the cold frame to start cuttings of shrubs, trees, and houseplants. Just be sure to keep the soil inside moist, and cover the frame with shade cloth during the height of summer.

FALL AND WINTER
IN THE FRAME

Cold frames really earn their keep during late fall and early winter. You can grow broccoli, lettuce, radishes, kale, or oriental vegetables long past the first fall frost if they're protected in the frame.

Choose the appropriate cultivars, then plant them in the frame early enough in the summer so that they're two-thirds grown by the first frost date. Once the plants are growing, place white plastic or aluminum foil under and around them to reflect light and brighten the frame on cloudy days. Because they give off heat as they freeze, containers of water placed inside the frame will help moderate cold temperatures.

COLD FRAME CARE

To work well, cold frames need attention. If possible, place yours near the house, where it won't be easily forgotten. It's also handy to have electrical outlets nearby, since some crops benefit from supplemental heat.

Choose a sunny, well-drained site for your cold frame. If you're sowing and transplanting directly into the soil in the frame, be sure you make it as fertile as the soil in your garden. If the frame is protected by a windbreak, it will stay more moist in summer and warmer in winter.

Controlling ventilation is one of the most important aspects of cold frame care. Excessive heat or cold will endanger your plants. Check your frame at least once a day or use an automatic ventilator. Some ventilators have thermostats that can be set high for keeping seeds warm and low for growing plants.

Thanks to plastic, there are now many different kinds of season extenders on the market. But the old-fashioned cold frame is still hard to beat.

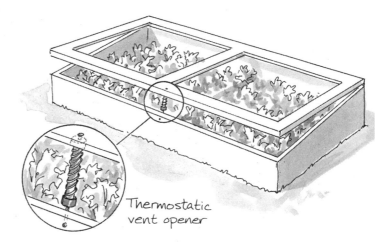

Thermostatic vent opener

Even in early spring, cold frames can heat up considerably. Although it may be too chilly to open the frame when you leave for work in the morning, heat can build up and fry sensitive seedlings by afternoon. The best way to avoid overheating is to install an automatic cold-frame ventilator, which opens the frame whenever inside temperatures trip its thermostat.

The Indispensable Hotbed

A hotbed is the Arnold Schwarzenegger of cold frames, a plant protector to the Nth degree. It allows you to take advantage of all the seasons so you can move the garden indoors and back out again for a full year without interruption. You can make even your wildest garden dreams come true when you build a hotbed.

But what is a hotbed? It's just a cold frame with a heat source. And that heat source is traditionally fresh manure mixed with straw or litter. When it's properly prepared, a hotbed will stay warm (15°F above garden soil temperature) for up to three months.

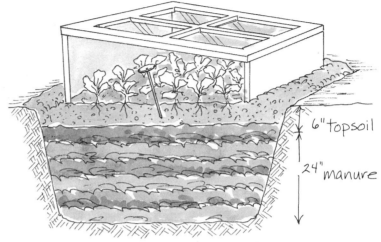

6" topsoil

24" manure

HOT—NOT?

To prepare the hotbed, allow fresh manure mixed with straw or litter to compost about seven or eight days so it can heat up. Then place a 24-inch-deep layer of the heated manure in the frame and top it with about 6 inches of good soil.

Use a soil thermometer to monitor how much heat is being generated. Keep in mind that composting manure can get very hot, and don't plant your seeds if the soil temperature rises above the maximum germination temperature for that particular crop.

THE HOTBED GARDEN

A properly working hotbed will give you a continuous supply of fresh salad greens all year. It's up to you to decide what suits your taste and growing conditions, but here are a few ideas to get you started:

In late summer or early autumn, you can dig up small herbs, such as chives and rosemary, or late greens, including celery, Chinese cabbage, kale, and lettuce, and transplant them into the hotbed. There they will continue to grow and provide you with plenty of ingredients for your winter salad bowl.

A hotbed is a cold frame with a heat source. Traditionally, the heat comes from a layer of fresh manure about 2 feet thick. You can sow seed directly into the 6-inch-deep layer of soil that covers the manure.

Meanwhile, back in the kitchen, you can be starting a couple of flats of greens in a sunny window for mid-winter eating. Sow your seeds of 'Bibb', 'Black-Seeded Simpson', and romaine lettuce in the fall, and transplant them into the hotbed in winter.

Spinach is fine for the winter salad, but remember that it takes more room than lettuce. Transplant from the flats to your hotbeds as you eat the salad greens that mature first.

PLAN FOR PRODUCTION

Since you want nonstop production, during the winter you should be planning ahead for spring and summer. While you're eating your way through the winter lettuce, start seeds indoors in cell packs for your first crop of early outdoor vegetables.

There are at least three advantages to starting transplants indoors in cell packs. First, starting from seeds means you have the widest possible choice of cultivars at the lowest possible cost. Second, using cell packs simplifies handling and transplanting. Third, the plants have a chance to establish themselves outdoors and to take hold before the hot, dry midsummer days arrive.

By mid- to late spring, the greens you sowed in late winter should be ready for the table. As summer swings in, the cycle has come full circle. And before you know it, it will be time to make late-summer plantings in the hotbed before the first frost arrives.

The hotbed, which makes such garden performances possible, is a time-honored, tried-and-true garden tool. I think it's nearly indispensable to a year-round growing program.

Fall gardening may seem risky, but it really is no more so than spring and summer gardening. You'll be surprised at how hardy some vegetables are. These crops are tough! They can take the cold. You have little to lose by aiming for fall vegetables. When the first frost comes and half the garden stays green, you will have your reward—some fine fresh eating come winter.

The Solar Greenhouse

Of course, the ultimate season extender is a solar greenhouse. Since I built mine, a whole new world of gardening has opened up to me.

Greenhouses come in all shapes and sizes (and with all kinds of price tags). The framing can be wood or aluminum. The glazing can be glass or one of the new miracle plastics. You can spend tens of thousands of dollars to have a greenhouse erected. Or you can order one ready-built from a mail-order supplier, or make your own from two-by-fours and 6-mil polyethylene. In fact, many Cooperative Extension Service offices have free greenhouse plans available.

USING YOUR GREENHOUSE

There are so many options, I'm not about to tell you how to build a greenhouse. But I *am* going to tell you how to use one.

There are a few things you need to know about the physical structure before you get started. In order to be a worthwhile investment of time and money, a greenhouse has to be big enough to work in.

I'd say the minimum workable size for a greenhouse is 12 feet by 15 feet for the outside measurements. Allowing for a foundation, walkway, and perhaps a small potting bench, that should leave a total usable area of 100 square feet.

For heat, you can install electric or gas heaters. Fifty-five-gallon drums, painted black and filled with water, can be used as passive solar collectors (if you have the room for them).

Or you can do as I do and include a "compost digester" as a backup heat source. That's a fancy name for a compost pile in the greenhouse. As the compost cools down, you can spread it on your garden beds and replace it with fresh manure for more heat.

LETTING IN LIGHT

Every solar greenhouse should be designed to admit the maximum amount of light possible in the cool season. It should also make the most use of that light once it's inside.

The simplest way to increase the amount of usable light for the plants is to paint the interior of the greenhouse—including all wooden beams and rafters—white or to coat the walls with aluminum foil. White paint scatters more light than foil does, so a little more light passes through the glass than if foil is used.

You can use supplemental lighting—fluorescent or high-intensity discharge lights—to extend the "day" in the greenhouse. This method is most cost-effective for seedlings, since young plants are more efficient than older plants at using extra light, and more plants can be raised under one light when they are still small.

Light Limitations

The best solar greenhouses, attached or freestanding, are designed so that they are shaded by their roof peak and perhaps an opaque roof in the summer. In such tight, well-insulated buildings, some shade is essential to avoid overheating during summer. Even with shading from the roof, light intensities during winter will still be ample for growth.

GREENHOUSE BEDS

For serious growing, you just can't beat permanent beds in the greenhouse. Wood-framed beds, 3 or 4 feet wide and 3 or 4 feet deep, are much easier to manage than pots or boxes on the ground or on benches. You can run the beds the full length of your solar greenhouse for maximum productivity. Another advantage of deep, permanent beds is that they require less watering once the crop is established.

You can bet that good soil is critical to greenhouse crop production. You'll need a depth of at least 15 inches of fertile soil for growing greens indoors. Use a mix of one part compost, one part fine washed sand, two parts mushroom compost, and two parts garden soil. (If you don't have access to mushroom compost, use composted manure.) Dolomite, rock phosphate, and nitrogen in the form of blood meal complete the formula. Add these if you find, on the basis of simple soil tests, that your soil is deficient.

In just 100 square feet (one 4-by-25-foot bed or two 4-by- 12½-foot beds), you can have tomatoes, onions, radishes, cucumbers, celery, lettuce, and other green leafy vegetables such as spinach all

growing at the same time. But not all of these crops grow well at the same temperature.

Lettuce, onions, and radishes do quite well when it is 45°F at night and 55°F during the day, but these temperatures are too low for tomatoes and cucumbers. When several crops are grown in one greenhouse, I've found that the best compromise is to use the temperature required by tomatoes: 60°F at night and 75°F during the day. At these temperatures, the tomatoes will flourish and the cold-tolerant crops will grow well, too.

READY, SET, GROW

When planning your crops for the solar greenhouse, it's a good idea to start simple. Start with the mainstays—the fast, easy crops such as greens—and leave the glamorous ones until after you have mastered the basics of growing and have gotten to know your greenhouse better.

Green leafy vegetables can be grown virtually year-round in the solar greenhouse. You can grow almost all the leafy types of vegetables from seed to harvest in greenhouse raised beds without having to transplant them.

Several cultivars of lettuce, including loose-leaf

The key to growing plants successfully in a greenhouse is light. During winter, light is a precious commodity. Your greenhouse should be designed to make the most of it, with reflective surfaces inside. At times, you may also need a supplemental light source like hanging fluorescent shop lights.

types and nonheading cultivars that mature in 40 to 50 days, do well with this method of planting. Radishes can be a continuous crop, if you stagger seed plantings.

If planting space is limited or if the beds are in full production at planting time, you can start seeds in flats and transplant the seedlings to the growing bed as soon as you've harvested a crop. With this technique, a small space goes a long way.

When you're scheduling planting dates, remember that as the days grow shorter, each crop takes longer to mature. This is one of the reasons why greens are better suited to greenhouses than root vegetables. In the fall in a solar greenhouse, it takes almost five months for root crops to grow large enough for harvesting, but greens are ready in less than half that time.

The Greenhouse Planting Season

You'll get the most from your greenhouse if you follow a seasonal schedule of soil preparation, planting, and harvest. Since I grow my summer crops outdoors, for me the greenhouse season extends from fall through spring. (Though I find that the greenhouse is a great place for starting seeds of succession crops in summer.) Here's what to do:

FALL

Beginning in August, cover the greenhouse beds with a 1- or 2-inch-thick layer of manure, rotted leaves, and compost. Sprinkle rock phosphate and granite dust or greensand plus fish meal over the top. Wet the beds down well and keep them moist as the organic matter decomposes.

At the same time, sow seeds of broccoli, cauliflower, and kohlrabi in flats indoors. At the end of the month, sow lettuce in flats. Till or work the beds and sow onions and long-growing root crops, such as turnips and beets.

By mid-September, the brassicas should be ready for transplanting into the beds. In the meantime, keep sowing lettuce, spinach, and other greens in flats so you'll have a constant supply of vegetables all winter long.

You can start fall greens as early as September. After a full year in the greenhouse, the beds are likely to be full of heavily bearing crops, so start all of your greens in small containers. Peat pots are a good choice for oriental greens because the plants sometimes bolt (go to seed) prematurely when their roots are disturbed. You can hold greens in their pots for four to six weeks, but don't let them get rootbound.

WINTER

Natural light levels aren't high enough in the winter to give seedlings a vigorous start, so you'll need to start early crops under lights. Artificial lights give greater flexibility during winter and spring.

Plants that will grow to maturity in the greenhouse are the first ones you should start. They all need the highest light levels possible in winter and spring, so clear a section of the brightest bed in the house for them.

If the minimum greenhouse temperature is averaging 70°F during the day and 50°F at night, you can start tomatoes right after Christmas. Peppers and eggplant are next, but wait until January to start them. Melons and cucumbers respond best to a 16-hour day during both their seedling and adult lives, so wait till after the vernal equinox (the first day of spring) to start them.

SPRING

Spring comes to the greenhouse when the days begin to lengthen. Kale, beets, lettuce, parsley, chard, turnips, and spinach are all good choices for early spring plantings.

Scheduling seedlings for the outside garden is a matter of counting backwards from the time they'll be set outside. That date is determined by the last frost date in your area and by the plants' cold-hardiness. In my greenhouse, I start parsley on March 7 for transplanting on May 5. I start broccoli on March 27 for transplanting on May 15. Although lettuce will be transplanted on the same date, I start it later, on April 10 to 17, since it grows faster than broccoli.

PART III

Let's Grow Vegetables and Herbs

10

A Gallery of Vegetables

ow we come to the fun part. Here's the heart of the matter, where you can finally stop fussing with the soil and learn how to grow it all, from asparagus to watermelon. Here's where you learn the individual quirks of vegetables both common and rare.

Organic gardening is an art, an opportunity for individual creativity. Far be it from me to crimp your style, step on your creativity, or steer you wrong. I believe that the gardener should make his or her own choices in order to derive the fullest satisfac-

tion from planning a garden. I don't want you to choose a cultivar just because *I* have grown and enjoyed it.

You'll find a few cultivar recommendations scattered throughout this vegetable section. If a cultivar is unique or stands head and foliage above all others, I've noted it. Other than that, you're on your own. Ask around. Find out what your neighbors and friends are growing. Experiment with heirloom cultivars. And above all, keep searching.

Basic Feeding Formulas

I've developed my own system for feeding various vegetable crops. First, I divided the veggies into categories—light feeders, such as beans; medium feeders, such as lettuce; and heavy feeders, such as corn. Then I came up with a formula for each category.

Look at the entry for each vegetable to find out whether it's a light, medium, or heavy feeder. Once you know that, you can apply one of these three formulas:

Light feeders: Apply 2 pounds of compost or composted manure per square foot (a 2-inch layer) in the fall. Till in spring.

Medium feeders: Apply 2 pounds of compost or composted manure per square foot (a 2-inch layer) in the fall. Apply another 2 pounds per square foot in spring, at least two weeks before planting.

Heavy feeders: Apply 2 pounds of compost or composted manure per square foot in both fall and spring. Before planting, broadcast blended organic fertilizer (3-6-3 or 4-6-4) at the recommended label rate.

I give all my crops a mid-season boost—I think it perks them up, no matter which type they are. Every three weeks, I drench plant foliage with liquid seaweed or fish emulsion fertilizer mixed at the recommended label rate.

ASPARAGUS

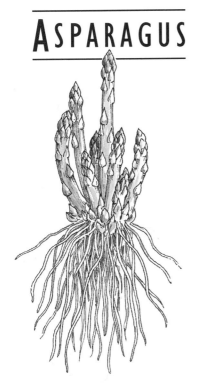

More than any other vegetable, asparagus requires a carefully chosen site. That's because it's a perennial crop. But asparagus differs from other perennials like rhubarb, since you plant a whole bed of it at a time. A good asparagus planting will continue to produce in the same spot for up to 20 years. Over that time, the roots will penetrate as deep as 6 feet into the soil.

SITE AND SOIL

Although a sandy loam soil produces the best asparagus, any well-drained garden loam will do as long as it is well fortified with organic matter. I like to grow a green manure crop in the future asparagus bed, then turn it and spade it into the bed in the fall. Next, I spade a 2-inch-deep layer of manure into the bed. The object is to get plenty of fertilizer in and on the asparagus bed before spring planting.

That way, the bed will need no additional spading after the crowns are established.

PLANTING

Plant strong, healthy one- or two-year-old crowns 20 inches apart in 12-inch-deep trenches spaced 3 feet apart. Set the center of each root on a small mound of soil so that the roots radiate out like spokes from a wagon wheel. Don't fill the trench completely at planting time. Instead, cover with just 2 inches of fertile soil—work it in carefully around each plant with your fingers and firm it down gently. Then, over the course of the summer, toss about 1 inch of soil around the young plants every time you hoe down the weeds. By fall, the trench will be filled in.

Planting crowns is the easiest and fastest way to get a crop, but you can start asparagus from seed, too. If you're starting from seed, sow in the spring, as soon as the soil is warm enough for germination—about 65°F. If you soak the seed in warm water for several days before sowing, it will germinate in about five weeks. Sow one seed every 6 or 7 inches along the row. If drought hits, flood the trenches once every two weeks.

CARE

Whether you're starting asparagus from crowns or seed, make sure to keep the bed weed-free all through the first summer. The following spring, spread a 2-inch layer of compost or aged manure over the whole bed. Then mulch the entire area with old hay, shredded leaves, straw, salt hay, or dried grass clippings. For a steady supply of thick, delicious spears, repeat this practice every spring.

To avoid problems with rust or fusarium wilt, choose resistant cultivars. You can also

Mulching Asparagus

Heavily mulched asparagus, though usually later than asparagus that is unmulched or lightly mulched, provides a longer picking season. A thick application (at least 12 inches) of leaves and grass clippings delays the emergence of the spears but seems to keep them coming for a longer time.

prevent fusarium wilt by disinfecting the seeds before planting: Soak them in a 10 percent bleach solution (1 part bleach to 9 parts water) for two minutes, then rinse them in clear water for one minute.

HARVESTING

There's a long-running debate among asparagus fanciers about the proper method for harvesting. Some say you should cut the spears at just about soil level. Others vote for cutting them off just below ground. Well, I've experimented with both methods, and as a result, I'm firmly in the underground camp. I've found that there's less damage to the spears if they're carefully cut off below ground. To do that, I slide a sharp knife down the stem about 2 inches below the soil surface and twist it to sever the spear. There also seems to be less insect damage if the spears are cut below ground.

Don't cut the shoots from a bed of one- or two-year-old plants. Wait until the third year, and then take just three cuttings. During the early years, the plants are still forming productive crowns beneath the surface and need plenty of foliage to grow. The more you cut, the less foliage will be produced.

CONTINUING CARE

After you have finished harvesting for the season, set a strong post at both ends of the row and string a ¼-inch rope between them. This trellis will hold the ferny tops up against prevailing winds and keep them from flopping into the aisles.

Once heavy frosts have browned the foliage, you can "put the asparagus bed to sleep" by cutting the foliage at ground level and laying it across the bed to hold the mulch in place over winter. To prevent inferior seedlings from sprouting in spring, dispose of any stalks that are loaded with red seeds.

CROW'S TIPS

Remember that asparagus must be fed and mulched with organic matter every spring if it is going to produce an abundance of thick spears. The more fertile the soil over the crowns, the more spears you will harvest as the years go by.

BEANS, DRY

Dry beans come in many intriguing and attractive sizes, shapes, and colors. Any mature edible legume seed that is dried in the garden (weather permitting) and used for baking, chili, soup, or other bean dishes qualifies as a dry bean. That includes garbanzo, French horticultural, kidney, navy, chickpea, black-eyed pea, scarlet runner, and pinto beans.

SITE AND SOIL

Preparing the soil properly is an all-important first step. Beans are light feeders and grow

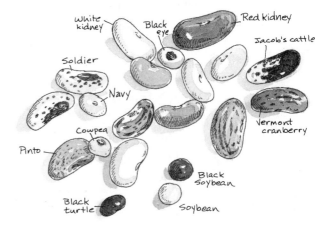

best in soil with a pH in the range of 6.0 to 7.5. A pH that is either above or below that optimal range could interfere with the plants' ability to utilize soil nutrients.

Beans are legumes and don't require a high amount of nitrogen in the soil since they can manufacture their own. (Too much nitrogen can actually reduce their productivity.) Like peas and other legumes, beans can fix nitrogen in the soil from atmospheric nitrogen. They do this through the action of rhizobium bacteria contained in their root nodules. You can buy a specific bean bacterial inoculum, called *Rhizobium phaseoli,* to help this process along.

However, beans still need some nutrients; so before planting, I till a 2-inch layer of compost or aged manure into the planting row. The compost or manure not only provides nutrients but also improves soil drainage and tilth.

PLANTING

When you're growing dried beans, starting with good seed is critical. Make certain that your seeds are whole and clean. Bean seed coats that are damaged carry a higher risk of infection and produce lower yields than those that aren't damaged. Seed freshness and vigor are also important because dry beans should germinate as rapidly as possible or they're liable to rot. Finally, the more genetically pure the seeds are, the better. Dry beans from a pure strain will all mature at the same time. If your seeds aren't good, maturation times may vary from bush to bush.

Bean seeds need warmth; if planted too early, they will rot in the soil. Wait until the soil temperature has reached at least 60°F. Sow the seed 2 inches deep and 2 inches apart in rows spaced 18 inches apart. Cover seeds with loose, friable soil, and tamp firmly to ensure a more uniform stand.

Once the seedlings emerge (usually within 7 to 14 days) and grow to finger length, thin them to 3 to 5 inches apart. Too-close quarters can lead to inadequate air circulation, which in turn can cause fungal diseases.

CARE

Keep the soil moist, but avoid wetting the plant foliage when watering, since damp foliage is prone to mildew attack. (This is where a soaker hose really comes in handy.) A 6-inch mulch of straw will cut watering in half. If mildew strikes, as it occasionally does in humid climates, you can control it with regular dustings of sulfur.

Aphids and Mexican bean beetles are the two main bean pests. They seem to be rare in some gardens but can be notorious crop-busters in others. Should beetles appear, rotenone applications will solve the problem. You can prevent pests before they become a problem by covering young bean plants with row covers. Some gardeners interplant with marigolds and nasturtiums to keep bean beetles away.

Beans are also susceptible to seed rot and damping-off, so don't put your beans in the same place each year. Rotate them around the garden with a cereal crop like corn or another non-legume. That way, the diseases can't get established in the soil. Try to avoid the peas-after-beans or beans-after-peas planting sequence because both crops can be infected by the same diseases.

Sanitation is the best tactic to control diseases. Dispose of all bean crop residues, don't till them back into the soil. This practice is critical, since rust can form overwintering spores in the fall that will germinate next spring. Don't work with the plants when the foliage is wet because it's easy to spread fungal diseases from one plant to the next.

HARVESTING

Most shell beans (those grown for their fresh beans) reach the "green-shell" stage from 9 to 11 weeks after sowing. At this point, the beans are fully formed in their pods and are ready to be shelled and then cooked, frozen, or canned. For dried beans, however, you must leave these pods on the vine until they're dry and brittle. Or, if rain or fog persists during the drying stage, pull the entire plant and hang it upside down in a well-ventilated shed or garage.

BEANS, LIMA

Foot for foot in the garden, lima beans provide more nutrition with less effort than any other vegetable crop. So who cares if they taste terrible? (Just kidding.) If you've never tasted a freshly steamed mess of lima beans straight from the garden, you're missing out on a protein-packed delicacy.

Don't pick lima beans too early! For best flavor and to avoid that mushy texture, wait till the pods are plump and completely filled out before harvesting.

SITE AND SOIL

Like other legumes, limas make their own nitrogen underground, but don't neglect their basic needs. During fall cleanup I spread leaves, grass clippings, pine needles, and vegetable stubble over the future bean site. I till that in and then sow winter ryegrass as a green manure crop for these light feeders.

Come spring, I till the rye into the soil just before planting the beans. The succulent tops and the roots of these plants provide excellent fertilizer for the young lima plants.

PLANTING

Limas seem to take to rows better than beds. I space the rows about 3 feet apart to allow room for my rotary tiller. Limas bush out quite a lot, so even if you're not tilling, it's a good idea to plant them at least 2½ feet apart.

CARE

I use the tiller to keep weeds down between the rows. Limas are among those crops that do well without mulch. They will grow in very dry soil, but if the weather is very dry at bloom time, I soak the soil thoroughly between the rows to encourage the pods to fill out. When the limas have finished bearing their first crop, I water again and loosen the soil around them with a hoe. In a few days, the limas will produce a new wave of blooms, with a second harvest of beans to follow a few weeks later. Plants will bloom again and produce a third crop after the second has been picked.

However, it's important to be careful watering your limas. Too much water causes the beans to rot and seems to encourage worms. For the most part, though, pest insects show minimal interest in lima beans. (For more on preventing or controlling pests and diseases that attack beans, see "Care" in the Dry Beans and Snap Beans entries on pages 99 and 102.)

HARVESTING

When the beans plump up in the pods all the way to the tips, pick them, leaving the flat pods for a later picking.

BEANS, SNAP

You've got one big decision to make before planting snap beans: bush or pole? Bean preference may be a genetic thing. It seems to me that there are two types of gardeners: those who grow bush beans and those who grow pole beans. You won't find too many who grow both.

In reality, your decision depends on some practical factors—for example, your growing season, available space, and preferred picking style. Still, it doesn't seem that simple. Folks get downright emotional when the subject of bean types comes up.

Pole-bean pushers tout the continuous production of their favorite bean type. The indeterminate growing habit of pole beans means that they keep producing flowers and beans as long as the vines are growing. Bush-bean lovers point to the concentrated harvest over a few weeks. In the long run, pole beans will bear more beans than bush cultivars, but the harvest will begin later and be stretched out over a longer period.

Pole beans make the most of vertical growing space, but you must be prepared to put up a tepee or trellis for them. Or you can grow pole cultivars up a porch or as a bean tent for children in the yard.

Bush beans are an ideal crop for succession plantings. You can stagger your sowings two or three weeks apart for a steady harvest. Just make sure you make the last sowing at least two months before the last frost date.

Bush beans are compact, ideal for tight spaces and intercropping. But if you have the room, pole beans are flavorful, productive, and fun to grow. Kids especially love pole bean tepees, and the tepees are great for shading heat-sensitive crops like lettuce.

SITE AND SOIL

As legumes, beans make their own nitrogen in root nodules. So add only moderate amounts of organic fertilizer at planting time. Too much nitrogen can actually discourage the plants from forming root nodules. An inch or two of compost, worked into the soil before planting, will provide a season's worth of fertilizer for light-feeding pole beans.

However, bush beans might need a boost since they bear over a concentrated period of only two or three weeks. They will especially appreciate supplemental feeding before fruiting. So when you first see blooms appearing, side-dress with a handful of blended organic fertilizer. Don't be tempted to overdo it with fertilizer. Too much nitrogen will cause the plants to fall over when loaded with pods, leaving you with dirty beans or with pods that have rotted from resting on the ground.

PLANTING

Bush beans will probably give you an earlier harvest than pole beans, but don't be in too much of a hurry to plant either kind. Bean seed just won't germinate if the soil temperature is below 60°F. If you're not the type of gardener who regularly takes your soil's temperature, you can watch for other natural signs that indicate when it's time to plant beans. For example, full bloom on redbuds, flowering dogwoods, crabapples, or lilacs usually indicates that the soil's sufficiently warmed.

For highest yields, sow bush beans 2 to 3 inches apart in rows spaced 18 inches apart. The plants will eventually grow together and shade the ground beneath them, so they'll require little weeding and watering. For bed planting, stick with only two bush bean rows in a 3-foot-wide bed.

Pole beans need more space than bush cultivars because their longer bearing season and higher yields require lots of foliage. Also, pole beans planted in rows seem to yield better than those planted in hills. Space row-planted pole beans generously, with at least 1 foot between plants. Space hills 4 feet apart, and thin seedlings to two or three per hill.

CARE

If you've sown your beans in moderately moist soil, your plants won't require additional watering until after they are up and growing. Light, frequent irrigation during early growth is best because bean roots are very sensitive to lack of oxygen in saturated soils and may rot. Keep the soil evenly moist by applying a straw mulch. Spray plants with kelp extract or liquid seaweed to prevent nutrient deficiencies.

Bean flowers are notoriously fragile. If the temperature is either too high or too low, it can affect their pollination. For example, if the temperature falls below 60°F during the day and 40°F at night, the young beans in the pods may abort. If a cold snap threatens, you may be able to save your bush beans by placing floating row covers over them.

Floating row covers placed over bean seedlings can also protect them from attacks by pests like leafhoppers, leafminers, and bean leaf beetles. Control the ¼-inch-long, yellowish brown, spotted Mexican bean beetles by handpicking them and their spiny orange larvae. For severe infestations, spray weekly with pyrethrins, sabadilla, or rotenone. Avoid bean diseases such as bean mosaic, anthracnose, rust, and powdery mildew by planting resistant cultivars.

HARVESTING

Pick the pods as soon as they fill out. Harvest them regularly for repeat blooming.

🐦 CROW'S TIPS

If you can't resist planting your beans early, dark-seeded cultivars like 'Royalty Purple', 'Provider', and 'Kentucky Wonder' are generally more cold-tolerant than the white-seeded types. Also, consider your soil type before you plant. Sandy soils will warm faster than heavy clay soils and may be more forgiving if you stretch the bean-growing season.

BEETS

Beets thrive in slightly sandy soil that allows the roots to develop smoothly. To help the soil retain moisture and nourish young plants, work in a 2-inch-thick layer of organic matter before planting.

SITE AND SOIL

Beets grow best in soil that is near neutral (pH 6.0 to 7.0). In more acid soil (below pH 6.0), they become stunted and spindly. If the soil is alkaline (above pH 7.0), the roots may develop scab and show rough brown spots on the surfaces.

Like other root vegetables, beets need adequate phosphorus. A good, safe, organic phosphorus source is bonemeal. If I haven't spread it on the beds in the fall, I sprinkle it in the rows at seeding time, applying just enough to cover the soil.

Healthy beets also depend on the availability of small quantities of boron in the soil. Beets that lack this trace element develop black, corky, bitter zones. Now, I know we must always be extremely cautious in applying trace elements. It's far better to err on the side of caution. But I don't want bitter beets, either. So if a soil test says my soil is low in boron, I provide some by dissolving $\frac{1}{4}$ teaspoon of common borax in 1 pint of water. That makes enough mixture to spray over a 16-square-foot area.

Even if the boron content of the soil is adequate, beets can suffer boron deficiencies in acid soil. So make sure the soil is neutral before you plant these light feeders.

PLANTING

You can sow beets as soon as the soil is workable in spring. I like to grow beets in double or triple rows. I sow the seeds 2 inches apart in shallow trenches $\frac{1}{2}$ inch deep. I space the rows 6 to 8 inches apart and leave an aisle about 12 to 18 inches wide between blocks of rows, then sow two or three more rows of beets.

I run the rows north and south so that the young plants won't shade each other. When the seedlings are about 3 or 4 inches tall, I thin them to 4 inches apart. Because beet seeds are really fruits containing two to eight seeds, many of the seeds sown will produce more than one plant. Still, beets are famous for their exasperating tendency to germinate spottily. I've found that they seem to need especially close contact with the soil to germinate well. To make sure there are no air spaces surrounding the seed, I press the seed firmly into the soil and water well. The soil should be fine to start with. If it is full of coarse crumbs or clods, the seed-to-soil contact will be poor.

Both cold-hardy and heat-resistant, beets are one of the best vegetables for succession planting. After the first sowing of beets, I keep planting every two weeks through mid-July.

CARE

In the hot months of summer, beets need ample water. Mulching with straw will help conserve moisture. If beets get dry, they'll become tough and stringy. If there are alternating dry and wet periods, white rings will appear in the roots.

Sow round cultivars for early plantings. For a fall harvest, use the longer-rooted cultivars, which store better in the root cellar.

Protect young plants from leafminers and flea beetles with row covers; when the weather warms up, remove the covers. Leaf spot can also threaten your beet crop, so choose disease-tolerant cultivars whenever possible.

HARVESTING

Like many vegetables, beets are best if harvested when they are still young and tender. For good keeping in winter storage, however, mature roots are necessary.

 ## CROW'S PICKS

At one time, you could get garden beets in any color—as long as it was red, as the old joke goes. But now you can have white beets, golden beets, and even striped beets, as well as red beets and some attractive hybrids. I like 'Red Ace' and 'Lutz Winter Keeper', a fall cultivar.

Beet cultivars differ substantially in the time required to mature. 'Lutz Winter Keeper', for example, matures more slowly than 'Red Ace' and needs to be sown a month earlier. 'Lutz' also grows large and requires 4 to 5 inches between plants, while smaller beets need only 3 inches between them.

BROCCOLI

Broccoli is one of the best vegetables you can grow. Not only does it taste good raw or cooked, it's really good for you. Broccoli is packed full of vitamins and minerals. And it even helps prevent cancer.

SITE AND SOIL

For the best broccoli production, nothing is more important than good soil preparation. Broccoli, a heavy feeder, requires a rich, well-drained soil chock-full of organic matter. Prepare the bed about three weeks before setting out transplants. Work in as much compost and well-rotted manure as you can—at least 2 pounds per square foot. Compost especially helps the soil retain moisture without becoming waterlogged.

To complete the soil recipe, broadcast thin layers of dolomitic limestone and wood ashes or greensand, and till them in. Wood ashes and greensand raise the potash value of the soil, while dolomitic limestone adds magnesium and calcium and neutralizes soil pH. (Broccoli prefers a pH of 6.7 to 7.5—anything lower, and your plants will be subject to club root.) Finally, work in 2 pounds of bonemeal per 100 square feet, and the garden is ready for transplants.

PLANTING

I always start my own plants from seed. That way, I have complete control right from the start. When you buy plants from a garden

center, you have no idea how old the seedlings are, what stress they have encountered, or what diseases they may be carrying.

For spring crops, I start plants in my greenhouse the first week of March. I keep the seedlings growing at a temperature of 60° to 65°F for about one month. After that, I harden them off by shuttling them between indoors and out for about a week. That brings me to mid-April—about three weeks before the last expected frost here, which is when I transplant broccoli to the garden.

Small one-month-old plants make the best transplants. Older plants are usually stressed and often doomed to failure. If their leaves are glossy with a bluish tinge, they're past their prime transplanting time.

Early broccoli is ready to harvest in June. The sweetest, most tender broccoli is harvested in cool weather, however. I sometimes direct-seed late broccoli near the end of June for harvest in the frosty days of fall. Like all cool-weather crops, broccoli prefers night temperatures of 60° to 70°F and day temperatures of below 80°F. The flavor is truly enhanced after a light frost or two.

CARE

Broccoli plants have shallow root systems, so close cultivation is risky. To control the weeds, conserve soil moisture, and keep the roots cool, I mulch the beds with several inches of straw, leaves, or grass clippings.

A living mulch of leafy crops can help make the most of valuable garden space, so I plant lettuce, spinach, and other leafy greens

Do the Dip

When transplanting, I think it pays to help get your plants off to a good start and alleviate stress. So I always dunk the transplants in a micronutrient-rich solution, such as liquid kelp, before setting them out in the garden.

around the broccoli plants. The greens shade the ground, keeping the soil cool and hindering weeds.

The scourge of the broccoli bed is a little green worm known as the cabbage looper. The best way to control this caterpillar is with *Bacillus thuringiensis.* Better known as BT, this totally natural pesticide kills only butterfly and moth larvae and is nontoxic to humans, animals, and beneficial insects. Infected cabbage loopers stop feeding within an hour after eating the bacteria and die within 24 hours. For best results, spray the broccoli with BT at weekly intervals, preferably in the early morning or evening so that the pests will eat the bacteria before it dries.

HARVESTING

Harvest heads when they are still small. If the buds have blossomed into yellow florets, the heads are past their prime. Broccoli plants will continue to produce heads over the next several weeks after the first cutting.

To harvest, cut the stem 4 to 6 inches below the head. Broccoli will keep in the refrigerator for one to two weeks.

CROW'S PICKS

There are scores of broccoli cultivars to choose from. For the best possible yields, select one that matures quickly, produces large heads, and makes many sideshoots. 'Green Comet' meets the first two requirements but produces few, if any, sideshoots. It's a great spring performer. And 'Green Duke' is a good heat-tolerant broccoli cultivar.

BRUSSELS SPROUTS

This hardy, slow-growing member of the cabbage family must have cool weather to mature. Forget that, and your sprouts are bound to fail.

As with all cool-weather crops, timing is critical for a quality harvest. The idea is to prime the sprouts to mature during the first few frosty days of fall, just as the trees begin to change color. That means planting at exactly the right time. Plant them too early, and the flavor may be too strong. Plant them too late, and the repeated frosts and thaws may cause them to rot. (A little frost is actually good for the sprouts, since it tends to sweeten them.)

To get the timing right, start by finding out the most likely date for your first fall frost. Then count back 90 to 100 days. Circle that date on your calendar. That's when you want to put Brussels sprouts plants in the ground. You can plan on buying garden center transplants at that time. Or count back

another four to six weeks before that date and start your own seeds then.

SITE AND SOIL

Before setting seedlings in the garden, use my heavy feeder formula. (See page 96.) Or apply a balanced organic fertilizer at a rate of 3 or 4 pounds per 100 square feet.

PLANTING

To start your own transplants, sow seeds in a light potting mix in small flats with good drainage and put them under lights. In about two weeks, when the first true leaves appear, transplant the seedlings to a 4-inch flat. Every other time you water, apply a liquid kelp fertilizer according to the directions on the label.

In a couple of weeks or so, when the roots are well established, transplant the seedlings to the garden. Space them 20 to 30 inches apart and water well to be sure the soil settles around the roots.

You can also direct-seed Brussels sprouts right in the garden, about 120 days before the first fall frost. Sow four to five seeds per foot. Plant them about ¼ inch deep, and cover lightly. Direct-seeded Brussels sprouts require thinning. Healthy plants will grow quite large (about 20 to 30 inches tall on an erect, unbranched leafy stem), so be sure to give them 2 feet of elbow room. Then keep them well watered.

CARE

A 4- to 6-inch layer of organic mulch will help the soil retain moisture. Brussels sprouts are heavy feeders, so side-dress each plant once a month with a handful of balanced organic fertilizer.

Cabbage loopers enjoy Brussels sprouts almost as much as they do broccoli. To control them, you can apply *Bacillus thuringiensis* (BT). (See "Care" in the Broccoli entry on page 105 for a description of BT and how to apply it.) Aphids may be more troublesome, however. Anyone who has grown Brussels sprouts has probably had the disturbing experience of seeing little black aphid bodies between layers of cooked sprouts. You can avoid these pests by planting late-maturing cultivars that don't form their sprouts until the weather has cooled and aphids have disappeared. Or, if you spot a few aphids on the plants, you can flush them off with a forceful stream of water.

CROW'S PICKS

The real secret to growing delicious sprouts is choosing a good cultivar. 'Jade Cross', a hybrid, is early, highly productive, and my personal favorite.

HARVESTING

Begin picking the lower leaves off the plants when the sprouts reach the size of marbles. This seems to concentrate the plants' energy on the future sprouts, now immature buds. To harvest sprouts, start at the bottom of the plant since these buds mature first. Don't delay: Pick the sprouts as quickly as they mature or they will toughen and lose their subtle flavor.

You can also easily encourage all the sprouts to mature at the same time. About a month before harvest, just nip out the plant's growing tip, leaving the top canopy of leaves intact.

To keep the harvest going into winter, pile dry hay or straw around the base of the plant and up as high as possible. You'll be able to pick sprouts well beyond the hard

frosts. As long as the ground doesn't freeze, the top part of the plant can take a surprising amount of cold weather.

If you'd rather not brave the cold for picking, you can pull up the whole plant by its roots before the ground freezes and hang it right-side up in the root cellar. The sprouts can then be harvested over several weeks.

CABBAGE

Cabbage is a reliable crop—and tasty, too, whether you eat it fresh, turn it into sauerkraut, or use it in coleslaw. But take my advice: Cabbage matures faster, tastes better, and is less prone to insect attacks when grown in the cooler weather of fall.

SITE AND SOIL

Cabbage is a heavy feeder, so prepare the soil well before you plant. Cabbage plants need a generous diet of nitrogen, phosphorus, potassium, and dolomitic lime. A 2-inch-deep layer of composted manure will supply sufficient amounts of the first three. Or apply fish meal, soybean meal, and cottonseed meal at the recommended label rates before planting.

If you have trouble with the heart of your cabbage dying out, there's probably a boron shortage in your soil. If so, use granite dust as your source of potassium since it also provides boron. Wood ashes will raise the pH while providing potassium, so use them if your pH is low. Otherwise, use dolomitic limestone, which is high in calcium and magnesium, and add granite dust, greensand, or composted manure for potassium.

PLANTING

Cabbage is easy to start from seed. I sow seed in my greenhouse four to six weeks before transplanting to the garden. I use cell packs and flats with a planting medium kept on the lean side: half soil and half sand, with just a touch of perlite.

I cover seeds with ⅛ inch of soil, firm it down well, and water. As soon as the seedlings develop true leaves, I transplant them into a cold frame, where temperatures reach 65°F during the day and drop to about 50°F at night. For the first couple of days they're in the frame, I make sure to shade the little plants. Then I gradually expose them to direct sunlight. Remember that cabbage plants need all the sun they can get, but growing temperatures must remain on the cool side. If you can get this combination, your plants will be short and stocky and will produce firm, massive heads.

I watch the weather carefully. When the cold frame thermometer reaches 65°F, I raise the cover slightly. Closing it at sundown holds in the soil heat, preventing night temperatures from dropping too low. I keep the soil moderately moist at all times. However, I don't feed the plants while they're in the cold frame because they'd grow too tall and lanky for good production.

I sow late cultivars in mid-July and transplant them to the garden by August 15. Cabbage needs a lot of water right from the start, so if it's possible, I transplant on a cloudy or drizzly day. Plants go in at 18-inch intervals in rows spaced 30 inches apart. Then I "mud-in" the plants by putting water in each hole to settle the soil gently around the roots.

CARE

To conserve moisture and keep the soil cool, mulch your cabbage rows heavily. Manure topped with a layer of straw makes an excellent mulch since it not only holds moisture in the soil but helps feed the plants as well.

The most important factor in producing healthy heads is soil moisture. Never allow the soil to dry out around cabbage roots. If it does, growth will slow down, and then when rains finally do come, plants grow so rapidly that the heads often split.

There are a few cabbage pests and diseases to watch out for, especially in summer crops. The cabbageworm and cabbage looper can be easily dispatched, thanks to *Bacillus thuringiensis* (BT). (See "Care" in the Broccoli entry on page 105 for a description of BT and how to apply it.) The armyworm can also be done in with BT.

You can keep cutworm damage to a minimum by wrapping wet tissue around the stems of your seedlings or by putting a can (with the top and bottom cut out) around each plant. Cutworms seem to run in cycles—they're bad one year and gone the next.

If you have had trouble in the past with cabbage yellows virus, grow yellows-resistant cultivars such as 'Golden Acre'.

HARVESTING

You can harvest early and mid-season culti-vars as soon as the heads are large enough to use. Late cultivars store well. Leave them in the garden until a hard freeze is expected, then cut them off and store them in an un-heated building. If you don't have an un-heated building, wrap the heads individually in newspaper and store them on shelves in the coolest part of your cellar or attic. You can also pull them up by the roots and heel them in upside down in a well-drained trench in the garden. Cover with a thick layer of straw to keep the cabbages from freezing.

🐦 CROW'S TIPS

If the heads are splitting on my cabbages, I grab hold of each head and give the plant a quarter turn to break some of the roots. This procedure puts maturation on hold for a couple of weeks. You can accomplish the same thing by cutting close to the plant with a shovel that has a sharp, narrow blade.

CARROTS

Spending a little extra time on the soil is the key to succulent carrots. More than any other vegetable, carrots need just the right soil con-ditions to succeed. In a favorable environ-ment they flourish, but in the wrong environ-ment they fail.

SITE AND SOIL

First, remove any stones that could cause carrot roots to split. The soil should be deep and friable. Sandy soils seem to produce the earliest and heaviest yields.

Composted manure is an excellent fer-tilizer for carrots, but it must be turned under during the fall before planting. Too much ni-trogen, especially in the form of fresh ma-nure, will result in branchy, fibrous roots, so I use the light-feeder formula: 2 pounds of ma-nure or compost per square foot of carrot bed. Plentiful potassium, on the other hand, is no problem—it promotes sweet, solid roots. Since I always make my compost with rock phosphate, 2 inches or so of compost provides all the phosphorus the plants need.

Carrots like a slightly acid soil with a pH of 5.5 to 6.5. When preparing beds for carrots, till the soil down to 9 inches or more. Carrots need that much loose soil to develop stout, straight roots.

PLANTING

You can begin sowing carrots as soon as the soil can be worked in spring. Young carrots are very hardy and can withstand late frosts.

Thin carrot seedlings when they are 1½ to 2 inches tall. Leave one plant every 2 inches.

Using a tight string as a guide, mark off rows 12 to 14 inches apart. Then, with a stick or the corner of a hoe, make a narrow trench about 1 inch deep beneath the string. Sow seeds about ¼ inch apart and cover with no more than ½ inch of soil. Or—even better—cover the seeds with compost, which won't crust over and slow the emergence of the sprouts. It's important to keep the seeds near the surface, where there is sufficient moisture and warmth for good germination. If wood ashes are available, sprinkle a thin layer in the seed furrows to keep nematodes and root maggots away.

Moist soil is critical to good carrot germination. When there is no rain, sprinkle the carrot patch with water every evening, using a nozzle or a soaker.

To extend the season of fresh, tender carrots, make consecutive plantings of an early cultivar every three weeks until June.

CARE

One of the most important steps in growing good carrots is proper thinning. Carrots will tolerate some crowding but do best when given plenty of room. When properly thinned, they will produce as much as 130 pounds per 100-foot row—far more than unthinned rows ever could.

Begin pulling out extra plants when they are 1½ to 2 inches tall, leaving one plant every 2 inches. Allow the stouter plants to remain, and remove the smaller, thinner ones. A month later, thin the rows again so that the plants stand 3 to 4 inches apart. You can use the roots of these larger thinnings in salads.

After the last thinning, loosen the soil in the aisles as deeply as possible with a grub hoe. Then mulch the aisles with straw. Take special pains to push the mulch right up

Winter Beds

As good as fresh food straight from the garden tastes in summer, it tastes even better when it's harvested still crispy while the snow is blowing. There are at least four dependable crops that can be harvested straight through the winter. They are perennial onions, carrots, parsnips, and leeks.

The best way to manage them is to grow them all together in one bed. That way, you can keep them all heavily mulched. Late in the fall, mulch the entire garden, surrounding—but not covering—the cold-weather crops with a snug blanket of hay or shredded leaves. Don't put the mulch over these crops until much later, when 20°F temperatures become frequent. Mark your rows with 2-foot-tall stakes so you'll be able to find them under the snow.

The most common perennial onions are Egyptian onions. In midsummer they bear tiny bulbs at the top of hollow stalks. Multiplier onions, another perennial type, bear flower clusters and seeds at about the same time. Both are year-round vegetables. In winter, the white portion of the stalks plus a few inches of the green tops are quite usable in soups and salads; in spring, these stalks lengthen into young scallions, which can be cooked or eaten raw. Grow both of these types in clumps in a permanent location.

When planting carrots for winter bedding, use cultivars that are good keepers, such as 'Imperator' or 'Danvers'. Some carrots, particularly the baby-finger cultivars, don't store well. The best soil for overwintering carrots is a light, sandy loam. Carrots won't keep well in a soil that holds water; they'll rot or be attacked by insects.

Plant your winter storage carrots in blocks or beds. A patch of ground is easier to keep from freezing than a narrow row, and you get more carrots per square foot as well.

If you're sowing a solid block of carrots, space them 2 to 4 inches apart in all directions. If you're planting in a bed, sow three rows 1 foot apart. Sow thickly, and thin seedlings to 4 or 5 inches apart in the row when the roots are large enough to eat.

You can also sow carrots in the parsnip bed. That way, you'll be able to cover both of them with leaves, conserving both space and mulch. Then in the winter, you can start at one end of the patch and gradually work your way to the other end, lifting carrots and a few parsnips at the same time.

Whatever you do, don't locate this winter bed near grassy areas that might be frequented by field mice or other rodents. Without fail, they'll find the warm earth and your stockpile of roots under mulch and consider it the best home ever! Plant carrots and parsnips where there will be bare ground around your pile of leaves.

When daily temperatures drop below 50°F and nightly frosts occur, it's time to gather leaves for mulch. Use maple, oak, or other large leaves. The aim is to trap the earth's heat, so make sure you cover your carrots before the ground freezes solid.

Carrots will let you know when it's time to cover them. After nightly frosts begin, many carrot leaves lie flat on the ground. This is the best time to cover your crops; if you cover them too soon, the plants will rot.

Cover carrots and parsnips with a layer of leaves at least 1 foot deep. The mulch pile should extend at least 6 inches out from all sides of your root patch.

After putting leaves on the bed, cover the pile with a large plastic sheet and anchor it with rocks. The plastic prevents the leaves from blowing off and keeps them dry. Not only are wet leaves poor insulation, but they'll also compress the water in the pile and cause it to freeze. The frozen mass will be difficult to remove for digging, and the ground itself will eventually freeze.

When you're ready to dig carrots, remove the snow (if there is any) from one edge of the bed. Pull back the plastic and lay aside the leaves, keeping the rest of the pile undisturbed to conserve heat. When you've dug as much of the crop as you need, put the leaves and plastic back down. Then shovel snow on top of the plastic to help conserve heat.

In the spring, you can use all those partially decomposed leaves to plant a great potato patch or make compost. Or you can just till them into the garden to increase the amount of organic matter in your soil.

You can overwinter spring-planted leeks where they grew in the garden. Space the leeks 6 inches apart in trenches 6 inches deep, filling the trenches in gradually as the leeks grow. In fall, when the first hard frost is forecast, cover the plants with a foot-thick blanket of shredded leaves or straw. Then harvest them as needed.

against the plants to shield the carrots from the sun as they grow larger—exposed carrots turn green and take on a bitter taste.

The best defense against pests and diseases is to keep the soil healthy and balanced with compost and other organic matter. To avoid carrot rust flies, skip your early planting, and cover the seedbed with row covers when you do plant.

🐦 CROW'S PICKS

Carrots come in all shapes and sizes. Among the short cultivars, I like 'Nantes Half-Long' and 'Danvers Half-Long'. For eating fresh or for freezing and canning, the Nantes strains are a gourmet experience. However, these cultivars are not meant for storage: The small-cored and so-called coreless types have a tendency to shrivel up and lose flavor after they are harvested.

'Danvers' keeps well and is a sweet, tasty root, even after six months of storage. The Imperator types 'Tendersweet' and 'Gold Pak' are excellent long-rooted cultivars for late planting and fall harvesting. 'Chantenay' keeps well in the ground.

CAULIFLOWER

The secret to producing big, tasty cauliflower is to grow this crop so that heading will not coincide with the extremely hot weather of midsummer. Cauliflower can be grown as an early or late crop. A spring crop is more difficult to grow since the variable or unfavorable spring conditions tend to stunt the plants and cause the cauliflowers to "button," or form small, unusable heads. If you don't want to take a chance, grow cauliflower as a fall crop.

SITE AND SOIL

Cauliflower is a heavy feeder and likes nothing better than a good dose of composted barnyard manure. I always scatter a liberal amount—a 2-inch-thick layer—over the entire plot just before setting out the plants. If you're not sure where you can get manure, grow a cover crop of rye in the cauliflower bed during the fall prior to your planting season. Then broadcast a granular organic fertilizer over the bed before setting out the transplants.

Cauliflower does best in a slightly acid soil: A pH of 6.0 to 6.5 is fine.

Blanch cauliflower by pulling the leaves over the developing head and holding them together with a rubber band. This keeps the head clean and white. You can also buy self-blanching cultivars with upright leaves that shade the heads.

PLANTING

Whether you're growing a spring or fall crop of cauliflower, it is far better to grow your own plants from seed since they're less likely to bolt than store-bought transplants. For best results, start seeds indoors about six to eight weeks before the outdoor planting date. For spring planting, set the young plants out about 2 feet apart in the garden when all danger of frost is past. Although cauliflower will survive a light frost, it is much more susceptible to frost damage than cabbage is.

CARE

Cauliflower does not like frequent hoeing. You should use a hoe only to break up the crust after a hard rain and to control weeds as necessary. The best labor-saving trick is to hill up the plants slightly after they reach 6 inches tall, then mulch the entire area heavily. The less you fuss with the earth around the shallow roots, the happier the plants will be.

Blanching is the key to tender, snowy white heads. (If you don't want to go to the trouble of blanching, grow purple cultivars like 'Violet Queen'.) Blanching is really easy: When the heads are about 2 inches in diameter, pull the leaves up over them. Leave a space for ventilation somewhere in the leaves so that there won't be excessive heat buildup inside the leaf cluster. Then tie the leaves at the top with string or a rubber band.

In hot weather, the heads may be ready to harvest within four days of tying. But in cool weather, the blanching process may take as long as a week. It's a good idea to check the heads daily so you can harvest them in their prime.

Plants need adequate moisture all through the growing season. However, they require extra water when the heads are forming. If moisture is not supplied by rainfall, irrigate the plants when you first tie up the leaves, and then every few days until the head is fully formed.

The two most common cauliflower pests are cabbage loopers and aphids. You can get rid of the loopers and other worms by using *Bacillus thuringiensis* (BT). BT is a natural pesticide that only kills the larvae of butterflies and moths; it is nontoxic to humans, animals, and beneficial insects. Infected cabbage loopers eat the bacteria, then stop feeding within an hour and die within 24 hours. For best results, spray plants at weekly intervals, preferably in the early morning or evening so the pests have a chance to eat the bacteria before it dries. A soap spray will take care of the aphids, which usually occur in hot, dry weather. Cutworms can chew through the stems of young transplants. To thwart cutworms in spring, place cans (with the top and bottom cut out) around the newly planted cauliflower.

HARVESTING

The best way to preserve cauliflower is by freezing, since all the cultivars freeze well. The heads will also keep well for a couple of weeks in a root cellar. Or you can place them in damp sand and leave them in a cool place, where they will keep for up to a month.

CROW'S TIPS

Cauliflower grows especially well in soil where snap beans grew the previous year. The bean roots produce and release nitrogen, which is taken up by the cauliflower.

CELERY

Most gardeners shun celery because it has a reputation for being hard to grow. To be sure, celery doesn't give the instant gratification that radishes do, but you *can* grow it successfully if you know a few tricks. Read on to find out how to get a fine crop of celery every time.

SITE AND SOIL

Boron is a key element for celery. A deficiency will result in cracked stems, brittle stalks, and brown spots on the leaves. If a soil test shows that your soil is low in boron, add a pinch of household borax to a gallon of water, then pour this mixture on the soil around the base of each celery plant.

PLANTING

First, start the plants from seed yourself, rather than buying transplants. Count backward from the final spring frost date in your area, and start your seed 12 weeks before that date.

To sow the seed, punch several holes in the bottom of 5-inch paper cups or peat pots. Fill them with a mixture of 2 parts garden soil to 1 part vermiculite and 1 part organic fertilizer.

Thoroughly wet the soil, then sprinkle the seeds over the top and cover with about ⅛ inch of vermiculite. Set the

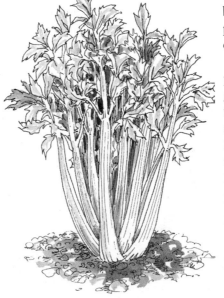

cups or pots in foil trays and place them in a greenhouse or cold frame or on a heating cable—anywhere that will provide a fairly steady temperature of 65°F.

In about ten days, the first seedlings will begin to pop through. After the first true leaves appear and the seedlings become crowded in their pots, transplant them one to a pot. The roots will be tightly packed and intertwined at this point, so make sure the soil is damp before removing the seedlings from the pots.

To transplant, tear away the paper cup or peat pot and lay the clump of roots and soil on its side. Carefully pull the young plants apart by grasping them by their leaves, not the roots. Transfer to individual 5-inch cups or peat pots filled with the same soil mixture as the original seedling mix. When the young plants have grown to 5 or 6 inches tall, they are ready for the garden.

Dig trenches 12 to 15 inches deep and long enough to accommodate two plants per row foot. Celery is a very heavy feeder, so improve the soil in the trenches by filling the bottom third with compost, well-rotted manure, or a combination of both.

The day before planting the celery in the garden, water the trenches thoroughly, soaking the soil deeply. Plant the seedlings about 6 inches apart. You can keep the plants in their paper or peat pots: Simply cut out the bottom with a sharp knife and set each one, pot and all, into the trench. Spray the transplants with a seaweed-based fertilizer. Then gather grass clippings or straw and tuck it around each plant so that only the leaves at the top of the stalks are exposed to the sun.

CARE

Covering the celery trenches completely with a deep mulch is important. Not only does this mulch help prevent the celery from becoming too dark, stringy, and bitter, but it also keeps the ground cool and damp.

Insects such as celery loopers enjoy celery nearly as much as people do. Loopers are light green caterpillars with a white stripe down the center of their back and a matching stripe down each side. They feed on celery leaves and tender stalks. You will often find them inside rolled leaves that have been tied shut with a filmy web.

Bacillus thuringiensis (BT) will control celery loopers as well as variegated cutworms. (See "Care" in the Broccoli entry on page 105 for a description of BT and how to apply it.) If the looper infestation is serious, you can use pyrethrins. The first dusting will make the larvae sick, and a second dusting will finish them off.

Be on the lookout for carrot weevils. These are ¼-inch-long brownish beetles that sport six spiffy speckles on their backs. They emerge from the soil in early spring and will lay eggs right on the young celery stalks. In just a week, the eggs hatch and the larvae move down to the crown of the plant. There they feed for six to eight weeks, and then migrate to the surrounding soil to pupate. A second generation emerges in mid-July to repeat the cycle. These weevils will stunt or kill celery plants. Rotate your celery plantings with other crops to control these bugs.

The green peach aphid is a speck of a bug, only ¹⁄₁₆ inch long. Although it generally lives on peach trees or other stone fruit trees, it will also attack celery. These aphids suck sap from the underside of celery leaves, stunting the plant. Ladybugs and spiders are good natural enemies. Insecticidal soap sprays provide control. You can also repel aphids by making an herbal spray from spearmint, marigolds, and tansy.

HARVESTING

You can begin to harvest celery as soon as the stalks are tall enough to suit you. To harvest, cut the root an inch or two below the crown of the plant. Store the stalks in a plastic bag in the refrigerator. Should the celery wilt, you can revive it by standing it in a pitcher of cold water.

If you plan to store a large amount of celery that has been harvested all at once, dig up the complete plants, roots and all. Plant them in boxes of earth so that the crowns are level with the soil's surface. Water the roots, leave the boxes in a dark place (a root cellar, if possible), and the plants should keep for three to five months.

CHICORY

Heading chicory has become chic, thanks to the red type known as radicchio, which is now considered a trendy salad ingredient. We Americans are finally beginning to understand why the beautiful, ruby red color and nutty, slightly bitter flavor have made chicory a favorite in Europe for years.

Chicory takes up to five months to mature, and it needs a cooling-off period toward the end in order to form proper heads. But it's well worth the wait. Anyone who has

❋ CHICORY

grown bitter chicory probably hasn't given it the consistently cool weather it needs. I make my first sowing in the middle to end of July. The heads are ready to harvest in September, but I allow some to overwinter until the following May.

Chicory

SITE AND SOIL

Chicory (a medium feeder) grows in a wide range of soil types, from well-drained sands to heavy clays. The crop is very tolerant of drought, but doesn't like waterlogged soil.

PLANTING

Chicory is simple to start. I just scatter seed on top of a bed, then rake the bed over—first in one direction, then the other—to cover it.

Some thinning will probably be necessary. When the seedlings are 4 to 5 inches tall or have eight well-developed leaves, thin so that individual plants are 8 to 12 inches apart. To some extent, chicory is self-thinning: The larger plants crowd out the smaller ones. Check the plot carefully in late summer for crowding. If the leaves touch, they often rot, especially if the weather is wet.

You can also start chicory indoors for transplanting outdoors when conditions are right. Plants should go to their permanent place in the garden when they have eight to ten well-developed leaves—generally 30 to 50 days after sowing.

CARE

Other than keeping weeds out, there is very little you need to do for the plants. You never have to water them since they're very drought-tolerant. And few, if any, pests bother chicory. However, plants are sometimes subject to Botrytis, a fungal disease that can damage outer leaves and, in some cases, hearts and leaf tips. If it strikes, just cut off the diseased leaves cleanly, leaving the healthier, undamaged ones beneath. Chicory is very resilient and, given time to recover, will often produce a harvest of usable leaves several weeks or even months later.

HARVESTING

To harvest chicory, use a knife to cut the head just above the soil level, being careful not to damage the crown. Plants resprout with great vigor after you cut the tight heart or the loose leaves. You can also cut just a few of the outer leaves as required, or take some outer leaves from the heart. The deeper you go into the heart, the more curled and pale the leaves are. These light-colored leaves tend to have a milder flavor than the outer leaves.

I always leave some chicory plants in the ground over winter to resprout in the spring. In their second season, they produce magnificent, eye-catching spikes that grow up to 5 or 6 feet tall and are laced with pale blue daisylike flowers. These edible blossoms open in the morning but tend to close by noon. They have a faint chicory flavor and add a great dash of color to a salad. However, because they close so soon after being picked, you should harvest them at the last moment and sprinkle them over the salad after it has been dressed.

CROW'S TIPS

The most common question I'm asked about chicory is how to make it form deep colors and dense hearts. The secret is in the seed. With most common vegetables, the seed planted by home gardeners has been selected over many years and is re-markably uniform. But red chicory (radicchio) is different. The seed is very variable, and the range of plants grown from any one seed packet is amazing. In one sowing of a non-hybrid cultivar, it's likely that only half of the plants will head up well, no matter what you do. However, new hybrids like 'Giulio' and 'Marina' are more uniform.

The Endive Experiment

Once you've mastered basic gardening, it's time to try something exotic. Belgian endive is a good place to start. Also called chicons, Belgian endive is really a name for indoor-forced chicories known as witloofs. This chic and expensive green can be grown in any garden, but it requires some extra steps, including digging, repotting, and some time in the dark.

To start, sow two 8-foot rows of witloof chicory behind the carrot patch or in the corner of a bed in late April. Make sure the soil is deep, mellow, and full of compost. Sow thickly—the plants may sprout haphazardly. Thin them to about 9 inches apart when they reach the size and shape of Swiss chard plants in midsummer.

Chicory's deep taproots seem to be able to find subsurface moisture even during summer droughts, so little watering is necessary. However, be sure to mulch well with grass clippings.

Let the plants grow undisturbed throughout the summer. When frosts demolish the garden, it's time to take the next step.

Dig the chicory roots carefully. Snip off the leaves an inch above the crown, and trim each long taproot to 9 inches. Mix up a wheelbarrowful of equal parts sand and garden soil, and "plant" the roots in a box filled with this mix. Leave 3 inches of space above the roots, and cover them with the sand-soil mix.

Now, bury the box in the garden, fitting it snugly into its hole. Shovel dirt around the outside of the box until it is buried. Then lay down a thick layer of leaves, more soil, and more leaves until the hole is filled and is level with the garden. In November, cover the hole with three bales of spoiled hay, then mound dirt around the base of the bales so everything will stay warm and cozy.

In January, pull off the bales, dig up the box, and take it to the root cellar. Remove the top 3 inches of soil mix so the soil just covers the roots. Water them and make sure the water drains out of the bottom of the box.

A dark, cool cellar, where the temperature stays about 60°F, is perfect for forcing. Keep the area dark and the roots moist, but not sopping wet. In a week or two, the roots will sprout tightly packed, creamy yellow-green spears of Belgian endive leaves. Slice them off and enjoy. Two dozen roots should give you salads for weeks during the dreariest part of the winter.

CHINESE CABBAGE

Gardeners looking for something new in green should take the Orient Express. But don't forget to bring your guidebook with you. There's a wide world of Chinese cabbage available to gardeners, and each type seems to have about half a dozen different names. I'll try to keep it simple here.

The Chinese cabbage that most of us are familiar with has a cylindrical shape and tightly wrapped yellow-green leaves. Inside, the head is nearly white. Then there's pak choy, also called bok choy or Chinese celery. It's a loose-leaf cabbage that sports dark green spoon-shaped leaves on smooth white stems.

There are at least four other common Asian brassicas worth trying in your garden. Choy sum is a loose-leaf cabbage that is harvested as it begins to flower. Dai gai choy is a mustard cabbage with large, tender leaves borne on thick, fleshy stems. Gai choy is a milder mustard cabbage, and gai lohn is a broccoli-like plant that is sometimes called Chinese kale.

SITE AND SOIL

Fortunately, you don't have to know 'em in order to grow 'em. Chinese cabbage needs a rich, well-drained seedbed. Use my heavy-feeder formula to improve the soil before planting. (See page 96.)

PLANTING

Most of the Chinese cabbages make perfect succession crops. They grow best when direct-seeded in a bed, and they germinate quickly under all sorts of conditions. They also add another crop to the garden while extending the season and saving space.

Not too many years ago, many Oriental greens could be grown successfully only after the summer equinox. They were so sensitive to daylength that they would flower prematurely if planted in the spring. To avoid that problem, gardeners pretty much grew them in late summer as a cool-weather crop. Now, however, there are cultivars that grow well in spring and summer.

Hybrid Chinese cabbage

Michihli Chinese cabbage

Choy sum

Gai lohn

Pak choy

CARE

Keep the bed thickly mulched and well watered—Chinese cabbage won't tolerate drying out. Because this is a hungry crop, you'll need to spray the plants with a liquid organic plant food like manure tea or fish emulsion every two weeks during the growing season.

Chinese cabbage will bolt when allowed to dry out, when subjected to sudden hot spells, or when grown at the wrong time of the year. Make sure you time your planting so that the plants will be growing in the cool days of spring or fall.

Chinese cabbages are prone to the same pests and diseases that attack regular cabbages. Cabbageworms and cabbage loopers are small green caterpillars that can reduce plants to a mass of lacy leaves in a few days. The best control is *Bacillus thuringiensis* (better known as BT). Spray plants with BT once a week, ideally in the early morning or evening. For more information on pest and disease control, see "Care" in the Cabbage entry on page 108.

HARVESTING

Most Chinese cabbages are ready to harvest 40 to 50 days after germination. This vegetable provides a range of exotic tastes and textures in salads, stir-fries, pickles, and slaws.

🐦 CROW'S TIPS

Many of the Asian vegetables are more temperamental than their American or European cousins. One of the most common mistakes in handling these plants is to transplant them the way you would broccoli or cauliflower. Asian brassicas are very susceptible to transplant shock—they go to seed quickly when transplanted. My solution: Always direct-seed Chinese cabbage.

CORN

Most people think of corn as a crop for big gardens only. But it can be grown to perfection in small patches if you work to overcome the pollination problem—the most common reason for poorly filled ears.

Corn is wind-pollinated, and for every strand of corn silk that doesn't get a grain of pollen, there will be a gap in the mature ear. When the plants stand in only one or two rows, the pollen often wafts away, never reaching the silk. To make sure your corn ears are filled, make your plantings square. So rather than two long rows, make five short ones, with the plants spaced equidistantly. That way, the middle plants are sure to catch ample pollen.

SITE AND SOIL

Corn, a heavy feeder, needs plenty of nourishment to attain good growth and a sweet flavor. Ideally, I like to prepare the corn bed in the fall. I spread a 2-inch-deep layer of composted manure and leaves over the entire area, then a thin layer of rock phosphate and greensand or granite dust. In the spring, before planting, I broadcast a granular organic fertilizer. A soil rich in organic matter and plenty of compost help retain moisture and encourage good root development.

PLANTING

I always wait until the weather has become fairly warm and settled before putting in corn seed. Too much moisture and low temperatures cause the seed to deteriorate, so there is no point in rushing. The soil temperature should be at least 60°F.

✺ CORN

Plant corn in rows spaced about 3 feet apart—corn roots may grow 3 to 4 feet across and just as deep. Sow seed about 1½ inches deep and 2 to 3 inches apart. Tamp the soil down firmly over the seeds using the back of a hoe or simply by walking down the row. This step ensures that each seed is firmly in contact with the soil, and it also helps conserve moisture in the cultivated row.

Thin the plants to about 12 inches apart in the row when they are 5 to 6 inches tall. Take out the weakest plants, and keep those that look the best.

CARE

Cultivate with a small hand tiller two or three times until the cornstalks are 8 to 10 inches tall, then mulch the entire plot with a 3- to 4-inch layer of leaves. Mulching controls weeds, keeps the soil loose after cultivation, and encourages fast growth by conserving moisture.

Unlike field corn, sweet corn tends to grow bushy by putting up extra stalks on the plant. Take these suckers off as they appear, and leave only the first big, sturdy stalk.

There are two major pests that attack sweet corn: the corn earworm and the European corn borer. To control the earworm, pour a few drops of mineral oil onto the silks about ten days after the silks appear. European corn borers bore into the stalks and will overwinter in them, so it's essential that you remove all cornstalks from the

garden at the end of the growing season.

In the disease department, there are no insurmountable problems. Sweet corn is susceptible to attack from soil fungi, which results in seedling blight. To avoid this problem, rotate your corn with other crops so that populations of fungi don't build up in the soil.

Corn smut is a fungal disease that can appear on the stalks, leaves, tassels, or ears. It is most apparent when it attacks the ears. As each kernel fills with spores from the fungus, the grayish black smut forms globs on the ears, which appear as if they were boiling. These spores are viable for five to seven years. Incidentally, there is no spray you can use to control this disease. The best remedy is to use garden sanitation, so smut can't get a foothold.

HARVESTING

In their eagerness for that first taste of sweet corn, many gardeners pick too soon. It's best to keep an eye on the silk and pick the ears only after it has turned brown. There is no question that the condition of the silk is a good indicator of corn's ripeness. But to be doubly sure, pull one side of the husk away from the ear to see how the kernels are doing. You will want to harvest when the majority of the kernels are full but (if it's a yellow cultivar) not a dull golden yellow. By that time, the ears are past their prime and they'll be tough and starchy.

CROW'S PICKS

There are hundreds of cultivars of corn, and everybody has a favorite or two. Some of my favorites are 'Country Gentleman' (an open-pollinated cultivar), 'Golden Cross Bantam', 'Gold Cup', and 'Silver Queen'.

CROW'S TIPS

I know some gardeners who do all they can to get their corn crop off to an early start—they're already thinking of ripe ears in winter! Their best trick is to start sweet corn seeds in peat pots indoors about six weeks before outdoor planting time. When the soil is warm enough, they set the entire pot in the ground. Corn does not transplant well, but leaving the little plants in the peat pots takes care of that.

I know other folks who just presprout the seeds indoors by wrapping them in paper towels and placing them in plastic bags. After just a few days, when the roots have reached ½ to 1 inch in length, they transplant the seeds into the garden rows.

CUCUMBERS

SITE AND SOIL

Cucumbers can be grown in almost any type of soil, but they prefer one with a pH of 6.0. The soil for these heavy feeders should have an organic matter content of 5 to 7 percent.

Don't plant cukes in or next to an area where cucumbers, squash, pumpkins, or melons have grown the previous three years. These crops are all members of the cucurbit family and harbor the same diseases.

PLANTING

Cucumbers are a warm-weather crop and will be killed by even a light freeze. The biggest mistake most gardeners make is to plant their seeds too early. Two weeks after the last frost is usually a safe time to plant cucumber, but make sure that the average air temperature is at least 60°F. The best average soil temperature range is 55°F to 95°F. The higher the soil temperature, the faster the seeds will germinate.

When sowing cuke seed in a row or bed, first dig a hole 1 foot deep and 2 feet in diameter. Place 2 to 4 inches of compost or rotted manure in the bottom, then put the soil back in the hole. Round off the top and plant the seeds in the center. Sow four or five

For easy picking, you can grow cukes up a trellis. Make the trellis out of 7- or 8-foot poles spaced 4 feet apart. Nail poultry wire to the poles. Plant cukes in hills placed 6 inches in front of the trellis and 2 feet apart down the row. Thin seedlings to two cukes per hill, then mulch with about 6 inches of straw. Cucumber vines produce tendrils and will cling to the trellis without tying, but you may have to train the vines up the trellis until they take hold.

seeds per hill, 1 inch deep and 2 inches apart in a circle. Planting in small mounds like this will concentrate cucumbers' favorite fertilizer near their roots, provide for extra drainage, and keep the soil warm.

When two or three true leaves appear, thin to the two strongest plants. Press the soil down slightly.

If you start your plants indoors, sow the seed about four weeks before you plan to transplant. Grow the plants in containers that will not disturb the roots when you transplant.

CARE

Cucumber roots are shallow, so cultivate carefully and sparingly. Then hill around the plants with soil taken from between the rows. After hilling, mulch the entire bed with a 6-inch-deep layer of straw to preserve moisture and to keep down the weeds. If the weather is dry, water well once a week.

The vines need a lot of extra energy when they're ready to set blossoms and bear fruit. When they're about 18 inches long, I feed each hill a handful of blood meal or a shovelful of well-rotted manure or compost. I place it 4 to 5 inches to the side of the plant, in a furrow a couple of inches deep, and then cover it. Then I water well to help carry the nutrients down to the root zone.

Yellow, bell-shaped flowers form within ten days after the appearance of the first true leaves. The first blossoms are male, and about a week later the females show up. (You can easily identify the female flower by the miniature cucumber between its base and the stem.) They both appear on the same vine, usually at alternating nodes. Bees carry pollen from the male blossom to the female blossom. They fertilize the cucumber-shaped ovary, which then develops into a full-sized cuke.

To discourage cucumber beetles or squash bugs from devouring your cucumber crop, cover the bed with floating row covers. (Compact cultivars with a bushy habit are the easiest to cover.) When female flowers appear, remove the cover.

Choose cultivars that are resistant to powdery mildew and other diseases. Unfortunately, there are no cultivars that resist bacterial wilt. However, nonbitter types are less likely to attract cucumber beetles, which spread the disease.

CROW'S TIPS

When grown on a trellis, cucumber vines produce prolifically. That's because they have abundant sunlight and good air circulation, both of which help prevent disease. I like to train cucumbers onto 20-gauge poultry wire—the thin wire provides good anchorage for the springy tendrils. The trellis should be at least 6 feet tall. Since the vines produce mostly at their tips as they grow longer, it's important to give them plenty of height in order to prolong the producing season.

Before planting, I place 7- or 8-foot poles every 4 feet along the row. I hammer them securely into the ground, then nail the wire to them, stretching it tightly between the poles. I make sure to sink a guy wire on each end of the fence to prevent sagging in the middle.

Whenever possible, I run the fence from east to west to keep all the vines growing on the south side. If I must run the fence the other way, I still try to keep the vines growing on one side for easier picking. I direct their growth by removing the vine tips now and then as they grow through the holes.

I sow the seed 6 inches away from the wire, placing a hill of seven seeds every 2 feet in the row. When sprouts first appear, I thin them out to stand four per hill. When the remaining plants reach 6 inches tall, I thin to only two plants per hill. As the vines grow taller, I train them on the wires.

HARVESTING

Pick cucumbers when they're young and the seeds inside are still soft. The fruits grow quickly, so check them daily. Harvest frequently to keep the plants productive.

The best time for picking cucumbers is in the morning. To avoid injuring the vine, be sure to hold the stem as you pull the fruit off. Refrigerate fresh-picked cukes immediately, then wash them just before you use them.

EGGPLANT

A perennial in the tropics, eggplant grows as though the season will never end, branching and flowering until frost. This exotic-looking plant has large flowers, shiny dark fruit, and 6-inch gray-green leaves. Even when bearing half a dozen fruits, it stands erect on its woody stem. But eggplant is more fragile than it looks. Cool weather, drought, and careless potting and transplanting can all lead to disappointment.

SITE AND SOIL

When preparing the garden bed for eggplant, keep in mind that this crop prefers a nearly neutral soil. However, you don't need to add lime unless the soil's pH is under 6.0. When liming, use dolomitic limestone—it's high in magnesium, which eggplant needs to thrive.

Although eggplant is a heavy feeder, it's possible to give it too much nitrogen. In that case, it will grow vigorously but set fruit rarely. But by all means, enrich your soil with compost or aged manure, at about the basic rate of 2 pounds per square foot.

PLANTING

Start seed early—as much as ten weeks before your last spring frost date. Both the seeds and seedlings like warmth. (Eggplant is a tropical crop, remember.) When the soil is 68°F, the seeds take about 13 days to germinate, but when the temperature rises to 77°F, the germination time drops to 8 days, and at 86°F the time is only 5 days. Try to provide the seedlings with a temperature between 70° and 80°F. A sunny windowsill may be fine by day but too chilly at night.

CARE

By midsummer, your plants should be bushy. When conditions are right, eggplant will branch at every leaf. Wait to fertilize the plants until after they flower and begin to fruit, then sprinkle them with manure tea every two weeks.

Eggplant has many pests, but the three most common and damaging are spider mites, flea beetles, and Colorado potato beetles. The red spider mite pierces the skin of the underside of eggplant leaves, has a meal, and moves to a new spot. If you suspect that your plants have spider mites, spray them frequently with strong blasts of water, taking care to reach the underside of the leaves. If the force of the water is strong enough, the mites will be knocked loose. Because they are so small, few of them complete the journey back to the plant.

Shiny and black and about the size of the period at the end of this sentence, the flea beetle is easy to spot in large numbers on the broad eggplant leaves. Flea beetles are quite agile. Once you try to catch one, you'll see just how it got its name. Dusting with lime, rotenone, or diatomaceous earth will keep the beetles in check. Once the transplants have grown larger, their leaves are tougher and therefore less appetizing to the beetles.

The Colorado potato beetle actually prefers eggplant to potatoes. Look for pumpkin-colored egg clusters under the leaves. Greedy feeders, the brick red humpbacked larvae grow rapidly. Do a thorough job of picking them off for a week or two so that none grow to adulthood, and you'll have no more trouble from the potato beetle.

I like to scatter my eggplant around the garden to make it harder for the pests to find. Planting two or more cultivars gives me additional insurance that I'll have an abundant crop over a long season. In most years, I wind up with more than I can possibly eat. But that seems to be the way gardening works. No matter what happens, you rarely go empty-handed.

HARVESTING

Harvest begins any time a fruit reaches a couple of inches long. Don't let it mature and lose its shiny luster, or the flesh will be bitter and the seeds will be hard. (You can use a fruit that has begun to dull if you pick it immediately.) Use a sharp knife or pruners to harvest eggplant. Cut the fruit stem—don't yank off the fruit.

CROW'S TIPS

The plants for sale in six-packs at supermarkets and nurseries, standing 6 inches tall in a pinch of soil, are almost always rootbound. Their growth has been checked early, so they will grow poorly in the garden. If you've planted nursery-grown eggplant and been disappointed with the results, try growing your own. I guarantee you'll see a big difference.

ENDIVE

Endive belongs in every salad garden. It's the one fresh green that you can enjoy from early summer until the snow flies. However, even though it can be grown in spring, summer, and fall, the spring crop is by far the easiest to grow. Plants are easier to start then, and the growing conditions stimulate rapid growth, which results in more flavorful and tender leaves.

SITE AND SOIL

If your soil is sandy or tends to dry out quickly, turn under the standard 2-inch layer of well-rotted manure or compost well in advance of planting time, preferably in the fall. The high levels of nitrogen in manure promote lush leaf growth in endive. Since this medium-feeder leafy crop seldom puts down roots deeper than 18 inches, it needs its food close to the surface. A 2-inch layer of manure or compost dug in over the row or bed to a depth of 6 inches should do the job.

Although endive prefers a neutral or slightly acid soil, it is quite tolerant of acid soils with a pH as low as 5.0. Endive and other leafy vegetables are susceptible to calcium deficiency, which causes the margins of the leaves at the center of the plant to turn brown, then black, and eventually die. Three pounds of dolomitic limestone per 100 square feet of garden will take care of most calcium deficiencies.

PLANTING

Nearly all endive cultivars take at least 85 to 95 days from seed to salad. There are two types of endive: curly and straight. Curly endive, with its loose head of notched and frilly leaves, is the most cold-tolerant and is the best for planting in early spring, though it makes a fine fall crop as well.

I recommend starting spring-crop seedlings indoors. Sow seeds in cell packs filled with rich, loose seed-starting mix. Plant them no more than $1/4$ inch deep, two or three seeds per pack, and cover with a light sprinkling of compost. They should germi-

nate in 10 to 14 days. If you don't want to be hit with a tidal wave of endive, stagger your plantings every two weeks to spread out the harvest.

If you want to direct-sow your spring crop, plant early. Sow the seeds outdoors as soon as the ground can be worked: They germinate best while the soil is still cool.

You can also start summer and fall endive crops right in the garden. Just sow the seed $1/4$ inch deep, about two seeds per inch, in rows spaced 18 inches apart. Then thin the plants to 10 inches apart when they are 4 inches tall. You can use the thinnings to add a tangy touch to salads.

CARE

Be sure to provide irrigation. Drip systems do a good job of keeping the soil moist—something that endive seems to love. Keeping endive growing rapidly under favorable conditions is very important to its texture and flavor. If the growth of this crop is retarded for any reason, the leaves become tough and very pungent, and your entire planting will be ruined.

When the plants reach 8 inches and begin to form rosettes, I use a hoe to loosen the soil in the aisles and sprinkle a handful of all-purpose organic fertilizer around each plant. Then I mulch the entire bed with straw

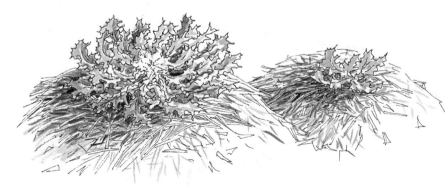

Endive adds a little bite to a salad—as well as iron and vitamins A and C. You'll get the most tender, mild-flavored endive if you grow it in hills and mulch thickly with straw to maintain even soil moisture.

to a depth of 4 inches. There's usually enough spring rainfall here on Long Island to keep endive growing rapidly. However, I periodically check the soil beneath the mulch. If it's dry, I turn on an overhead sprinkler system and let it run for half an hour or until the soil is soaked down to 6 inches.

If endive is overlooked by some gardeners, it is ignored even more by most pests. Rotate your crop every year and don't allow water to stand in the crowns of the plants, and disease will never be a problem.

Air pollution is an increasing hazard for garden plants, and endive is no exception. Pollution damage shows itself in a silvering on the undersides of endive leaves and in small black specks on the leaves. If you notice that your endive leaves have a silvery cast, douse them with water and hope for the best.

HARVESTING

If you're growing endive for the first time, don't make the mistake of waiting until most of your plants have matured before you begin to use them in salads. Start cutting and using heads of endive as soon as the plants are as large as your fist. Although the central rosette may not be fully formed by then, the outer leaves will be as tender as the inner ones and just as good. If you don't begin harvesting at this stage, some plants may rot before you can reap the full benefit from your planting.

If you harvest endive when it is fist-sized, you don't need to blanch it. In fact, health authorities maintain that unblanched endive, celery, and other crops contain a great deal more of the nutritional vitamins than blanched produce does. But if you prefer endive with a less pungent flavor and a lighter color, blanch away.

Blanching doesn't have to be complicated. It's as simple as covering the plants with overturned fruit baskets to shut out light. In two or three weeks, the rosettes will be blanched and ready for the salad bowl.

CROW'S TIPS

Rows are fine for endive, but I've developed another sowing method that I like even better. Instead of dropping the seeds into a long straight furrow, I sow endive in hills. First, I dig a hole and amend the soil with compost. Then I drop a pinch of seed into each hole and cover it well. With this method, I'm saving seed and also simplifying weeding, since I can clean everything out of the row between the hills.

When the young plants are 2 inches tall, I thin each hill to three healthy plants. A week later, I thin them down to just two plants. Finally, when the plants are 6 inches tall, I thin them to one plant per hill. That leaves me with one plant every 12 inches in the row.

GARLIC

Here at Spring Meadow, it seems that we just can't grow too much garlic. Garlic literally grows like a weed. It takes up very little room and actually looks ornamental during the seed stage. And it's an ideal insect-repelling companion plant for almost any crop.

We grow it outdoors, scattered throughout the garden around tomatoes and other crops. We even grow it indoors in flowerpots on the kitchen windowsill.

SITE AND SOIL

To plant medium-feeder garlic outdoors, dig a trench about 8 inches deep and 10 inches wide. Place a 5-inch-deep layer of compost in the trench, then fill it with a mix like the one I use for my indoor garlic pots: 4 parts peat humus, 1½ parts perlite, 1 part clean sand, and ½ part bonemeal.

PLANTING

Plant large garlic cloves about 2 inches deep in the soil mix in the trench, water thoroughly, and cover lightly with straw mulch.

You can plant garlic in the spring and harvest it in the fall. But the biggest bulbs come from a fall planting that is allowed to overwinter. Elephant garlic, a truly gigantic cultivar, should be planted in mid-August so that it has time to make root growth before cold weather sets in.

Garlic

CARE

Water your garlic trench thoroughly every three weeks with a weak seaweed solution. If you're going to harvest your crop in late September, stop regular watering and feeding in late July or August to give the bulbs a chance to size up.

For winter protection, mulch all overwintering garlic plants with straw. In spring, these plants will send up a center stalk, and a bud will develop. Snip the buds off—if you don't, the plants' energy will go into making seed rather than making large-sized bulbs.

To prevent onion maggots, wireworms, and other pests from attacking your garlic crop, avoid planting where onions grew the previous year. Bulbs are susceptible to rotting and molds, so be sure to provide good air

circulation in the garlic bed. (For more on controlling pests and diseases, see "Care" in the Onions entry on page 143.)

HARVESTING

If the soil is heavy, or if the root systems of the plants are well developed, garlic can be tough to pull. To save yourself the frustration of having stems pop off underground, use a spade to dig the plants up.

🐦 **CROW'S TIPS**

For indoor planting, mix 4 cups of peat humus (not peat moss), 1½ cups of perlite, 1 cup of clean sand, and ½ cup of bonemeal. Pour 1 inch of the mix into a 4-inch pot. Carefully divide a head of garlic, and plant three unpeeled cloves upright (root side down) in the bottom of the pot. Then fill the pot with planting mix, covering the cloves completely. Repeat until you have as many pots as you want.

After watering, place the pots on the sill of a south-facing window. For best growth, the plants will need about 13 hours of sun per day. In seven to ten days, you should be able to see shoots poking up through the soil. When they reach 3 inches tall, you can begin to cut the shoots to use as chives.

GOURDS

Gourds are easy to grow if you've got the time. They need about 130 days of warm, frost-free growing weather; warm nights are especially important for rapid growth. And gourds can't handle the slightest touch of frost. When sowing, you have to try to squeeze the crop in after the last frost in the spring and hope that the first frost in autumn doesn't come too early.

SITE AND SOIL

In the garden, gourds need full sun, plenty of room, and a light, well-drained soil with a pH of about 5.5. A little extra care in preparing the soil will help your medium-feeder gourds beat the frost deadline.

To prepare the soil for planting in hills, dig holes measuring 2 feet deep and 2 feet in diameter. Allow 8 feet between each hole. Make a mixture of equal parts well-rotted chicken manure and rich, friable soil. Then put a 1-foot-deep layer of it in the bottom of each hole. Place a 1-foot layer of topsoil on top of that, and then build up the outer perimeter to form a concave, dished-out hill that will hold water.

Gourds

PLANTING

Gourd seeds germinate reliably in a week to ten days, but if you soak them overnight, they'll germinate in half that time. Sow eight to ten seeds about 1 inch deep around the inside lower slope of each hill. If you prefer to plant in rows, space plants about 5 feet apart and allow 8 to 10 feet between rows. You can buy packets of mixed gourds or focus on a single type like birdhouse gourds.

CARE

After planting, keep the seedbed moist. As soon as the young seedlings are a few inches tall, tuck newspaper around them and cover it with straw. Together, the newspaper and straw will keep weeds down and conserve moisture.

When the seedlings are about 8 inches tall, thin them to two plants per hill. When thinning, try to leave a variety of plants of different sizes and leaf types. The idea is to wind up with as many different shapes, sizes, and colors of gourds as possible.

HARVESTING

In late September, ease up on the water. Watering once every two weeks should be plenty. By October, begin keeping one eye on the weather forecast and the other on the gourd stems.

When the vine stops sending out sap, the gourd's stem will wither, and the flesh will become hard. That's the time to harvest. Even though the gourds may feel like rocks, you must handle them carefully to avoid bruises that may later lead to rot. Don't rip the gourd from the vine—cut it with pruning shears, leaving 2 to 3 inches of stem attached to the fruit.

After washing and drying the gourds,

spread them out in a dark, well-ventilated room so they aren't touching. For faster drying, you can make holes in the bottom of the gourds with an ice pick and hang them by their stems to dry.

HORSERADISH

If any garden crop qualifies as an invasive weed, horseradish is it. This fiery-flavored plant spreads ferociously from its roots, cropping up throughout the garden. To keep horseradish under control, plant it in a corner of your garden where it won't be spread by tilling, hoeing, raking, or weeding.

SITE AND SOIL

Like a weed, horseradish will grow in any type of soil, from sand to clay. But if you're after thick, tangy roots, it pays to prepare the soil carefully. The very best soil for growing horseradish is a deep, moist loam. If possible, avoid sandy soils and heavy clays, or amend them with compost and mulch.

PLANTING

To plant horseradish roots, make furrows 3 to 4 inches deep in rows spaced 2 feet apart. Lay the roots down lengthwise in the furrows, leaving about 1 foot between them. Cover the roots and firm the soil. Don't add manure when planting horse-

radish. If you do, your plants will end up with too much topgrowth or irregularly branched roots.

CROW'S TIPS

There are several ways to get your first piece of horseradish. My first choice is rooted crowns. You can either buy them at a garden center in the spring or dig them from a friend's garden. Take the root with the crown attached and split it lengthwise into as many strips as possible, each with a piece of crown still attached. This method gives you a complete plant to start with. You'll get quicker initial growth and ultimately end up with larger roots to harvest.

You can also use root cuttings, which are available at garden centers. They're usually little pencil-thick side roots that come ready to plant.

Finally, you can take larger roots from a friend's garden, slice them lengthwise, and plant each piece. However, I don't recommend this last method, since it is greatly inferior to the other two.

CARE

Because gardeners think of horseradish as a weed, they often neglect it and don't get the most from it. But I've found it worthwhile to give horseradish a shot of fertilizer every year. Add 2 pounds each of blood meal and dolomitic limestone per 10 square feet of horseradish patch. Horseradish outgrows its weed competition if given an occasional cultivation. A thick mulch will help keep weeds down and maintain even soil moisture, which horseradish needs to thrive.

HARVESTING

Horseradish roots grow best in the cool, short days of fall. If possible, wait to dig the roots until two or three frosts have nipped the plants. For some reason, frost brings out the full pungent qualities of the roots.

Don't worry about replanting. If you leave even the smallest piece of root in the ground, it will spring to life the next year. Once you plant horseradish, you'll have horseradish for life.

JERUSALEM ARTICHOKES

The funny thing about Jerusalem artichokes is that they're neither from Jerusalem nor true artichokes. Instead, this native American plant is a sturdy, upstanding member of the happy sunflower family. A hardy perennial, it has a widespread root system that produces clusters of tubers under the ground, just like the potato.

This completely frostproof crop grows from Nova Scotia to the Mexican border and produces up to 1 pound of tubers for every square foot of garden space in just about any kind of soil. As a bonus, it crowds out the weeds and produces delightful sunflower-like flowers.

SITE AND SOIL

Jerusalem artichokes are light feeders and aren't fussy about soil. But, like horseradish, the plants spread rampantly, so wise growers keep them confined to a bed by themselves.

Once the plants take off, they will race up 6 to 12 feet tall, producing flowers in late summer and early fall. So be sure they are in an area where they won't shade other plants.

PLANTING

Like potatoes, Jerusalem artichoke plants are propagated by cutting large tubers into chunks or by planting small whole tubers. Plant the tubers 6 inches deep and 1 foot apart in rows spaced 3 to 4 feet apart.

CARE

Keep weeds and grass out of the row until the young plants reach about 2 feet tall. From then on, they'll be able to outpace the weeds. Now I'll tell you something else that you're bound to be glad to hear: Don't cultivate between the rows once plants are up. You have a good excuse for avoiding this work: Cultivating disturbs clusters of growing 'chokes. Instead of cultivating, you can keep weeds down and conserve moisture by spreading a layer of straw, hay, or other mulch between the rows.

HARVESTING

Plump tubers are ready for harvesting when the stalks die down—about November here in southern New York. Or you can store the whole tuber crop right in the soil. Just cut the stalks back to 12 inches above soil level, apply a 6-inch mulch of straw, and leave the tubers through the winter for digging in spring.

When spring planting time arrives, dig the whole crop, using a potato fork rather than a digging spade to avoid injuring the tubers. Start digging about 2 feet from the stem, then slowly work your way toward the plant. If the soil is loose, you may not need to dig—just tug at the dried-up stems to pull the tubers from the soil. Once the tubers are exposed to the air, their skins shrivel up easily, so store them as quickly as possible. They will keep well in the vegetable crisper of your refrigerator.

KALE

Kale is an easy and extremely hardy crop. There's nothing that extends the season as much as kale does. It keeps right on growing as long as the average temperature doesn't drop below 35°F. Once hardened, kale will survive frost after frost—and even brief dips into the teens or lower—as long as it warms up afterward. For gardeners with limited space, a few kale plants will go a long way for a long time.

Kale

SITE AND SOIL

For the most flavorful leaves, kale should be grown as rapidly as possible. That means ensuring that soil conditions are optimal. If your soil is heavy, it pays to double dig before planting kale. Then sprinkle dolomitic lime or wood ashes to bring the soil pH to nearly neutral. Whatever your soil type, mix about ½ pound of compost or well-rotted manure into the soil per foot of row for this heavy feeder.

PLANTING

For extra-early kale, I sow seeds in flats in my solar greenhouse in January and transplant the seedlings into the garden as soon as the soil thaws in late winter. I sow seeds in 4-inch-deep flats filled with sterilized potting mix, spacing the seed carefully about 3 inches apart. With weekly feedings of manure tea or fish emulsion, the plants grow vigorously in the flats until they are ready for transplanting.

I know I could follow the standard spacing by transplanting kale 12 inches apart in rows spaced 18 inches apart, but I like to plant in beds. So I simply run three rows of kale down the length of a 3-foot-wide bed.

❋ KALE

Since lettuce and kale share the same growing seasons and habits, I often interplant them in a row. This type of companion planting seems to benefit both, and also reduces insect damage.

If I'm feeling ambitious, I might make a second sowing of kale in August, preferably on ground that was previously planted with a legume like fava beans or peas. It isn't really necessary to start a second kale patch, though, since most of the plants from the first patch will continue to be productive until they send up seedstalks the following spring.

CARE

Aside from watering (whenever the ground begins to dry out) and harvesting, I just ignore kale until fall. At that time, I sprinkle a narrow band of blood meal along each row and put down straw mulch for winter growing.

Because kale is a brassica, it is subject to attack by cabbageworms and cabbage loopers. While the little white butterflies are fluttering around, I spray or dust kale weekly with *Bacillus thuringiensis* (BT), available in either dust or liquid form.

HARVESTING

Throughout the summer, you can harvest the outer leaves by snipping them with scissors or breaking them off by hand. The leaves will remain tender as long as you harvest them this way regularly.

When cold weather comes, growth slows down considerably, causing the outer leaves to become tough. So once the August patch begins producing, I harvest the entire growing top of plants from the first sowing, strip off the outer leaves, and save the inner rosette for a tender, mild-tasting winter salad.

KOHLRABI

Kohlrabi is a great crop to plant if you want to impress your neighbors and mystify the kids on the block. It's about the oddest-looking vegetable you're likely to find, resembling a chartreuse sputnik.

But there are plenty of other reasons to grow kohlrabi as well. It's such an early-maturing crop that you can harvest the first sowing and still have time to plant it again for a fall harvest.

SITE AND SOIL

Kohlrabi thrives in most soils, but does especially well in a good, loose, loamy soil that's high in organic matter. It is not a particularly heavy feeder—a balanced fertilizer regimen for medium feeders should be sufficient to ensure rapid, even growth.

PLANTING

To get an extra-early crop, I sow kohlrabi seeds ½ inch deep in cell packs in the greenhouse in March. They sprout in about ten days. When the seedlings are 3 or 4 inches tall, I transplant them to the garden, setting them 4 to 6 inches apart.

Kohlrabi makes an ideal crop for interplanting. Since the tops are sparse, they don't shade other row crops grown next to them. For example, I like to plant rows of squash on either side of the kohlrabi. The early crop is gone before the squash gets too big, and the squash eventually occupies the space vacated by the kohlrabi.

CARE

Kohlrabi requires little care, but it does like evenly moist soil, so I always mulch with straw about 6 inches thick. Kohlrabi forms its "sputniks" above ground—the plant stems gradually enlarge into a bulbous shape several inches above the soil. Spring rains bring the kohlrabi along quickly, so when the bulbs are plum-sized, I begin to thin them to a foot apart. I add the thinnings raw to salads.

As for insects, those ubiquitous cabbageworms and cabbage loopers are happy to snack on kohlrabi leaves. But by now, you know how to control them: Spray or dust plants weekly with *Bacillus thuringiensis* (BT), available in either dust or liquid form.

HARVESTING

The mature vegetable is best when it is 3 inches across. Cut the bulb off at the base of the plant. To prepare for eating, discard the leaves, cube or slice the kohlrabi bulb, and boil it a few minutes until tender. Because the spring garden has mostly leafy vegetables to offer, the kohlrabi bulb gives your menu a nice change of pace.

LEEKS

The mildest and, in my opinion, most delicious members of the onion family are the leeks. They are also the best-tasting of the cold-weather vegetables. Plant them in spring or summer, and you can enjoy them fresh right through the winter. And leeks don't need any special storage conditions. They'll happily survive all but the fiercest winter under a thick blanket of mulch.

SITE AND SOIL

Like other onion-family members, leeks are light to medium feeders. For best results, add a 2-inch layer of compost or composted manure to the leek bed in the fall prior to planting. Then add another layer in early spring, at least a month before planting.

PLANTING

Leeks are agonizingly slow growers, taking four to five months to mature, so it's best to start them indoors in late winter or early spring and then transplant them outdoors. As soon as the ground can be worked in spring, set the seedlings (which look like tiny blades of grass) into the ground. As they grow, you'll have to bank soil around the stems to blanch them.

Or, if you prefer, you can plant in shallow (5-inch-deep) trenches, then fill in the trenches as the plants grow. You may find this old Amish method easier than hilling.

Full-grown leeks should stand about 6 inches apart; set the seedlings at that distance so you won't have to thin.

CARE

Once frost hits in the fall, begin to mulch the plants with loose hay or straw. By late fall, they should be covered with at least 1 foot of mulch.

To prevent pests and diseases from threatening your leeks, rotate them with crops other than onions and garlic. (For more on how to control problems affecting leeks and other onion-family members, see "Care" in the Onions entry on page 143.)

HARVESTING

Leeks can be harvested and served raw anytime during the season, but they reach perfection when they are fully mature. They are especially tasty after they've been subjected to cold temperatures. Leeks will maintain their quality under a blanket of mulch

Grow leeks the Amish way! Set the seedlings, which look like tiny blades of grass, into 5-inch-deep trenches of rich, well-prepared soil. Plant the leeks 6 inches apart, and gradually fill in the trenches as the plants grow.

through the winter, so you'll be able to harvest them at your convenience to enliven a winter meal.

LETTUCE

Cos

Iceberg

Bibb

Looseleaf

Ever wonder why so many small organic farms specialize in lettuce? It's because lettuce is a cinch to grow. If there's one trick you need to learn, it's growing the right cultivar at the right time.

SITE AND SOIL

Lettuce grows well in a wide range of soils, but it prefers a soil with a pH between 6.2 and 7.0. Because of its limited root system, lettuce needs fertile ground with nutrients readily at hand. For example, healthy lettuce requires lots of nitrogen, which stimulates leaf production. Use a high-fertility formula of aged chicken manure and balanced organic fertilizer in the spring before planting.

PLANTING

You can grow lettuce from seed right in the garden or sow it in flats in a greenhouse or under lights and transplant it later. For an early crop, sow two to three seeds per cell in cell packs filled with a loose seed-starting mix. Sow about five to seven weeks before the ground thaws in spring.

Lettuce needs lots of light—maybe more than any other young seedling. So as soon as the seedlings break ground, move them outdoors to a cold frame. If the weather is still cold, bring them in at night. Once the first true leaves appear, thin to one plant per cell. Feed with a liquid kelp fertilizer once a week. Keep the soil evenly moist.

With any luck, by the time the seedlings are 2 or 3 inches tall, the weather will have mellowed and you'll be able to transplant them to the garden. When you do plant them outdoors, be sure to set the plants no deeper than the soil line in the cell, and set the taproot straight.

At the same time, you can sow a second crop directly into the garden bed. Just make a ¼-inch-deep furrow, and place a few seeds every 6 inches. As the plants get larger, thin them so that they are 8 inches apart. You can use the thinnings in salads.

Lettuce germinates only reluctantly if the weather is too hot and dry. Keeping lettuce seed in the refrigerator before planting helps germination somewhat. Watering well with cool water also helps. If the soil is dry, first soak the furrow thoroughly. Then scatter the seeds in the furrow, press them lightly into the wet soil, and cover them very lightly with peat moss. If the weather is hot, shade the furrow with boards or shade cloth.

While you're harvesting your summer crop of lettuce, continue sowing for a fall crop. Sow seeds every ten days from the be-

Self-Sown Lettuce

There are several garden plants that will come back year after year with little help from you. That's because they set seeds and self-sow faithfully.

The best vegetable crop for self-sowing is lettuce. Choose a cultivar that matures gradually and doesn't bolt (go to seed) early. Let a few plants grow a flowerstalk, ripen seed, then die. Let the plants fall over by themselves, or pull them up and leave them lying in the bed. Mark the site and cover it with a light straw mulch. You can lift the thick clumps of seedlings that may appear in late fall and move them to a cold frame.

Dig up the seedlings carefully, then separate and transplant them. These little lettuce plants will surprise you with their hardiness, sturdy root development, and quick growth.

ginning of August until a couple of weeks before your fall frost date.

CARE

Once the plants are up or transplanted into the garden, side-dress with a 1-inch-wide band of blood meal. Then spray with a liquid organic fertilizer every five weeks.

Lettuce doesn't like the heat and drought of summer. But there are ways you can nurse it through. Mulch the lettuce beds with straw, and irrigate when the mulch starts to dry out and the soil beneath it is dry. To help the plants start the day with a cool

Year-Round Lettuce

I've found that I can grow lettuce for over 300 days of the year. The only requirement for such a steady supply is a cold frame exclusively devoted to lettuce growing. I rely on the cold frame for lettuce during early spring and late fall, when freezing prevents growth in the garden, and in midsummer, when garden conditions are too hot for lettuce.

Start preparing the cold frame in the fall. First, prepare the soil inside the frame by adding a 1- or 2-inch-thick layer of composted manure. Turn it over with a fork, pulverize it well with a rake, and firm it down by treading over it on a plank. Rake very lightly again, and all will be ready for the seedlings next spring.

In February, sow lettuce seed in the house or greenhouse. Keep the seedlings watered and begin to thin them as soon as they're 1 to 2 inches tall. Aim for an eventual stand of seedlings just 1½ inches apart.

About a week before setting the seedlings out in the cold frame, begin to harden them off by reducing the amount of water they've been getting. You should allow the soil to dry out almost completely between waterings. Wet the soil again before transplanting.

Around March 1, it's time to set the seedlings into the cold frame. Figure on an average distance of about a foot between plants and rows. Space leaf lettuce about 9 to 10 inches apart in rows set 12 inches apart. Space head lettuce a little farther, about 14 to 15 inches. One-foot spacing means that a 6 × 6-foot cold frame will hold 36 lettuce plants.

By March 15, you should be able to start eating lettuce by thinning out alternate plants. When the soil outdoors can be worked, you can move some plants out of the cold frame every two weeks—at the same time you're sowing seed in the garden for succession crops.

During cold weather, the cold frame requires close attention. On sunny days it needs ventilation, so you need to open the frame. Then well before sundown, close the frame to retain heat, and unless the weather is quite mild, cover the frame at night.

In April and May you may leave the cold frame uncovered, except when the temperature gets down near freezing. Continue to sow succession rows in the garden. Thin, cultivate, and water if rain doesn't fall freely once a week.

By June all the mature lettuce should be gone from the cold frame. Just before really warm weather sets in, transplant young seedlings from the garden to the cold frame, leaving room to sow seeds in the frame for late-summer lettuce.

In July and August, cover the bed with slat covers or shade cloth when the sun shines; take them off at night and during cloudy or rainy weather. Keep the soil moist with regular watering. By late August, you can set out some of the seedlings started in the cold frame. You can also start seeding directly in the garden, spacing small sowings two weeks apart.

In September and October, harvest the lettuce from both the garden and cold frame, and fill the frame with young seedlings from garden sowings made in late September and early October.

In November and December, your challenge is the same as in early March: Be constantly vigilant to carry the plants over the first freezes. But with good management, you will have lettuce to take you into January.

head, use overhead irrigation early in the morning. Be careful not to overwater, though. If the mulch stays too wet, rotting will begin on the undersides of the leaves that touch the soggy mulch, and soon the whole plant will become a slimy mess.

Insects such as aphids, leafhoppers, and flea beetles, as well as larger creatures like rabbits, like to munch on lettuce leaves, so cover your crop with floating row cover after planting, and build a chicken-wire fence around the bed. To prevent mosaic virus or downy mildew, choose disease-resistant cultivars.

CROW'S TIPS

I'll guarantee you good lettuce if you remember these four points:

1. Lettuce likes moderate temperatures. It is hardy but will not withstand freezing. It tends to go to seed prematurely in dry, hot weather.

2. If you want lush, tender lettuce or you want heading cultivars to head, you must keep the plants growing. Because lettuce is a leaf crop, it needs plenty of nitrogen-rich organic material and soil amendments.

3. Leaf lettuce will withstand a little crowding.

4. Frequent cultivation holds down weeds and keeps the soil loose. But cultivate lightly since lettuce roots are near the surface and are easily injured.

CROW'S PICKS

Once you have those lettuce-growing basics down, it's time to learn a little more about lettuce cultivars and types. There are four distinct kinds of lettuce. Let's look at all four.

Leaf lettuce: *Leaf lettuce is the hardiest and fastest, reaching full maturity in 40 to 50 days. I think 'Salad Bowl' is one of the best loose-leaf cultivars for the home garden because it stays in prime*

condition throughout the growing season. 'Ruby', another loose-leaf cultivar, is noted for its ruby red color. It should be picked when young because it doesn't keep its color or sweetness well. 'Black-Seeded Simpson' is an old favorite that still belongs in every garden. It takes about 45 days to mature, but it can be harvested well before maturity and holds its quality well in the garden. It does not become tough and bitter with time. 'Slobolt' is a leaf lettuce that is often grown in greenhouses during the winter and does well in summer, too.

Butterhead lettuce: *Butterhead types like 'Bibb' and 'Boston' form loose heads in 60 to 75 days. They do well in the spring and fall, but they lose quality if they reach maturity in the hottest part of the summer. However, you can raise some cultivars in summer if you provide shade and plenty of water. I think that 'Buttercrunch' is the most delicious lettuce you can grow.*

Romaine lettuce: *Romaine takes 75 to 85 days to form the characteristic long, loose, cylindrical heads of deep green, vitamin-rich leaves. Romaine lettuce is used in the classic Caesar salad.*

Crisphead lettuce: *Crisphead lettuce (including the familiar 'Iceberg') takes 85 to 95 days and is the slowest to mature. This type is also the hardest to grow because it is the least heat-tolerant. 'Great Lakes' and 'Imperial' are the most reliable headers. 'Hot Weather' is an exceptional head lettuce—its name says it all. This crisphead cultivar doesn't seem to be affected adversely by heat or cold. Give it plenty of nitrogen and water, don't wait for the heads to get too solid, and even in midsummer you'll have lettuce that's nearly as good as any spring cultivar.*

HARVESTING

With most crops, you want to wait until they reach the peak of flavor at maturity before harvesting. However, you must pick midsummer lettuce early, or it will bolt, go to seed, and get bitter. Pick the leaf types anytime they're half-grown to nearly full-grown, and discard the outer leaves, which tend to be tough and bitter. Pick head lettuce as soon as the head has formed, but while it still gives a little when squeezed.

If left in the ground, late lettuce is liable to face frost damage, but you can save it by pulling it before a hard frost. Pull up the entire plant, roots and all, and plant it in a bucket of moist sand in a cool but protected place, such as a garage. Keep the leaves dry, and the plant should stay fresh for up to one month.

MUSKMELONS

Muskmelons?" you may be asking. "What about cantaloupe?!" Well, fact is, almost all the "cantaloupes" we grow in this country are really muskmelons. True cantaloupes are smooth-skinned French cultivars that are rarely seen over here. The fragrant, flavorful, rich orange-fleshed melons with netting and ribs are—trust me—muskmelons.

SITE AND SOIL

When choosing the site and soil for your melon patch, look for a southern exposure and a sandy, well-drained soil with a pH no lower than 6.0. The plants will let you know if the soil is too acidic: Their leaves may turn yellow or curl and dry out at the edges. Prepare the soil with plenty of well-rotted manure before planting. Melons also need boron for full-flavored fruit. Apply it sparingly, though: Use no more than 4 ounces of household borax per 1,000 square feet.

Rotate your muskmelons with other crops from year to year so that nematode populations won't build up in the soil. It's best to alternate with legumes (for example, beans, peas, or clover), since they add nitrogen to the soil.

PLANTING

Muskmelons require a long frost-free season. Most cultivars take 80 to 100 days to mature. If you love muskmelons but don't think you can grow them because you live in a short-season area, try starting them from seed in peat pots indoors. Sow them about four weeks before the actual outdoor planting date.

My favorite soil mixture consists of two parts rich garden soil, one part leaf mold, and one part sifted compost. Fill each peat pot to within $1/4$ inch of the rim, then drop three seeds into each and cover lightly.

Place the planted pots into seed flats, allowing about $1/2$ inch of space around each. Pour vermiculite around the pots all the way up to the rim, tamp it down evenly, and moisten it. The wet vermiculite prevents the fiber pots from absorbing moisture too rapidly from the soil. Otherwise, the soil in the peat pots, if allowed to dry out too rapidly, can slow down or harm proper germination.

Place the flats under lights or on a very sunny, warm windowsill. Temperatures should never drop lower than 55°F. You can expect to see green sprouts in about one week.

About a week before transplanting time, harden off the melon seedlings by exposing them to the outdoor sun and air a little each day, until they can take a full day without wilting. An easy way to harden off melons is to place the flats in a cold frame and leave the lid closed for the first few days. Be careful not to allow your seedlings to get too hot during the day. After a day or two, open the cold frame, and continue to open it a little more each day. Gradually withhold water to harden the foliage sufficiently.

When all danger of frost has passed, remove each peat pot from the vermiculite, being careful not to damage the mass of tangled roots that have grown through the walls. Make hills large enough to accommodate three peat pots each, spaced 12 inches apart in all directions. The hills should be from 5 to 7 feet apart. Dig a shovelful of granulated organic fertilizer into each hill and mix it in well.

Place the seedlings, pots and all, in the holes. Then tamp the soil up over the rims and pile it loosely around the stems of the plants. When the vines begin to creep, thin the plants to three per hill.

CARE

When you thin the plants, rework the soil in and around the hills. (As you do so, be sure you don't disturb the plants.) Then scatter a liberal amount of bonemeal over the entire area, and rake it in. To discourage weeds, mulch with 7 inches of straw or grass clippings. There will be little else to do until it's time to harvest your melons.

Muskmelon plants are shallow-rooted, and the roots often extend beyond the vines, so be very careful when weeding. Pull the weed, rather than chopping down deep with a hoe. You can avoid weeding if you use a good mulch.

Sometimes melons are attacked by the yellow-and-black-striped cucumber beetle. The adults and larvae feed on plant tissues and transmit bacterial plant diseases. You can defend your melons against the beetle in several ways. None gives perfect control, but at least you will get some melons.

Provide early protection by covering your entire melon patch with a floating row cover. This light, porous material allows light, air, and water to pass through, but keeps insects out. Make sure to fasten it firmly to the ground with rocks, soil, metal staples, or sharp sticks, and remove it when the blossoms form so bees can pollinate the plants.

Single-crop monocultures make things too easy for bugs, so rotate the melon bed every season and separate the individual hills. Separate melons and cucumbers, and try to plant them in different spots in succeeding years, so that the newly hatched larvae must at least work for their first meal.

If some of your muskmelons form perfectly while others form a half-moon and crack in the hollow part, the problem could be mosaic virus. Mosaic sometimes causes the fruits to be misshapen because infected plants have insufficient foliage to supply food and to cover the fruits. Usually the virus is transmitted by aphids. Control measures to curtail the activity of these pests, including row covers and insecticidal soap sprays, will help prevent mosaic.

There are additional tricks for discouraging mosaic and other diseases. Don't grow muskmelons near their relatives, like squash, and keep areas bordering the melons free from weeds. You can also keep the losses from disease to a minimum by maintaining vigorous growth: Use plenty of compost, and constantly add generous amounts of organic matter.

After the tiny melons form, it is remarkable how fast they grow. When they are nearly full-sized, hold back on the watering. Let the soil dry out, and the melons will ripen into delicious sweet fruit.

HARVESTING

Muskmelons are ready for harvest when they pass the "slip test." Apply light pressure to the stem at the base of the melon. If the melon doesn't slip off the stem, it has not yet reached maturity. Don't pick melons early and expect them to ripen. Once it has been picked, it will not ripen further; in fact, it will begin to lose some of its sweetness.

OKRA

If you say you grow okra, most people will assume that you're from the South. But there's no reason this crop can't be grown throughout the country. Sure, it likes hot summer weather, but once planted outdoors, it needs only 50 to 60 days of heat to begin to mature. Almost every part of the country can provide that much summer weather.

SITE AND SOIL

Okra isn't too picky about soil, but it prefers a neutral soil with a pH between 6.0 and 8.0. I like to work up a special furrow for okra, mixing in 1 pound of aged rabbit manure or blended organic fertilizer per row foot to give plants a boost for extra-good growth.

PLANTING

In long-season areas, you can direct-seed okra into the garden about a week after your last frost date. Space seeds about 5 inches apart. If the weather is dry, water before covering the seeds. If you apply a light mulch of straw over the seeded row, the seeds will germinate more rapidly. When the plants are 2 inches tall, thin them to 10 to 12 inches apart in the row. Plant okra again one month after the first planting, when you have more room in the beds.

Those of us north of the Mason-Dixon line are better off planting transplants in the garden. You can start plants up to a month ahead of time in the greenhouse or under lights. Okra resents root loss, so start seed in peat pots so you can transplant with minimal disturbance. Plant outdoors when the soil has warmed to 60°F and all danger of frost has passed.

CARE

As the plants grow, pull soil around them as you hoe, then mulch with 4 inches of straw. Within a month, the tall plants will begin producing beautiful hibiscus-like flowers. The pods will soon follow.

During the growing season, aphids or corn earworms may attack the okra pods. But nematodes are the worst problem since they damage the roots and keep the plants from getting adequate nourishment. Nematodes attack other crops besides okra, and once the soil becomes infested, it can take up to three years to get rid of these pests.

Fortunately, nematodes are hindered by crop rotation. If you plant cold-weather crops, then sweet corn, then nematode-resistant limas, there won't be any nematode food in the soil for an entire season, and the pests will starve. Marigolds also help control nematodes, but it takes a full season for this method to work. You have to plant the entire nematode-infested bed as a solid block of marigolds, then let them mature and plow them under at the end of the season, so you don't get a crop—but you do get rid of the nematodes!

Okra continues to grow upward as it produces, and by the end of a long season, pods may be 7 feet above the ground. You may need a stool or ladder to harvest the tallest pods. Leaves, stems, and pods of okra are covered with short spines that can irritate your skin, so wear long sleeves and thick gloves when you harvest or work around the plants.

HARVESTING

Most Yankees don't know how or when to pick okra. That's why it has gotten such a bad reputation. You must harvest frequently since pods mature very rapidly. Tiny pods are very tender, but within a week a tender pod will become fibrous and inedible. Furthermore, leaving pods on the plant too long slows production. Harvested regularly, okra will continue bearing until frost.

When harvesting, cut the stem, leaving it attached to the pod. Once harvested, pods need to be handled carefully. They bruise easily, and they wilt quickly and become tough if they're left lying around.

For short-term storage, put unwashed okra in plastic bags in the refrigerator. For long-term storage, simply pack the whole pods in freezer bags or containers and freeze them raw; no blanching is necessary. Before cooking, cut the cap off each pod carefully so that you don't cut into the pod.

ONIONS

Onion cultivars fall into two main categories: long-day and short-day. You must grow the proper type for your area, or you won't get any bulbs at all. Long-day onions are programmed to mature during the long summer days of the North, while short-day onions mature during the cool, short fall and spring days of the South.

You can buy onions as seeds or as sets. The best long-keeping onions are grown from seed. Stems on seed-grown onions seem to be thicker and tighter than those grown from sets. And the thick stems seem to seal the onions better for their many months of storage.

Still, onion sets have their advantages: They're easy to buy and handle, and they produce a quick crop. When shopping for sets, keep in mind that the best ones are firm and about the size of a large marble.

❋ ONIONS

SITE AND SOIL

Onions grow best in soil that is moist, well-drained, and rich, with a pH of 5.5 to 7.0. Since they have shallow roots (I call them surface feeders), the soil must be rich and loose in the top 6 to 8 inches. Organic matter will keep the soil from drying out, and moisture is very important for onions. A temporary drought causes the outer scales on the bulbs to mature or dry out. So after the next rain comes or you water again, you end up with a lot of split and double bulbs.

You can improve the water-holding capacity of the soil by adding manure, but it must be at least a year old and well composted. Keep fresh manure out of the onion bed because it harbors weed seeds that will quickly sprout and take over your bed.

If you can't find well-aged manure, take the time to hunt down another source of organic matter. Try straw, hay, grass clippings, shredded leaves, or, failing all else, shredded newspaper. The object is to get material into the soil that will hold moisture. Once you've worked the organic matter in, break up any clods and pick out all the stones you can find. Then firm the seedbed by rolling it with a lawn roller or by walking all over it.

If you have the time and the space, you can also improve the soil by green-manuring the onion bed. Sow a crop of buckwheat, oats, or rye late in the summer of the year before planting onions. Then till the residue under in the fall or next spring.

PLANTING

Many beginning gardeners pick up a bag of onion sets at the garden center and pop them in the ground for a satisfactory crop. If you decide to buy onion sets, plant them about 1 inch deep and 6 inches apart in the garden. (One pound of sets will plant a 50-foot row.) Five weeks after planting, you'll be able to pull scallions for cooking or salads.

I much prefer growing onions from seed. Not only do you have a much wider selection of cultivars, but the resulting bulbs are often bigger, healthier, and better for storing. The only drawback to growing onions from seed is that they do take a long time to grow. You must start onions in flats indoors or in a greenhouse six to ten weeks before the last frost.

Use a rich version of my standard Spring Meadow seed-starting mix, which includes garden soil, peat moss, fertilizer, vermiculite, and perlite. Sow the seed thickly—about a half-dozen seeds per square inch. Onion seedlings need plenty of light, so you'll have to grow them in a greenhouse

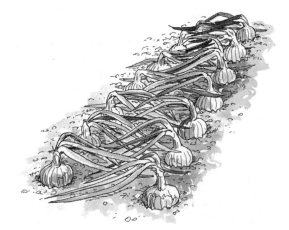

Your onion crop won't keep well unless you cure it before storing. When the bulbs are full-sized, pull the mulch and soil back to expose the bulbs, then bend the tops over to one side until they have yellowed. Next, pull the onions and lay them on a screen until the foliage has dried. Then braid the tops together and hang the onions in bunches, or cut off the tops an inch above the bulbs and store the onions in mesh bags, baskets, or crates.

or under grow lights for 12 to 18 hours a day. To keep them growing vigorously, spray with a liquid organic fertilizer every two weeks.

When it comes time to transplant, pull the plants from the flat, separate the individual plants, and cut the top half of the leaves off. This forces new growth and also reduces the amount of water lost from the plants as they adapt to the outdoors.

Set the plants about 6 inches apart in rows or beds. Onions don't like to be buried, so plant them shallowly in the bed. They should be just deep enough for the soil to cover the roots. As they mature, half the bulb should be sticking up above the surface.

CARE

Weeds are the bane of onions, so be sure to hoe and weed regularly between the plants and the rows. Once the plants are about the size of a pencil, put down a straw mulch about 3 inches thick. This amount of straw should be heavy enough to cover the soil and retard the weeds, but thin enough to allow the sun to warm the soil.

Be very fussy about keeping the bed free of weeds until July. In the early stages of seedling growth, weeds will really slow the onions down. The seedlings are so thin and frail that weeds quickly shade them out. A weed-free environment also helps eliminate insect problems.

During the growing season, trim the tops of the onion plants back to about 18 inches maximum to prevent the plant's energy from going into the production of a seedhead at the top. When it is kept trimmed, the plant puts more effort into the root bulb, and large onions result. When the bulbs reach the size of a baseball, draw the soil away from them, exposing them to as much air and sunshine as possible to help them ripen.

When the leaves start to turn yellow, bend them down to the ground. Bend them so that those of adjoining rows are turned toward each other, leaving one side of each row clear of leaves so it's easy to work among the onions.

Wireworms and onion thrips are both attracted to onions. To prevent infestations, don't plant onions where they've been grown in the past three years, and avoid rotating them with sweet potatoes, alfalfa, oats, or wheat. Be on the lookout for onion maggots and cutworms—if you've had problems with them in the past, apply parasitic nematodes to the soil before planting, and cover the bed or plants with a floating row cover after planting.

Onions are subject to a whole host of diseases, including pink root, Fusarium bulb rot, onion leaf blight, and smut. The best way to prevent disease-related problems is to plant resistant or tolerant cultivars.

HARVESTING

Once the leaves have died, pull the onions or carefully lift them out of the ground with a spading fork, and allow them to dry in the sun. Lay them out on wooden tables, screens, or boxes where they can dry on all sides. (Laying them on the grass or soil would result in one dry side and one soggy side.) When the tops have dried completely, cut off the foliage at the neck and store the onions in mesh bags, baskets, or crates.

If you've completely dried the onions before storing them in a cool, dark, well-ventilated place, you can enjoy them for several months during the winter. Warm, humid conditions may cause the onions to sprout and rot.

ONIONS, SPANISH

Huge, sweet Spanish onions: Can't you just taste the slices on a juicy burger or in a salad now? You'll get the sweetest onions ever if you grow your own.

SITE AND SOIL

To get really large onions, dig a 4-inch-deep trench and cover the bottom with 2 inches of sifted compost. Cover this with 1 inch of soil, then you're ready to plant.

PLANTING

Large, sweet onions are almost always grown from plants. You can usually buy the plants or grow your own from seed, just as you would for cooking onions. Sow the seed thinly in flats of rich, organic potting soil about ten weeks before outdoor planting time, and germinate them at 50° to 65°F.

Set the plants in the prepared trenches about 6 inches apart. Spanish onions grow twice as large as ordinary onions and need more room. Don't plant the seedlings too deeply. Cover only the lower ½ inch with soil, then firm the soil very well around each plant. If there's no rain in the forecast, water the entire bed after planting.

CARE

Spanish onions need only shallow cultivation. After each rain, loosen the soil around the plants down to 6 inches with a grub hoe so roots will have good air circulation. Once the soil has warmed, mulch the rows with 3 or 4 inches of hay, straw, or grass clippings. If you use clippings, be sure to keep them away from the stems or they'll burn them.

Sweet onions need plenty of moisture. If the soil stays dry around the roots for a prolonged period, the onions will split, and each plant will form two smaller bulbs instead of one large one.

HARVESTING

As the bulbs mature, pull the soil away so the upper half of each is exposed to the sun and air. When most of the tops have fallen over, push the rest down with a rake. A week later, pull up the onions and leave them on the ground for three days to cure in the sun.

When the outer skin is dry, snip off the tops 1 inch from the bulbs. Then place the bulbs in a well-ventilated outdoor building to cure until cold weather sets in. Before storing, check the onions for rot and discard any with soft spots. Then place them in open trays and store in a cool, dry cellar or attic.

PARSNIPS

As far as I can tell, there are only two problems in growing parsnips. One is training yourself to keep out of the parsnip patch until the first frost, and the other is planting enough roots to keep you satisfied all winter.

SITE AND SOIL

Parsnips, like other root crops, respond wonderfully to generous applications of rock phosphate and potassium. Add rock phosphate every few years at the rate of 10 pounds per 100 square feet. One pound of wood ashes per 100 square feet, applied annually, will take care of the potassium. Also, add dolomitic limestone to maintain a pH between 6.0 and 6.5.

A 2-inch-thick layer of compost or well-rotted manure, dug into the rows before planting, takes care of nitrogen. But don't go overboard: Too much of this nutrient can cause the roots to become stringy and flavorless.

Since parsnips will grow a foot long without coaxing, the deeper you loosen the soil, the easier it will be for the roots to penetrate and thicken. So begin in early spring with a deep and thorough tilling of the soil.

PLANTING

After putting in all the fertilizer, rake the seedbed smooth. Then dig ½-inch-deep furrows spaced 18 inches apart.

Next comes the most critical phase of parsnip cultivation. This crop has a short seed life and a slow germinating habit, so take care to ensure a good stand.

Time your planting correctly. Parsnips prefer a cool season, so that means sowing in early spring. Use only the freshest seed. If you have old seed around the house or find a "terrific bargain" on last year's seed at the local supermarket, forget it—parsnip seeds lose their viability after a single season. If you plant old seed, you could get anywhere from a spotty stand to practically zero germination.

After sowing, cover the seed with fine sand or a mixture of sand and peat moss to help retain moisture. Also, keep the soil loose in the furrows. Parsnip seedlings are very delicate little things and can't push through surface crusts easily.

When the plants are about 3 inches tall, thin them carefully so that they stand 3 inches apart in the row. Because the seedlings sometimes become intertwined as they grow, be especially careful to leave just one plant in each spot.

CARE

Water parsnips regularly throughout the season. Irrigate every time the top ½ inch of the soil dries out. Dry soil during peak growth periods leads to dry, mealy, tasteless roots.

Although parsnips need lots of moisture, water falling hard on the seedbed fosters puddling, which promotes crusting. So water gently, and keep your furrows moist but not wet.

HARVESTING

You can dig up your crop and store it in a root cellar, or you can allow the roots to remain in the ground until you need them. If you leave your parsnips in the garden, protect them from alternate freezes and thaws with a heavy mulch of shredded leaves or straw. For best flavor, try not to use the roots until they've gone through the season's first couple of frosts, since cold weather really sweetens them.

PEANUTS

Peanuts are a fun crop to grow. As mysterious as potatoes, they're even more fun for kids to harvest, roast, and eat. They don't take up a lot of space and are relatively trouble-free. I think there should be room for a few peanut plants in every garden.

SITE AND SOIL

The soil for these light feeders should be well drained, light, and on the acid side, with a pH of 5.0 to 6.0. A sandy loam is ideal. Since peanuts are legumes, they don't need a soil rich in nitrogen. However, unless other legumes have been grown in the soil previously, you should inoculate the seed with nitrogen-fixing bacteria. Before planting, apply plenty of bonemeal—about one handful per row foot—to the bed or row, then work it in with a cultivator.

PLANTING

When the soil has warmed to 60°F and it's time to plant beans in the garden, carefully shell the peanuts and plant them 1 inch deep. Place two peanut kernels in hills spaced 12 inches apart in rows spaced about 2 or 3 feet apart. If you're gardening in the North, try to provide a south-facing slope in a sheltered area for this long-season, warmth-loving crop.

The seedlings should be up within a week. When they poke through the ground, you'll see why you planted two per hill. Germination is spotty at best, and many of

the kernels do not sprout. In spots where two seedlings emerge side by side, you can either pull the weaker member of the pair or leave them be.

CARE

Peanuts are remarkably drought-resistant. It's amazing how they can take hot sun and drought and still produce a sizable crop. Peanuts are also surprisingly problem-free. They aren't bothered by insects, and the only disease that bothers them is just a touch of leaf spot, usually not enough to worry about. The only thing you have to do is keep the weeds down.

About a month after germination, the plants will start to bloom, producing two different kinds of flowers. The conspicuous orange pealike flowers are male. The inconspicuous female flowers, which produce the crop, grow on the ends of pegs that penetrate the ground after pollination. The nuts form about an inch below the soil surface. At bloom time, put down a layer of straw mulch around the plants to conserve moisture, keep weeds down, and provide the nuts with a friendly place to form.

HARVESTING

About 100 days from planting, depending on the cultivar, you can start checking the nuts for ripeness. Dig under a plant with your fingers, pull out several of the larger nuts, and take a look (and a taste). Immature peanuts have soft, white, spongy shells with watery, white-skinned, bland-tasting kernels. As they mature, the shells grow darker. The kernels plump up and develop pink skins that turn dark red at maturity.

If the nuts aren't ready, let the plants continue to grow. Light freezes don't seem to hurt the mature plants, and you can always

pile mulch over them to extend the season a couple of weeks, depending on how nasty Jack Frost is that year.

At harvest time, simply dig up the plants with a shovel, then shake the soil loose from the roots and nuts. To cure the nuts, leave them on the plants until the foliage dries out completely. Then pick the nuts from the roots and place them in a burlap sack or mesh bag. Hang the sack in a warm, airy room to dry thoroughly.

PEAS

The flavor of fresh peas, like that of corn, is fleeting. Within two hours of picking, much of the sugar will have turned to starch. That's why frozen peas are so much sweeter than "fresh" ones that may have been sitting around the grocery store for a week.

SITE AND SOIL

Peas aren't too picky about soil. But when picking a patch to put your peas in, keep in mind that they prefer cool conditions. You'll want to plant them as early as possible in spring. And if you have any light, sandy, well-aerated soil in your garden, that's the place to put your peas. On the other hand, a low-lying, waterlogged site will slow them down by promoting rot.

Peas are legumes, of course, and make their own nitrogen, so use my light-feeder fertilizer formula on page 96. A rich soil that has previously grown heavy feeders like broccoli or eggplant is ideal. Peas profit from phosphorus and potash, so add about 3 pounds of bonemeal and 10 pounds of greensand (or 1 pound of wood ashes) per

✳ PEAS

Peas are easy to pick when you grow them on a sturdy trellis. Place a stake or broom handle every 3 feet along the row, and attach 3-foot-high chicken wire. Plant a row of peas on each side of the trellis.

100 square feet. Also, add dolomitic limestone as necessary to bring the pH to nearly neutral (about 6.5).

If you have one perfect patch for peas, you may be tempted to plant them in the same spot every year. Don't. In order to cut down on disease, make sure you rotate the crop, and don't return peas to the same ground for at least three years.

PLANTING

Because peas prefer cool weather and aren't injured by frost, you should sow them in the garden just as soon as the ground is workable in the spring. That's late March here on Long Island, or about six weeks before the last spring freeze.

To assure a long season of pea picking, I always plant several cultivars with different maturity dates. They can all be planted at the same time, so you don't have to concern yourself with successive sowings. As with all legumes, the pea seed should be inoculated with nitrogen-fixing bacteria. Just moisten the seeds with water and dust them with a powdered legume inoculant. The inexpensive powder inoculates the soil with bacteria that help the plant create its own nitrogen. I've found that using it increases the yield considerably.

As for hastening the yield, the faster you get the seed in the ground, the sooner you'll be picking peas. To get the earliest start possible, I always prepare the ground in the fall, before the ground freezes hard. I choose a well-drained, south-facing spot and dig and rake it smooth. Then, in the spring when the ground is thawing, I simply push the peas into the rows with my fingers.

CARE

Once my pea fence is in place (see "Crow's Tips" on the opposite page for how I build my fence), I side-dress the rows with just enough compost to cover the soil, and add a dusting of bonemeal, greensand, and kelp meal. After working all of that in with a rotary tiller, I cover the entire area with a 3- to 4-inch-deep layer of hay mulch.

There's not much more to do till pea-picking time. Oh, sure, you can pull the occasional weed that pokes up through the mulch. And it wouldn't hurt to spray the plants with a liquid organic fertilizer every three weeks or so. But basically, peas are trouble-free once you've put up your fence.

Occasionally, leafhoppers, leafminers, cucumber beetles, or other pests may feast on pea plants. If this has happened to your crop, protect your next planting with a row cover when the seedlings appear. To prevent problems with downy mildew, pea root rot, and other diseases, plant resistant or tolerant cultivars.

HARVESTING

Depending on the cultivar, your peas will be ready to pick in 50 to 80 days. Pick the pods as soon as they are plump and bright green. For the finest flavor and the greatest vitamin content, steam or stir-fry the peas rather than boiling them.

Unlike most other annuals, the young pea vines grow best in cool weather and cease to produce when it is too hot. When the vines have finished bearing, you can pull them up and use them on the spot as mulch for the next crop. Some of the roots of the vines may be so heavily covered with crinkly nodules of nitrogen-fixing bacteria that you can hardly see the roots themselves.

CROW'S TIPS

It seems that everybody I talk to has a different technique for growing peas. I'm convinced my system produces healthier plants and makes feeding, cultivating, and mulching much easier. I grow them in double rows and train them up 3-foot-tall wires. With this method, picking becomes a pleasant operation. You don't have to bend over so much, and the pea pods hang where you can see them.

Here's how I do it: I sow the seed in twin rows spaced 7 inches apart, leaving 3½ to 4 feet between each double row. I make sure I run my peas in rows that are perpendicular to the path of the sun. That way, one row faces east to catch the morning sun, and one row faces west to catch the afternoon sun.

When the pea plants are 8 to 10 inches tall and just beginning to develop tendrils, it's time to start staking them out. For dwarf and early cultivars,

I use 3-foot-tall poultry mesh, 3 feet wide by 40 feet long. Old broomsticks make perfect fence stakes.

I run the wire between the two rows, then put in a stake every 3 feet. I weave the stakes through the wire strands, pounding them 1 foot deep into the ground.

That's the best way to do it. The worst method of staking peas is to train them to a series of strings. The weight of the vines usually makes the strings sag and the vines collapse on themselves, shutting off light and creating damp conditions that contribute to fungus and rot.

PEPPERS

If you've had problems with the peppers in your garden, you've probably been pampering them too much. Peppers don't need as rich a soil as tomatoes. If your plants grow exuberantly but never seem to set fruit, you've used too heavy a hand with nitrogen fertilizer. On the other hand, peppers do need a steady supply of nutrients all season. If the size of the peppers growing on your plants decreases as the weeks go by, you haven't provided enough nitrogen to get them through the season.

SITE AND SOIL

For best results, use my medium plant prescription when preparing the soil (see page 96), with applications of nitrogen in fall and spring. Be prepared to supplement with side-dressing or foliar feeding as the season progresses.

PLANTING

Peppers require a long growing season and need some extra attention when they're

Peppers can take the heat, but they're wimps when it comes to cold. Get yours off to a fast—and safe—start by setting out transplants through a black plastic mulch and covering the crop with floating row cover supported by hoops. The black plastic will warm the soil quickly, while the row covers provide frost and pest protection.

starting off indoors. If you've ever spent the whole spring waiting for a flat of pepper seeds to sprout, it was probably because the soil temperature was too cool. Peppers need soil temperatures of 70° to 90°F to germinate. That's about 10 degrees warmer than the temperature required by tomatoes. If you're going for peppers in a big way, it would be worth your while to invest a few bucks in a heating cable.

Start with the standard Spring Meadow seeding mix formula. (See page 57.) Sow two or three seeds per cell in a cell pack. Move the packs to a heating cable, and cover them with plastic to keep the heat in. Don't get discouraged if there's still no sign of seedlings in a week or so.

You'll need to start peppers at least eight weeks before the last spring frost to give yourself sizable plants to set out. The plants should be bushy and on the verge of blooming at transplant time. Peppers are perfect for beds and intensive planting: They actually seem to give better yields if planted closely together. They can get by with as little as 2 square feet per plant.

CARE

I've read that pepper yields can be increased up to fivefold by using a combination of black plastic mulch and drip irrigation with organic nutrients fed at frequent intervals through the irrigation water. Even if you don't have the technology to feed fertilizer through a drip system, you can get similar results by side-dressing your pepper plot.

Make the first application three weeks after transplanting and successive treatments three weeks apart. The first application should consist of compost mixed with a dusting of kelp meal and fish meal; apply 2 pounds per square foot. Three weeks later, apply a mix of compost and bonemeal at the same rate. For the final application, spread compost and Sul-Po-Mag.

You may have seen leathery, black patches at the bottom of your pepper fruit. That's blossom end rot, which is caused by water stress and a calcium imbalance. Calcium deficiency symptoms in peppers show up in the leaves, which turn a bronzy color and develop basil-like crinkling. To provide sufficient calcium, add 10 pounds of dolomitic limestone per 100 square feet of soil. This application will also meet the magnesium needs of the pepper plants.

Peppers are sometimes subject to diseases, especially viruses. The main troublemakers are tobacco mosaic, tobacco etch, and potato Y viruses. If the plants look stunted and have patchy, mottled coloration on the leaves, they've probably contracted a virus.

Aphids are the primary virus carrier. It's critical to control them with insecticidal soap from the time your plants are just little seedlings. That's because there's no cure once a plant is infected. The only other prevention against viruses is disease resistance bred into the plants. For example, more than 70 percent of the commonly available bell pepper cultivars are resistant to tobacco mosaic virus.

HARVESTING

Green and red bell peppers are simply different stages of ripeness of fruit on the same plant. If you like green peppers, pick them when they're full-sized but still green. For a higher vitamin C content and a sweeter flavor, let them ripen to a rich red before you pick them.

Cut bell peppers from the plants, leaving ½ inch of the stem attached—don't just pull the fruit off. Store them in the vegetable crisper, or freeze or pickle them. Some cultivars mature to yellow, orange, or purple ("chocolate"), so you can grow a range of colors to brighten salads.

If you're a hot-pepper fan, remember that these peppers can burn—and not just when you eat them. Wear gloves and sunglasses when you harvest, and don't touch your face until you've taken off your gloves and washed your hands! You can dry these peppers in the traditional long strands or *ristras,* make dried pepper wreaths, freeze them, or pickle them.

🐦 CROW'S TIPS

I normally don't like to use or even recommend black plastic mulch, but peppers are one crop that really seems to thrive with plastic. If you lay black plastic over the bed first, then set pepper plants into it, you'll gain about a week and boost yields considerably. Combine that with a floating row cover over hoops, drip irrigation, and supplemental fertilizer, and you'll have created a veritable pepper-producing machine.

POTATOES

Potatoes are a simple crop, but they do require a little advance planning. For one thing, they're grown from "seed potatoes" (small potatoes set aside for the following season) rather than from seed. (You'll find more about seed potatoes under "Planting" on page 152.) You also need to think carefully about site and soil preparation when you plant potatoes. Once you've got your seed potatoes and have prepared your site, though, potatoes are easy and fun to grow. And they're especially fun to harvest.

SITE AND SOIL

When deciding where your potatoes are going to grow, pick a location where potatoes, tomatoes, eggplant, peppers, and petunias have not been grown for at least three years. These plants are all related, and growing potatoes where their relatives have previously grown invites diseases and leads to soil deficiencies.

encourage leafy growth at the expense of tuber formation. Fresh manure and lime both lead to scabby potatoes.

Potatoes need a loose, well-drained soil. A waterlogged soil will produce rotted or sickly tubers. To improve the tilth and drainage of the soil, sow a cover crop of winter rye in the potato bed in the fall. Till thoroughly in the spring, or spade well, breaking up all the clods.

Fortunately, potatoes grow fairly well in acid soils, so you shouldn't need to raise the pH. On the other hand, make sure the soil gets plenty of phosphorus, a mineral essential to maximum yield in tuber crops. Bonemeal and rock phosphate are perfect for this purpose. For normal soils, add about 3 pounds of bonemeal or 6 pounds of rock phosphate per 100 square feet in the fall. (Don't add wood ashes, since they can encourage the formation of scab on the tubers.)

PLANTING

The most important step in avoiding disease comes right at the start. Always buy certified virus-free seed potatoes. You may be tempted just to plant eating potatoes from the cupboard that have gone soft or started to sprout. Even if you save money in the short run, this type of bargain too often leads to late blight problems.

To make the seed potatoes go further in the garden, you can cut them up before planting them. Slice the potatoes into 1- to 2-ounce pieces, making sure there are no more than two eyes on each piece. For best results, cut them to about the size of a small egg—smaller pieces just don't seem to grow well. Since the new plants draw on the starchy reserves of the seed pieces for a good start in the garden, the more they have to draw on, the better they'll grow.

You should improve soil for potatoes in the fall or between seasons, not as a last-ditch effort while the plants are growing. Potatoes require a fairly rich soil, but there are three things they don't like: nitrogen, fresh manure, and lime. Nitrogen-rich fertilizers, such as blood meal and alfalfa meal,

Milk-Carton Potatoes

Here's an interesting potato-planting technique. It involves some additional props, most notably an empty milk carton.

First, prepare a ½-gallon milk carton by cutting off the top and cutting around three sides of the bottom. When the carton is inverted in the potato patch, the bottom will serve as a trapdoor that you can close on cold nights after the potatoes are up.

But we're getting a bit ahead of ourselves here. In the garden, dig a hole about 6 inches deep. Mix 2 cups of moistened peat moss and 2 tablespoons of greensand into the soil at the bottom. Then set a potato piece firmly in place, eyes up. Now, set the ½-gallon milk carton over it, tilting the carton a bit toward the south for good sun exposure. Next, push soil up around the sides, right up to the top of the carton, and sprinkle just enough inside to cover the potato with about an inch of soil.

This completed "potato well" will collect the heat of the sun, and the soil around the sides will hold the warmth at night. As the sprouts appear, sprinkle soil around them so just the tips show. As they grow, keep adding soil inside while gradually lifting the carton.

Meanwhile, put down 8 to 10 inches of straw mulch between the plants. Finally, when the plant seems squashed inside the carton, pull the carton off and level the soil. There's nothing more to do till harvest, except to push the straw up around the plants when they're tall enough—no weeding, no hilling, no cultivating, and if your soil was moist when you applied the straw, no watering. The only drawback to planting this deep is that you have to dig deeper to get all of your potatoes.

You don't want to plant a freshly cut tuber directly in the soil, since it would be likely to rot there. Instead, after cutting the seed pieces, allow the cuts to heal in a sunny window for about a week, turning the pieces slightly each day. By the end of the week, a protective skin will have formed over the cuts, and the eyes will just have begun to show signs of sprouting.

You can plant whole seed potatoes as well. They are less likely to rot in the ground than cut seed potatoes, and they may result in larger, more productive plants.

Plant potatoes as early as you can. Potato plants like cool weather—their tuber production is highest at air temperatures ranging from 59° to 64°F. Don't be afraid to plant as early as two or three weeks before the last expected frost. Even if the sprouts get nipped, the food reserves in the seed potatoes will send out new shoots, and your crops will be all right.

Plant your potatoes about 4 to 6 inches deep. You can either drop them into a furrow or use a bulb planter to make individual planting holes. Space the potatoes about 12 to 15 inches apart in the row, and allow 24 to 36 inches between rows.

CARE

The first shoots may not emerge for weeks in cool soil. Don't give up! Once they're up, hoe the soil well around them and hill an inch or two of soil up around the base of the plants. Then toss a loose mulch of hay or straw, 6 to

12 inches deep, over the entire patch. This keeps the potato tops from turning green once they've grown big enough to push to the surface. Green potatoes contain a poison called solanine and can be harmful to eat.

If you don't want to mulch the bed, you can plant potatoes in trenches, then draw soil up around the stems as the plants grow. The theory is that the new potatoes form above the planted seed potatoes. Therefore, if you put the seed pieces in the bottom of the trench and add soil as the plants grow, the potatoes will be encouraged to set more tubers, and the soil itself will protect them from greening. This system works, but I think it involves too much digging at both sowing and harvesting time.

The Colorado potato beetle is the most troublesome insect in the potato patch. These fat, 1/3-inch-long, yellow-and-black-striped beetles feed on the foliage, weakening the plants. Late plantings are usually bothered less than early ones. Handpicking is still an effective way to deal with these pests. Potato beetle larvae are fat orange blobs, with black legs and two rows of black spots along each side. If you catch the infestation in its larval stage, you can apply a special kind of BT, *Bacillus thuringiensis* var. *san diego,* to kill them.

HARVESTING

When the plants begin to blossom, you can start checking for "new potatoes" (actually, they're just the baby tubers of regular potatoes). Carefully dig into the mulch or soil directly under the stems with your fingers, and you should find some golf ball–sized new potatoes. As you dig them out, be careful not to disturb the plants. These new potatoes are delicious when boiled, skins and all. They are very sweet, moist, and tender, because not much of the sugar has

been converted into starch yet.

Let most of your potatoes mature. You can leave them right in the ground until fall if you wish, as long as the weather isn't wet enough to cause decay or encourage them to sprout.

Dig the spuds with a three-pronged potato fork during a dry spell, and let them dry out on top of the soil for a few days. Some people skip the drying process because they're afraid the potatoes will turn green, but a few days in the sun won't do them any harm. Rather, this sun drying helps toughen the skins. Once cured, they store well in a cool, dark place, where they will last all winter.

When you harvest, make sure you pick up *all* the potatoes. Don't dump piles of diseased or culled potatoes in or near the garden. Fungal spores will overwinter and can travel on the wind to infect next year's planting.

PUMPKINS

Is pumpkin pie your favorite? Or do you think of pumpkins as Halloween decorations? However you like to think of them, these big winter squashes are easy to grow and a lot of fun for kids—and for some of us adults, too!

SITE AND SOIL

As you might guess, producing these prodigious fruits requires quite a bit of food. Pumpkins are very heavy feeders. I like to give them a special diet, starting with the soil. In the fall—or at least six weeks before planting in spring—I mark out the pumpkin patch in a sunny, well-drained area, and then I start digging. By the time I'm done, I've dug a 2 × 2-foot hole for each hill. Then

I fill the holes with my special mix of compost, to which I've added a sprinkling of bonemeal and wood ashes. I also give pumpkins my heavy-feeder fertility formula. (See page 96.)

PLANTING

Once the weather is settled and warm, and there's absolutely no chance of a frost, I sow two pumpkin seeds per hill. The plants are usually up within a week, and then I just let them run.

CARE

The only care pumpkins need is an occasional hoeing to keep the weeds down—and maybe a little help with pollination. Within a month of sprouting, pumpkin plants sport huge, bright orange blossoms. Like summer squash, pumpkins have male and female flowers on the same plant and must be insect-pollinated to set fruit. If you don't want to leave this process to chance, especially if you're growing just a few plants, you can pollinate the flowers yourself. Just transfer the pollen from the male flowers onto the pistils of the female flowers with a fine paintbrush. (See "Make Your Own Squash" on page 168 for more on plant pollination.)

Pumpkins share the same pests and diseases as other winter squash. For information on how to control them, see "Care" in the Summer Squash entry on page 169.

HARVESTING

Before you harvest your pumpkins, make sure they're fully mature. Thump the pumpkin much the same way you would a watermelon, and listen—if you hear a hollow sound, it's time to harvest. You can also test for ripeness by digging into the skin with your thumbnail—if the skin is hard and resistant, the pumpkin is ready.

Let pumpkins cure in the garden for a week or two on the vine before bringing them in, taking care not to bruise them. Then cut the stem with a sharp knife, leaving an inch or so attached to the fruit.

CROW'S PICKS

Think you don't have enough space to grow pumpkins? Think again. There are a number of bush pumpkins available these days. My favorite is an open-pollinated cultivar, 'Cinderella'. Five square feet is all you need to raise this cultivar. And in just 95 days, each plant will produce two or three bright orange, 7- to 15-pound pumpkins.

RADISHES

Radishes are such a quick-and-easy crop, they're perfect for beginning gardeners. But their spicy flavor and crunchy texture make them favorites of experienced gardeners, too. And they come up so fast that you can use them to mark the rows of slow-to-show crops like carrots—they'll be out of the ground and in the salad before they start crowding the slower-growing vegetables.

SITE AND SOIL

As with all root crops, you'll get the shapeliest radishes if you grow them in a loose, well-drained soil. A sandy loam is ideal. The best pH range for radishes is 5.5 to 6.8. I always work compost into the soil before planting my radishes. Because they're in the ground such a short time, I use the light-feeder formula—too much nitrogen could cause deformed roots. (See page 96.)

PLANTING

Radishes can take the cold, so you can start planting as soon as the soil is workable in spring. But don't overplant radishes—they don't store well once they're harvested. Instead, keep the salad trimmings coming by sowing a short row of radish seed every ten days to two weeks until early summer, then again when temperatures don't exceed 75°F in early fall.

Sow seeds $\frac{1}{2}$ inch deep and 1 inch apart in rows spaced 8 to 18 inches apart. Once the seedlings are up, thin to 2 inches apart.

CARE

Once your plants are established, mulch them to conserve moisture. Heat and drought make the roots tough and stringy. So water as needed to maintain even moisture, and time your plantings so the radishes are out of the ground before the weather really starts heating up.

Radishes have few pest or disease problems. If yours are bothered by soilborne diseases, look for resistant cultivars. If cabbage maggots attack your crop, cover the seedlings with floating row covers to keep the parent flies from laying eggs on the plants.

HARVESTING

You can harvest radishes anytime from the moment the roots start to swell until they're about an inch around. After cutting off the tops, refrigerate them and use them as quickly as possible.

CROW'S TIPS

Try Asian radishes if you enjoy stir-fries or pickles. Japanese radishes are called daikons. They're long and white and look like carrots, but they can reach practically baseball-bat size. Unlike salad radishes, daikons remain edible no matter how large they get.

Work the soil deeply before sowing Asian radishes. Plant them in midsummer as you would salad radishes, but thin them to 3 or 4 inches apart. Let them grow through the season and provide even moisture. Harvest them after the first frost.

You can store Asian radishes in the refrigerator or in a root cellar or other cool, moist place. Slice them for stir-fries, or grate them for spicy oriental pickles like the Korean kimchi.

RHUBARB

Rhubarb is such a beautiful plant that you should grow it as an ornamental even if you're not a fan of rhubarb pie. It requires no more care than the perennials in your flower beds. And just a couple of plants should produce enough rhubarb for the average family.

SITE AND SOIL

Since rhubarb is one of the few perennial crops in the vegetable garden, it calls for special soil care. A new planting will occupy the same piece of ground for a long time, so it pays to make sure the soil is fertile and well worked.

Choose a location with plenty of sun and good drainage. Rhubarb needs a lot of water, but your bed should not be in a low-lying area where water accumulates and doesn't drain away.

Dig a trench about 30 inches deep and wide—the length will depend on the number of plants you want to start. In the bottom of the trench, put in a layer of manure or compost about 5 inches thick, then a layer of soil a few inches deep. Repeat the layers until the trench is almost filled to the top.

PLANTING

Like perennial flowers, rhubarb is usually grown from plants or roots rather than from seed. To set plants or roots, start about 18 inches from one end of the trench with your first plant. Set the rhubarb in the center of the trench, roughly 4 inches deep if you are using roots. If you're using plants, set them slightly deeper than they had been growing in the nursery. Space plants about 30 inches apart. From your last plant, allow about 18 inches to the end of the trench. If you're planting more than one row, space the rows about 30 inches apart.

CARE

After setting out plants or roots, water them well, and they should take off quickly. As the leaves emerge and grow, check plants for seed heads. These will be more bulbous than the leaves on the regular stalks and should be pulled off as soon as you can see their stems. Don't cut the seed heads off—instead, pull them off the crown. If the stalks or stems are pulled off the crown, it will heal quickly.

In the fall, after a good hard frost or two, rhubarb will gradually die back. Pull the leaves off as they turn yellow. Keep pulling off the dying leaves and stalks until the bed is cleaned up completely. Then put a 2- to 3-inch-thick layer of manure over the whole bed. Don't dig it in; just leave this manure blanket on until spring. As soon as the weather begins to warm up, pull it back from the crown area of each plant to expose the ground to the sun and warm up the soil around the plants.

The secret to a productive rhubarb bed is very fertile soil and proper moisture. Add manure every year and water during prolonged dry spells, and your bed will continue to produce for many years.

Rhubarb is seldom bothered by pests or diseases. However, be on the lookout for rhubarb curculio, a yellow-gray beetle measuring about $\frac{1}{2}$ inch long. This pest bores holes in the stalks and crowns of rhubarb plants and lays its eggs there. Pick the adults off by hand; if the problem is severe, use rotenone. Curly dock (*Rumex crispus*) is also a host to the larvae, so destroy any plants that you find growing nearby.

HARVESTING

Harvest rhubarb in spring by snapping off the stems at the base. As with asparagus, you should harvest lightly the first year after planting, and take only stems that are at least an inch thick the second year. After that, you can harvest for one to two months every spring. The red or green stems are the edible part of rhubarb; the leaves are poisonous, so cut them from the stems as you harvest.

 CROW'S TIPS

Rhubarb spreads slowly. Every year, each plant sends up one or more new growths alongside the old plants. You can separate these newcomers and transplant them to enlarge your bed, or just leave them. If your plants become too crowded, thin them by pulling some stalks out from time to time. After four or five years, you may even want to remove some of the plants. Thinning will allow the remaining stalks to get bigger and better.

SALSIFY

Salsify is usually given short shrift by gardeners. But wise growers know that it has some outstanding and unusual qualities that make it worth growing. Where else can you get the taste of oysters in the garden? That's right—salsify is also known as "oyster plant" for its distinctive flavor. And it's a flavor that can be enjoyed starting very early in the spring. Like parsnips, salsify can be left in the garden over the winter to be dug in spring when the ground thaws.

Salsify is a biennial. It produces a mature root in 120 to 150 days and will set seed the following year. The plant sometimes produces seed the first year if it's grown in a mild climate.

SITE AND SOIL

The soil for salsify should be deep, free of rocks, and neutral in pH. As with most root crops, shallow soil, fresh manure, or large rocks will ruin your chances for a really first-class crop. Till or spade the soil to a depth of about 1 foot, and add a light application of well-rotted manure or aged compost.

PLANTING

The most common cause of salsify failure is poor seed. The seed must be absolutely fresh, or it will not germinate reliably. Even fresh seed should be planted about 1/2 inch deep and sown quite thickly. Thin seedlings to 4 or 5 inches apart in rows spaced 18 inches apart.

CARE

Salsify can withstand moderate frosts, both when it's small and when it's reaching maturity. It will keep on growing in the fall after light freezes as long as the days are warm and sunny.

HARVESTING

Salsify roots mature at about 1 inch in diameter and 8 inches long. You can store them indoors or leave them in the garden to harvest as needed. If you want to store salsify, wait until just before very cold weather sets in. Then dig and place the roots in very damp sand.

If you leave the roots to overwinter in the garden, cover the patch with old hay or straw to keep the ground unfrozen so you can dig them. Be sure to dig the roots before growth starts up again in the spring. Once the plants start growing, the roots become stringy and tasteless.

CROW'S PICKS

'Mammoth Sandwich Island' is the most common cultivar. Black salsify and Spanish salsify are related, but they are rarely grown in this country.

SHALLOTS

Shallots are a versatile vegetable—you can use both the tops and the bulbs in salads, soups, and stir-fries. Shallots also make tasty seasonings. They're a wonderful asset in the garden as well as in the kitchen.

SITE AND SOIL

Shallots grow best in a sandy loam soil, but they will produce in a wide range of soil types. They like a balanced diet similar to that preferred by onions. Use a light-feeding mix of either blended organic fertilizer or well-aged manure. The best crops are grown in beds that have been planted with a green manure of buckwheat, oats, or rye the previous year.

✳ SHALLOTS

Shallots

PLANTING

Buy shallot sets as early as possible in the spring, and plant them as soon as the soil temperature reaches 40°F. Use 1½ pounds of dry sets to cover a 50-foot row. Plant them 1 inch deep and 8 inches apart in rows spaced 18 inches apart.

CARE

The plants will begin to sprout in 7 to 14 days, and once they are up, frost will not damage them. Cultivate carefully as the plants grow. Don't mound the soil up around the developing bulbs—pull it away. That way, part of the bulbs can form on top of the soil, which helps keep them from rotting during very wet weather.

Shallots are ideal for interplanting. While the shallots are still young, you can grow early-maturing vegetables such as turnips, mustard greens, or radishes as companions without inhibiting either crop.

HARVESTING

You can begin to use the tops as scallions in about 40 days. Much like onion bulbs, the bulbs of shallots aren't ready for harvesting and storage until the plants are fully mature. You'll know a plant has reached maturity when it bolts and then starts to wither.

When mature, the bulbs can be dried and stored for use during the winter. (You can dry and store them like garlic and onions.) They are every bit as pungent as onions but with a slightly different flavor.

CROW'S TIPS

Make sure to save a few cloves to plant the following year. You can also divide shallots during the growing season. Select strong, healthy clumps, divide them in half, and then transplant some to another area of the garden.

SHUNGIKU

Shungiku, also known as "chop suey greens" and garland chrysanthemum, is a cut-and-come-again crop. Plant it once, cut it early, and the plant will grow back time and time again, saving you time, effort, seed, and garden space. You get two, three, or often up to six harvests without having to work the ground again or raise more seedlings.

SITE AND SOIL

For a leafy crop, shungiku needs rich soil. Use my fertility formula for medium feeders. (See page 96.)

PLANTING

Here in New York, shungiku grows best as a fall crop. I start the seeds in flats eight to ten weeks before the first fall frost date. It's best to start the seeds in flats so they're protected from heat stress, which can induce premature flowering. I set the plants in fertile ground, spacing them 6 to 12 inches apart.

CARE

Shungiku plants must have plenty of water for the rapid and succulent growth that produces tender leaves. This crop favors cool weather and will grow vigorously in the weaker light of autumn. Where winters are mild, it will winter over and sprout again in spring. It also self-sows readily.

HARVESTING

I start harvesting shungiku when the plants are about 6 inches tall. It grows back from sideshoots, so I pick it like amaranth greens or New Zealand spinach, taking 3- or 4-inch-

Shungiku

long tender shoots with tiny leaves and, sometimes, small flower buds. Then I chop the deep green, spicy stems and leaves for steaming or stir-frying.

SOYBEANS

I can't figure out why soybeans are still a sort of stepchild in most home gardens. They're among the easiest garden vegetables to grow. They do well anywhere that corn will grow. And they're incredibly nutritious, whether you steam and eat them green or dry them.

SITE AND SOIL

Prepare the soil for soybeans beforehand, using my medium-fertilizer formula. (See page 96.) Soybeans grow best in soil containing nitrogen-fixing bacteria (*Rhizobium* spp.) that can produce nodules on the plants' roots. If your soil hasn't previously grown soybeans, you should inoculate the seed first with these bacteria, which are available in powder form at garden centers and through mail-order catalogs. Different bacteria work best for different crops, so buy a powder labeled for soybeans. Without inoculation, the crop yield will be less, and the beans will fix less nitrogen in the soil.

PLANTING

Plant soybeans after the last frost date. Sow seed 1 inch deep, using about six to ten seeds per foot in rows spaced 15 to 30 inches apart. Thinning is not necessary. A pound of seed normally plants 150 to 200 feet of row.

❋ SOYBEANS

Soybeans

CARE

Soybeans do best when the soil is kept evenly moist through the growing season. Be sure the plants get plenty of water when the pods are developing. Don't let the ground get soggy, though, or the plants may become stunted and the pods may drop. Mulch with grass clippings to keep weeds in check and conserve moisture.

Soybeans are bothered by many of the same pests and diseases as other beans. If you've had problems with leafhoppers, Mexican bean beetles, aphids, or other bean-loving insects attacking your plants in the past, cover the young plants with floating row covers. To combat powdery mildew or blight, choose disease-resistant cultivars and thin the plants to improve air circulation. To prevent the spread of disease, don't harvest or work around the plants when the foliage is wet. (For more on controlling pests and diseases, see "Care" in the Dry Beans and Snap Beans entries on pages 99 and 102.)

HARVESTING

Many gardeners and cooks consider soybeans somewhat difficult to shell. But there's not really that much to it. As soon as the pods have fully filled out, clip them from the plant and toss the stalks on the compost heap. Then open the pods, pulling them open from the clipped end, and strip out the beans.

If you intend to serve the beans green and don't want to let them mature, pour boiling water over the fresh-picked pods and let them stand three to five minutes. After draining the pods, break them crosswise and squeeze out the beans. Then cook them until tender.

 ## CROW'S TIPS

Why not try something different and inter-plant soybeans in the same row with black-eyed peas? Alternate black-eyed peas and black soybeans, planting them about 6 inches apart in the row. The black soybeans tend to grow with their branches held vertically, while the black-eyed peas flop over and start rambling along the ground.

The black soybeans will be well above the peas and able to receive plenty of the warm sunlight they need. At the same time, the peas shade the ground and conserve moisture. The peas mature first, so the black soybeans will have more room just when they need it the most.

SPINACH

I happen to like cooked spinach, but I know that many people don't. Even if you remember Popeye with fondness, you may still have unpleasant childhood memories of overcooked green gunk. If that's the case, think about delicious, nutritious spinach salads instead. Or maybe spinach lasagna, spinach quiche, or Greek spinach pies. Spinach is easy to grow, too.

SITE AND SOIL

Choose a sunny, well-drained location for spinach. Although this crop grows in just about any soil, it fares best in one that is fertile, with plenty of moisture and good tilth. Light, sandy soils with only a little organic matter will yield poor-quality, spindly, light green spinach.

Like most leafy green vegetables, spinach needs lots of nitrogen for rapid growth. Use my heavy-feeder formula of 2 pounds of fresh manure per square foot, and apply it to the soil at least six weeks before planting time. (See page 96.) At the same time, add enough lime to bring the pH to about 6.0 to 6.5.

PLANTING

A cool-weather crop, spinach grows best at temperatures of 60° to 65°F, so plan to have yours up and growing when temperatures reach this range in your area. Here on Long Island, I make several plantings from early February to early May, and I sow a late crop in August.

Water your spinach plot thoroughly a day or two before you plant. By the time the seeds are in the ground, all excess water will have percolated through the soil or evaporated, yet there will still be plenty of water held around the seeds by dirt particles.

Sow spinach seeds $\frac{1}{2}$ inch deep and 1 to 2 inches apart. Space standard rows at least 1 foot apart. Or you can save space by broadcasting seeds in a wide row, up to $2\frac{1}{2}$ feet across.

As long as the soil doesn't dry out, wait to water again until the seedlings have emerged. By holding back on watering, you will greatly reduce the possibility of moisture-related diseases attacking your spinach.

Crowding encourages the plants to bolt or flower prematurely, so thin to one plant every 4 inches. Thinning also increases air circulation and reduces fungal diseases.

CARE

After the plants are established, water whenever the top $\frac{1}{2}$ inch of the soil dries out. Cultivate shallowly around the seedlings to remove weeds and promote rapid growth. When the soil has warmed, mulch the plants with 3 to 6 inches of straw, hay, or grass clippings.

Stretching the Spinach Season

Spinach is more versatile than most gardeners think. There are several ways to stretch the harvest season. One is to over-winter fall-sown spinach; this gives the earliest spring growth.

You can also sow spinach just as soon as the snow melts by taking pains to prepare the soil thoroughly the preceding fall. To advance your planting time two to four weeks in spring, cover the autumn-prepared bed with a cold frame sash or a plastic tunnel. The ground will soon be warm enough to plant.

You can gain a few more days by starting seeds indoors in cell packs. However, the cost in space and effort is high, since you'll need a lot of spinach plants to get an adequate number of leaves at a picking. That's because spinach is not an abundant greens producer, so you'll need about 30 plants to feed one person.

If you're working with a greenhouse or cold frame, spinach is an excellent crop to plant in February for harvest at the end of March. 'Monnopa' and 'Benton #1' both do very well under these conditions. Just be prepared to ventilate the greenhouse or cold frame when daytime temperatures exceed 80°F.

However, just because spinach is super-hardy doesn't mean it's a good crop for mid-winter production. In fact, it's one of the worst. Despite its ability to survive extreme cold, the plants don't grow big when days are short. Spinach needs a fair amount of light, and mid-winter levels are just too low.

Powdery mildew can be a major problem for older cultivars, especially in wet weather. The fungus causes spinach leaves to become discolored with yellow spots. In severe cases, the spots will converge, killing the plant. Downy mildew is also a problem for spinach. The best protection against these diseases is to buy resistant cultivars, thin the plants to promote good air circulation, and avoid working among the plants when the foliage is wet.

If leafminers or flea beetles have been a problem in your garden, cover your spinach seedlings with floating row covers to keep these pests out. They can quickly deface spinach leaves if not controlled. You can leave the row cover on until harvest as long as temperatures remain moderate.

CROW'S TIPS

Bolting is a serious problem for spinach. Even under the best growing conditions, plants will begin to bolt (go to seed) when the daylength exceeds 14 to 16 hours. When spinach is about ready to go to seed, you'll notice that a flower bud begins to form and elongate in the center of the plant's crown, reaching a height of 3 inches in four days or less. At the same time, new leaves will be smaller and thinner. All the leaves will take on a bitter taste.

Daylength isn't the only factor that triggers bolting. Spinach will also bolt faster when grown in temperatures over 80°F. This is why gardeners who experience an unexpected spell of hot weather in late May end up with tiny plants that have just a few leaves and a flowering stalk. You can minimize this problem if you plant early and use bolt-resistant cultivars.

CROW'S PICKS

Spinach breeders have developed some wonderful new bolt-resistant cultivars. 'Melody' was one of the first, and it has become a regular in my garden. Although 'Melody' doesn't bolt as rapidly under longer daylengths or in hot weather, it doesn't grow quite as rapidly as 'Tyee' and 'Skookum', two other hybrids.

'Tyee' is truly amazing. I've harvested huge leaves from it in as few as 37 days from sowing. 'Olympia' is another hybrid cultivar that is even more bolt-resistant than 'Tyee', but doesn't grow quite as fast. In my garden, it matures about five to six days later than 'Tyee', and even a couple of days later than 'Melody'.

I like 'Olympia', though, because the leaves are erect and smooth—there are no wrinkles to hold dirt. This may sound like a minor point, but it's important for gardeners like me who have heavy spring rains that splatter dirt up onto the leaves. 'Tyee' and 'Melody' produce erect leaves, too, but they are semi-savoyed (wrinkled) and not nearly as smooth as those of 'Olympia'.

Other bolt-resistant cultivars of spinach are 'Long Standing Bloomsdale', which is wrinkled, and 'Indian Summer', which is a smooth-leaved cultivar. Besides being long-standing, all of these new hybrids are resistant to, or at least tolerant of, downy mildew.

HARVESTING

You can start picking spinach leaves as soon as they're large enough to use, usually starting about 35 to 45 days after sowing. Pick the larger outer leaves first so the inner leaves can continue growing. If you see signs of bolting, cut off the entire plant at ground level.

Wash wrinkled-leaf types thoroughly to remove any clinging soil. You can refrigerate fresh spinach up to a week; blanch and freeze extras for winter use.

SPINACH, MALABAR AND NEW ZEALAND

If you miss fresh spinach during the hot summer months, try an exotic substitute—either Malabar spinach or New Zealand spinach. Malabar spinach leaves are thicker, more succulent, and crunchier than almost any other green around. The leaf surfaces are smooth and shiny, without deep curly pockets where soil can hide, so you won't have the unpleasant experience of tasting grit as you chew your greens. And the plant is a vine, so you can train it up off the ground, away from the dirt that can splatter onto the leaves when it rains.

New Zealand spinach is a native of—you guessed it—New Zealand and, as you might expect, will thrive in the heat that causes common spinach to become bitter. The flavor is not exactly like that of regular spinach, but it does make a good substitute in the hot summer months, when other greens can't be grown. While common spinach is a rather modest rosette of a plant, New Zealand spinach may sprawl over an area of about 5 feet and grow to a height of 2 feet, so you'll have plenty to pick.

SITE AND SOIL

A fertile, slightly alkaline soil will grow the best of these medium-feeder crops. Both Malabar and New Zealand spinach do fairly well in poor soil, but the plants don't grow as large, nor do they produce as big a crop.

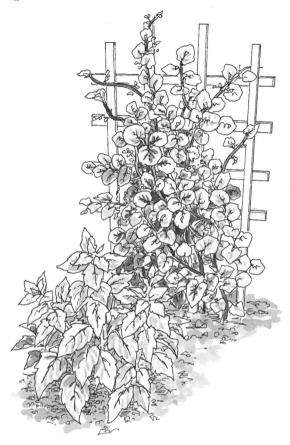

New Zealand spinach (front) and Malabar spinach (back) are heat-tolerant substitutes for spinach. Harvest the tips and small leaves of New Zealand spinach and steam them; Malabar spinach leaves are good raw or cooked. Malabar spinach is a vigorous vine—grow it on a trellis so it doesn't take over your garden.

PLANTING

A tropical plant that grows wild throughout the Orient, Malabar spinach is very frost-tender. I start seeds early in my solar green-house in order to have sturdy vines that are crowded with leaves by midsummer. Seeds take two or three weeks to germinate, so you can start them about ten weeks before the last expected frost. To reduce root shock, I dip the roots in liquid seaweed before transplanting the seedlings to the garden bed.

I'm in no hurry to transplant Malabar spinach to the garden. I know that the plants can't survive spring frosts or even night temperatures much lower than 58°F. In general, I plant it out at about the same time I'm setting out eggplant or sowing lima beans.

New Zealand spinach seed is large, tough, and heavy-coated, and it will resist germination if not soaked for 24 hours before planting. Sow seeds about 1 inch deep and 4 inches apart in the row, after the soil has warmed. Because the plants tend to sprawl, leave 4 feet or so between rows. When the plants are well up, thin them to about 18 inches apart. This vegetable is prolific, so the average family will need only eight to ten plants to harvest an ample supply.

CARE

If started in May, Malabar spinach will thrive through the summer months and produce until the first frost in autumn. This crop is pretty much problem-free, except for one type of leaf spot, the same fungus that makes holes in beet leaves. In Malabar spinach, it leaves a red-rimmed hole about $\frac{1}{4}$ inch in diameter—not a large bite, but enough to spoil the appearance of a bowlful of leaves.

Keep a sharp eye out for leaf spots. If you see any infected leaves, pick them off and remove them from the garden. To discourage the fungus, practice good garden sanitation and rotate your crops. Hot weather favors the disease, though the spores are able to overwinter on leaves in the garden. As soon as frost comes, clean up every leaf that has fallen off both Malabar spinach and beets.

New Zealand spinach will keep producing all summer if it is regularly harvested and watered. Most garden books recommend shading the plants during the really hot part of summer, but I've grown New Zealand spinach without shade, too. If you want to shade your plants during the hottest part of a summer afternoon, simply plant them on the east side of a tall-growing crop like corn or caged tomatoes. A mulch will reduce the need for excessive watering and keep the leaves cleaner, so you won't have to spend as much time washing them before eating or freezing them.

HARVESTING

Start picking Malabar spinach as soon as there are several leaves on each plant. Pick only one leaf per plant at first. After the plants have branched, you can gradually reap a larger harvest. Use a sharp knife to cut the stem just below the leaf. Because the leaves are so thick, it takes fewer of them to make a meal than most greens.

To harvest New Zealand spinach, pick off the tips (about 4 to 6 inches) of the branches. Eat them stems and all, fresh or steamed, or freeze them.

SQUASH, SUMMER

Summer squash lives up to its name. It likes hot weather and can't be planted until the air temperature stays in the 65°-to-75°F range. Summer squash grows fast, though. Almost all cultivars bear fruit in less than two months, and most zucchinis ripen in less than 50 days. I can safely sow squash in May and be eating it by July. From then on, I can pick it day after day until the first frost ends the harvest.

SITE AND SOIL

Squash needs rich soil. It's best to prepare the beds in the fall by adding a 2-inch-deep layer of composted manure and tilling it in thoroughly. Then, for a quick boost at planting time, broadcast blended organic fertilizer according to package directions. Summer squash needs this boost so it can keep pumping out fruit all summer (even though we sometimes wish that it would slow down a little, especially if it's zucchini).

PLANTING

You can rush the summer squash season a bit by starting seed inside, then moving the seedlings to the open garden at the same time you transplant tomatoes. Just make sure you sow in peat pots so you can transfer the seedlings into the ground, pots and all, without damaging their roots.

Or, if you don't want to fuss with indoor growing and transplanting, sow squash seed outdoors three weeks before the regular planting time and protect the emerging plants

Get your summer squash off to a great start by planting them in hills of rich, well-prepared soil. Put cardboard collars around your seedlings to protect them from cutworms, and mulch them to maintain even soil moisture for best growth. Hotcaps will protect frost-sensitive seedlings until all danger of frost is past.

Make Your Own Squash

You can develop new cultivars, or keep certain characteristics in an existing cultivar, by playing a hand in pollination. If you want to try hand-pollination, experiment on squash or pumpkin. Both have large blossoms, making them easy to work with.

Watch carefully as buds form on your plant. When you feel that blooming is imminent, gently tie the female blossoms closed with soft yarn, rubber bands, or twist ties. The next morning, pick an open male blossom from the plant you wish to cross with the mother plant, and remove the petals.

This procedure will expose the male blossom's anthers, where the pollen is located.

Then remove the yarn from the female blossom and gently rub the anthers across the stigma, which is usually located at the center of the blossom. Tie the female blossom closed. Mark the stem of that blossom with a tie or marker. As the fruit develops, the blossoms will slough off.

Wait for the fruit to ripen fully, then remove the seeds. Wash them off and dry them carefully on a screen, then store them in a glass jar in a warm, dark place. Plant the seeds the following year to see what you've created. Who knows? you could be another Luther Burbank!

Make your own squash! Who knows what you'll come up with if you try experimenting with cross-pollination? But whatever you get, it's easy and fun! To make a cross, strip the petals off a male flower on one parent plant. Cut off the flower and rub the pollen-coated anthers against the stigma of the female flower you've chosen as the other parent. (Female squash flowers look like they already have a tiny squash forming at the base.) Once you've pollinated the female flower, tie its petals together with a twist tie to make sure bees don't destroy your experiment! Harvest the mature squash, save the seeds, and plant them out next year to see what you've produced.

with hotcaps. On very chilly nights, you can toss a light mulch of straw over the hills for extra protection. Early-seeded squash grows rather slowly, but it also ripens about two weeks earlier than squash that's direct-seeded in the ground at the regular time.

Sow three or four squash seeds per hill, and space the hills 4 or 5 feet apart. After a few weeks, thin each hill to the one or two strongest plants, and put a cardboard collar around the stem of each young plant to thwart cutworms. Ideally, just one bush squash plant should occupy about a 4 × 4-foot area. Summer squash is a husky grower in good soil, and if the plants get too crowded, they often form tiny fruits that turn brown at the blossom end.

CARE

Summer care is minimal. Just spray the plants once every three weeks with a micronutrient-rich foliar feed like kelp or liquid seaweed, and keep them well mulched and watered.

Watch for the reddish brown egg clusters of the squash bug on the undersides of leaves. Destroy the eggs and handpick any gray nymphs or adult brown bugs that may hatch out. Wood ashes bother the pests; apply them when the leaves are wet.

The squash borer is an inch-long, fleshy white caterpillar that eats inside the stem near the base of the plant, sometimes severing the stem. A weak plant will wilt and die. Prevention is the best way to control these pests. If you've had borer problems in the past, cover your plants with floating row covers before the vines begin to lengthen, or spray the base of the plants with pyrethrins or rotenone weekly. If you find a borer hole in your squash stem, slit the stem, extract the borer, then cover the stem with soil.

Proper spacing helps to keep powdery mildew in check. If your plants have leaves coated with white or gray powdery spots, pull out every other plant to provide maximum sunlight and air circulation. Where the problem is common year after year, make sure the leaves of one squash plant don't touch those of another. You can spray the plants with sulfur according to package directions to keep mildew at bay. New research in the field has shown that you can also control mildew by spraying a solution of baking soda and water (1 teaspoon of baking soda and 1 quart of warm water) on the leaves.

HARVESTING

Harvest summer squash when they are still immature and tender—you should be able to pierce the skin with your thumbnail. The fruit grows quickly, so check the plants daily. Frequent harvesting will also encourage the plants to continue producing. To harvest summer squash, cut the fruit from the vine, leaving about 1 inch of the stem attached.

CROW'S TIPS

I have a special technique that allows me to concentrate soil fertility where the individual squash plants will be growing. For each hill, I dig a hole about 15 to 18 inches deep and wide, and backfill it with a mixture of $1/3$ compost, $1/3$ good garden loam, and $1/3$ shredded leaves, sphagnum moss, or similar humusy material. To that I add $1/2$ cup each of greensand, blood meal, and rock phosphate, and 1 cup of blended organic fertilizer. In soils with a pH of 6.5 or lower, I add $1/2$ cup of dolomitic limestone.

This mix will give the plants enough to go on for most of the season. For an extra boost, I feed them every three weeks with a liquid fertilizer like manure tea or fish emulsion.

CROW'S PICKS

The main types of summer squash are yellow, green, and scalloped. But there's one cultivar of yellow squash that really stands out in my garden. It's called 'Custard Marrow'. The fruit resembles 'Pattypan' squash and grows to about the same width—7 or 8 inches—but it's much thicker. The young fruits, up to 4 inches in diameter, have very firm yet tender flesh without the undesirable seediness and soft centers of other summer squashes.

SQUASH, WINTER

Huge, lumpy, blue-gray hubbards. Striped, snakelike cushaws. Club-shaped butternuts. Turkish turbans. Stringy spaghetti squash.... Winter squash comes in a whole spectrum of shapes and colors, from the fantastically flavorful acorns, buttercups, and butternuts to the simply fantastical. Whichever winter squash you choose, provide a rich soil for the huge, rambling vines that keep growing throughout the summer to produce their fall crop. And make sure you give them plenty of room to spread.

SITE AND SOIL

Plant winter squash in very good organic soil. Dig a hole 1 foot deep and twice as big around for each plant. Fill each hole with rotted manure and add ½ pound of balanced organic fertilizer. I think composted citrus rinds make an excellent addition to soil intended for winter squash, since the plants can really use the minerals in the rinds.

PLANTING

After all danger of frost has passed and the soil has warmed to 70°F, plant two or three seeds in each hill. Sow the seeds 1 to 2 inches deep. When the seedlings become established, thin to the best one.

CARE

Like its summer cousins, winter squash requires relatively little care. Keep the soil evenly moist, and mulch with straw or grass clippings to conserve moisture and control weeds. Foliar-feed plants every three weeks with kelp or liquid seaweed for an extra boost. To keep developing fruit healthy, place small boards underneath, or train the vines up a trellis or other vertical support.

Watch for signs of pests or diseases that can threaten your crop. For control information, see "Care" in the Summer Squash entry on page 169. Feeding by squash bugs causes leaves and shoot tips to blacken and die back. Borers tunnel into stems near the base of the plant, causing the stems to wilt and eventually die. Powdery mildew produces dusty white or gray spots on leaves.

HARVESTING

By the time the first frost comes, the stems of the fruit should be dry and the fruit itself should be ready to harvest. Take hand shears to the winter squash patch and cut each fruit from the vine, leaving an inch or more of the stem. Handle the fruit carefully to avoid breaking the skin or pulling the stem off accidentally.

If the stem comes off the fruit completely, the fruit won't keep nearly as long. Use any stemless fruit first, and cure the rest of your winter squash crop. Lay the squash out in the sunshine for a few days, turning them so the ground side is up. If rain threatens, gather them up and take them to shelter—prolonged dampness could cause squash to rot through the stem. Let the squash sun-cure for about a week, then take them to a cool, dry attic.

Spread newspapers and place the squash on the floor so they're not touching. They should keep there for months, but check them occasionally. There are always a few that cave in and go soft during the winter. (The acorns seem the most difficult to keep.) By March, the remaining squash will lose some quality and be drier and stringier than when first harvested, but they should still be perfectly usable.

Crow's Tips

For something different, try melon squash. It looks, smells, and tastes like a melon, but is in fact a winter squash. When eaten raw, melon squash has a subtle cantaloupe taste. When baked, it tastes like a yam. It can be steamed, boiled, or stuffed, and the toasted seeds are as tasty as pumpkin seeds.

The growing season for melon squash is quite long: 160 days from seed to fruit. You can get a jump on the season by starting seeds indoors under grow lights about one month before the last spring frost. Sow one seed per peat pot in a mixture of potting soil, peat moss, and vermiculite. All the seeds should come up within a week's time.

After a couple of weeks, move the seedlings outside during the day to harden them off. Set the young plants out in the squash patch when they're about one month old and after all danger of frost has passed. Mulch with straw.

Because melon squash plants are gigantic and really compete for space, choose a site for them outside your main garden. Green at first, the fruits continue to grow until the leaves die back. Harvest them as you would winter squash. Then store them in a cool, well-ventilated outbuilding until they ripen. The fruit is ripe when the skin turns a dull orange color.

Crow's Picks

I think butternut is the best-tasting of the winter squashes. I also like acorns, which are bush types and grow into lovely green mounds of leaves 4 feet wide and 3 feet high. Both types produce about seven fruits per plant.

SWISS CHARD

Swiss chard is an almost indestructible perennial member of the beet family. It's just as easy to grow as beets, and that's plenty easy.

SITE AND SOIL

When choosing a site to plant Swiss chard, remember that in milder climates, one planting will last for several years. So pick an out-of-the-way spot that won't be disturbed by annual tilling.

Soil requirements are simple—any rich, mellow soil will do. Just work in about a 2-inch-deep layer of compost or composted manure, my soil prescription for a light

☀ SWISS CHARD

Swiss Chard

feeder. (See page 96.) A lack of magnesium or potash in the soil may result in brown spots on the leaves. If this occurs, just add a bit of bonemeal or ground potash rock. In general, though, Swiss chard is not a heavy feeder and can produce fair yields on pretty slim rations.

PLANTING

Swiss chard is a cool-weather crop that can be planted from as early as four weeks before the last expected spring frost all the way until midsummer. Before planting, soak the seed overnight to hasten sprouting and encourage more even germination. Soaking really helps when you're planting in dry soil during warm weather. One early planting will provide an abundant crop over a long season.

Sow Swiss chard seed ½ inch deep, spacing each seed 3 inches from its neighbor. Keep your rows at least 2 feet apart. The "seeds" of Swiss chard, like those of all beet-family members, are really fruits that contain many seeds. Therefore, several seedlings will

sprout from each "seed." Although these can be thinned to the largest plant once the first true leaves develop, you don't really need to bother thinning Swiss chard.

CARE

Swiss chard needs regular rainfall or irrigation, but once the plants are well established, they'll tolerate a surprising amount of drought. Unlike some other types of greens, this crop has the ability to thrive during scorching summer days. It doesn't turn sulky and wilt under the sizzling sun, provided it gets enough water. Growing chard in a mulched garden bed will eliminate the moisture problem entirely.

In an extreme heat wave, leaf growth may be slowed, and smaller leaves may emerge. If this happens, you can plant new seed and have plants ready for harvest in four to six weeks.

Except for leafminers, chard is just about pest-proof. Cover the seedlings with floating row covers to keep this pest from ruining your crop. If miners are bad in your garden, keep the cover on all season.

HARVESTING

You can begin harvesting as soon as the plants have several leaves that are at least 5 inches long. To harvest, cut the outer leaves near their junction with the main stalk of the plant, leaving the smaller, inner leaves to mature. This is a cut-and-come-again vegetable, so after a few days, a new growth of tender leaves will start appearing. The cycle of cutting and regrowth can continue all summer and even into winter, when the plants finally bolt to seed.

Use the stems and leaves of Swiss chard as you would beet greens or spinach. The leafstalks may be cooked like asparagus.

CROW'S TIPS

To keep chard producing into January, cover it at night and during cold spells. If rainfall isn't regular, give the plants occasional water to keep growth going. In areas where the ground freezes solid for extended periods, a thick mulch over the dormant chard plants will protect them from freezing damage.

About six weeks before the last expected spring frost, trim back all the dead leaves and prune the stem back to within 1 inch of the ground. At the first sign of warm weather, the plants will send out new leaves, providing some of the earliest tender garden greens.

During the second and subsequent growing seasons, chard plants form seed heads. However, by cutting the heads back in June, you'll be able to harvest fresh leaves again by late July. To ensure good summer growth, feed the plants with fish emulsion when you prune the seed heads.

CROW'S PICKS

'Rhubarb' Swiss chard is an eye-catching cultivar with reddish leaves and brilliant crimson stems. I also recommend 'Fordhook Giant', with dark green, glossy leaves and white stems; 'Lucullus', a standard cultivar with white stalks and light green crumpled leaves; and 'Spinach Beet', with smooth leaves and slight midribs.

TOMATOES

Tomatoes are so easy to grow, it's tempting to plant too many. But hey, they're easy to eat, too. And there are lots of great cultivars to try, from sugar-sweet cherry tomatoes to whopping beefsteak types. Try several each year until you find your favorites. Maybe your neighbors will want the extras!

To make sure your tomato plants are putting their energy into heavy fruiting, pinch out the vegetative suckers that grow between the stem and the leaf branches (top). If they don't have to support suckers, your plants will produce bumper crops of beefsteak, plum, pear, and cherry tomatoes.

Tomato Blossom Drop

It's frustrating to see all the flowers fall off your prized tomato plants before they set any fruit. Tomato blossom drop has a wide variety of causes, but the best cure is prevention. With a little careful planning before planting the tomato patch, you can greatly improve your chances of having successful blossom set all season long. Here's what you should look for:

Nutrient deficiency: The soil's mineral content plays a major role in tomato blossom set. Deficiencies in potassium, phosphorus, or nitrogen will affect the plant's ability to set fruit. Mineral deficiencies don't even have to be severe enough to show other symptoms in order to cause blossom drop. Once symptoms do appear in the foliage, however, it's a sign of critical starvation.

Potassium deficiency results in stunted, woody plants with grayish green leaves. Phosphorus deficiency causes dull, bluish green leaves and soft, acid fruits with poor keeping quality. Nitrogen deficiency turns top leaves yellow, while stems become deep purple. Tomatoes rarely suffer from nitrogen deficiency, although excess nitrogen can also cause blossom drop. Too much nitrogen also causes rapid, succulent growth.

You can correct nutrient deficiencies by adding greensand or granite dust to boost potassium, bonemeal or rock phosphate to boost phosphorus, and blood meal, cottonseed meal, or poultry manure to boost nitrogen. But it will take a while for the rock dusts to release their potassium and phosphorus. So for fast relief, first spray your tomatoes with a foliar feed of liquid seaweed. Then add the other materials to the soil for long-term benefits.

Proper pH: Tomatoes prefer a slightly acid soil with a pH of 6.0 to 6.5. Maintaining the pH factor within that range will help keep the plants' fruit-setting machinery running smoothly.

Hot weather: A major cause of blossom drop is high temperatures. Tomatoes are native to the tropics, where they are perennial. But unlike their smaller native ancestors, today's large plants can't tolerate temperatures lingering in the 90s or higher. When daytime heat is combined with nighttime temperatures that remain above 70°F for several nights, tomato plants conserve energy by not setting fruit.

Cool weather: Cool weather can also cause blossom drop. When nighttime temperatures drop below 60°F, you can pretty well forget fruit set, especially with late-bearing cultivars. Pollination just doesn't take place. This is a common problem for eager-beaver gardeners who just can't wait until warm weather settles in before setting out their tomato plants.

Wet soil: Too much moisture is most often a problem early in the season, when heavy spring rains can flood the tomato patch, saturating the soil and literally drowning the tomato vines. Leaves turn yellow and wilt, and blossoms drop almost before they form. In poorly drained areas, roots may even rot. If your garden is in such a location, plant in raised beds, or dig trenches just outside the root zone to carry away excess water.

When blossom drop is at its most severe, the blossoms are shed before the pollination process is finished. You can ease the problem by pinching out some of the terminal plant growth. If the plant is really growing wild, you might even try severing the roots with a spade at two or three places around the plant. If you do, you should definitely pinch back some of the terminal growth to make up for root loss.

Lucky for us, most causes of blossom drop eventually take care of themselves. Unless the cause is a nutrient deficiency, tomato plants rarely continue to drop their flowers. As soon as temperatures moderate or rainfall either increases or slackens, blossom set nearly always resumes. If the plant is in reasonably good health, production will be as heavy as if it had never been interrupted. But if the plant's health has been adversely affected, its reproductive ability may have been permanently damaged.

SITE AND SOIL

Tomatoes are lush, vigorous growers. They need a fertile soil to provide plenty of food to keep them going. But be careful not to over-fertilize this tropical plant. Too much fertilizer results in rampant foliage growth at the expense of fruit.

Start with my medium-feeder formula (see page 96), supplementing later if your plants need a mid-season boost. Apply compost or composted manure to the planting area in the fall, then add another 2-inch layer to the soil in the spring.

Get the ground ready for your tomatoes at least a week before you transplant them. If the ground was mulched over the winter, till the mulch under to allow the soil to warm up. To help prevent blight, don't plant tomatoes in a patch where eggplant, peppers, or potatoes were planted last year.

PLANTING

Because tomatoes are tropical, long-season, hot-weather plants, they must be started indoors in all but the hottest areas of the country. Choose an early cultivar—early-season tomatoes grow faster, are usually cold-resistant, and may ripen in 60 days or less. (Note that the number of days in a catalog description indicates the time it takes for the first fruit to ripen after the young plants have been set out, not the time from seeding to harvest.) A main-crop or mid-season tomato may take 75 to 80 days.

Tomato seeds are big enough to sow individually. Plant them an inch or so apart, cover thinly with soil, and press down to firm. Before germination, keep the flats in a warm, dark place. When the seeds sprout, move the flats to a greenhouse or under grow lights. When the seedlings reach a few inches high, transplant them to stand 3 × 3 inches apart.

Some gardeners transplant tomatoes twice. Some don't transplant at all, simply thinning out and discarding crowded plants or else sowing seed far apart in the first place. On the whole, though, I think it pays to transplant: You get a stockier plant and a stronger root system. And don't forget to harden off the seedlings in a cold frame a few weeks before they're ready to go outside in the garden bed.

In the spring, wait until all danger of frost has passed, then transplant your tomatoes on a sunny day, when the soil and air are as warm as possible. It's best to do the deed early in the evening so that the seedlings can avoid the shock of exposure to full sun.

Just before planting out, water the flats until water runs out of them. Water the plants again just after transplanting, then cover the bed with a thick mulch of straw or grass clippings. The mulch will keep the moisture content of the soil more uniform, which helps prevent blossom end rot.

Set the early tomatoes deeply—new roots will form along the submerged stem. Protection is a must for tomatoes that are set out early in the spring. If there's any danger of a light frost or even chilly nights that might damage the plants, place floating row covers firmly over the plants and draw the soil up over the edges to seal it.

CARE

I believe in pruning and staking my tomatoes since I like to grow the tall, vining types. (They're called "indeterminate" since they keep on growing until killed by frost, unlike the bushy determinate types that stop growing at a certain height.) Tomato plants that are permitted to sprawl will produce more fruit than plants that are pruned; but the fruit will be smaller, and much of it may rot on the damp ground. Unstaked fruit is also more subject to damage from slugs and other insects. When the foliage is dense, some fruit may be overlooked and allowed to rot unseen—a problem with tomato cages, too.

If you don't prune, your tomatoes will produce branches at each leaf node, and sometimes fruit cluster stems will extend to form additional branches. Whether you decide to train the plants or not, pinch off these fruit-cluster branches just beyond the cluster in order to channel all the nourishment from that stem into the fruit.

If you're training the vines to one stem, pinch out all side branches after they have produced one set of leaves. You should also remove any suckers arising from the root after the main stem has made sturdy growth. Tie the main stem to a sturdy stake, using a figure-eight twist so the twist tie or twine won't cut the stem. If you'd like to allow two or three stems to grow, let the branches on the first leaf nodes develop. Then tie each branch to its own stake.

Once you've begun pruning, you must do so every week throughout the growing season. If you start pruning and then stop, the tops of the plants will develop strongly, and many suckers will take the strength from the plants without providing much fruit.

Six weeks before the first expected frost in autumn, nip out all the growing tips, including those on the main stem. This will stop the vine from developing and permit the plant's nourishment to be concentrated on the maturing fruit. You can also prune out new blossoms after this date, since fruits that set late won't be large enough to use.

The biggest garden pest of tomatoes is

the tomato hornworm, a huge (up to 4½-inch), hungry, green caterpillar. Despite their size, hornworms are surprisingly hard to spot when they're camouflaged among tomato stems and foliage. Check your plants carefully—especially if something's been eating them—and handpick these pests if you find any.

Tomatoes are subject to many diseases. When selecting cultivars, look for the initials V, F, N, or T following the name, which indicate the cultivar's resistance to Verticillium wilt, Fusarium wilt, root knot nematodes, and tobacco mosaic virus, respectively. If the leaves on your plants are speckled or falling off, your tomatoes may be suffering from a leaf spot disease; pinch off the infected leaves, and spray the plants with compost tea.

HARVESTING

There's not much to say about harvesting tomatoes. Pick 'em when they're ripe, colored up fully, and smelling like tomatoes—and enjoy them. Yum!

CROW'S TIPS

If you're like me, you'll want to have a few plants just for fall use. That means by the time the first frost hits, they'll still be in prime condition and bearing top-quality fruit.

For this late crop, start seeds inside at least three weeks later than main-crop tomatoes, then set the young plants outside several weeks after the others. Or sow seed directly in the ground in May.

Whichever planting method you use, these plants will begin bearing later than those set out for mid-season, but well before the first frost. They'll still be vigorous vines when the plants of main-crop tomatoes are spent, and they'll be laden with good fruit that keeps better, too.

CROW'S PICKS

Everybody wants to have the first ripe tomato. But mid-season cultivars like 'Celebrity' and 'Better Boy' have many advantages. Their fruit is bigger, and their output per plant is far greater than that of early cultivars. They also stand up better under prolonged production. Their luxuriant foliage protects fruit from the sun and acts as a mulch during drought.

Late tomatoes like 'Burpee's Long Keeper' extend the harvest at the fall end. To be sure that yours do, protect the vines and fruit from the first frost with floating row covers, and green fruit may still ripen through Indian summer. If days are cool but not really cold, ripe fruit will stay in better condition on the vines than in the refrigerator. Continue to protect the plants at night if temperatures drop well below 40°F.

TURNIPS

If one plant can serve two purposes in the garden, so much the better. Turnips produce both a root crop for cooking and greens for fresh eating, and some cultivars mature as fast as radishes. In fact, it's possible to get three crops of turnips in the time it takes to get one crop of carrots.

SITE AND SOIL

Turnips appreciate a rich, loose soil that's high in organic matter, but they'll grow in just about anything. For normal soil, add 2 to 4 pounds of rock phosphate and 3 to 4 pounds of blood meal for every 100 square feet of planting bed. If the soil is naturally high in potassium, you can improve it further with a high-potash seaweed mulch. If

Turnip

it's deficient in potash, apply 8 to 9 pounds of greensand per 100 square feet.

PLANTING

Fresh turnip seed is very viable. Even a sparse sowing can mean laborious thinning. I sow about 1 seed to the inch and then thin to 3 inches. The seedlings make good greens but get tough as the roots start to develop rapidly. When the roots grow out enough to meet those of neighboring plants, thin every other plant for fresh eating. The remainder will be 6 inches apart, a spacing that is just right to mature well-cultivated roots in moist, rich ground.

CARE

The key to getting that sought-after mild turnip taste is planting at the proper time, frequent cultivation, and ample water. Grow turnips early and late, before May 15 and after August 15. Cool weather and moist conditions favor optimum production, though you can grow acceptable crops during the summer if you apply a thick mulch and provide plenty of water.

Turnips must grow fast or they get woody and bitter. Moisture, coupled with shallow cultivation, seems to promote fast growth. Make your first cultivation within a couple of days after the seedlings are up, and follow with a second immediately after the first thinning, and a third when harvesting roots from their 3-inch spacing. Frequent cultivation in the early stages not only takes care of weeds around the plants but also loosens the soil so the roots can expand easily.

The only pest that causes trouble for turnips is the root maggot. You can keep root maggots in check by using parasitic nematodes, a totally safe biological control. Unlike chemicals, which kill indiscriminately, parasitic nematodes only attack harmful insects.

CROW'S TIPS

Many large-growing turnip cultivars grow only to fill the space available, then stop. If you have extra room, broadcast seed over a prepared bed— some seed may be 6 inches apart; other seed, 2 inches apart. The plants with the wide spacing will grow up to 6 inches in diameter. The ones with the 2-inch spacing will grow to 2 inches in diameter. This self-limiting factor makes turnips an ideal crop for broadcast sowings where you want to use up all the available space.

CROW'S PICKS

As far as cultivars go, 'Purple Top White Globe' seems to be the tastiest and most dependable turnip under the widest range of conditions.

HARVESTING

For finest flavor, harvest turnip roots before they're mature, when they're still mild and tender. The mature roots tend to develop a tough skin and stronger flavor that's suitable for soups and stews. Eventually, the core will get woody, the skin will get thick and tough, and the roots will taste bitter.

WATERMELONS

Watermelons mean summer to me—wolfing down the refreshing red fruit, spitting seeds, or trying to pick a perfectly ripe melon from a field of contenders. If the large, red-fleshed cultivars aren't enough for you, there's an exciting range of less common but equally tasty types for you to try. If space is limited, grow a compact icebox type, like 'Sugar Baby'; you can even train them up trellises if you support the developing fruits with nets or slings. If exciting color is what you're after, try a yellow-fleshed cultivar like 'Gold Baby' or 'Golden Midget'. Or experiment with an heirloom cultivar such as 'Moon and Stars', which has unique yellow markings on a dark green background. Like muskmelons, watermelons need a long, frost-free growing season. They prefer hot weather and must have 80 to 120 days to mature.

SITE AND SOIL

Watermelons grow best on newly cleared, well-drained, sandy loam. If your soil is heavy clay, loosen it well before planting by tilling under compost or aged manure. The soil should be slightly acid to neutral, with a pH of 6.5 to 7.0. Use my heavy-feeder formula to prepare the soil for watermelons. (See page 96.)

PLANTING

For best results, start seeds indoors as you would for muskmelons. (See "Planting" in the Muskmelons entry on page 138.) A few days before setting the plants out, spread about 3 inches of composted manure over the entire area to be planted. Next, run the rotary tiller, as deeply as it will go, over the area a few times to work the manure in.

Set the watermelons, peat pots and all, in the ground so as not to disturb their roots. Plant the melons in rows spaced 4 feet apart. Water after planting, and keep watering for the next three or four days unless it rains.

CARE

When the vines start to run, it's time to mulch with several inches of straw. Mulch will keep the soil moist and protect developing fruits from soilborne rots. Rely on the mulch for weed control, too, since cultivation can injure shallow-rooted plants. Like its relatives, the watermelon has a shallow root system, so you should be careful even when hand-weeding.

Watermelons are thirsty plants—the melons themselves are 90 percent water. Normal rainfall in most areas provides enough moisture for watermelon plants as long as you mulch them. During long, dry stretches, irrigate every week to ten days to maintain steady growth. Soak the soil thoroughly, but don't use an overhead sprinkler since wet foliage is susceptible to leaf spot disease. Try running water through the furrows between hills, or use a soaker hose in each furrow.

Because the vines and fruit get so big, watermelons need lots of nutrients, too. Foliar-feed every two weeks with liquid seaweed to keep the plants growing rapidly.

The striped cucumber beetle is a common pest of watermelon. It goes after young seedlings before they get a strong start. One countermeasure is to cover the seedlings with floating row covers until they develop half a dozen leaves. Always remove the row covers before the first flowers open; otherwise, bees won't be able to pollinate the flowers, and you won't get any fruit for your efforts.

Watermelons are also subject to several diseases, including anthracnose and Fusarium wilt. Your best bet is to choose disease-resistant cultivars. Rotation on a three-year plan and good garden cleanup in the fall are also effective preventive measures.

HARVESTING

Harvest your watermelons when they're fully ripe and sweet. When a melon is ripe, the tendril near the stem turns dry and brown, and the stem itself becomes quite brittle. Thump the melon, listening for that ripe, hollow sound. An underripe melon won't be as sweet as a ripe one. After studying, thumping, and sampling a few, you will develop the knack of judging ripeness fairly accurately.

Until you get the knack, go by what I call "Crow's rule of thumb for harvesting watermelons": If in doubt, leave the melon on the vine for another day or two. One that's overripe will have a slightly mushy texture, but it will have better flavor than an underripe melon.

CROW'S TIPS

Watermelon vines require considerable space in which to sprawl, but even a small garden can accommodate a few hills. That's because you can interplant watermelons with other vegetables to make the best use of available space.

If your garden is small, space hills half as far apart as recommended, in a single row next to your potatoes, then train the vines to run into the potato patch. Since the potatoes are grown under a straw mulch and not cultivated, the watermelons can grow over them undisturbed. You can intercrop watermelons with any early low-growing vegetable. It's not a good idea to plant watermelons with corn, as is often done with pumpkins, because they need a lot of sunlight and the corn would shade them.

Fall Planting Schedule

Planting a fall and winter garden requires watching the calendar. Here's my sowing schedule for my garden, where the first fall frost strikes in October or November:

I sow Chinese cabbage and fennel about July 5, and lettuce a week or two later. For fall brassicas, I sow cabbage, broccoli, and cauliflower about July 15, and set the seedlings out four to six weeks after seeding time.

Carrots for the cold winter months are sown about August 1. I sow beets right in the bed about August 10. In most cases, I just reuse space left empty by early crops.

Most fall and winter vegetables should mature well before frost comes and growth stops. Lettuce, beets, cabbage, kale, chard, and Chinese cabbage may all be harvested and used when immature. Broccoli, cauliflower, and Brussels sprouts must head up before you can harvest them.

Remember to plant plenty for fall and winter harvests. In winter, when the choice is limited, quantity counts.

Vegetable Gardening— The Last Word

Of course, you won't be planting every one of these vegetables in your garden every year. I don't think I know of anyone who does. In fact, it's a good idea to set your sights low when starting out. Poll your family and find out just which of these vegetables they really want to eat fresh. Then start with those. As your successes mount and your menu expands, you can gradually work some of the more exotic entries into your garden.

If you have tough luck with a particular crop in any given year, don't give up on it. Try a different cultivar in a different spot with a different fertilizer regime, and you might be surprised at the results.

Above all, keep growing, keep experimenting, and keep observing and recording. Year by year, your garden—and your gardening skills—will just keep getting better.

11

Herbs for Many Uses

Don't get me wrong—I love vegetables and flowers. But for pure pleasure, herbs are hard to beat. Most of them smell good, and many of them taste good. But besides that, they look good. Herbs look great in my vegetable garden, where they attract pollinators to my plants. They also look great in a flower garden or all together in an herb garden.

The ways to enjoy herbs are almost endless. If you like to cook, experiment with herbs that have flavorful foliage. Tangy herb leaves spice up salads, sauces, and grilled meat and veggies like nothing else. Or perhaps you'd like to make your own herb teas. Some brews are regarded as general tonics;

others are said to ward off colds, aid digestion, or soothe jangled nerves. Every organic gardener should grow some aromatic herbs as bee attractants to increase fruit and vegetable yields.

It would be easy to write a whole book just about growing and using herbs. There are so many herbs out there that people sometimes get lost in the huge variety of choices available or get confused about how to use them in the garden and in the kitchen. So instead of trying to cover the whole world of herbs, I'd like to focus on a few of my favorites, which I've divided into categories according to how I use them.

CHIVES

Well, maybe chives (*Allium schoeno-prasum*) don't smell so great, unless you think of onions as fragrant. But they *look* great, with their 6- to 12-inch upright grassy foliage and purple pom-pom flowers. And they taste great—they're just right in a salad, or chopped and sprinkled on a baked potato.

You can buy chive plants or sow seed indoors in late winter and transplant seedlings to the garden in spring. Plant chives in full sun and rich, well-drained soil; space plants 5 to 8 inches apart. For more plants, divide clumps every three years in spring. Chives are perennial and are hardy (will overwinter) in USDA Plant Hardiness Zones 3–9—that's most of the country. (See the "USDA Plant Hardiness Zone Map" on page 366 to find your area and zone on the map.)

Garlic chives (*Allium tuberosum*) are perennials that are as beautiful as they are flavorful. Plants grow 8 to 12 inches tall and bear flowers on 1½- to 2-foot-tall stems in summer. The deep green straplike leaves add a garlicky flavor to salads and stir-fries. And the 2-inch-wide, starry white flower heads have a lovely tuberose fragrance—just don't cut them, or you'll smell the garlic from the stem! Garlic chives are hardy in Zones 4–8.

OREGANO

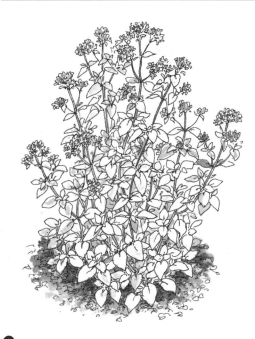

Oregano (*Origanum vulgare*) is a shrubby perennial. This highly scented herb is grown mainly for its spicy leaves, which are most

often used in salads and Italian cooking. The tiny white or pink flowers are very attractive to bees. For the best flavor, look for Greek oregano (*O. heracleoticum*, also called *O. vulgare* subsp. *hirtum*).

The plants, which eventually reach 12 to 30 inches tall, can be started from seed, but for consistent flavor, I recommend buying plants. Grow in well-drained soil in full sun. You can divide oregano if you need additional plants. Oregano is hardy in Zones 5–9.

PARSLEY

Many gardeners overlook the ornamental aspect of parsley (*Petroselinum crispum*), but this herb looks as good in perennial borders as it does in the vegetable garden. Although it is often treated as an annual, parsley is really a biennial. It grows a mass of crisp green leaves the first year, winters over in milder climates or where protected with mulch, then bolts to seed soon after it resumes growth the next spring—unless you take steps to stop it.

If you have difficulty getting a good stand of parsley in your garden, don't blame the seed or your soil. Chances are, you aren't giving it an early enough start. Parsley demands very cool temperatures for good germination. This requirement often creates a problem in gardens that can't be worked in early spring.

To avoid disappointment, try sowing parsley in October. Fall

plantings have two advantages over spring sowings. First, if the seed is planted in late fall, it will be able to sprout in spring as soon as conditions are favorable. Second, the alternate thawing and freezing of the soil throughout the winter softens the hard seed hulls, thus greatly increasing the percentage of germination. Of course, you can also buy parsley plants at a garden center.

Parsley is about the most versatile herb I know. Once the plants become established, they can withstand extremes of both heat and cold. This herb thrives in any soil that is well fortified with organic matter. Rich, sandy loams are excellent for parsley.

Parsley requires very little attention once it's up and growing. To retain moisture and to cut down on weeding, mulch your beds with straw as soon as the plants are tall enough. To keep the leaves nice and green, spray them with a micronutrient-rich foliar feed like liquid seaweed or compost tea every five weeks.

You can preserve your outdoor planting from the first season to the second by mulching the bed heavily with straw or leaves after the weather turns cold but before the ground freezes hard. Remove this mulch as early in spring as possible so that the plants can resume growth.

To keep your second year's stand growing, remove the seed heads as soon as they appear. (I just swat off the topgrowth with a sickle right before the seed heads form.) This encourages fresh new growth from the roots.

It's always a pleasure to have fresh parsley around the house in the winter—it has a way of driving out those winter blues. So I transplant three plants into a large flowerpot about the middle of August. After cutting off two-thirds of the topgrowth, I give the plants a good watering, then sink pot and all in a cool, partially shaded area. When cold weather hits, I bring the pot in and place it in a south-facing window. You can also keep potted parsley in a well-protected cold frame or in the greenhouse.

Because parsley is so high in health-giving vitamins, I think it should be grown in *every* garden and used as much as possible in foods. It's great in salads or with carrots and potatoes. Once you've gotten into the habit of using this herb, you will never be without it. Parsley is hardy in Zones 5–9.

ROSEMARY

Rosemary (*Rosmarinus officinalis*) is a great plant for herb gardens, containers, and hanging baskets. The upright form, with its incredibly fragrant needlelike leaves, looks like a little pine tree. There are many cultivars to choose from. Plants bear tiny pale blue, pink, or white flowers. If you'd like to try growing rosemary in a hanging basket, choose the prostrate cultivar (*R. officinalis* 'Prostratus'), which will trail nicely over the edge of the pot.

Rosemary grows best in full sun and average soil. You can sow seeds indoors in early spring and transplant seedlings to the garden, or buy plants. Set plants 3 feet apart. (If you want to grow cultivars, always buy plants, since cultivars don't come true from seed.)

Rosemary is a tender perennial that can form a large bush (reaching 6 feet!) in warm-winter areas (Zones 7–10). Farther north, where plants seldom grow taller than 2 feet, overwinter rosemary indoors or take cuttings in the fall to start new plants.

Use the fragrant leaves of rosemary to add a pungent flavor to salads, roasted meats, and soups. Dried leaves also add a piney fragrance to potpourris and sachets.

SAGE

The ancients held sage (*Salvia officinalis*) in the highest esteem as a medicinal herb. Today, it's grown as a seasoning herb and an ornamental. The thick, straplike leaves come in many colors, including variegated cultivars with yellow and green leaves ('Aurea') and purple, white, and green foliage ('Tricolor'). Sage leaves make a strong-flavored tea that is really enjoyable when the weather is cold. It seems to have a stimulating effect. Sage has bee-attracting pink, purple, or white flowers.

Sage

It's easy to start sage from spring-sown seed. (Buy plants of the cultivars since they won't come true from seed.) Allow 3 feet between your sage plants, which need ample sunshine and well-drained soil of average fertility to thrive.

If your sage plant has blossomed during summer, you can gather seed from it in late fall. Cut off the flowering branches and shake them over a pan, and the large, dark brown seeds will drop out. Make sure they're dry, then save them for spring sowing. Sage is hardy in Zones 4–8.

Pineapple sage (*S. elegans*) is a great garden plant. It grows 24 to 42 inches tall, with dark green leaves that smell like pineapple, and it has stunning tubular red flowers. This species of sage is grown as an ornamental rather than an herb, and it's a wonderful plant for attracting hummingbirds and butterflies.

Pineapple sage is a tender perennial that's usually treated like an annual. It's one of the first plants to die in the fall. But I've got a trick so I don't have to buy new plants each year. To obtain more plants and hold them throughout the winter, I cut small stems and place them in a vase of water, where they root easily. As a result, I have nice little plants in the winter to pot and hold over until they can go into the garden.

Clary (*S. sclarea*) is another of my favorite sages. It can reach 5 feet tall and bears stalks of beautiful lavender flowers. You can use the aromatic foliage just like garden sage. Grow clary in full sun. This species is hardy in Zones 4–7.

SWEET BASIL

I can't imagine my vegetable or herb garden without at least some sweet basil (*Ocimum basilicum*). It's the classic complement to any tomato dish, and sweet basil and tomatoes are good garden companions.

There are several different species and lots of cultivars available, and many are ornamental in the garden. 'Dark Opal' and 'Purple Ruffles' have purple leaves that "spice up" the garden and can be used to make beautiful pink herb vinegars. 'Spicy Globe' produces a compact mound of small but flavorful bright green leaves, making it a perfect choice for the edges of a bed or front of a border. And lemon basil ('Citriodorum') adds a lemon tang to the basil flavor.

Basil grows best in full sun and rich, moist soil. This bushy plant grows 1 to 2 feet tall and about 18 inches wide. Sow seeds indoors in spring and transplant them after all danger of frost is past, or sow outdoors when temperatures are reliably warm. Thin plants to 1 foot apart. You can also buy and plant bedding plants.

Harvest the aromatic leaves as needed for salads, pesto, and tomato sauce. To keep the leaves growing vigorously, cut off the flower heads as soon as they form. Basil is an annual, so when the first frost is predicted, harvest the entire plant, strip off the leaves, and freeze them for best flavor. One neat trick is to freeze chopped leaves in an ice cube tray full of water; pop the frozen basil cubes into a freezer bag and use them as needed.

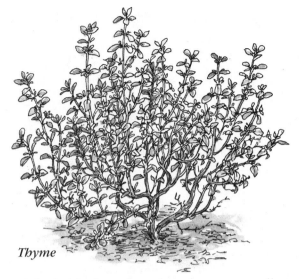

Thyme

THYME

There are about 50 different species of thyme (*Thymus* spp.). And there are probably just as many ways to use it, from landscape accent to soothing tea to cooking spice. For most of us, though, a few of the most common species will provide plenty of variety.

The first and most popular is common thyme (*Thymus vulgaris*). It is a rather woody perennial, with small leaves and a more upright habit than the other thymes, usually growing about 8 inches tall. It's what you're most likely to end up with if you buy a packet of seeds simply marked "Thyme," with no indication of species.

Another type is mother-of-thyme or creeping thyme (*T. praecox* subsp. *arcticus*). This one has a low-lying habit—it hugs the ground closely and sends out roots along the stem where it touches the soil. The plant won't grow much taller than a few inches and makes an attractive groundcover, especially when it's covered with twinkling white, red, or purple flowers.

A third thyme that I enjoy is the small-leaved lemon thyme (*T.* × *citriodorus*), named for its lemony fragrance. It, too, is a rather sprawling plant (though it can reach 1 foot), with wiry, yet woody stems. Lemon thyme must be grown from plants or cuttings, since it won't come true from seed.

Thyme does best where it can receive full sun most of the day. It will grow in a shadier spot, but don't expect it to be as full and healthy as it normally would. As for soil, thyme has a decided preference for well-drained sites. Aside from that, it isn't particular about soil and will even grow in dry, gravelly spots that wouldn't support many other plants.

When selecting a location, keep in mind that bees have a strong affinity for thyme. So plant thyme near tomatoes, melons, cucumbers, fruit trees, and other plants that need to be pollinated in order to set fruit.

Regardless of where you decide to plant them, thyme seeds should be sown outdoors after the last frost, or four to six weeks ahead of time in your greenhouse. Seeds germinate in two to three weeks. When the plants are a few inches tall, you can thin them to stand about 12 inches apart. You can also plant stem cuttings or divisions from a mature plant. However you plant thyme, be sure to keep the soil moist until the plants are established.

You can use thyme fresh, as needed throughout the season, but the best time to harvest it in quantity is when the plant is in full bloom. Cut it back to one-third of its former height (preferably in the morning, after the dew has dried from the leaves), gather the stems into small bunches, and tie them at the base with string. Hang them upside down in a warm, shady, well-ventilated room to dry. Since thyme has such small leaves, drying seldom takes more than a few days. When the stems and leaves are without any trace of moisture and are brittle to the touch, strip off the leaves and store them in airtight containers to use during the winter.

If any herb ever deserved a little space in your garden, thyme is it. It's easy to grow, beautiful to look at, a beekeeper's delight, and a delicious seasoning.

HERBS WITH EDIBLE SEEDS

CARAWAY

Caraway (*Carum carvi*) is a 2- to 3-foot-tall biennial with feathery foliage that remains green most of the year here on Long Island. Although most folks grow caraway for its seeds, I find it to be a very valuable green in late fall and early spring. I use the licorice-flavored leaves to add zest to salads.

Caraway does best in loamy soil and full sun or partial shade. To avoid disturbing the long taproots, plant in early spring and sow the seed directly in the garden. Thin to 8 to 12 inches apart.

During the first year, only carrotlike greens will appear. The following year, white flower umbels form. Shortly, the crescent-shaped brown seeds will mature, then the entire plant dies. Ripe seeds must be harvested before they fall, but a few seeds are bound to escape and self-sow. Caraway is hardy in Zones 3–7.

CORIANDER

DILL

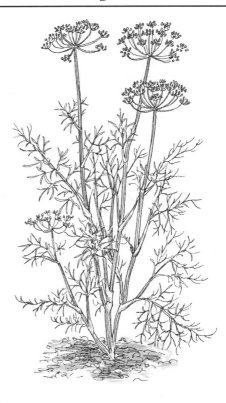

Coriander (*Coriandrum sativum*), an annual that grows 2 to 3 feet tall, is often scorned because of the extremely pungent scent of the fresh greens. (Also known as cilantro or Chinese parsley, these same leaves are an integral ingredient in Mexican cooking—they're what gives a good salsa its distinctive flavor.) Surprisingly, when dried, the leaves emit a pleasant, clean-smelling scent reminiscent of lemons. But coriander is most often grown for its seeds, which are used in pastries, sausage, and pickling.

To start coriander, sow seeds shallowly in early spring. Seed germinates easily in about two weeks. For best results, grow coriander in a light, well-drained soil in full sun. Thin plants 8 to 10 inches apart. When in bloom, the umbels of tiny pinkish white flowers make a welcome garden addition. Pick the leaves as needed for fresh use. If you are growing coriander for its seeds, watch the seed heads and harvest when the seeds turn from green to brown.

Dill (*Anethum graveolens*) is grown for its fresh foliage as well as the seeds that form on large yellow-flowered umbels. Dill weed is delicious in soups, bread, and salads. Besides being the quintessential pickling herb, dill seed makes a nice tea. (Do *not* drink dill tea if you're pregnant, though.)

Dill seed, which remains viable for three years, germinates in one to two weeks. For fresh dill all summer, make successive sowings from mid-April until the end of May. Sow at two-week intervals in a sunny site with well-drained, fairly good soil. When planted in single rows, this 3- to 4-foot-tall annual tends to fall over, so I plant in patches. Harvest the seeds before the heads can shatter, and leave a few to self-sow.

FENNEL

Fennel (*Foeniculum vulgare*) is a 5-foot-tall perennial with lovely ferny foliage similar to dill's. However, the plant is bushier and more branched at the base than dill, and the leaves smell like licorice. Because of this fullness and the delicate yellow-green leaves topped by numerous umbels of tiny gold flowers, fennel makes an attractive background plant in a border. There are even fennels with purple foliage, usually sold as "bronze-leaved fennel." Fennel flowers will attract many beneficial insects to your garden.

Fennel may live for years. Sow seed in a permanent location since fennel transplants poorly. Plant in spring in a sunny site with light, well-drained soil. Thin plants to 12 to 18 inches apart. Harvest the licorice-flavored seeds before the heads shatter, and use them in cookies, cakes, and other baked goods. Fennel seeds are also good in salads and with steamed vegetables. Hardy in Zones 6–9.

HERBS FOR TEA

CATNIP

This 2- to 3-foot-tall hardy perennial herb has triangular, mintlike leaves and tiny lavender flowers. You can buy plants of catnip (*Nepeta cataria*) or grow it from seed planted in early spring. Give plants a rich, moist soil and space them 18 inches apart. Don't let them go to seed, or the plants will be weakened and you'll have seedlings all over the garden.

Cats love this herb, of course—and so do people. Dry the leaves and steep them in hot water to make a delightful, soothing tea. Catnip is hardy in Zones 4–9.

GERMAN CHAMOMILE

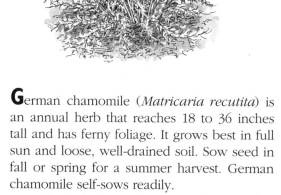

German chamomile (*Matricaria recutita*) is an annual herb that reaches 18 to 36 inches tall and has ferny foliage. It grows best in full sun and loose, well-drained soil. Sow seed in fall or spring for a summer harvest. German chamomile self-sows readily.

The little button flowers make a tea that is said to be calming. They have a yellow center surrounded by white petals, much like a small daisy.

MINT

If there's a more vigorous plant in the garden than mint (*Mentha* spp.), I'd like to see it. Mints are 1- to 3-foot-tall hardy perennials. They grow so rampantly that they often have to be contained to prevent them from overrunning the garden.

Mint plants are characterized by square stems and pointed, deeply veined leaves. Bees are attracted to the spikes of tiny white or pastel blooms. Gardeners are attracted to the cool, refreshing scent. There are many popular cultivars and species of mints, with scents ranging from peppermint and spearmint to pineapple, apple, and even chocolate. The leaves of all mints can be dried and steeped to make refreshing teas.

Plant cuttings or plants of mint in spring or fall. Give them a site with moist, well-drained soil and full sun or partial shade. If you don't confine your plants in bottomless metal cylinders, they'll quickly form a mint patch, with new plants growing from the creeping roots. So if you're not willing to fool with the cylinders, I advise planting mint in an isolated spot where it won't invade the rest of the garden. You can also keep mint in check by growing it in containers. Mints are hardy in Zones 5–9.

AROMATIC HERBS FOR BEES

BEE BALM

Although bee balm (*Monarda didyma*) is grown primarily as an ornamental in the perennial garden, it was once grown for its citrusy leaves, which were used to make tea. And, as its name suggests, it's a powerful attractant to bees—hummingbirds, too!

Bee balm, which reaches 3 to 4 feet tall and grows in bushy clumps, is an eye-catching plant in the perennial border. In early summer, plants sport 2-inch-wide, double, scarlet flowers that look like upside-down mop heads. Some cultivars have pink, violet, or white flowers.

Plants started from seed seldom grow true to the mother plant (especially if it's a cultivar) and take years to bloom. Buy plants or take a start from a neighbor.

Every few years, you can increase the number of plants by division. When dividing bee balm, dig up the clump, then cut it into sections with a sharp spade. Replant only the outer roots, and discard the older, woody inner portions.

Space plants 2 feet apart in a sunny location. If grown too close together, bee balm plants are often troubled by mildew. If mildew has been a problem in your garden, try a resistant cultivar like hot pink 'Marshall's Delight'. Bee balm is hardy in Zones 4–9.

BORAGE

Bees love borage (*Borago officinalis*). They swarm around the small, purple, star-shaped flowers of this hardy annual. Once you plant a packet of borage seed, you'll have borage forever. Although it's not a perennial, it self-sows year after year. (See "Volunteer Herbs" on page 194.) Sow seeds in a dry, sunny site, and thin plants to stand 18 inches apart.

Borage is an attractive plant in the landscape, with flower stalks reaching 2 to 3 feet tall and mounds of silver-green leaves. And its pretty, delicate flowers can be added to salads and to drinks like lemonade and iced tea.

LEMON BALM

Another minty-looking plant, lemon balm (*Melissa officinalis*) is named for the tangy, citrusy scent and taste of its leaves. The small flowers of this perennial attract bees and are even said to calm them.

To start lemon balm, order plants for spring delivery. You can also take cuttings or divide an older plant in spring or fall. Lemon balm is not the slightest bit fussy about soil, although it makes a more handsome plant if the soil is rich and well watered.

Set plants 2 feet apart in either partial shade or full sun. They will grow 1 to 2 feet tall. You can harvest the glossy leaves several times each year for potpourri or to dry for a fragrant tea. Lemon balm is hardy in Zones 4–9.

PENNYROYAL

Pennyroyal (*Mentha pulegium*), often called English pennyroyal to distinguish it from a native wild herb, is a strong-flavored mint that's easy to grow from seed either indoors or out. This small-leaved groundcover grows no taller than 1 foot and bears purple flowers in summer. Plant pennyroyal in early spring. Give it a site with moist, humus-rich soil and full sun.

Harvest pennyroyal before it blooms. Mature plants can be dried easily by hanging up the leafy stems. Although bees enjoy this herb, other insects don't. If you make pennyroyal tea, you can use it as an insect repellent—just swab the cooled brew on your arms and legs before heading outside. You'll smell great, too! Pennyroyal is hardy in Zones 5–9.

☀ Volunteer Herbs

Many herbs self-sow with ease, "volunteering" in your garden. Herb volunteers are a great low-work way to keep annual herbs coming back year after year without having to buy and sow seed every time.

Borage is one annual herb that can't wait to volunteer. Once you've sown it in your garden, it will probably be there forever. Borage drops dozens of black seeds, and almost as many seedlings come up. But don't think of volunteer borage as a nuisance. Clumps of 3-foot-tall, blue-flowered borage here and there in a vegetable garden are a colorful sight. But to keep your garden from being overrun by borage, don't let more than three plants go to seed.

Dill is another herb that you only need to sow once. After that, new plants will come up on their own each spring. In fact, dill plants grow so quickly, they often self-sow twice in one year. You can let quite a few of them go to seed, but thin the seedlings diligently. The plants, which can grow 3 to 4 feet tall, need plenty of room to mature. Dill is killed by frost.

Chives also self-sow readily. But take care—one plant will produce dozens of seedlings. Although the lavender pom-poms of chives and the starry white flower heads of garlic chives add color to the garden, you should cut off most of the stalks before they go to seed. I use the excess seedlings, which are flavorful and tender, as salad greens.

Of course, even volunteer herb seeds need good garden conditions to sprout and grow. They won't come up well in bare, exposed ground. You'll get the best results if your site is lightly mulched. (A thick mulch will keep the seeds from sprouting.) Keep the soil evenly moist, and don't disturb it by digging or tilling.

❧ ⋯⋯⋯⋯⋯ PUNGENT LANDSCAPE HERBS ⋯⋯⋯⋯⋯ ❧

LAVENDER

This shrublike, woody member of the mint family derives its name from the Latin word *laver*, meaning "to wash." That's because it was used in ancient times to scent baths. There are several species and many cultivars of lavender (*Lavandula* spp.), each lovely in itself. English lavender (*L. angustifolia*) is the hardiest, and it's the species I've found most reliable.

Lavender grows from 1½ to 3 feet tall and sports narrow, gray-green leaves that are about 2 inches long. The tall, slender spikes of lavender-to-purple flowers make a lovely specimen shrub fit for an emperor's courtyard.

For an appealing accent, place one plant of lavender where it can grow unhindered and show off its bright flowers all summer. For a purely decorative effect, plant in groups of three to five among your perennial flowers, or tuck a plant here and there near steps, walks, or doorways. In England, lavender is planted in lavish beds, masses, and hedges.

Dry lavender flowerstalks to use in sachet bags, or scatter loose leaves lightly through linens for a lovely fragrance. Crush some in your hands and toss them into the tub for a refreshing bath. You can make a luxurious lavender oil by hanging small clusters, with stems and leaves downward, in a big bottle of unscented oil and placing it in full sun for several weeks.

You can buy plants or sow lavender from seed. If you find it difficult to start in flats or peat pots, try sowing seeds outdoors in early spring after the ground has warmed. Plants prefer a well-drained, limy soil and a sunny spot.

Wet the soil lightly to hasten germination, and sow seeds $\frac{1}{4}$ inch deep. Then cover the seedbed with floating row covers or plastic held in place by stakes set along the row. Weigh down the edges with rocks as an extra precaution against winds and heavy rains. To provide shade for the tiny seedlings and to retain moisture, leave the cover on even after the seeds have sprouted. Seeds are slow to germinate, so if tiny traces of green do not appear right away, don't give up.

When the seedlings are sturdy and all danger of frost has passed, remove the cover and transplant them to their permanent sunny location in the herb patch. To get the most fragrance from lavender, provide a poor soil rather than an overly rich one. A mulch will protect against winterkill in areas with relatively mild winters, but if you want to be doubly sure, bring two or three prize specimens inside to spend the winter on a sunny windowsill.

You can take lavender cuttings in spring. Snip off pieces about 3 inches long and set them into wet sand. Keep the new plants in partial shade the first year, then move them to their permanent locations the following season. Hardy in Zones 5–8.

SOUTHERNWOOD

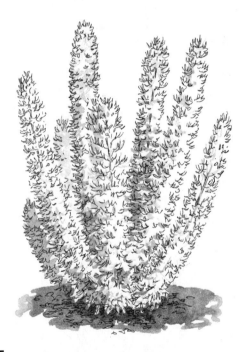

From earliest times, southernwood (*Artemisia abrotanum*) has been grown to repel insects. But even if you don't grow southernwood as a repellant, this herb earns its keep with its distinctive aroma and attractive appearance. The stately plants send up 3- to 6-foot plumes of feathery foliage. They bear inconspicuous flowers in late summer.

Plant southernwood in full sun and well-drained soil. Plant cuttings 2 to 4 feet apart or divide plants in spring or fall.

You don't need to cut southernwood back severely to harvest it for moth bags or insect sprays. Wait until the foliage is at its height in August. Then prune your bushes to shape them as you gather material.

A well-shaped southernwood is an asset to any organic garden. The plants are nearly evergreen, and will still look colorful after frost has blackened other plants. Southernwood is hardy in Zones 4–8.

TANSY

Tansy (*Tanacetum vulgare*) is commonly used as an ornamental for the back of the perennial flower bed. Country folks have long believed that tansy planted next to the foundation of a house will keep ants out, and that dried tansy scattered where ants congregate will send them away.

Plants grow 3 to 5 feet tall and have very nice flower heads with dozens of little yellow buttons in summer. These dry well and are attractive in both fresh and dried flower arrangements. The long, fernlike aromatic leaves are nicely scalloped and curled. Their rich dark green color is a nice foil for the gray-green of wormwood.

Sow tansy seed indoors in late winter for spring transplanting. Plant in full sun to partial shade and in well-drained soil, spacing plants 4 feet apart. Plants may need staking or other support. You can divide tansy in spring or fall. Unfortunately, this plant has a bad habit of spreading in an ungainly manner. To control this growth, pull up the runners in spring. Tansy is hardy in Zones 4–8.

A species called curly tansy (*T. crispum*) is available from most herb nurseries and may be a better choice for small gardens. The plant grows only 2 feet or so, and bears flowers similar to those of the common tansy. The edges of the leaves have a nice wavy appearance.

YARROW

Yarrow (*Achillea millefolium*) is a useful perennial herb and also a common meadow weed. It keeps bugs at bay and makes a superior tonic for coughs and colds. And yarrow is a beautiful plant in the landscape.

This herb has different names, but it is best known as yarrow, milfoil, or thousandleaf. The ancients used it in medicine and magic. Today, yarrow is grown primarily for its beautiful foliage and flowers.

What first attracted me to this plant were its summer-flowering heads in a rainbow of pastels, its very finely divided fernlike leaves, and its pungent aroma. Once you see it and smell it, you will recognize it for the rest of your life. Some people get yarrow confused with Queen-Anne's-lace because of the similarity in the flowering heads, but Queen-Anne's-lace doesn't have a strong smell or fernlike leaves.

Yarrow is invaluable as a companion plant in the garden. According to biodynamic principles, it makes other herbs stronger. If you'd like to test that theory, plant yarrow in the same bed with mint, chives, thyme, parsley, basil, oregano, or other culinary and tea herbs. It is also believed that when yarrow is planted among vegetables, it makes them more flavorful.

Some organic gardeners have found yarrow helpful in the battle against insects. No one knows what triggers this beneficial effect, but yarrow does contain several chemical substances.

Others use yarrow as a home remedy to cure an oncoming cold or cough. They make a yarrow tea by stripping off all of the leaves and steeping them in a teapot for approximately 15 minutes. The stronger the tea, the better. The taste may be less than great, but a cup every three hours, along with a clove or two of garlic and some lemon juice, is said to do the job. (Don't try this until you're sure you're not allergic to yarrow.)

If you'd like to transplant a few wild plants, divide the roots in early spring and relocate them to a sunny, well-drained spot in your garden. You can plant yarrow anytime as long as you keep the soil moist until the plants settle in. If you'd like to grow one of the many beautiful cultivars of yarrow, buy plants either at a garden center or by mail order. (You'll find them in perennial catalogs.)

Yarrow thrives in adverse conditions, including poor soil, partial shade, and bad handling. Only the cultivars need a bit more than minimal care—they prefer moderately rich, well-drained soil in full sun. Yarrow is hardy in Zones 2–8.

Yarrow

Winter Protection for Herb Beds

There's nothing like a permanent mulch to keep an herb garden happy. In summer, the mulch conserves moisture, keeps the foliage clean, and holds down weeds. In winter, this same mulch helps maintain a uniform temperature around plant roots and provides protection against heaving caused by frequent freezing and thawing of the soil. To my mind, the best all-around mulch for herbs is straw. It's light, it's weed-free, and it looks good—always a consideration in the herb garden.

During your early herb-growing years, you might become anxious in autumn and harvest as much as you can just before the first frost. Don't. Late harvesting prompts the plants to put out a spurt of rapid, tender growth just before winter, which in turn makes them prime candidates for winterkill. My rule is to stop all major harvesting about one month before the first expected killing frost.

THE TOUGH AND THE TENDER

The following herbs should fare well down to temperatures as low as −20°F, with no more protection than a few inches of mulch around their base: bee balm, caraway, catnip, chives, comfrey, lemon balm, mints, oregano, rue, sage, southernwood, tansy, thyme, wormwood, and yarrow. After an extra-severe winter, a few of these—such as rue, sage, southernwood, and common thyme—may appear brown and dead. But in time, new growth should appear.

Harsh, drying winter winds can prove as fatal as cold temperatures to some of the more tender perennial herbs. Windbreaks are lifesavers for many herbs that don't take kindly to below-zero temperatures. Herbs that need protection from the icy winds of winter are English lavender, English pennyroyal, lemon verbena, Roman chamomile, and rosemary.

Rosemary and lemon verbena are normally treated as tender perennials and moved inside before the first frost. Under certain conditions, however, I've seen rosemary survive winters here on Long Island. Lemon verbena, on the other hand, is not only tender, it's a perennial shrub—it's deciduous and will lose its leaves while wintering inside.

Some species of creeping thyme can withstand −20°F temperatures. But others, like silver and lemon thyme, may need to be covered with a few evergreen boughs to prevent them from drying over the winter.

OVERWINTERING RULES

Here are a few of "Crow's Rules of the Road" to help see perennial herbs through cold winters:

♣ Obtain plants raised in a climate as cold or colder than the one they will grow in, to make sure that you have the hardiest possible stock.

♣ The more cold-sensitive herbs have a better chance of surviving the winter if you give them a sheltered spot in your garden.

♣ Most herbs demand a well-drained soil and, if subjected to heavy damp soils, may perish from rot or mildew damage over winter. Keep in mind that slopes or rocky sites usually have good drainage. Amend poorly drained soil by tilling in lots of organic matter and making it lighter.

♣ If you have only damp, poorly drained soil for your herb garden, choose herbs that will adapt to it, such as bee balm, mints, and pennyroyal.

Follow my guidelines, and get ready to sit back and enjoy a gardenful of herbs.

PART IV

Let's Grow Fruits and Berries

12

Fruit-Growing Basics

Even with all the vegetables I grow, my garden just isn't complete without including organic fruits. I harvest fresh organic vegetables all season long—why not fresh fruits, too?

Fruit growing is easier (and takes up less space) than most people think. The hardest part is choosing which fruit to start with. With such a variety of fruits suited for the small home landscape, all it takes is planning and timing. If you grow five to seven kinds of fruit and plant cultivars of each fruit that ripen at different times, you can stretch the harvest from early summer to late fall.

Make Room for Fruits

What? You say you don't have room for fruit trees? Nonsense! If you can find 20 sunny square feet, then you have room for dwarf apples, pears, peaches, or apricots. Dwarf trees are a real godsend for the home gardener. They produce much sooner than old-fashioned standard trees. And they can be planted, mulched, pruned, and harvested with less effort, time, and money. You can grow a dozen dwarf fruit trees in a 150-square-foot area. And that's not a lot of room, even in modest-sized gardens.

Take a tip from me: If you're going to go to the trouble of growing fruit, don't plant just one cultivar of fruit tree. Plant an early and late cultivar of each different type of fruit you grow. That way, you'll double the season you can expect from a single kind of fruit. For some fruits, you'll extend the picking even further than that.

If you're still nervous about the idea of raising fruit trees, start with something a little less demanding: berries. They require less space, yield earlier, and are usually less troubled by insects and diseases than the fruit trees. It's easier to find room for berries, too, because they're smaller plants and much more easily trained and confined than even the smallest dwarf fruit trees.

Finally, if your yard seems too small for any fruit, look again. Think of fruit trees, grape vines, and berry bushes as landscape features. Blueberries, for example, are handsome shrubs that can stand alone or form a hedge. Dwarf fruit trees can be squeezed to fit in a narrow space along a driveway or a property line. Grapes on an arbor create inviting shade over a patio. You can even grow blueberries and some peach, plum, and apricot cultivars in containers on your deck or patio.

You really don't need a lot of bushes or trees to pick a lot of fruit. A single blueberry bush at maturity yields up to 15 quarts of fruit and occupies only a 4-foot circle. A dwarf apple tree needs just an 8-foot circle and easily yields two bushels of fruit each year.

The Natural Orchard

If you have the room, I think it makes sense to keep all of your fruit trees and bushes together in a home orchard. That's the way we do it here at Spring Meadow. By concentrating the fruit in one area, we can enrich the soil intensively in a small planting and give each plant plenty of nourishment. Also, we find ourselves visiting the planting area often, tying up canes and thinning the fruit. And since we can inspect and clean up all the plants in one place, we're more likely to stay ahead of pests.

Getting off to the right start is even more critical with fruit than it is with vegetables. True, it takes discipline and foresight to spend time working on a crop that won't come to fruition for three, five, or even ten years, but the investment will pay off in a big way.

SITING YOUR ORCHARD

Before you do anything else, consider the location of the orchard. Sloping land is best because it offers natural air and water drainage. Cold air and blossom-killing frosts move down slopes, away from tender fruit trees. Water on sloping land moves freely, too, which means it won't waterlog the soil and cut off the supply of air to roots.

Soil is also an important consideration. The best soil for growing fruit is a deep, well-drained loam. If the drainage and tilth are good, test the soil for deficiencies and amend as needed. But if the prospective orchard site is poorly drained or in a frost pocket, don't waste time and money on it.

SETTING UP

For best results, you should start working the orchard site well in advance. Till it thoroughly and sow a green manure crop a year before planting your young fruit trees. Sow buckwheat in the summer or winter rye in the fall. (See Chapter 4 for information on green manures.)

Let the green manure grow to full maturity, then till it down and plant your trees. After planting, keep the area within a 5-foot radius of each tree trunk mulched and weed-free. You can then seed the rest of the orchard with a permanent grass cover. Bluegrass, fescue, and clover are the best mixture.

Mulch is a must in my orchard, and it should be in yours, too. I use mulch as a weed deterrent, soil builder, and moisture conserver all in one. I lay it down thickly—6 to 8 inches deep—keeping it a foot or two from the trunk of each tree and extending it out past the drip line where the feeding roots are. I like straw mulch best; if applied heavily every year, it can supply a lot of the nutrients a growing tree needs.

You don't have to have an orchard to grow fruit trees and bushes. Think about ways to incorporate fruit in your landscape. A blueberry hedge, a grape arbor, and apples or pears grown as shade trees are all ways to make fruit a part of your yard.

PRUNING

Everything I've said about site, soil, green manuring, and mulch may sound fairly familiar to you if you're a vegetable grower. Now we come to the mysterious element that scares more people away from fruit growing than any other: pruning.

Pruning *does* require some practice for sure. Young trees and mature trees require different types of pruning. Most young fruit trees should be trained to a central leader (one main trunk) with well-spaced lateral (side) branches. Older trees must be thinned out to allow sun and air to reach every part of the tree.

In general, pruning requires mastery of just a few straightforward techniques. For a discussion of the slightly different pruning practices recommended for different types of trees, see Chapter 13.

PEST AND DISEASE CONTROL

If you're thinking about growing fruit organically, the experienced orchardist may tell you, "It can't be done, period! If the insects don't defoliate the trees and deface the fruit, disease will." Sure, this might be true if you suddenly stopped using pesticides in chemically dependent orchards. Without poisons, the trees would be in sad shape because the soil they live in is dead.

But today, fruit trees are being grown successfully in organic orchards throughout the country. These organic growers know how to keep their soil healthy and to follow the basic principles of natural pest and disease control.

Cleaning Up

The most important step in halting the spread of disease and insect pests is to eliminate all their sources. That means removing infected fruit, twigs, and leaves from the orchard.

For example, apple scab, the worst fungal disease of apples, is spread to new growth in the spring from last year's leaves that have fallen to the ground. All winter, the spores lie dormant, ready to be released by rain and warm temperatures in the spring. By removing leaves after they've fallen, you are eliminating the source of infection. Although scab fungus may still find its way in from other apple trees in your area, there's much less chance of finding the right conditions to attack your trees.

Every fall, I make sure I take the time to clear out all fallen fruit, prunings, loose scaly bark on older trees, and any other possible sources of infection. Only by following extremely cautious sanitation practices can you stop insects and diseases from starting up in your orchard.

Controls

Even so, diseases and insects may find their way into your organic planting. If they do, there are several natural substances that you can apply safely.

Black spots on the leaves, for example, are an indication of fungal infection and can be treated with an organic spray of sulfur or bordeaux mix. I make my own bordeaux spray by mixing 4 pounds of copper sulfate, 4 pounds of hydrated lime, and 50 gallons of water. (You can adjust the quantities to make as much or as little spray as you need.) Then I thoroughly drench the leaves of the infected trees with the mixture as soon as the spots appear. Bordeaux mix controls many fungal diseases, but it can also burn plant leaves. To avoid damaging your plants, don't spray when temperatures are below 50°F or when humidity is high.

Actually, sunlight may be the most effective fungicide. So I always plant my trees in the sunniest spots and prune to keep the shape open.

How about controlling

bugs? *Bacillus thuringiensis* (BT) is a wettable powder that kills leaf-eating caterpillars, including gypsy moths. Insects that ingest BT stop eating in two hours and die in three days.

Dormant oil is another organic control. It's such a useful insecticide that even chemically inclined orchardists use it regularly. This oil-and-water mixture can be applied to fruit trees before any signs of growth (like bud swell) appear in the spring. Once applied, it smothers overwintering pests such as mites, scales, and fruit moths. There's also a lightweight summer oil that you can apply even when the trees are actively growing.

Finally, I make sure I treat my plants regularly with a liquid seaweed spray like Seacure. Seaweed helps fight diseases and pests by maintaining maximum plant vigor.

There's a whole world of biological controls available to the natural orchardist. There is no better way to answer a disbeliever than to do it right and prove it can be

Mature fruit shows scab symptoms.

Infected leaves fall to ground.

Lesions may appear on twigs and bark.

Scab fungus grows on dead leaves.

Scab symptoms appear on new foliage and young fruit.

Spores are ejected during wet weather in spring.

Good sanitation is one of the best ways to stop fruit diseases in their tracks. Apple scab, for example, is spread to new growth from last year's leaves on the ground. If you rake up the fallen leaves and clean up fallen fruit, you can break the scab cycle.

done. The fruits of your labor will certainly shine for years to come.

Standard and Dwarf Trees

What about the trees themselves? Now you have a choice between standard (full-size), semidwarf, and

dwarf fruit trees. Generally, you can get the same cultivar in all three sizes to suit your needs and available space. No matter what size tree you choose, it will bear full-size fruit.

DWARF TREES

Dwarf trees are usually the best choice for backyard gardeners. They're easier to reach for chores like pruning, spraying, and netting, and they take up less space. For example, you can grow 40 dwarf apple trees in the space needed for 4 standard trees.

These days, you can find just about any cultivar in a dwarf version. That's good because you'll almost certainly want to plant more than one cultivar, if only for variety's sake. Also, planting different cultivars can aid pollination since many cultivars can't pollinate themselves. (See "Pollination for Productivity" on page 212.)

There's really no mystery to the dwarfing process. Dwarf trees are made by grafting wood from standard trees onto dwarfing rootstocks. Semidwarfs are simply

Dwarf fruit trees are one of the best things that ever happened to home fruit growers. They're just a fraction of the size of standards (full-size trees)—as much as 75 percent smaller—so you can fit up to ten times as many trees in the same amount of space.

Standard tree

Dwarf tree

grown on less-dwarfing rootstocks.

For example, standard apple cultivars, such as 'Red Delicious' or 'McIntosh', are grafted onto dwarfing rootstocks, which were developed primarily at the East Malling Agricultural Experiment Station in England. The rootstocks are called M7 (for Malling), MM106 (for Malling Merton), and so on. Each one confers a different degree of dwarfness. Some rootstocks were also developed for special soil conditions (like clay), and some can resist certain diseases.

To make dwarf pear trees, wood from a standard pear is grafted onto rootstock of a quince bush, a close relative. The result is a bush-size tree that grows full-size pears. And, as with most

dwarfs, the pear trees bear early, when they are only three years old. (For more on dwarfing rootstocks, see "Grafting" on page 208.)

Pollination

Most apple cultivars are not self-fertile. In order to set fruit, they must be cross-pollinated by another cultivar planted nearby. The same goes for pears and cherries. Peaches and apricots are usually self-fertile, but they set a better crop when two or more cultivars fertilize each other.

Of course, for best results you'll need to plant cultivars that flower at approximately the same time. With apples, you're safe if you choose mid-season cultivars such as 'Jonafree', 'Empire', 'Liberty', 'Cortland', and 'Red

Delicious'. The first three cultivars are also highly disease-resistant. It's a bit easier with pears, since all cultivars except for 'Seckel' and 'Bartlett' will pollinate each other.

Planting and Care

You can purchase young fruit trees either container-grown or bareroot. I prefer the bareroot plants because they're easier to handle and I've found that they're less likely to suffer from transplant shock.

To plant a bareroot fruit tree, I dig a generous hole in well-prepared soil and set the tree in the hole so that the graft union is above the soil line. Then, I tamp the soil down well and stake and mulch the tree. (To plant a container-grown tree, dig a hole the size of the container and just pop the plant into the hole, removing the container first.)

PRUNE AFTER PLANTING

Believe it or not, you'll need to start pruning and training your tree as soon as it's planted. Success with bareroot fruit trees begins with pruning back the topgrowth at transplanting time. (If you're planting in fall, wait until the following spring.)

Pruning after planting is a simple process. Usually, a

new fruit tree is sold as a branchless trunk, called a whip. Just cut back the trunk by about one-third. This will restore a reasonable balance between the first season's leaf surface and the moisture-absorbing capacity of the root system, which was sharply reduced when the plant was dug. Pruning this way will also result in vigorous regrowth and keep the vulnerable new plant from drying out too fast. Just be sure the nursery didn't pre-prune your whip for you before you take out the pruners!

FEED YOUR TREES

The next task is a simple one: feeding the trees. You can choose one of the many slow-release organic fertilizers on the market today, or you can make your own, as I do.

To supply nitrogen, I add a mixture of cottonseed meal and fish meal to the soil; for phosphorus, I apply rock phosphate and bonemeal; for potash, I add greensand and dolomitic limestone; and for trace elements, I add kelp meal. I apply about 1 pound for every year of the tree's age. To build up the soil's organic matter content, I also work in about 3 inches of compost each spring. Finally, I spray on a liquid seaweed mix—just enough to wet the leaves—every five weeks throughout the growing season.

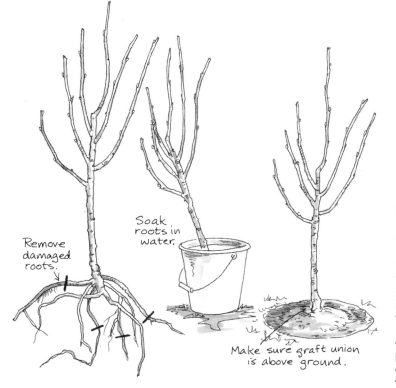

Remove damaged roots.

Soak roots in water.

Make sure graft union is above ground.

When planting bareroot trees, first cut off any damaged or dead roots, then soak the roots in a bucket of water. Dig a hole as deep as the root ball and twice as wide, loosening the soil on the sides of the hole. Mound soil in the bottom of the hole, then gently spread the plant's roots over the mound. Make sure the graft union is above the soil line. Backfill around the roots with soil, firming the soil down. Then water well.

Plant a Seed

It's hard to believe, but many cultivars of apple, pear, plum, or peach originated from a seed or stone. And a great many of the finest were raised by amateurs in a casual sort of way. If you've got the room, it seems to me that experimenting with seeds or stones is worth trying! Don't be put off by the expert pessimists. I heartily recommend that you raise at least one seedling apple, pear, plum, or peach. I've seen many instances where stone-raised peach trees have borne huge crops of first-class peaches. And remember that the 'Red Delicious' apple and 'Bing' cherry started life as seedling trees.

Just how do you begin? Let's talk about apples. Take the seeds from your favorite apple and sow them in a 6-inch pot. In a year's time, you'll have several tiny apple trees that are 3, 4, or 5 inches tall. Select one of these to develop (not necessarily the biggest, since size doesn't always indicate quality).

Replant your favorite seedling in fresh soil in a pot. When it's two years old, your tree should be a foot or so high; you can now plant it outside in the ground. Choose a place where it will get good light and air circulation and have plenty of space to develop.

After three or four years, dig it up and examine its roots. Most likely it will have a thick, deep taproot. If so, shorten it, but leave all the small fibrous roots. Replant. Pruning the taproot in this way helps to prevent rank, sappy growth and can hasten the fruiting stage.

What sort of tree will you have after all this waiting? Almost certainly not an exact replica of its seed parent. However, your homegrown fruit will be your own particular cultivar, and you can name it what you will. No other cultivar in the whole country will be exactly like it. It may be a really good eating apple that's worth propagating, or it may be a good cooker. It will definitely be an original.

What do all the experts think about this? They'll say that grafted trees of known cultivars would be a better value. And usually that's true—the seedling may not even be as good as its parents. But obviously, you can't put a price tag on an apple seed or peach stone whose growth can bring us so much personal pleasure and satisfaction. Starting fruit from seed is an adventure.

Propagating Fruit Trees

Most fruit trees won't grow true from seed. That means the seedling will not resemble the parent at all. So, to reproduce a certain desirable cultivar, a nurseryman must propagate it vegetatively, either by grafting or taking cuttings. You can also take cuttings of brambles and shrubs, plant out suckers, or propagate them by a low-work technique called layering.

GRAFTING

The most common method of propagating fruit trees is grafting. To make a graft, you take a piece of the desired cultivar (the grafting stock) and attach it to another tree (the rootstock), where it will grow and bear fruit. Old cultivars have been handed down this way for centuries.

Making grafted trees yourself is not only simple,

it's economical, too. For the price of four or five ordinary apple trees, you can buy the rootstocks and grafting stocks for 30 of the most unique cultivars available, including delicious heirloom fruits.

Getting Your Stock

If you grow your own rootstock from seed and collect the grafting stock (called scionwood) from your favorite apple trees, you'll be carrying on an old farmers' tradition. You will also be raising an orchard very inexpensively. If you want dwarf, early-bearing, or extra-hardy trees, you can buy special rootstocks. If you want particular named cultivars of apples, you can order scionwood of them as well.

Since a rootstock and the material grafted onto it become a single organism, the two parts naturally affect each other. The rootstock influences the ultimate size of the tree, its hardiness, the age at which it comes into bearing, its disease resistance, and the heaviness of the crop. The disadvantage of using a seedling rootstock is that you can't predict its effect in those areas. Therefore, most growers use special, uniform strains of rootstock.

Some fruit tree catalogs include listings of rootstocks for sale. They may offer a wide variety, such as EMLA 7, EMLA 27, Malling 9, and MARK for apples, and 'Old Homestead' × 'Farmingdale' for plums. The rootstocks are generally inexpensive—as little as $1 each when purchased in quantity. I'm partial to the dwarfing rootstocks of the Malling series. They produce smaller apple trees with full-size fruit. Many Malling rootstocks also bring the trees into bearing at an early age.

This Bud's for You

You'll find it easier to follow and implement the how-to of grafting if you know how grafting actually works:

Only one layer of cells of a tree's branch or trunk is capable of healing a wound. This layer, between the bark and the wood, is called the cambium. Grafting is simply cutting a bud-bearing piece off the parent tree so that the maximum amount of cambium is exposed, and then attaching it to a place on the new tree where an area of cambium has also been exposed. Where the two cambiums touch, the cells will multiply and join the two pieces into one organism. Then the new bud will grow to form the top of the tree.

If the cambium layers of the two pieces do not touch, the bud piece put onto the new tree will die, and the rootstock tree will just heal over the wound. So you have to be sure to put the grafted material in the right place and to bind the graft tightly to keep it there. There are a few different ways to do this.

The T-Bud Technique

T-bud grafting, also known as summer budding, is the method I prefer to use on young trees. It's quick and has the greatest chance of success of any grafting method, especially for apples and peaches. The grafting is done in August because that's the only time of year when the bark will slip easily from the wood underneath. Here's how you do it:

Early in August, check the trees that you want to propagate by pulling downward on a leaf in the middle of a shoot. Buds are mature enough for grafting if the leaf stem breaks off cleanly without tearing.

Cut your grafting stock, called a bud stick, from the end of a branch or shoot of the cultivar you want to propagate. This will form the top, or fruiting part, of the tree. Cut the bud stick from wood that has developed during the current growing season. It should be about the thickness of a pencil.

Just as soon as you cut the bud stick from the tree,

Here's how to make a T-bud graft:

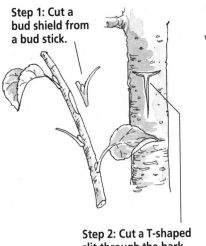

Step 1: Cut a bud shield from a bud stick.

Step 2: Cut a T-shaped slit through the bark of the rootstock.

Step 3: Slide the bud shield into the slit with the bud pointing up.

Step 4: Wrap the graft tightly with rubber strips, leaving the bud exposed.

remove the top inch or two of the shoot. Strip off all the leaves, leaving about 1/2 inch of each leaf's stem for use as a handle. Wrap the bottom of the bud stick in moist material and keep it in a plastic bag. If it dries out, the bud will die, so graft as soon as possible.

Needless to say, budding takes some skill. But the steps are easy to learn. If you practice, you can master them quickly.

First, cut a bud shield from your bud stick. To do this, make a shallow horizontal cut above a leaf bud. Then, put your propagating knife 3/4 inch below the bud and make a shallow cut up

to meet the first cut, removing the bud and a "shield" of surrounding bark. Avoid using fruit buds (they're much fatter than the narrow, pointed leaf buds) because they'll bloom in the spring instead of making strong shoots.

Next, make a T-shaped cut through the rootstock's bark at least 4 inches above the ground. If you cut the north side of the tree, the graft will be less likely to dry out. Make your cut quickly and smoothly with a very sharp knife; ripped or bruised tissue may not heal. With your knife blade, lift the flaps you've just made in order to loosen them.

Then fit the bud shield into the T. Holding the bud shield by the leaf stem handle, slip it under the flaps on the rootstock. Cut off the part of the shield that extends above the top of the T.

Wrap the graft tightly with rubber strips to keep the two parts moist and in close contact. You'll usually need two strips for each graft. You can also use masking or electrical tape. It's not necessary to cover the whole area, and you should leave the bud itself uncovered.

Sometimes it takes a while for a grafted bud to swell, even after the rootstock branches have opened their leaves. However, its ability to survive is amazing. Once the bud has sprouted in spring, cut off the top of the rootstock just above it, sloping the cut away from the bud.

FRUITS FROM CUTTINGS

A cutting is simply a piece of a plant that has been removed from its parent and developed into an entirely new plant. You can sever a cutting from the branches (stem cutting), from the roots (root cutting), or from a single leaf (leaf bud cutting). (Taking cuttings from the roots is a tricky technique and is best left to professionals.) You can take a stem cutting when the plant is dormant and the leaves are off (hardwood cutting) or when the plant is actively growing in the spring or early summer (softwood cutting).

With a little experience and experimentation, you'll find that cuttings are an inexpensive and enjoyable way to increase your fruit stock.

Leaf Bud Cuttings

Although many home gardeners have never tried it, I think the most fascinating propagating method is taking leaf bud cuttings. I've found that you can start huge numbers of black raspberries or trailing blackberries by using the leaf bud method. (This technique is great for black and purple raspberries, but it doesn't work for red and gold cultivars.)

A bramble leaf bud cutting is a leaf with the stem and a small piece of the cane attached. Taken in early summer, the leaf cutting is treated like a softwood cutting. Just bury the piece of cane in a light, porous potting medium with only the one leaf visible above it.

Hardwood Cuttings

Grapes and currants are easy to propagate from hardwood cuttings. Some growers take the cuttings in the fall; others prefer to take them in early spring, before any sign of growth starts. Either way, be sure to make the cuttings with a sharp knife.

Cut 6 to 12 inches from the end of the current year's growth if you're working in the fall, or of the previous year's growth if you're taking cuttings in the spring. Once

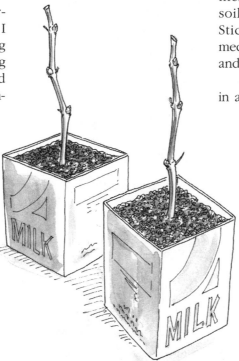

Cut a 6- to 12-inch piece from the tip of this year's growth on a grapevine. It should be about as thick as a pencil. Place this cutting, with its bottom end about 2 inches deep, in a milk carton, pot, or flat of vermiculite topped with potting soil. The cuttings will root faster if you cover them with clear plastic.

cut, the wood doesn't need to be rooted right away. You can bury bundles of cuttings in moist sand in a cool place for several weeks or until you're ready to plant them.

You can place the cuttings in a prepared propagating bed as soon as the outside soil has warmed up. Use a 2-inch-deep layer of vermiculite, covered with a 1-inch-deep layer of potting soil, as a rooting medium. Stick the cuttings into the medium about 2 inches deep and 2 inches apart.

New growth may start in a few days, or it may take as long as a few weeks. If you prefer, you can hasten the rooting process and increase your chances of success by covering the cuttings with a tent of clear plastic. Use a garden hose with a misting nozzle to keep the rooting medium thoroughly moist.

As soon as the cuttings are well rooted, remove the plastic cover and allow the plants to grow naturally. I use a liquid seaweed spray every four weeks to feed the new plants. A mulch of leaf mold helps keep the plants growing well and prevents the new roots from drying out.

Softwood Cuttings

Blueberries are easy to grow from softwood cuttings. The process for taking softwood cuttings is virtually identical to taking hardwood cuttings. The only difference is the timing and the age of the wood—softwood is soft, green, and actively growing. Young pieces from the current year's growth are cut in mid- to late summer and planted about 2 inches deep in a light rooting medium such as that used for hardwood cuttings.

Softwood cuttings of blueberries take a long time to root. They need high humidity and warm temperatures both day and night. New cuttings survive better if you leave them in their propagating bed until the following spring.

Feed blueberry cuttings with composted manure and kelp meal, and apply foliar sprays of liquid seaweed. Cottonseed meal, peat moss, and shredded pine needles are all good soil amendments for acid-loving blueberry plants.

SUCKERING

Suckering is the easiest way to propagate upright blackberries, as well as red and gold raspberries and straw-

berries. If the runners or suckers that shoot out underground from the mother plant are left undisturbed, they will root readily and sprout in early spring. You can then separate them from the main plant and use them to start new plants.

Gold and red raspberries are so easy to propagate by digging up and replanting their abundant suckers that any other propagation technique just isn't worth the effort. And once you have a strawberry patch, planting out runners is the only way to go.

LAYERING

You can also encourage your brambles to form new plants by an easy technique called layering. To layer a plant, you simply make sure that some branches touch the soil and stay there. If they aren't already touching, you'll need to bend some flexible canes down to the ground, bury them under a couple of inches of soil, and hold them in place with a rock or a forked stick.

Leave the layer in place until roots form (this can take a season or two), then sever the new plant from its parent, dig it up, and move it to its permanent location. To get a layer to root faster, you can cut a slit in the part of the

stem that will touch the ground and hold the cut open with a toothpick or small pebble.

Black raspberries are commonly propagated by tip layering. The end of the cane stalk is buried in the soil, where it roots and grows into a new plant.

Pollination for Productivity

When it comes to pollinating fruits and berries, honeybees, hornets, and bumblebees do practically all the work. But sometimes conditions interfere and make their job more difficult. You should suspect a pollination problem if your fruit trees produce lots of blooms but no fruit, or if tiny fruits form on the trees and fall off soon thereafter.

Most fruit trees need to be cross-pollinated the pollen from one tree must be moved to another in order for it to bear fruit. Apple blossoms are usually readily cross-pollinated because there are almost always two or more cultivars of apple trees growing within flying distance of bees. Wild apples growing in the vicinity of an orchard are often excellent pollinators as long as they bloom at the same time as the trees you want pollinated.

Crabapples also make

excellent pollinators. Most orchardists plant one crabapple tree for every 25 apple trees to help with pollination. You can plant an ornamental crabapple in your front yard and enjoy its beauty while it helps pollinate those apples out back.

POLLINATION PROBLEMS

Pollination problems often occur when trees bloom early in the spring. Sometimes the few wild bees that survived the winter just aren't able to handle the thousands of blooms that appear at the same time. Not only are there too few bees in early spring, but the cold, wet days can limit their activities. Many blossoms may come and go without visits from bees. And even if the blossoms have been pollinated, frequent rains during the blooming season can wash off the pollen before it sets.

The Danger of Frost

Frost is a major cause of crop failure. If frost occurs at the end of the blooming season, there is usually no damage unless the temperature gets extremely low. However, when frost hits before the blossoms are fertilized by the bees, the tiny tube from the pistil to the ovaries may be damaged. As a result, the pollen can't move down the tube, and no fruit will form.

There are steps you can take to minimize the danger of frost-induced failure. For example, you can delay blooming—and thus allow the bee population to build up while the spring weather improves—by manipulating the microclimate around your trees. Plant early-blooming fruit trees on the north side of a windbreak. Or use a heavy mulch to help keep the roots of the trees cool in the spring.

Pollinating by Hand

If your trees still bloom early, if cool or windy weather keeps the bees in their hive, or if rain washes out the pollen, you can always do the job yourself. Although it may sound like an enormous task to pollinate a fruit tree by hand, it's not that difficult.

You can collect the pollen yourself or buy it from a supply house. If you collect pollen yourself, use a small, soft brush, such as an artist's paintbrush, and collect the yellow powder from the stamens of several blossoms on one tree. Then, with the same brush, dust the flowers on another tree, marking the limbs as you go so you can tell where you've been. It will be time well spent if it means the difference between a crop of fruit and no fruit set at all.

One old-timer's trick is to put the pollen you've collected in your beehive so that the bees will walk through it as they leave the hive on their way to the trees. But there's a simpler way to help the pollinating process: If your fruit tree doesn't have a satisfactory mate in the neighborhood, cut a few blooming branches from a friend's tree and put them in your branches. The bees will do the rest.

Fruit Thinning

Even after you've planted, pruned, and pollinated, you still can't leave a fruit tree to its own devices. If left alone, many types of fruit trees tend to overbear; they produce too much fruit in the space available. The result is runty fruit with disappointing flavor, broken branches weighed down with fruit, and poor production the following year.

So you must take matters into your own hands and remove some of the excess fruit before it has a chance to mature. Thin to leave enough room for each fruit to expand its girth. For example, you may want to remove every other fruit. If the fruits are naturally small at maturity, like apricots, don't space them very far apart. If the tree isn't in good health, if it was set back by a freeze last year, or if you're having a drought, remove more.

HOW TO THIN

When you're up on the ladder surrounded by boughs laden with fruit as thick as bunches of grapes, how do you keep track of where you've thinned? One trick I like is to reach everything you can on the right side of the ladder as you go up and all the branches within reaching distance on the left side as you go down.

Some folks prefer to climb to the top and work at arm's length on both sides on the way down. There are no strict rules for thinning; each orchardist has his own preference.

WHICH FRUITS TO THIN

How do you break up a cluster by hand? Which fruits should you leave? If some fruits are undersized or deformed, the decision is made for you; just pull these off and leave the good ones.

You shouldn't automatically thin out all fruit with marks on it, though. Frost marks aren't any worse than freckles if you're raising fruits just for your family. Likewise, people don't like to buy fruit with limb rubs, but it's still

To get bigger fruit and more reliable yields year after year, it pays to do some fruit thinning on apple, apricot, peach, and pear trees. When the fruits reach marble size, remove enough of them so that the remaining fruits can reach full size without touching each other.

okay to eat. However, you should remove any catfaced fruit or fruit that has been badly damaged by insects.

While you're thinning fruit from a branch, try to imagine how it will look at harvest. If you can picture the fruits pressing against each other, remove more.

Soft fruits such as apricots, peaches, plums, and prune plums tend to bear heavily one year and lightly the next. You'll break the cycle and get a more consistent harvest every year by thinning.

Each time you finish thinning a tree, the ground below will be covered with a lumpy green carpet of fruit.

Looking back up into the tree, you may think you either picked too many or not enough. Don't worry about it. Just leave enough room for each fruit to grow to a good size, and you can't lose. It doesn't matter how much fruit is on the ground.

Thinning allows the remaining fruit to grow larger, and it will taste better, too, since competition for the tree's limited supply of sap will be reduced. Interestingly, thinned fruit matures earlier, perhaps because it gets more sugar and sun.

Make Time for Fruit

Given the wide variety to choose from and the modest amount of growing room required, you have every reason to include fruit in your garden plan. Your plantings will mature in a few years, and you'll have the pleasure of fresh, chemical-free fruit harvests all season long for many years afterwards.

There are many mail-order nurseries that feature dwarf fruit trees. Specialists like NAFEX (North American Fruit Explorers, Route 1, Box 84, Chapin, IL 62628) and the New York State Fruit Testing Cooperative Association, Inc. (P.O. Box 462, Geneva, NY 14456-0462) offer interesting heirloom cultivars and new breeding developments to their members.

But which fruits should you grow? In Chapter 13, I'll tell you about each tree fruit and how to grow it, so you can decide which ones you want. And in Chapter 14, you can look up all the brambles and bush fruits, then make your choices.

13

Fruit-Growing Guide

Apples, apricots, cherries, grapes, nectarines, peaches, pears, plums—if you enjoy these fruits from the store, just imagine how good they'd taste if you picked them straight from the tree or vine! And think about the lack of toxic chemicals all over them, too. You *know* homegrown fruit is as fresh and wholesome as it can be because you're the one who's grown it.

Choosing from among all the different fruit trees can be tough—if you're like most gardeners, you want to grow one of everything. But keep these points in mind before you start buying all the trees you can get. First, allow enough room for each tree to develop fully. They'll be small at planting time, but they grow surprisingly quickly. Crowded trees are hard to maintain and more prone to pest and disease problems.

Also remember that some fruit trees— like many apples—will need a partner for pollination; that means you need room for at least two trees. Time is another factor: To produce a good crop, your plants will need some regular attention throughout the year for pruning, pest control, and harvesting. Exactly how much time depends on the crop you decide to grow.

Fortunately, fruit growing isn't too hard if you know what you're doing. And in this chapter, I aim to make sure you've got everything you need to know. But above all, remember that you must spend time with your plants. The secret of successful organic orcharding is to always keep an eye on the trees—let them tell you what needs to be done in the orchard. After all, they live there.

APPLES

Baseball, hot dogs, and apple trees—what could be more American? If you're planning on planting any fruit at all, chances are that apples are near the top of your list. That's good. There's an incredibly wide variety of apples to choose from, not to mention a number of ways to grow them. You'll find the perfect cultivar and growing system for any taste and location. Apples are hardy in Zones 3–9, depending on the cultivar.

Generally, I recommend dwarf apples for home gardeners. Besides saving space, they're so much easier to take care of and harvest. A dwarf apple tree should start to bear a few apples in the third year after planting. By the fourth year, you can expect to pick 15 to 30 pounds of fruit from a single tree.

I think the best way to buy apple trees is through mail-order nurseries. And the best trees to buy are one-year-old whips. Go for trees with the largest caliper (trunk diameter) you can find. These whips won't look like much when they arrive. Each is just a bare-root, 4- to 6-foot-tall central trunk, typically without side branches.

CHOOSING A ROOTSTOCK

You can choose from among literally hundreds of apple cultivars to suit your climate, conditions, and taste. I wouldn't presume to tell you exactly which apple belongs in your garden. But no matter which cultivar you choose, I *will* strongly recommend that you order it on the Malling 9 (M9) rootstock. This rootstock provides the greatest dwarfing effects of those that are commonly available. A mature tree on M9 rootstock will grow about 8 feet tall and equally as wide.

Depending on the cultivar and season, a single tree can produce as many as three to five bushels of fruit, though one to three bushels per tree is a more common yield. Apples on this rootstock must be staked. If you'd like to grow a dwarf tree that doesn't require staking, try one of the MARK rootstocks.

PLANTING

You can plant apples in early spring or fall. But even before ordering your trees, you

About Hardiness Zones

Hardiness zones are your key to a plant's cold-hardiness—whether the plant will make it through the winter where you live. If you turn to page 366, you'll find the "USDA Plant Hardiness Zone Map." Look on the map for your zone. (Here on Long Island, I'm in Zone 6.) The zone key tells you the average low temperatures for your zone (0° to −10°F for my area).

Lots of gardening books and nursery catalogs tell you the hardiness range for perennial and woody plants, so it's really useful to know your zone. That way, you can tell at a glance if you can grow a certain cultivar or species where you live. If you live in Zone 5 and read that an apple cultivar is only hardy to Zone 6, don't take a chance—find one that's hardy at least to Zone 5. On the other hand, if the description says "hardy in Zones 4–8," you'll know that it's safe to buy that cultivar.

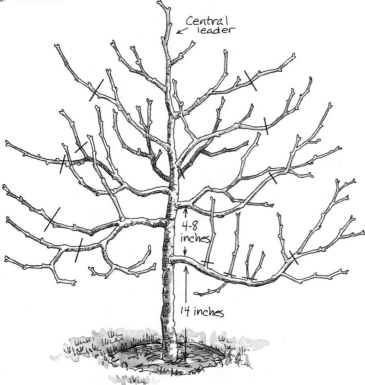

Central
← leader

4-8
inches

14 inches

Train apples to a central leader. Allow a dominant central trunk to develop, with branches spaced evenly around the trunk about 4 to 8 inches apart. Remove any branches lower than 14 inches.

If the trees are on Malling 9 rootstocks, you can plant them 10 feet apart, or even closer together. You'll find complete planting information in Chapter 12.

As soon as you've set out the tree and thoroughly watered it, place a 6-inch-deep layer of mulch around the base, extending out beyond the root system. Keep the mulch 4 to 8 inches away from the trunk; otherwise, mice may burrow under it and girdle, or strip the bark from, the trunk of the newly planted tree.

PRUNING NEW TREES

Immediately after planting, you'll need to prune your one-year-old whip. (If you're planting in fall, wait until the following spring.) This initial pruning will affect later yields, growth, and appearance. The guidance you give the tree during the first year, plus regular care thereafter, will decrease upkeep and ensure that you'll have plenty of fresh fruit.

Once you've planted the whip, carefully cut the trunk off about 30 to 36 inches above the ground. That's right: Just lop off the top. Do this early in the spring, before any growth appears. After you've cut the trunk, three or four buds that are 4 to 6 inches below the cut will break and start to grow. Leave the uppermost shoot, which will form the main trunk, called a central leader. The other shoots will form sharp-angled—and thus weak—crotches and should be removed.

should select a site. Rule out heavily shaded spots or low-lying areas that are susceptible to frost. Also, avoid areas with poorly drained soil. Once you've chosen a site, prepare the soil for planting as described in Chapter 12.

Plant the tree so the stem of the rootstock extends about 2 inches above ground level. (You can tell where the scion, or top part, joins the rootstock by looking for the place where the trunk crooks; that's the graft union.) It's important to make sure the graft union is a couple of inches above ground. If the stem of the scion is planted below ground, it might root. Then it would grow into a standard (full-size) tree and negate the effects of the dwarfing rootstock.

Usually, several shoots will form lower down on the trunk—you can select these for future scaffold (side) branches. The lowest branch should be about 14 inches above the ground. Space subsequent branches 4 to 8 inches apart in a sort of spiral pattern around the trunk. If you follow these simple steps, there will be little need to prune the first winter.

CONTINUING CARE

You'll need to provide support for the trees during the first four or five years after planting, or until a strong root system has developed. Some dwarfing rootstocks, like Malling 9, require permanent staking. To stake, drive a sturdy wooden pole into the ground 8 to 10 inches from the tree, preferably on the west side. Use a piece of garden hose or similar material to loop around the trunk and tie to the stake. Position the loop just beneath the lowest branch.

You'll also need to protect the trunk of your new tree from sunscald. Wrap the trunk with white tree wrap, or paint it with diluted white latex paint.

Apple trees need plenty of water, especially the first year, when they're getting established, and from bloom through bearing. Water the trees deeply out to their drip lines—don't let them dry out. To grow and bear well, apples also need food. Apply 5 to 10 pounds of compost to the soil around each tree every year in late winter or early spring, before growth starts. Plants will also appreciate a boost from liquid seaweed; spray from the first sign of green in spring until the flower buds show pink.

Often, a tree will set more apples than it can carry to maturity, so you should remove some of the apples before they reach the size of golf balls. Most modern cultivars bear fruit on short (1- to 2-inch), nubby branchlets called spurs. If your apple tree is a spur-bearing type, thin to the best fruit on each spur. If your apple isn't a spur-bearer, thin so that the fruit won't touch when it's full-size—about 6 inches apart.

Just remember that if you give your apple trees the right training right from the start, they'll be more productive and easier to care for, and they'll make a more handsome contribution to the landscape.

PEST AND DISEASE CONTROL

Apples have a few serious pests and diseases, but if you take sensible precautions and keep an eye out for problems, you can keep them under control.

One effective control for a variety of pests, including scale, spider mites, and aphids, is dormant oil. Spray it on the trees in late winter.

Codling moths are a major pest of apples. You'll know they've reached your trees if you hang pheromone traps, which lure the pests to their deaths. Put up one or two traps per tree two weeks before bud break. Replace the lures in the traps six to eight weeks after you put them out. Check your traps weekly. If you're catching moths, you can spray the trees weekly with *Bacillus thuringiensis* var. *kurstaki* (BTK) mixed with insecticidal soap and ryania.

Apple maggot is another pest that attacks apple fruit in the eastern and central states. Luckily, they're easy to control. You can trap the adults on sticky red spheres that look like apples. Buy the spheres or make your own from apple-size red balls. Coat each sphere with a sticky substance like Tanglefoot. Hang one trap in each dwarf tree about five weeks after bloom. Place the trap at eye level and about 2 feet within the tree's canopy.

Despite its name, plum curculio can also be a major apple pest. Curculios usually strike within six weeks after bloom. Trap them the same way you catch apple maggots—with sticky spheres. But paint these 'Granny Smith' green (you can just spray-paint the red traps you bought or made for apple maggots). Then give them a sticky coating. You can also shake curculios from your trees onto a sheet on the ground, then gather and destroy them.

Apple scab is a fungal disease that can disfigure your fruit with brown, corky patches. It also produces brown or black spots on the leaves. Plant resistant cultivars like 'Jonafree' and 'Liberty', or keep it under control by spraying your plants with lime-sulfur spray before the buds open in spring. Once the leaves are fully open, spray twice a week during warm, wet weather. By mid-summer, you can stop spraying; scab should be under control for the season.

Fire blight is a bacterial disease that can kill a tree if it's not controlled quickly. If the leaves blacken for no reason, hanging on curled, blackened twigs like they've been burned, cut the infected branches right away. Make the cut 6 inches below the last sign of disease and destroy the clippings. Sterilize your pruners in alcohol between cuts.

HARVESTING

Pick apples carefully to avoid bruising the fruit. Harvest summer apples when they're ripe, but pick winter apples when they're not quite ripe since they'll continue to ripen in storage. Store apples in a root cellar, extra refrigerator, or unheated garage where the temperature is cold (but not freezing) and the humidity is high.

FALL AND WINTER CARE

In fall, pick up any dropped fruit from the ground and rake up fallen apple leaves from around the tree to prevent pest infestations and disease outbreaks. Remove old mulch and replace it with 6 to 12 inches of fresh straw; keep a 6- to 12-inch area around the trunks bare to protect the trees from rodents. To prevent sunscald, paint your trees' lower trunks with diluted white latex paint, then wrap them in hardware cloth sleeves. If deer are a problem in your area, hang several bars of deodorant soap in your trees. Leave the wrappers on so the soap lasts longer.

PRUNING ESTABLISHED TREES

Prune your apple trees in late winter, before growth starts up. After the first year, your biggest pruning job will be removing unwanted and broken branches. The less pruning you do, the earlier the tree will bear fruit. If your apple trees bear fruit on spurs, thin out any crowded or unproductive spurs. As the trees grow, the only additional pruning required will be to keep growth within bounds.

PROPAGATION

Propagate your apple trees by grafting. See "Grafting" on page 208 to find out how.

CROW'S PICKS

Choose apples that are adapted to your area. Some of the best apple cultivars for the North are 'Empire', 'Liberty', and 'Cortland'. In the South, you'll get good crops with 'Adina', 'Anna', and 'Dorsett Golden'. If you live in the West, grow 'Red Melba', 'Stayman Winesap', and 'Yellow Transparent'.

APRICOTS

There's something exotic about apricots; the sun-ripened fruits make you think of distant climes, like Persia or Madagascar. But the trees are easier to grow than you might think, and they're productive, too. Even a family that's crazy about apricots should be able to pick all the fruit it can handle from a pair of dwarf trees.

Apricots don't require a lot of room, either—15 feet between trees is ideal. Where space is scarce, 10 or 12 feet is adequate for the dwarf stock.

When it comes to apricots, you won't be confounded or overwhelmed by cultivar selection. In fact, you can't go wrong if you choose two companion cultivars meant to be planted in pairs: 'Moongold' and 'Sungold', both of which can survive winter temperatures of −25°F (Zone 4). Most other apricot cultivars are self-pollinating and hardy in Zones 5–9.

Apricots integrate nicely with other fruits in the landscape. The only exception is plums. They shouldn't be planted nearby, since certain insects and other pests share an affinity for both fruits.

Because apricots can endure some shade, they are fine trees for today's landscapes. But for really good fruiting, they need sun most of the day.

PLANTING

For best results, plant apricots in a sunny, well-drained site. Your bareroot trees should be about 5 to 6 feet tall. Make sure the branches and well-developed buds are evenly distributed along the trunk, down to about 12 inches above the roots. Before planting, soak the roots in water.

Dig the holes at least 1 foot deeper and 1 foot wider than the roots require. Plant the tree and backfill with the topsoil. Then top-dress each tree with about ¾ bushel of good compost and a handful of bonemeal, mixed together. Mulch with straw, leaving 6 to 12 inches bare around the trunk.

PRUNING NEW TREES

Cut the main trunk of your new apricot off about 2 feet above the graft. Cut the side branches back to stubs.

CONTINUING CARE

When your new trees begin to grow, sprinkle a thin layer of aged manure or organic fertilizer over the mulch around each tree. Also, spray the foliage every seven weeks with a liquid seaweed fertilizer. Seaweed will increase yields, give better color, increase bud and blossom set, and make the trees more resistant to stress caused by adverse soil and weather conditions.

The young trees' growth the first summer is important. During this time, don't water extravagantly. Even in drought, 2 or 3 gallons per tree, applied every second morning, should be plenty. Your goal the first year should be to keep the roots viable and growing—don't worry about the tops.

PEST AND DISEASE CONTROL

Fortunately, there are few insects or fungal diseases that seriously injure apricots. The principal insect enemy of apricots is the plum curculio. Larvae of this ¼-inch-long, black or brown long-beaked beetle bore into the fruit, often causing it to drop before it matures. The best way to control these pests is to clean up fallen fruit so they can't complete their life cycle.

If you have only a few trees, there's also a mechanical method that works well. Place a sheet under your apricot tree and shake the branches. The bugs will fall from the tree onto the sheet, making it easy for you to gather up and dispose of the pests. Do this daily, just after fruit set, and you may be able to control the problem.

Another control technique is to catch the adult curculios on sticky traps made of apricot- or apple-size spheres. You can make your own or buy the red traps sold for catching apple maggots; just paint them 'Granny Smith' green and cover them with a sticky substance like Tanglefoot. Soon after bloom, hang one trap in each tree, at eye level and about 2 feet within the tree's canopy. If the traps get full, scrape off the trapped pests and apply a fresh layer of sticky coating to the sphere.

HARVESTING

Harvest apricots frequently. Pick over the trees several times, removing ripe but firm fruit. The fruits bruise easily, so handle them carefully. Don't pour apricots from one container to another; instead, place them by hand in a box in a fairly shallow layer to protect the firm quality of the fruit.

FALL AND WINTER CARE

In most climates, it's a good idea to mulch the ground around apricot trees heavily after picking. Rough up the area beneath each tree lightly with a hoe, scatter a handful of lime and a couple of quarts of greensand, then apply a mulch of either straw or aged compost. If the ground is dry (as it often is in late fall), water well before applying the mulch and before the ground freezes hard.

Apricot trees seem to be especially susceptible to damage from frost and freezing weather. The fruit buds may freeze and the entire fruit spur may be killed. If only the bud is affected, it turns brown and the flower never opens. Sometimes only the pistil is killed. You might try inspecting the flowers to see if the pistils are still as small as they would be in the dormant buds. If they are, the fruit buds have winter kill, which means you won't get a fruit crop.

PRUNING ESTABLISHED TREES

Prune apricots in late winter, while they're still dormant. For easy care, train to an open-center (vase) shape. Choose three or four main scaffold branches around the tree and remove all others.

After the fourth year, prune to remove old growth since the fruit forms on new wood. Head the branches back so that the new growth forms on the trunk and main branches and the fruit is evenly distributed. Remember that your goal is to let the sunshine in to ripen and color the fruit. When you prune, be sure to remove all broken branches and diseased areas.

PROPAGATION

Propagate apricots by grafting. See "Grafting" on page 208 to find out how.

CROW'S PICKS

Some of the most disease-resistant apricot cultivars are 'Jerseycot' and those in the 'Har-' series (like 'Harcot' and 'Harglow'). These cultivars are all late-blooming, which makes them good choices for areas that get hit with late-spring frosts.

CHERRIES

Sweet cherries for fresh eating and sour cherries for pies and jam—few fruits have such a powerful appeal. Sweet cherry trees and sour cherry bushes (which are really small, bushy trees) are attractive, and the fruit is easy to grow. Choose a dwarf sweet cherry cultivar to save space and to make care and harvesting easier.

If your summers are hot and wet, sweet cherries won't be happy, so choose sour cherries instead. Most sweet cherry cultivars need a different cultivar for cross-pollination, but not all cultivars are compatible, so check before you buy. Sour cherries and some sweet cherries are self-pollinating. You can find cherry cultivars that are hardy in Zones 4–9.

CHOOSING A ROOTSTOCK

Like most tree fruits, sweet cherries are grafted onto rootstocks. Choose 'Mazzard' for heavy, wet soil and 'Maheleb' for light, dry soil.

PLANTING

Plant cherries in spring unless you live in a mild-winter zone, where you can plant in fall. Pick a site in full sun with well-drained soil— a north-facing slope is ideal. Don't plant your cherries near wild chokecherries, which can host pests and diseases.

Your new cherry tree should be 4 to 5 feet tall and have one to three branches. Space dwarf cherries 8 to 12 feet apart. Water well, then mulch the trees with 6 to 12 inches of straw, leaving 6 to 12 inches around the trunk bare to prevent rodent damage. You'll find complete planting information in Chapter 12.

PRUNING NEW TREES

Train sweet cherry trees to a modified central leader form: When the leader is 6 feet tall, cut it back to a side branch. Train sour cherries to an open-center (vase) form.

CONTINUING CARE

Keep your cherry trees well watered all season; uneven moisture can cause developing fruit to crack. Sweet cherries are especially prone to cracking. If you've had problems with cracking, you can help prevent it by spraying your plants with chelated calcium three times, starting when the fruits are about ¼ inch around and repeating every ten days to two weeks. Here's some good news, though: You don't need to thin cherries.

Like all fruit trees, cherries appreciate a yearly feeding. In late winter, spread 5 to 10 pounds of compost around each tree. If your trees look stressed during the growing season, give them a boost with a liquid seaweed foliar feed.

PEST AND DISEASE CONTROL

Birds are the biggest pest of cherries. To keep them from consuming your crop, drape bird netting over each tree when the cherries begin to color up. Tie the netting securely around the trunk so the birds can't fly under it. They don't seem to go for yellow-fruited sweet cherries—I guess they keep waiting for them to turn red—so you can also plant yellow cultivars to foil them. If you want bird-free sour cherries, try the late-bearing bush cherries 'Jan' and 'Joy', which birds tend to avoid.

Cherry fruit fly maggots burrow into cherry fruits, causing shrunken fruits that drop early. Control them with apple maggot traps—sticky red spheres that look like apples. Buy the spheres or make your own from apple-size red balls. Coat each sphere with a sticky substance like Tanglefoot. Hang one trap at eye level in each dwarf tree about five weeks after bloom. If the maggots were a serious pest in your orchard last season, spray rotenone when the fruit begins to color up.

Black aphids may feed on leaves and shoots, coating your tree's foliage with sticky honeydew or black sooty mold. If there aren't too many aphids, it's safe to ignore them. If the infestation is severe, spray your cherry trees with insecticidal soap.

Black knot, which shows up as knobby black swellings on the branches, is a fungal disease. Prune out branches with knots on them in late winter, and spray lime-sulfur when buds swell in spring. Spray again in seven days if your tree had black knot last year.

Cherry leaf spot is a fungal disease that forms tiny reddish to purplish black spots on the leaves. As the disease progresses, the centers of the spots drop out, leaving tiny holes. Leaves may turn yellow and fall early. If the disease isn't treated, it can eventually kill the tree. Control cherry leaf spot by spraying affected plants with sulfur every 10 to 21 days until leaf drop.

Powdery mildew can bother your trees when nights are cool and days are warm. This fungal disease coats the leaves and fruit with a white or gray powdery coating; leaves can also be twisted. Control powdery mildew with sulfur sprays.

Cherries also have many of the same pests and diseases as peaches. If you see a problem on your trees that isn't described here, check "Pest and Disease Control" in the Peaches and Nectarines entry on page 233.

HARVESTING

Cherries don't keep ripening after you've picked them, so make sure they're ripe before you harvest. Don't wait too long, though, or they'll rot. Once the fruit has colored up, taste for ripeness. Pick carefully to avoid bruising the fruit or injuring the spur. Cherries will keep longest if you leave the stems on. Store them in the refrigerator until you're ready to can, preserve, freeze, or eat them. Tart cherries will keep up to one week in the refrigerator; firm-fleshed sweet cherries will keep up to three weeks.

FALL AND WINTER CARE

To cut down on pest and disease problems, pick up dropped fruit and rake fallen leaves and compost them. Apply a thin layer of composted manure or organic fertilizer all around the tree when it has gone dormant in the fall, then mulch for winter. Paint the trunk with diluted white latex paint at the start of each dormant season to protect it from sunscald.

PRUNING ESTABLISHED TREES

Once cherries are trained, they don't need much pruning—just remove diseased, damaged, and crossing branches.

PROPAGATION

Propagate cherries by grafting. See "Grafting" on page 208 to find out how.

🐦 CROW'S PICKS

It pays to look for cherry cultivars that are resistant to brown rot, like 'Windsor' (a sweet cherry) and 'North Star' (a sour cherry). If your yard is a magnet for birds, try the sour cherries 'Jan' and 'Joy'.

GRAPES

Raising grapes is a great way for gardeners to get started with fruit growing. Regardless of your climate or your soil type, you can find a cultivar of grape to grow.

Plant grapes and you'll be rewarded quickly. Grapevines come into bearing only two or three years after planting. Given good care, they'll continue to bear for the rest of your life. If you combine a few different cultivars of grapes in your backyard vineyard, you can harvest from August to November. Grapes fit well into every landscape and can be grown on trellises, stakes, fences, arbors, and porches.

If you live in the Deep South, you can grow muscadine grapes. Otherwise, you'll have three types to choose from: European wine or vinifera grapes (*Vitis vinifera*), the classic wine grapes; American or fox grapes (*V. labrusca*) like 'Concord', best known for jelly and juice; and French-American hybrids. All can be eaten fresh.

European wine grapes prefer dry summers and mild winters, so they're best suited to the Southwest and drier areas of the West Coast (Zones 6 or 7–10). On the East Coast, plant American grapes (Zones 4–7), which tolerate more humidity and colder winters. You can grow French-American hybrids anywhere the particular cultivar is hardy; check with your local nursery to find out which cultivars do best in your area. Except for muscadines, grapes are self-fertile.

PLANTING

Siting is important for grapes. In commercial vineyards, grapes are often grown on hills and mountains. Southern slopes are best for early and very late grapes; northern slopes retard blooming until after spring frosts, a benefit in colder areas. Some American cultivars, such as 'Concord', 'Niagara', and 'Delaware', can make do in just about any type of soil. However, most grapes don't grow well in wet soil, so make sure your site is well drained. Grapes also require full sun and good air circulation.

Since grapevines will produce for decades, they need plenty of nourishment right from the start. If possible, plant a green manure crop the year before planting grapes. Then, when you turn under the green manure, work in a 2- to 4-inch-deep layer of aged manure throughout the vineyard.

You can plant grapes in either early spring or fall. Before planting, trim off injured or unhealthy roots and soak the roots in water or compost tea. Dig planting holes at least as deep and wide as the roots, and space them 8 feet apart. When you plant, make sure the graft union on grafted vines is at least 2 inches above the ground.

PRUNING NEW VINES

Once you've planted your grapevines, you need to train them. Training involves arranging the canes on a support system so the leaves will get maximum sunlight and it will be easy to harvest the fruit. There are plenty of ways to do it, but my favorite is the two-wire trellis.

I set 8-foot posts 2 feet deep in the ground and 8 feet apart in the rows. I string the lower wire 36 to 40 inches above ground and the upper wire 30 inches higher. (I use 10-gauge wire.) Then I plant one vine between each set of posts.

The first year, I simply tie the permanent main stem loosely to a temporary 4- or

✳ GRAPES

5-foot-tall stake in order to train the grapevine to grow straight—I don't worry about tying it to the wires. By the second spring, I train the main stem to reach the top wire and tie it carefully to both wires. I also train two branches in opposite directions along this upper wire. Close to the lower wire, I train two branches in the same way. The third year, I cut the horizontal branches back to five or six buds.

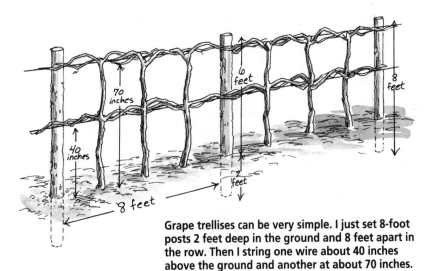

Grape trellises can be very simple. I just set 8-foot posts 2 feet deep in the ground and 8 feet apart in the row. Then I string one wire about 40 inches above the ground and another at about 70 inches.

It's important to choose sturdy shoots to train as horizontal branches. That's because the stubs of these shoots, along with the main stem or trunk, are the permanent foundation from which all the fruiting canes will grow during the life of the grapevine.

CONTINUING CARE

Mulch your grapes with 6 to 12 inches of straw or other organic mulch, leaving 6 to 12 inches of bare soil around each trunk. Once the plants are established, you shouldn't have to water them unless there's a drought. If you spray with a micronutrient-rich foliar feed like liquid seaweed every two weeks throughout the growing season, the grapes may be less susceptible to diseases. It certainly can't hurt, anyway!

As the vines grow, tie the canes to the trellis wires in several places to prevent damage during summer storms.

Thin the fruit when the vines set a very heavy crop, or you'll be inviting fungal diseases and exhausting your vines. Thin when the grapes are still small and hard. Remove some bunches completely and take off individual fruits to open up others.

PEST AND DISEASE CONTROL

Novice grape growers could work themselves into a lather by reciting the litany of grape pests and diseases: phylloxera, grape rootworm, flea beetle, rose chafer, grape leafhopper, grape berry moth, black rot, downy mildew, and powdery mildew.

Don't let these bad guys scare you away. As a practical matter, these insects and diseases present little hazard to the organic grower. You can give your plants the best possible start by selecting disease-resistant cultivars (there are many to choose from) and healthy plants, and siting them where they'll get full sun, good air circulation, and excellent drainage. (And don't forget foliar sprays of liquid seaweed to combat disease.)

With all grapes, good sanitation is the first line of defense in controlling or eliminating disease. To prevent the spread of fungus, inspect the fruit as it forms and remove any grape showing a dark spot. This may sound like a big task, but it just takes a few minutes a day.

Black rot usually affects only a few grapes or bunches at the most. This fungus appears first as light spots, then progresses to shrivel the fruit into hard, black "mummies" coated with black pimples, which contain the spores of the disease. If black rot seems extensive, dusting sulfur on the soil and on the mulch around the grapes will help to control it. If you've had problems with black rot before, spray lime-sulfur when the buds swell in spring. Respray twice a week until midsummer. Spraying lime-sulfur will also help control downy and powdery mildew.

Grape berry moth larvae feed on leaves, causing the leaf edges to roll over. They also attack fruits (look for telltale webbing). You can control them by spraying BTK (*Bacillus thuringiensis* var. *kurstaki*) weekly from the time fruit buds appear until midsummer.

Birds love grapes. You can protect your grapes from birds—and keep insects off, too—by putting a small paper bag over each bunch and stapling the bag for a tight fit around the stem. (Make sure the bag is big enough so the grapes have room to grow.) Cut a small hole in the bottom of the bag for water to drain out. If you don't want to bag your grapes, you can also foil birds by netting your plants.

HARVESTING

Like cherries, grapes won't continue to ripen after you've picked them, so make sure they're ripe before you harvest. Wait until all the grapes in a bunch have colored up, then taste for ripeness. Store in a cold (but not freezing), humid place like a refrigerator or root cellar.

FALL AND WINTER CARE

After the leaves drop in fall, rake up and dispose of any fallen leaves or dropped fruits. Also, make sure you pick off and destroy any "mummies" still clinging to the vines.

Rake away the old mulch in early fall and compost it, then replace it in late fall with 6 to 12 inches of fresh straw. (Be sure to keep the mulch a few inches away from the trunks.) In late winter, mulch the vines with a layer of compost. I use about 10 to 15 pounds for every 10 feet of row.

PRUNING ESTABLISHED PLANTS

If there's one thing that scares gardeners away from grapes, it's the regular pruning

Container-Grown Grapes

If you would like to try growing grapes but you don't have the space, try growing grapes in a container.

Pot a compact cultivar like 'Delaware'. Support the vine with three or four stakes—make sure your pot is large enough to accommodate both the vine and its supports comfortably.

Train the growing shoots around the stakes. When your grapevine reaches full size, repot it each year during its dormant period. Keep the vine pruned, taking off slightly more than you would for a vine that is planted in the ground.

During very cold winters, protect your grapevine's roots by piling garbage bags filled with leaves around the pots.

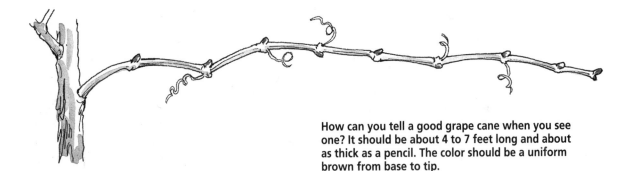

How can you tell a good grape cane when you see one? It should be about 4 to 7 feet long and about as thick as a pencil. The color should be a uniform brown from base to tip.

required to keep the plants productive. To most beginners, the process seems incomprehensible. But it's really pretty simple if you remember a few basic principles.

Grapes are prolific growers, putting out a lot of excess stems and leaves every year. And each year they bear fruit—but only on new growth. The old wood merely serves as a base for the new twigs on which fruit is formed. If you don't prune back the old canes enough, the vines keep growing longer and wider, and eventually there's no more energy in the vine to produce fruit. On vigorous vines like 'Concord', the lack of pruning can lead to rampant growth and reduced yields.

Of the 750 or so buds that you'd normally find on a vine before pruning, 100 to 150 will grow. Since pruning removes all but 50 to 75 buds, it spares the vine the burden of overproducing. The smaller crop gets more nourishment, and the grapes grow larger and finer than they would without pruning.

Before you start pruning grapes, you must first select the right canes to train. Since a pruned vine has fewer buds, the canes you choose must be strong and fruitful. Look for canes that are 4 to 7 feet long and about as thick as a pencil. Good canes have a uniform brown color from base to tip. They are also

firm to the touch and have smooth, tight bark and plump buds.

The best time to prune grapes is during the dormant season, which begins after the first freezes of fall and ends when the buds begin to break in spring. Where late-spring frosts are common, there's a slight advantage to pruning as late as a week before the buds begin to break. Late pruning can delay budding by as much as ten days, and this grace period can mean the difference between having a crop and losing it to frost.

Generally, you'll only need to make two kinds of cuts when pruning grapes: one to shorten a cane, and another to remove a cane. To shorten a cane, you should make the cut square and ½ inch beyond the last bud. A closer cut causes the bud to dry up; a cut made farther from the bud causes part of the cane to wither, which in turn invites borers and disease. To remove a cane, make the cut flush with the trunk. That way, the vine won't have to put out as much energy to cover the wound.

When pruning grapes, keep in mind that you want to choose new wood that is most likely to be fruitful. At the same time, you need to leave spurs and canes to maintain the shape of the vine. Naturally, these two guiding principles conflict at times. I always place shape before crop. That way, I can keep the pruning wounds small. If you put off pruning for shape in favor of reaping bigger crops, sooner or later you'll have to pay the price by inflicting a large wound on the vine. And don't forget that a strong vine will produce more grapes than anyone could ever use (except a vintner, of course), so the slight loss of fruit caused by pruning for shape is almost a blessing.

Spur Pruning

Pruning systems differ in the shape of the vine they create and in the length of the pruned canes. The spur-pruned head system and the spur-pruned cordon system both clip the canes back to stubs with only two or three buds on each. These spur systems work best for cultivars with European ancestry—traditional wine grapes and the French-American hybrids. These species are so fruitful that they'll even bear fruit from buds that are close to the base of the canes. But spur pruning is severe, leaving only 25 to 30 buds per vine, and it's rapidly losing favor among commercial growers.

Cane Pruning

American grapes such as 'Concord' and 'Delaware' have unreliable basal buds, so they should be cane-pruned rather than spur-pruned. Cane pruning leaves four to six long, one-year-old arms on each vine. With 10 to 15 buds on an arm, each vine pruned to this system can have 40 to 90 buds. Cane pruning yields much larger crops than spur pruning.

When you start cutting each spring, you must shape bearing branches for that year and make provisions for a renewal spur near each. The renewal spur will produce the bearing cane for the following year. Remember that grapes bear fruit only on the new wood. The challenge is to encourage the production of healthy buds and to plan the system so that the arms of the vine don't gradually get longer and longer.

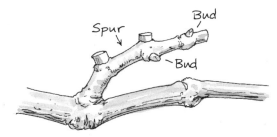

When spur pruning (above), clip the canes back to stubs, leaving only two or three buds on each stub. The idea of cane pruning (right) is to encourage the production of plenty of healthy buds without letting the cane grow out of control. Cut back each arm to one fruiting cane with 10 to 15 buds, and one renewal spur with two or three buds.

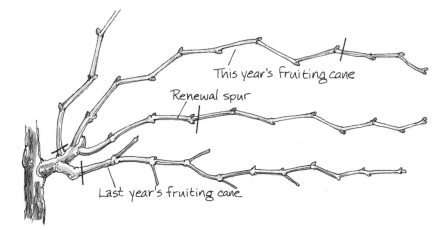

Spur-pruned grapevines can be trained to a stake, but cane-pruned grapevines must grow on a trellis. (See the illustration on page 226 for my favorite kind.) The type of trellis you use will help to determine the shape of the grapevines. Train arms coming off the trunk at each wire or crosspiece of the trellis. Prune each arm to one renewal spur bearing two or three buds, and one (or sometimes two) canes bearing 10 to 15 buds. On a large, healthy arm you can prune a cane to 15 buds, but on a small arm you must leave fewer buds.

In the course of a few years, you can strengthen weak arms and give the vine a balanced look by leaving more buds than normal on these arms and then removing about half the fruit clusters as soon as they appear. The burst of growth that results will rebuild the weak arm.

Summer Pruning

During the summer, after the grape bunches are about half-grown, you can prune a second time to increase air circulation and inhibit fungal growth. Thin the leaves around the grape clusters, and remove excess lengths of vine that grow much beyond the fruiting area of the canes. Grapes also grow suckers, much like those on tomato plants. You can cut these out, too.

PROPAGATION

You can propagate grapes by cuttings or layering. See "Hardwood Cuttings" on page 211 and "Layering the Lazy Way" on this page for details.

CROW'S PICKS

Like many fruits, grapes are adapted to certain parts of the country. You'll have healthier plants and heavier crops if you choose cultivars that grow well where you live. Up North, grow 'Concord', 'Himrod', and 'Interlaken'. In the South, buy 'Tokay', 'Pierce', and 'Thompson Seedless'. In the West, choose 'Champanel', 'Golden Muscat', and 'Flame'.

Layering the Lazy Way

Layering is the best—and easiest—way of filling bare spots in the vineyard. A layer is simply a branch of a plant that you bend to the earth, then cover with soil so that it will root while it's still a part of the parent plant. You can layer grapes in either fall or spring.

Bury a section of stem about 1 foot back from the tip, stripping the leaves off first. Weigh down the soil over the buried part with a brick or a rock. You can also bend a wire into a U-form and push it down over the buried stem.

The buried portion of the cane will eventually form roots, while the buds will develop into shoots. This process can take a long time, however. (The season after layering, you can tug on the buried stem gently to see if the layer has rooted.) For faster rooting, cut a shallow, 2-inch-long slit in the underside of the cane where it comes in contact with the ground, then put a toothpick or small pebble into the cut to hold it open. Once the new plant has rooted, you can cut it free from the parent vine, dig it up, and transplant it.

PEACHES AND NECTARINES

If you love peaches, there's no excuse not to grow your own. Choose cultivars that are adapted to your area and follow my guidelines, and you'll soon be harvesting mouthwatering fruit. You can grow nectarines, which are really just fuzzless peaches, the same way.

Unlike most tree fruits, peach and nectarine trees aren't too huge (about 20 feet tall), so you can grow standard (full-size) trees or choose space-saving dwarfs. If nematodes are a problem in your area, buy plants that are grafted onto 'Nemaguard' or 'Okinawa' rootstocks. In cold-winter areas, 'Siberian C' rootstock will increase plant hardiness.

Most peaches and nectarines are self-fertile, so you can plant just a single cultivar if you like. Of course, you can still grow several cultivars if you want to add variety and stretch the season. But regardless of how many you decide to plant, make sure you buy cultivars that are adapted to your area. In the North, buy high-chill cultivars that are less likely to bloom too early and lose their crop to frost. In the South, go for low-chill cultivars to be sure you get a good crop. Depending on the cultivar you choose, peaches and nectarines are hardy in Zones 5–9.

PLANTING

Plant your peach trees in early spring. They're pretty picky about where they put down roots, so choose the site carefully. Peaches require full sun and good drainage. Although 90 percent of the peach's roots grow in the top 18 inches of soil, some roots penetrate much deeper. Ideally, then, the soil should drain fast and deep—a wet soil stresses the tree and stunts growth. Consider planting your peaches on a north-facing slope, which would offer good drainage as well as protection against frost damage (from buds opening too early).

To get your trees off to a good start, dig a bushel-size hole for each tree. Before planting, prune off any broken or damaged roots. Soak the roots for an hour or so in cool water, then place the tree in the hole so that the graft is well above ground level. Don't plant the tree straight up. Instead, position it so it leans slightly in the direction of the prevailing wind. Plant dwarf peaches 8 to 12 feet apart and standard (full-size) trees 15 to 20 feet apart. Top-dress your new peaches

Hold That Mulch

Mulch has its place under peach trees during winter to prevent cold damage to roots. But during the growing season, I think regular hoeing is the best way to kill pupating soil-dwelling pests.

Your first cultivation may kill larvae of the oriental fruit moth. After that, regular cultivation helps control borers and plum curculios. Remember that peach roots are shallow; work only the top few inches of soil and be careful not to damage the bark. If you cultivate the soil one to three weeks before blossom time, you can also help protect the blossoms from frost damage—cultivated soil seems to release more warmth than either mulched ground or uncultivated ground.

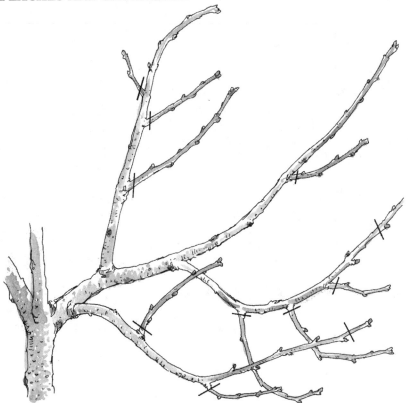

Peach trees need fairly heavy pruning. Every spring, remove any branches that grow straight up or hang down. Prune out crossing, weak, and diseased branches. After six years, remove all the new wood that has grown over the previous two years.

with compost, then cover with 6 to 12 inches of straw or other organic mulch, leaving 6 to 12 inches bare around the trunk.

PRUNING NEW TREES

Immediately after planting, cut each little tree back severely. When you've finished wielding your pruning knife, the trees should be about 35 inches tall, with only three or four of the strongest outward-growing (as opposed to upward) branches remaining. Even these should be cut back to the first or second bud, since the root system can support very few limbs and leaves the first year. This kind of pruning will create an open-center, or vase, shape that will let light in to leaves and fruit.

CONTINUING CARE

Young peach trees need plenty of water. Since their tiny feeder roots are killed by transplanting, water is extremely important the first summer. For healthy trees and succulent fruit, provide an inch of water a week.

Be careful not to overfeed your peach and nectarine trees. In spring, pull back the mulch and incorporate a bit of well-rotted, finished compost into the soil. During the growing season, spray plants with a foliar feed like liquid seaweed or compost tea every four to seven weeks.

Your crop will be slim at first, but after a year or so you may want to thin the fruit to get really big peaches. Wait until after the normal June drop. Then, as the year progresses, remove any odd-shaped, undersized, scarred, or off-color fruit. Compost these culls and any dropped fruits.

PEST AND DISEASE CONTROL

Peach trees are a bit more susceptible to diseases and insects than apples, cherries, or pears are. So it's important to get into the habit of practicing wise pest control right from the start. Here are the basics.

First, late in winter or early spring, while the trees are still dormant, coat them with a dormant oil spray. The oil will kill any overwintering scales and insect eggs.

Throughout the spring and summer, keep your eyes peeled for lumps of drying sap on the trunk of the tree. That's a sure sign that the peach tree borer has burrowed under the bark. Borers hatch in the soil around the tree. To control them before they get to the tree, apply beneficial nematodes to the surrounding soil. If you see signs of borers, look for their holes (usually in the bottom foot of the trunk). When you find one, stick a sharp wire into the hole to kill the borer.

Plum curculio can also be a pest of peaches east of the Rocky Mountains. Shake these weevils from your trees onto a sheet on the ground, then gather and destroy them. Or trap them with green spheres. Buy the red spheres sold for trapping apple maggots or make your own from peach-size balls; paint them light green and coat them with a sticky substance like Tanglefoot. Set the traps out after the peach flowers have fallen.

You can control oriental fruit moths by placing one or two pheromone traps in each tree at bud swell; replace the pheromone lures in the traps about six weeks after bloom. Or spray trees with *Bacillus thuringiensis* var. *kurstaki* (BTK). You can also release a batch of parasitic *Trichogramma* wasps every two weeks during the growing season to prey on the moths' eggs.

A number of fungal diseases can attack peach fruit, especially during wet, humid weather. Spray with lime-sulfur at bud swell as a preventive measure. Sulfur sprays, applied at bloom and when fruits begin to color up, will control brown rot. (Pick and destroy any rotting fruits to keep the disease from spreading.) Spraying sulfur or lime-sulfur will also control peach scab, which forms olive-green spots on fruit, and bacterial leaf spot, which causes dark spots on the fruit. Spray every ten days to three weeks until harvest.

You'll know your trees have peach leaf curl if new leaves are crinkled and distorted. Liquid seaweed sprays can help prevent this fungal disease. Spray the trees when the leaves open, then monthly during late spring and summer. Remove and destroy any infected leaves.

HARVESTING

Peaches are another fruit that won't keep ripening after harvest, so make sure they're fully colored and ripe before you pick them. (A great excuse for a taste test!) Be careful when you harvest—ripe peaches are slightly soft and bruise easily. Peaches don't keep well, so plan to can or eat your harvest right away.

FALL AND WINTER CARE

Pick up dropped fruit and rake fallen leaves and compost them to cut down on pest and disease problems. Apply a thin layer of composted manure or organic fertilizer all around the tree when it has gone dormant in the fall, then mulch for winter (leaving 6 to 12 inches of bare soil right around the trunk). Peach trees need full sun, but they're susceptible to sunscald in winter. Paint the trunk and the south and west sides of larger limbs with diluted white latex paint at the start of each dormant season. Then wrap the trunk with commercial trunk wrap to protect the tree from strong, cold winds, which aggravate winter drying and cold damage.

PRUNING ESTABLISHED TREES

For best growth, health, and production, peach trees need annual pruning. Do the deed as late as possible in spring, and never before bud swell. Late pruning lets you spot winter injury and adjust for it as you remove wood. Dress the large wounds with tree paint.

Fruit is borne on new wood produced the previous year. A healthy peach tree can put out twice as much fruiting wood as it needs; you have to cull it out. The second year after planting, do minimal pruning—just enough to shape the three or four limbs that you chose to grow out into an open vase shape. From then on, keep the interior of the tree open. Remove all crossing, diseased, leggy, and thin branches. Keep major limbs and branches growing laterally by cutting back any that are starting to grow upward.

PROPAGATION

Propagate peaches by grafting. See "Grafting" on page 208 to find out how.

 ### CROW'S PICKS

For reliable crops, make sure you choose peach and nectarine cultivars that are adapted to your region. Some of the best for the North are 'Elberta', 'Reliance', and 'Golden Jubilee'. In the South, grow 'Flordaprince', 'Early Elberta', and 'August Pride'. Westerners should choose 'August Pride', 'Desert Gold', and 'Orange Cling'.

PEARS

Pears are ornamental trees that are also easy to grow. They thrive on moderation—not too much food or water. And they're long-lived, looking good in the landscape for years.

Pears need pollinators, so you'll need to plant two or more cultivars for good fruit set. (Ask your nursery which pears will cross-pollinate each other.) Because pears are upright growers, it pays to choose dwarf trees—they're easier to take care of. Dwarf pear trees will yield about a bushel of fruit per tree, while standard (full-size) trees bear three to five bushels. Depending on the cultivar you choose, pears are hardy in Zones 4–9.

CHOOSING A ROOTSTOCK

Pears are grafted onto rootstocks that do different things for the tree. 'Bartlett' seedling rootstocks are used for standard trees, which mature to about 40 feet tall. There are a number of dwarfing rootstocks, which can cause mature trees to be as short as 8 feet tall.

There's also a rootstock series, 'OH × F' ('Old Home' × 'Farmingdale'), which provides resistance to fire blight and pear decline. The rootstocks in this series produce standard, semidwarf, and dwarf trees ('OH × F51' is the most dwarf). Quince rootstocks are also very dwarfing, but don't provide disease resistance.

PLANTING

Plant pears in early spring or fall. They need full sun and good air circulation, but aren't as fussy about drainage as other fruit trees. Once you've chosen a site, prepare the soil for planting as described in Chapter 12.

Buy trees that are 4 to 5 feet tall and have one to three branches. If you're planting dwarf cultivars, space them 8 to 12 feet apart. Allow 15 to 20 feet between standards.

Plant the tree so the stem of the rootstock extends about 2 inches above ground level. (You can tell where the scion, or top part, joins the rootstock by looking for the place where the trunk crooks; that's the graft union.) As soon as you've set the tree out and thoroughly watered it, place a 6-inch-deep layer of straw or other organic mulch around the base, extending out beyond the root system. Keep the mulch pulled back 6 to 12 inches away from the trunk. Otherwise, mice may burrow under the mulch and girdle the trunk of the newly planted tree.

Stake your tree to provide support until a strong root system has developed. To stake, drive a wooden pole into the ground 8 to 10 inches from the tree, preferably on the west side. Use a piece of garden hose or similar material to loop around the trunk and tie to the stake. Position the loop just beneath the lowest branch. You also need to protect the trunk of your new tree from sunscald. Wrap it with white tree wrap, or paint it with diluted white latex paint.

PRUNING NEW TREES

Like apples, pears should be trained to a central leader or dominant branch, with several strong scaffold (side) branches. Remove new branches that are growing directly over each other, and leave the stronger one. If two branches sprout from the same place, remove one, again leaving the stronger. The lowest branch should be about 14 inches above the ground. Space subsequent branches 6 to 8 inches apart in a sort of spiral around the trunk.

CONTINUING CARE

If you want plenty of pears, there's something else besides pruning you have to do to shape the tree. Pear branches tend to grow vertically rather than horizontally, and vertical branches bear less fruit than horizontal branches. Your job is to make the branches grow sideways instead of straight up. To do that, you'll need to weight the branches down with rocks, plastic soda bottles filled with water, or cans filled with concrete with a hanger embedded in each one. Or you can put wooden spreaders (clothespins or pieces of board) between the branch and the main trunk. Besides producing more pears, your plants will bear fruit earlier.

Keep your pears watered, especially during droughts. The mulch will help keep the soil evenly moist.

I think the real secret to successful pear growing is fertilizer—and not a lot of it. When fertilizing pear trees, aim for $1/2$ to $3/4$ pound of actual nitrogen per mature tree. That's about 5 to 8 pounds of blood meal or cottonseed meal, or about twice as much dried poultry waste. Always apply it early in spring so that the nitrogen has a chance to reach the roots and the shoots by late summer.

Why so sparing with the fertilizer? Because in pears, nitrogen and fire blight go hand in hand. High applications of nitrogen cause more succulent shoot growth over a longer period, giving the destructive bacteria more chance to attack the tree. In addition, insect pests such as aphids like the fast-growing, succulent leaves on the shoot tips. Excess nitrogen also aggravates calcium deficiency, which leads to fruit that won't keep more than a few weeks before the flesh around the core softens and turns brown.

Go easy on the lime, too. Crown gall is

caused by a soil-inhabiting bacterium that invades subsoil wounds on pears and other fruit trees, creating a knotty, health-threatening gall on the roots. It prefers soil with a high pH, so always go by what your soil test tells you and curb the urge to lime indiscriminately.

Foliar feeding is a great way to get nutrients to your pears fast. If, for example, a leaf test indicates an abnormally low magnesium level and the soil pH is below the ideal range for pears (6.4 to 6.8), you can apply a spray of Epsom salts (up to 10 pounds per 100 gallons) to the fully leafed-out tree. (If you need less spray, reduce the quantities accordingly.) To correct a calcium deficiency, you can also apply micronized calcium sulfate or powdered gypsum (I mix 1 pound per 100 gallons) in this manner—spray once a month in May, June, and July. Liquid seaweed sprays will correct calcium, boron, and many other nutrient deficiencies.

Pears need thinning to produce a healthy crop of sizable fruit. Thin pears one or two months after bloom, leaving one or two pears per cluster.

PEST AND DISEASE CONTROL

Pears can be attacked by pear psylla and are susceptible to fire blight. If your trees are bothered by pests or diseases other than these, check "Pest and Disease Control" in the Apples entry on page 219. Pears and apples share many of the same problems.

Spray your pears in late winter or early spring with dormant oil to keep pear psylla in check. You can barely see the tiny ($1/10$-inch) reddish brown insects, but if you look closely, you'll see the sticky honeydew they excrete. (If the tree is really infested, the leaves may become coated with honeydew, which in turn can attract black sooty mold.) If you find signs of psylla during the growing season, spray your trees with superior oil or insecticidal soap.

You'll know your pear has fire blight if the leaves and twigs look like someone scorched them with a torch. They turn black or brown and curl up, but the leaves still hang on the branches. If you don't stop it, fire blight can eventually kill a tree. You can protect your pears from this bacterial disease by spraying with streptomycin or copper just before the flowers open, then every four days during bloom. After bloom, spray every week until the fruit has formed.

Prune out and destroy fire blight–infected shoots, cutting at least 6 to 12 inches below any sign of infection. Your pears will be less likely to get fire blight if you don't overfertilize with nitrogen, which encourages soft, susceptible growth. If you know that fire blight is a problem in your area, plant resistant cultivars like 'Magness', 'Moonglow', and 'Kieffer'.

HARVESTING

Unlike most tree fruits, pears should be picked *before* they're ripe—they'll keep on ripening after harvest. (An exception is 'Seckel', which should be ripe when picked.) Harvest pears when they're full-size and the green color starts to lighten or turn yellow. You can store them in a cold, humid place like a root cellar or extra refrigerator, then ripen them at room temperature.

FALL AND WINTER CARE

In fall, pick up dropped fruit and rake up fallen pear leaves to prevent pest infestations and disease outbreaks. Remove the old mulch and replace it with 6 inches of fresh straw; keep a 4- to 8-inch area around the trunks bare to protect the trees from rodents.

Paint your trees' lower trunks with diluted white latex paint to prevent sunscald, then wrap them in hardware cloth sleeves.

PRUNING ESTABLISHED TREES

Prune your pear trees in late winter, before growth starts up. After the first year, prune as little as possible. Remove only crossed, diseased, or broken branches and vigorous upright growth, like suckers and water sprouts.

PROPAGATION

Propagate pears by grafting. (You can use either pear or quince rootstocks.) To find out how, see "Grafting" on page 208.

🐦 CROW'S PICKS

Choose pears that will grow well where you live. In the North, you can't go wrong with 'Bartlett', 'Seckel', and 'Sure Crop'. But down South, choose 'Douglas', 'Kieffer', and 'Monterrey'. And in the West, plant 'Cascade', 'Fan Sill', and 'Hood'.

PLUMS

There are generally two types of plums grown in the United States: Japanese and European. Japanese plums are more adaptable to varying soil conditions than the Europeans, but their shallower root systems make them more susceptible to drought damage. A good rule of thumb is to plant Japanese plums only in areas where peaches will survive.

Most European plums are self-fertile, but will produce heavier crops if two or more cultivars are planted near each other. Japanese plums are not self-fertile. To ensure proper pollination and fruit set, you'll need to plant at least two different cultivars.

Most plums begin bearing two to four years after planting and continue bearing for 15 years or more. Mature standard trees produce more than 100 pounds of plums, while dwarfs yield about two bushels, sometimes more if conditions are ideal. Like other fruit trees, dwarf plums are easier for backyard gardeners to manage. European plums are hardy in Zones 4–9, depending on the cultivar, while Japanese plums are hardy in Zones 6–10.

PLANTING

To plant either type, first remove any damaged roots, then dig a hole large enough to accommodate the root system comfortably. All commercially sold plums are grafted, so be sure the graft union remains above soil level when you plant your tree. Give the tree a good soaking, then mulch with several inches of straw and rotted manure keeping a ring of bare soil a few inches wide around the trunk.

PRUNING NEW TREES

Plums seem to respond best when pruned to a vase shape. Prune the main leader back to 3 feet (2 feet for dwarfs), just above a healthy bud. Shorten the side branches to two buds, cutting to an outside bud to promote open growth. See "Pruning Established Trees" in the Apricots entry on page 222 to find out more about pruning to a vase shape.)

CONTINUING CARE

Many plum trees—Japanese cultivars in particular—tend to overbear. If this happens, thin fruits to approximately 4 inches apart when they're about the size of grapes. Without this thinning, the plums will be stunted. Also, overcrowded fruits pressed snugly against each other are likely to fall prey to brown rot.

PEST AND DISEASE CONTROL

Japanese plums are somewhat more susceptible to brown rot fungus than European types. Check your trees every spring for the white fungus fluff, and remove and destroy all infected twigs before the buds open. The best preventive measure is to apply a liquid copper fungicide at bud swell. Conscientious pruning helps, too, since it encourages open growth and good ventilation.

If plum curculios strike, remove all damaged or fallen fruit. If they become a big problem, pull back the mulch in autumn and lightly till the soil around each tree to expose the overwintering pests. Leave the ground exposed for a week to give birds time to pick through the clods. Then put down some kelp meal and mulch with fresh straw. The following spring, spread newspapers under the tree at blossom time and shake the tree vigorously. Destroy the curculios that drop onto the newspapers until the infestation is under control. You'll find more on controlling curculios under "Pest and Disease Control" in the Apples and Apricots entries on pages 219 and 221.

HARVESTING

Plum trees bear fruit from June to September, depending on the cultivar. Pick plums for cooking and jellies when they're fully colored up, but still firm. Dessert plums should remain on the tree until they are fully ripe. Pick plums carefully to avoid bruising the fruit.

FALL AND WINTER CARE

Fall and winter care for plums is the same as for peaches. Pick up dropped fruit and rake fallen leaves and compost them to cut down on pest and disease problems. Apply a thin layer of composted manure or organic fertilizer around the tree when it has gone dormant in the fall, then mulch for winter (leave a mulch-free zone a few inches wide around the base of the tree). To protect the tree from sunscald, paint

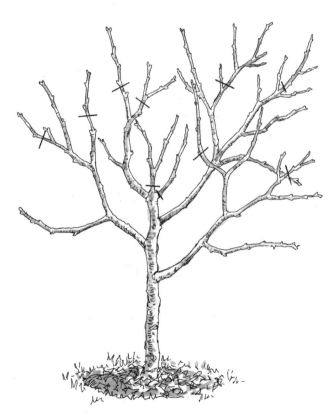

Plums grow vigorously and should be pruned hard to hold them to an open-center form. Choose three or four scaffold branches, head them back before the second year, then let them grow. Remove all other scaffolds growing from the central trunk.

the trunk with diluted white latex paint at the start of each dormant season.

PRUNING ESTABLISHED TREES

The first winter after planting, remove weak branches and those with narrow crotches. Once they've been trimmed to an open vase shape, European plums require only light pruning to remove crossed, damaged, or diseased limbs. Japanese plums, on the other hand, tend to produce long whips each year—you'll need to cut these back by one-half, always to an outside bud. When pruning, keep in mind that long-lived fruiting spurs develop on two- to three-year-old wood. Don't remove nubby spurs, and avoid removing well-placed new wood.

PROPAGATION

Propagate plums by grafting. See "Grafting" on page 208 to find out how.

CROW'S PICKS

Like peaches and pears, some plums do better in certain parts of the country. In the North, try 'Burbank', 'Green Gage', and 'Santa Rosa'. In the South, grow 'Satsuma', 'Stanley', and 'Queen Ann'. And if you live in the West, choose 'Burbank', 'French Prune', and 'Late Santa Rosa'.

14

Let's Grow Berries

Growing berries and brambles is the perfect way to get started with fruit. In nearly every case, these bush fruits produce fruit faster, take up less space, and are easier to grow than tree fruits. And, in many cases, I think they're even more of a treat. What tastes better than a freshly picked red raspberry straight from the plant? Or how about a bowl of fresh blueberries in cream? They're hard to beat.

As long as you have a few feet of sunny space, you can grow berries. From Zone 2 in the far North to Zone 10 down South, you can find plenty of berry types that will thrive and grow as vigorously as wild plants. (See the USDA Plant Hardiness Zone Map on page 366 to find your zone.)

With berries and brambles, pruning is usually simple and straightforward, and you'll begin harvesting in as little as two years. So what are you waiting for? Let's grow berries!

BLACKBERRIES

There are two different types of blackberries: upright and trailing. Trailing blackberries (left) sprawl to the ground if not trellised and fruit all along their canes. Upright blackberries (right) have erect canes and bear their fruit at the tips of the canes.

Blackberries grow like weeds throughout most of the East. They can be cultivated in the garden all the way down to Texas. They don't require extremely fertile soil, although it should be well drained. Blackberries even grow well in partial shade; in fact, that's where you'll invariably find the best wild berries.

But don't settle for wild berries—the best cultivars offer fruit that is bigger, juicier, tastier, and longer-lasting. And there are plenty of new cultivars that don't have the worst feature of wild blackberries: thorns.

There are two distinct types of blackberries, which are categorized by their growth habit: upright and trailing. (Trailing types are sometimes known as dewberries.) The upright cultivars are the hardiest and will grow as far north as Zone 3. But most gardeners agree that the trailing kinds are the most flavorful. The two are grown pretty much the same way, except that the trailing types must be trellised.

When choosing a blackberry cultivar, check to see if it requires cross-pollination.

You may discover that planting two or more cultivars will increase your berry crop, even if they don't need pollinators. With good care, blackberries will keep producing for ten years or more. They're hardy in Zones 3–10, depending on which cultivar you choose.

PLANTING

For highest yields, choose a site carefully. If possible, locate your blackberry patch where it will get filtered sun all day. The plants should also be shielded from winds, which can chill them in the winter and dry them out during the summer. Frost pockets are another potential problem, since blackberries are relatively tender. The ideal site for this crop is probably a gentle northern slope.

Blackberries don't mind acid soil and

aren't particularly heavy feeders, but the soil should have lots of organic matter since the plants need constant moisture. It should also be well drained—standing water around the plants' shallow roots will sharply reduce yields.

If you have time, sow and turn under a cover crop of rye, clover, or oats the year before planting. Any of these crops will supply all the organic matter and nutrients the plants need the first year.

Early spring and late fall are best for setting out canes or young plants. Before planting, cut the tops back to 6 inches. Then plant the blackberries so that the center crown is covered by no more than 2 or 3 inches of soil. Give them plenty of room since they're rampant growers. Allow 4 to 6 feet between bushes, and space rows 8 feet apart. This spacing may seem wide at first, but it won't once the bushes begin to fill out.

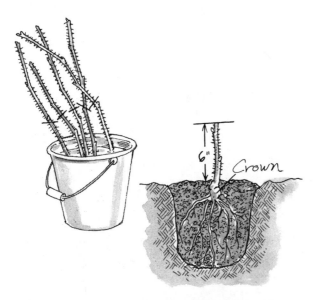

Soak the roots of your blackberry plants in water before planting. Cut the tops of the canes back to 6 inches. Plant so that the center of the crown is no more than 2 or 3 inches below the soil surface.

CONTINUING CARE

To keep weeds down, hoe shallowly around the plants until midsummer. Then mulch with 6 inches of straw or weed-free hay. Blackberries need plenty of water until the berries reach full size; then cut back on water as they ripen. (Don't let them go dry, though—just give them about half as much water as before.)

PEST AND DISEASE CONTROL

Insects generally don't bother blackberries much, though spider mites may attack if the weather is hot and dry. You'll know they're in the neighborhood if the leaves turn gray and lose their luster. Try controlling the mites by misting the plants—especially the undersides of leaves—with water, or by applying an insecticidal soap spray according to label directions. If aphids become a problem, these controls will take care of them, too.

Several diseases are common in blackberries. Rust first appears as yellow dots on the leaves; the dots soon erupt into powdery, orange fungal spores. Anthracnose starts as small, purplish spots that enlarge and form sunken gray fungal lesions. If you spot either of these diseases, cut out and burn the infected canes immediately.

HARVESTING

Blackberries usually ripen in August, after the raspberry harvest and before most peaches, pears, apples, and grapes are ripe. But control yourself: Never pick blackberries when they first turn black. Even if you see birds pecking at the fruit, resist the temptation. It's not until the bees are hanging around the berries that they're sweet and really ripe.

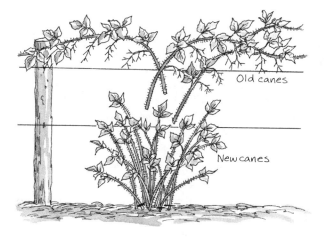

Old canes

New canes

FALL AND WINTER CARE

Rake back mulch from the plants in the fall. Once the weather is reliably cold, replace the mulch, adding fresh mulch as needed. In late winter, apply 1 to 1½ pounds of compost per foot of row.

PRUNING

Upright, or erect, blackberry canes will grow 6 feet high or more. The berries form on one-year-old canes; remove these after fruiting. To encourage branching and more fruit the following year, cut off the tips when the canes reach 36 inches in their first year.

As the lateral branches begin to grow, cut or pinch off the tips when the shoots reach 16 inches. Keep up the pruning until midsummer or just before the fruiting buds begin to form. At the same time, keep an eye out for suckers that may sprout up several feet from the main plant. If you let them go, your blackberry patch will soon become an impenetrable thicket.

As long as you keep erect blackberries pruned within bounds, you won't need to trellis them. But if you're a neatnik, you can train them by putting up posts and confining

Pruning erect blackberries is simple. Just remove the one-year-old canes after they fruit, then cut back the new canes to 36 inches. You can leave them to grow on their own or tie them to a wire stretched between posts.

the canes between them. To construct a trellis, set posts 15 to 20 feet apart in the row and stretch wire between them. For erect cultivars, use a single wire and attach it to the posts about 30 inches from the ground. Tie the canes up with soft string where they cross the wire.

Trailing blackberries put on a tremendous amount of growth. After fruiting, cut the one-year-old canes right back to the ground—new growth will quickly take over.

You'll need to trellis trailing blackberries so you can reach them for care and harvesting. For semitrailing and trailing types, make a trellis with posts and two wires. Set the posts 15 to 20 feet apart, as for erect blackberries. Then attach one wire to the posts 1 to 3 feet from the ground, and the other wire 5 feet from the ground. Using soft string, tie the canes horizontally along the wires, or fan them out from the ground and tie where they cross each wire. Do not tie the canes in bundles.

In summer, as soon as you've picked the last berries, cut out all the old canes and burn them. Also, thin out the new canes: Leave 3 or 4 canes on the erect cultivars, 4 to 8 canes on the semitrailing cultivars, and 8 to 12 canes on the trailing cultivars.

PROPAGATION

Propagate blackberries by tip layering. See "Making More Black Raspberries" on page 255 to find out how.

Crow's Picks

You'll have the best luck with blackberries if you grow cultivars that are specially adapted to your region. In the North, buy 'Logan', 'Thornless Logan', and 'Darrow'. Down South, choose 'Thornfree', 'Brazos', and 'Rosborough'. Out West, the best bets are 'Boysen', 'Cascade', and 'Marion'.

BLUEBERRIES

The great thing about blueberries (aside from the true blue taste, of course) is their looks. Blueberry bushes are well-behaved and attractive. They produce pretty white flowers in spring, and the leaves turn a rich red in fall. In fact, they make lovely landscape plants. That means you can plant them just about anywhere in your yard.

Blueberries are easy to grow, care for, and harvest. They need less space than fruit trees and have very few insect problems. The fruit ripens over a period of six or more weeks, depending on the cultivar. And if kept properly fertilized and pruned, blueberries should produce for a lifetime.

There are four kinds of blueberry bushes: lowbush, highbush, "half-high," and rabbiteye. Lowbush cultivars are natives of the Northeast, where they grow wild in meadows. In the landscape, these low-growing plants function like shrubby groundcovers. The berries are small but extremely flavorful. Lowbush cultivars are the best choice where space is limited since they don't get too big. However, you should still prune them periodically to keep them dense and compact—4 to 8 inches high is ideal. Pruning will also lead to larger fruiting clusters.

Highbush blueberries are the most commonly available in catalogs. They're the ones that grow into large bushes, some up to 6 feet tall. "Half-high" blueberries are shorter versions of highbush blueberries and grow 2 to 4 feet tall. Rabbiteye blueberries are the best choice for the South. These cultivars were developed from the native southern species, *Vaccinium ashei,* and can grow into really huge plants, topping out at 15 to 18 feet.

Whichever kind or kinds you choose, plant at least two cultivars of each type for cross-pollination purposes. The blueberry is self-pollinating, but a self-pollinated cultivar is slower to set fruit than one that's been cross-pollinated.

Blueberries are such handsome, easy-care shrubs that they fit perfectly into just about any landscape. With their glossy green leaves, clusters of white flowers, showy blue berries, and stunning red fall color, they're a treat for the eye as well as the palate. You can mix them with other acid-loving ornamentals like mountain laurels, azaleas, and rhododendrons, or grow them as a hedge.

PLANTING

You can grow blueberry bushes as single specimens, or you can plant them 4 to 6 feet apart in groups. You can also plant them 3 to 4 feet apart to create a mass effect for hedging.

It's best to plant blueberries when they're dormant. Plant in spring as soon as the ground can be worked, or in the fall as soon as the leaves drop but before the ground freezes too hard to be workable.

Remember that there's one thing blueberries demand, and that's an acid soil. They grow best in soil with a pH of 4.5 to 5.5. If your soil is slightly acidic, you can add organic matter like peat moss, oak leaves, or pine needles to lower the pH. But if it's more alkaline, you'll need to add sulfur as well. (See "Playing with the pH" on page 35 for application rates.)

Prepare the soil a bit deeper than you would in your vegetable garden, and work in a 6- to 12-inch-deep layer of organic matter like peat moss, compost, or shredded leaves. If possible, till under a green manure crop like buckwheat, oats, or rye the season before planting to provide more aeration in the soil. You can work in a layer of acid compost (made from peat moss, shredded oak leaves, pine needles, or a combination of these) and composted cow, horse, or chicken manure when you till the green manure crop under.

When planting, prepare a hole 2 to 3 feet wide and at least 18 inches deep. It should be large enough for the roots to spread out flat rather than hang down deep. Plant at the same depth as the soil line on the main stem, or slightly deeper. Never let the sun or wind dry out the roots—keep them protected while you are preparing your hole.

Mounds of Blueberries

Mounding is an easy way to start new blueberry plants. To propagate by mounding, build a wooden frame about 1 foot high and 3 feet square around the blueberry bush. Fill this structure with a mixture of moist peat moss and rotted sawdust, mounding the medium around the canes of the bush. The canes will form roots beneath the surface of the medium. Once they've rooted, you can pull back the medium, cut them off below their new roots, and plant them. Mounding will reproduce the parent plant exactly to give you more plants of a specific cultivar.

CONTINUING CARE

Apply a mulch 3 to 6 inches deep around the bush, extending out beyond the drip line of the branches. Use an acid mulch such as shredded oak leaves, pine needles, or peat moss, and replenish it yearly as it decomposes. (If you use peat, mix it with shredded leaves so it won't dry out and form a crust around your plants.) Apply the mulch when the soil underneath is full of moisture.

Some folks recommend sawdust as a mulch for blueberries, but I don't like it. Sawdust will dry out in the hot summer months and will steal moisture from the soil around the roots. As it decomposes, it will also deplete the nitrogen content of the soil. So, unless you're prepared to water regularly and to add two or three times the usual amounts of nitrogen each year, it's best to avoid using sawdust.

Wait until your blueberry bush has

leafed out and the leaves have matured, then fertilize and water well. The best fertilizer for blueberries contains nitrogen, phosphorus, and potash in approximately equal amounts—a balanced organic 5-5-5 fertilizer would be perfect.

When you use manure for nitrogen, be sure it's well composted. Keep it away from the crown, and apply it only when the plant is dormant. I use blood meal and apply it right on top of the mulch in spring. One pound of blood meal for every 10 feet of row is about right.

To keep up the mineral health of your soil, apply bonemeal, rock phosphate, and kelp meal once every three or four years. You can apply these liberally at any time of the year, though I recommend doing it in fall or winter.

Don't forget that blueberries need a

Blueberries from Seed

If you're keen on native plantings and starting plants from scratch, try growing your own lowbush blueberries. My favorite way is to start them from seed.

You'll find the plants growing wild from Maine to Minnesota and south to the Carolinas. For best results, go berry hunting in the fall. Since lowbush blueberry seed enters a rest (dormant) period soon after harvest in August, it's best to obtain the seeds from berries that have been frozen at least 90 days. If you harvest berries in the summer, place the fruit in your freezer and leave it there for 90 days or more to break the dormant period.

The best time to sow the seed is in January. New seedlings will then be ready to set out when the growing season begins. Here's what to do:

Remove the seed from the berries. The easiest way to do that is with a kitchen blender. Put $1/2$ to $3/4$ cup of thawed berries in the blender and fill to the $3/4$ cup mark with water. Blend for 15 to 20 seconds at high speed, then allow the mixture to stand for 5 minutes.

The seed will settle to the bottom, and you can pour off the pulp floating at the top very slowly with the water. Refill with water and repeat the operation, allowing the seed to settle and pouring off the pulp. Then remove the seed and spread it on a paper towel to dry. Once dry, it is ready for planting.

Fill a 3-inch-tall flat with finely ground sphagnum moss, sprinkle the seed evenly over the surface, then cover with a very thin layer of moss. Place the flat in a greenhouse or under lights and cover with newspaper to retain moisture. Keep the moss moist but not soaked. Maintain the soil temperature between 70° and 80°F. The seedlings should emerge in three to four weeks.

Once the tiny seedlings begin to appear, place the flat in full sun. When the plants reach 3 to 5 inches, transplant them into pots filled with either compost or a mixture of $1/3$ sand, $1/3$ peat, and $1/3$ leaf mold, amended with a pinch of organic fertilizer. Grow them in a nursery area through the season, then put them in a cold frame for the winter. Next spring, plant them in their permanent location.

steady supply of moisture to grow and bear well. Make sure they get plenty—and don't spare the mulch!

PEST AND DISEASE CONTROL

Blueberries aren't bothered much by pests. A little commonsense sanitation will keep most of them in check. Pick fruit when it's ripe. Don't leave any overripe berries hanging or fruit flies will lay eggs in them. Clean up all old trimmings—they provide a breeding place for insects. If you find a wilted tip on a branch, clip or break it off and burn it. Chances are, you'll be frying a stem borer along with it.

Diseases? Not much to worry about there, either. Just make sure you buy disease-free plants from a reputable nursery. Once the plants are growing, remove any wood that looks damaged and destroy it immediately. To avoid mummy berry (a fungal disease that causes some berries to drop early and others to shrivel and harden), keep all fruits picked—don't let them shrivel on the bush.

If this short list of potential minor problems sounds too good to be true, it is. There's one pest that loves blueberries as much as you and I do: birds. Drape each bush with bird netting when the fruit starts to color up, and weight the edges down to keep 'em out. Or build wire-and-frame blueberry "cages" around your plants as a permanent barrier. (Make sure one side opens up!)

HARVESTING

Blueberries are not ready for picking when they first turn blue. Restrain yourself and remember that it takes five more days for them to ripen once they're blue. To test for ripeness, pick a berry and check the scar left where the stem pulls off. If there's a reddish ring around the edge of it, the berry isn't quite ripe. You'll notice that the berries get larger as they ripen, so if you pick them before they're completely ripe, you'll lose volume as well as flavor.

Pick each berry by hand. You should get about four or five pickings about five days apart from each cultivar. Pick the fruit early in the day before the sun gets hot. Never pick immediately after a rain; the water often dilutes the flavor, and the skin may crack open if the fruit is too moist. For best flavor, harvest on a cool evening after a warm day.

Don't wash the berries until you're ready to serve them. If you're not going to eat them immediately, remove any soft berries, and keep the rest cool and dry. Blueberries freeze well, too.

FALL AND WINTER CARE

In the fall, rake up and compost the old mulch, and replace it with a 6-inch layer of fresh shredded oak leaves, peat moss, or pine needles. Sprinkle blood meal around the plants to repel rabbits, which may otherwise eat the bark; renew as needed.

PRUNING

Blueberry bushes need some pruning, but not much compared to fruit trees. The object is to make them produce tall, erect canes directly from the root crown. They won't need much cutting the first few years; just snip out all small, twiggy growth at ground level.

Prune in late fall, winter, or early spring, when the plant is dormant. Cut back damaged wood to strong, healthy growth. When the bush is six years old, you may find older branches that aren't producing good lateral growth; cut back to a strong branch. Renew your bush constantly and get rid of old wood.

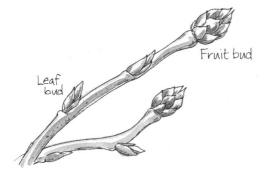

Leaf bud

Fruit bud

When pruning blueberries, you have to be able to tell the difference between the fruit (flower) buds and the leaf buds. The fat fruit buds are usually near the tips of the branches, while the leaf buds are lower and tighter to the branches. By pruning off some of the fruit buds, you'll get larger, sweeter berries.

The fruit buds are fat and usually near the tips of the branches; the smaller, pointier leaf buds are just below and are tighter to the branch. If you have a heavy crop set, trim off the shorter laterals that have only two or three fruit buds, since these will produce only small berries.

PROPAGATION

You can propagate blueberries from cuttings; see "Softwood Cuttings" on page 212. But it's simpler to propagate them by mounding—learn how in "Mounds of Blueberries" on page 245. And if you're feeling adventurous, it's easy to grow blueberries from seed; see page 246 for details.

🐦 CROW'S PICKS

Where you live affects which blueberries you'll grow. In the North, some of the best are 'Northsky', 'North Country', and 'Elliot'. Favorites for the South are 'Sharpblue', 'Beckyblue', and 'Southland'. In the West, try 'Olympia', 'Bluecrop', and 'Sharpblue'.

ELDERBERRIES

I'd be glad to lead an elderberry revival in the United States. This American native deserves to be a lot more popular in the home garden than it is. Selected elderberry cultivars, cross-bred from the wild bushes, produce great quantities of purplish black fruits year in and year out. Rich in iron, natural sugars, vitamin C, and flavor, the fruit makes wonderful pies, jams, and even wine. And the bushes can make a dramatic statement in the landscape—some grow over 15 feet tall and several yards wide.

An elderberry in full bloom is a glorious sight. The whole clump becomes a mass of white, like a gigantic snowball. The fragrance permeates the whole area. Hummingbirds and butterflies spend much of their day fluttering about. Shortly after the blooms appear, the bush is covered with purplish black fruits, which stand out against the fernlike foliage. And if that's not enough, elderberries are almost pest free, and they aren't attacked by any serious fungal or viral diseases that I know of.

Elderberries are easy to transplant and easily adapted to garden conditions. They're especially valuable in cities since they can tolerate smoke and dust. They'll grow vigorously in partial shade or full sun. And they're hardy in Zones 2–9, depending on the cultivar.

Even if you don't like elderberry jelly, take a tip from me and plant a few bushes to spruce up the landscape and attract wildlife. More than 100 species of birds feed on elderberries. Plant these bushes, and I guarantee you'll soon see birds you've never seen before!

PLANTING

Elderberry bushes thrive in almost any fertile soil. Ideally, the soil should be deep and friable—a deep sandy loam is just about perfect. To encourage vigorous root growth, add a lot of woodsy organic matter like shredded leaves. Elderberries require a little more than average moisture.

If you plant your elderberries in full sun, keep the soil cool and moist by underplanting the bushes with dense-foliaged groundcovers like periwinkle (*Vinca minor*), pachysandra, or English ivy, or by applying a thick mulch of shredded leaves or well-rotted manure. Keep in mind that these bushes don't like sawdust, wood chips, or other mulches with a high acid content. That's because, unlike blueberries, elderberries prefer a slightly alkaline soil (pH 7.1 to 7.5).

For best results with elderberries, it pays to take some extra care at planting time. Here's what I do: For each plant, I dig a hole about 3 feet in diameter and 2 feet deep. I throw the topsoil into a heap and mix it, two parts to one, with well-rotted compost. Then I place the plant in the hole and backfill with this mixture. I tamp the soil down firmly against the roots and water thoroughly. The water will firm the soil even more and prevent air pockets that can damage the roots. I plant the bushes about 10 feet apart; in a few years, they'll spread to fill the spaces between.

CONTINUING CARE

Remember that elderberries need plenty of water—never let them get dry. Don't fertilize your elderberry bushes the first year; just spread a 6- to 12-inch-deep layer of mulch. After the first year, instead of cultivating, maintain a mulch of 4 inches or

more. Allow the mulch to extend a few inches beyond the drip line, and keep it 4 to 6 inches away from the main trunk. After the first year, apply a mixture of 2 cups of bonemeal or rock phosphate and 1 cup of greensand to each bush. For an extra boost, spread a handful or two of wood ashes around each plant annually.

HARVESTING

Elderberries ripen in August and September. When the berries turn dark purple-black, taste-test for sweetness. If they're ready, cut off the entire cluster.

FALL AND WINTER CARE

Rake off old mulch each November, then apply 4 inches or more of fresh mulch. Leave 4 to 6 inches bare around the trunks to discourage marauding rodents.

PRUNING

Routine pruning includes removing dead, weak, and diseased wood. Cut out any canes that are at least four years old, but make sure you leave five to nine strong canes on each plant.

PROPAGATION

Propagate elderberries from cuttings. See "Fruits from Cuttings" on page 210.

CROW'S PICKS

Unlike many fruits and berries, elderberries aren't region-specific—you can grow the same elderberry cultivars no matter what part of the country you live in. I think the best cultivars are 'Adams' and 'Johns'. Plant both for the heaviest fruit set.

GOOSEBERRIES

Most folks think of gooseberries as a very tart pie fruit. True, you can pick them at an early stage and use them that way. But if that's the only way you handle gooseberries, you don't know what you're missing. Let them ripen to fully red or purple for a fantastic fresh-fruit treat!

Gooseberries are attractive bushes with pretty lobed leaves that turn yellow in fall. You can grow them in Zones 3–7.

PLANTING

Site your gooseberries in full sun in Zones 3–5 and partial shade in Zones 6 and 7. Gooseberry bushes need fertile, well-drained soil, but will do well in many soils if grown with a heavy mulch. Fall planting is often recommended, but I've had good luck with spring planting. You can space the plants as far as 5 feet apart or as close as 2 feet to form a dense hedge.

CONTINUING CARE

Mulch your plants with 6 inches of straw, shredded leaves, or compost. (Gooseberries have thorny stems, so you don't have to leave a mulch-free zone around the trunks.) These bushes need plenty of water while they're actively growing; don't let them dry out.

Gooseberries are heavy feeders and thrive on organic fertilizers like cottonseed meal and bonemeal. But top-dressing with these powders will encourage shallow root growth, so try to work them in deeply.

Here's a little trick I've learned to get the fertilizer down to a depth of 8 to 10 inches: Force a spading fork into the ground to the full length of the tines and rock it back and forth. Space these holes around the bush at the outer branch line, then fill them approximately half-full with the bonemeal and cottonseed meal.

PEST AND DISEASE CONTROL

Although gooseberries do have their share of insect enemies, these pests are pretty easy to control. Your most serious problem may be aphids. As soon as you see the tiny green or black bulbous bugs, spray them with a mix of garlic oil and Palmolive Green liquid soap. If they're allowed to get a foothold, they cause the leaves to curl and the spray won't touch them. The best thing to do if they get that far is to pick off and destroy the curled leaves.

Green gooseberries are fine for pies, but if you let them ripen to a deep red or purple, they're delicious eaten right off the bush. The ripe ones will be bigger—juicier, too!

Handpicking can also control another pest, the imported currantworm. Wrens seem to be extremely fond of this pest, so it probably won't be a real problem on your bushes if there are lots of birds on your property. If you see wilted canes, suspect the currant borer. Control this pest by cutting off the canes below the hole where the borer entered the stem.

Gooseberry plants are susceptible to powdery mildew, but you can keep it in check by making sure the bushes receive at least a half-day of full sun and have adequate air circulation. If mildew is a serious problem in your garden, try a preemptive strike by spraying the bushes with a baking soda solution every two weeks from the time the buds start opening.

Black currants are relatives of gooseberries and are alternate hosts for white pine blister rust, a devastating disease of pines. Before it was discovered that only black currants were carriers, some states restricted the importation of gooseberry plants. In some cases, these laws are still on the books, so check your state's restrictions before you buy gooseberries for your garden.

Here's the best way to fertilize gooseberries: To get the fertilizer down to a depth of 8 to 10 inches, force a spading fork into the ground to the full length of the tines and rock it back and forth. Space these holes around the bush at the outer branch line, and fill them approximately half-full with bonemeal and cottonseed meal.

HARVESTING

The color tells the tale of gooseberry flavor. If you want a tart flavor, let the berry ripen on the plant at least until the green color begins to change to yellow (or, in some cases, to white). The fruit will be larger then, with better texture and flavor than unripe berries, and it will need much less sweetening. If you harvest your gooseberries at this half-ripe stage, you can store them, juice them, or make them into sauces or pies.

If you leave your gooseberries on the bush until they turn pinkish red, the fruit takes on a new sweetness. At this stage, the succulent berries make delicious jam, jelly, or a truly thirst-quenching juice. And as the fruit changes from light red to dark red and then to purple—if you can wait that long—it makes a delicious fresh-fruit dessert.

FALL AND WINTER CARE

In late fall, rake off the old mulch and compost it. This is a good time to feed your gooseberries, too. After applying cottonseed meal and bonemeal (see "Continuing Care" on page 250), replace the old mulch with 6 inches of fresh mulch.

PRUNING

Prune gooseberries by cutting out some of the older branches from year to year. The growth coming up from the center will renew the bush, and your gooseberries will continue to produce for many years.

If you're growing the bushes just for fruit, you should also remove all low-growing limbs that are touching the ground. If you're training a gooseberry hedge, leave the lower limbs and just ignore the fruit they produce.

Of course, improved fruit production is the basic reason for pruning, but it's also important to develop an open, spreading shape to discourage mildew. Do your pruning as soon as possible after picking. In fact, it's best to prune as you pick since you can easily see which branches are past their prime and snip them out on the spot.

PROPAGATION

You can propagate gooseberries from cuttings. See "Fruits from Cuttings" on page 210 to find out how.

Crow's Picks

Like elderberries, the same gooseberry cultivars can be grown all over the country. My favorites are 'Poorman' and 'Pixwell'. Plant both for heaviest fruit set.

RASPBERRIES

I don't think there's any plant on earth that rewards its grower as handsomely as raspberries. I've found them to be virtually trouble-free. They grow vigorously under all types of conditions and bear fruit in one year, sometimes sooner. And, oh, the fruit—it melts in your mouth. It's like fruit of the gods. Something that good shouldn't be that easy to grow. But it is.

There are two distinct types of raspberries: black raspberries and red raspberries. They require slightly different growing techniques. If you master them, you'll be able to pick that luscious fruit for a month or more.

Black raspberries are the easier of the two to care for. Just plant them about 6 feet apart, provide a simple trellis, and cut out fruiting canes after you've harvested. That's all there is to it. Red raspberries are not much more difficult, but the pruning technique is a bit different. Both types are hardy in Zones 3–9, depending on the cultivar.

PLANTING

Plant raspberries in early spring, in a location that provides at least a half-day of sunshine. Because these brambles are susceptible to soilborne diseases of the nightshade family, don't plant them where tomatoes, eggplant, potatoes, or peppers have grown during the past three years.

Weeds can make raspberry cultivation a misery. The key to controlling weeds is good soil preparation before planting. To rid the soil of all grass and weed roots, cultivate deeply. If possible, grow a cover crop the year before to get rid of the sod.

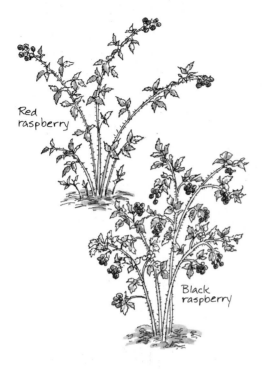

CONTINUING CARE

All the cultivated bramble fruits have not been civilized for long, so they still like the woodsy soil where their wild ancestors grew. Mulching heavily helps recreate these soil conditions—cool, moist, and full of bacterial life and decaying organic matter. Mulch also helps kill weeds and eliminates the need for cultivation. My favorite mulch for raspberries is maple leaves.

To increase soil fertility, apply a shovelful of organic fertilizer to each plant as growth begins, then renew the mulch. As the small fruits begin to form, make sure the beds receive 1 to 2 inches of water a week; otherwise, the berries won't be plump and juicy.

During the first year, resist the urge to harvest. Instead, pick off all the flower clusters and let the plants' energy go into making canes. That way, the plants will have a chance to build strong root systems. Each fruiting cane lasts only two years, but the roots of the plant are perennial and, if properly cared for, can live 20 years or more. That's why it's important to choose the best location you possibly can when you plant.

PEST AND DISEASE CONTROL

Aphids and spider mites can both be a problem on raspberries. If you see aphids or webbing, spray the plants with a steady stream of water, making sure you hit the undersides of the leaves. Often, one or two sprayings will control the pests, but if you've got a heavy infestation, a soap spray will knock them out. Use an insecticidal soap and apply it according to package directions, or try my homemade version. (See "Pest and Disease Control" in the Gooseberries entry on page 250.)

Red raspberries (top) bear fruit at the tips of their canes, and they spread by suckers to form large clumps. Black raspberries (bottom) fruit on side branches, and they don't form suckers; instead, they spread by tip-layering.

Good drainage is essential; these berries can't stand wet feet. And black raspberry roots can reach downward as far as 3 feet. Work the soil deeply before planting. Since raspberries are also heavy feeders, the soil should be rich in nutrients, especially nitrogen. Before planting, I till in a 3- to 6-inch-deep layer of manure, compost, grass clippings, and shredded leaf mold.

When the plants arrive, soak the roots for a few hours. Dig holes about 1 foot in diameter. Then spread the roots and place them in the holes, setting the plants 2 inches deeper than they grew in the nursery. Space the plants 4 to 6 feet apart, mark them with stakes, and cut them back to just above ground level.

Control raspberry rednecked cane borers by pruning off wilted canes below the telltale borer holes. Destroy the infested canes.

Only certified disease-free plants should ever go into your garden. Once disease symptoms (deformed growth, stunting, discoloration, or permanent wilting) appear, it's essential to cut out and burn all infected canes. By removing old canes regularly, you'll help prevent infection from black raspberries' biggest enemy: viruses.

If powdery mildew strikes, beat this fungus by spraying bushes with a baking soda solution every two weeks, or use a sulfur spray. Spraying with compost tea will help prevent gray mold from forming.

HARVESTING

Here's another great thing about growing raspberries: You get to taste-test for ripeness. But you'll know they're ripe when they drop into your hand with just a gentle tug. Pick them when the dew has dried and handle them like the priceless jewels they are—rough treatment (and moisture from the dew) results in moldy berries within a few days.

FALL AND WINTER CARE

Fall is the time to renew the mulch around your raspberries. Rake off and compost the old mulch, then, when the ground is cold, replace it with fresh mulch. (Raspberry stems are thorny, so you don't have to leave a bare space around the base of the canes.)

PRUNING

I've seen plenty of raspberry patches fail long before their time because they were allowed to become crowded with weak or dead plants. Pruning is simple, so don't let this happen to your patch.

Although the roots of the raspberry are perennial, the tops are biennial. Each cane or stem grows one year, produces fruit the second year, then dies. These old canes must be removed as soon as the fruit is harvested. Cut them close to the ground, then take them from the area and destroy them to prevent any insects from overwintering or diseases from building up in them.

After the leaves have fallen in autumn, thin the remaining canes. Cut out

It's easy to prune everbearing and fall-bearing red raspberries: With a sickle bar mower, cut all canes right down to the ground in early spring, while the plants are still dormant.

Making More Black Raspberries

Unlike red raspberries, which reproduce by sending up new shoots from the roots, black raspberries tip-root to start their next generation. Tip-rooting means that the plants root at the ends of arching canes where they touch the ground. This process happens fairly quickly—within about three weeks in October.

As the tops of the plants reach the ground, you can help them along by scratching up the soil a bit, keeping it slightly moist, and covering the tips of the canes with handfuls of mulch. By the time cold weather sets in, the buried shoot tips will have developed enough roots to give them a good hold in the soil. To protect the developing young raspberry plants through the winter, surround them with a 10-inch layer of mulch.

The following spring, pull back the mulch layer and cut the new plants free from the parent plant, leaving two or three buds above the roots. You can transplant them or leave them where they are. If you leave them in place, don't worry about spacing; the arching canes will have naturally given the right spacing.

all weak and broken canes, leaving only healthy ones, spaced about 6 to 7 inches apart. The remaining canes should be sturdy, straight, and 4 to 5 feet tall. If you cut back the tops to this height, you won't even need a trellis to hold them up when the berries ripen.

Everbearing red raspberries must be pruned differently. Cut them right to the ground every year before growth starts in the spring. The best way to do this is to run over them with a sickle bar mower. (A lawn mower probably wouldn't be tough enough for this.) You won't get any summer crop from your plants this way, but the fall crop will be larger.

PROPAGATION

You can propagate black raspberries by tip-layering the stems; see "Making More Black Raspberries" on this page to find out how. Dig the suckers of red raspberries and transplant them to increase your stock; see "Suckering" on page 212 for details.

CROW'S PICKS

Each region has its favorite raspberry cultivars. Black raspberry fanciers in the North prefer 'Allen', 'Black Hawk', 'Bristol', and 'Huron'. Down South, try 'Cumberland'; out West, choose 'Munger'. For all you red raspberry fans, if you're up North, try 'August Red' (everbearing), 'Heritage' (everbearing), and 'Latham'. In the South, pick from cultivars such as 'Dormared', 'Sentinel', and 'Scepter'. In the West, plant 'Canby', 'Sumner', and 'Willamette'. Raspberries don't need pollinators, so you can grow a single cultivar for a one-time crop, or you can try several different cultivars to stretch the harvest season from summer all the way through fall.

STRAWBERRIES

If you're in a hurry for luscious fruit, you just can't beat strawberries. Plants set in the spring will produce a full crop the second year. And you can accelerate the process even more: Plant day-neutral cultivars in the spring, leave the blossoms on, and you'll be picking strawberries in 60 days. (See "Strawberries in 60 Days" on page 258.) Day-neutrals bear fruit all season, while June-bearers fruit in spring or early summer, and everbearers fruit in spring and again in fall. Strawberries are hardy in Zones 3–10, depending on the cultivar.

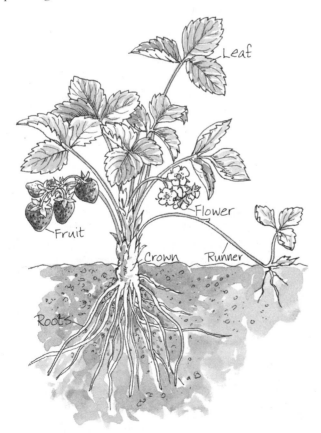

Leaf

Flower

Fruit

Crown   Runner

Roots

PLANTING

However you decide to manage them, it pays to take care when selecting a site for strawberries. Since they are subject to spring frosts, choose a location on ground that is slightly higher than the surrounding areas. Avoid depressions because cold air flows downward to form frost pockets.

Plants will do well in most any well-drained soil that has a liberal supply of organic matter. You can add organic matter before planting by turning under a green manure crop. (Legumes, which take nitrogen from the air and fix it in the soil, are the best green manures.) If you don't have time for that, add a 3- to 6-inch layer of compost or well-rotted horse manure before planting.

Have your soil tested to see if you need to add lime or fertilizer. Strawberries grow well in soils with a pH ranging from 5.7 to 6.5. If the pH falls below 5.0, certain nutrients—particularly phosphorus—may not be available to the plants. The deficiency will show up as wilted plants with reddish purple leaves. You can correct this deficiency with a top-dressing of bonemeal or dolomitic limestone. Use as much compost as you can at planting time to add plenty of organic matter to the soil. But stay away from fresh manure because the excess nitrogen will give you plants with too many leaves and not enough fruit. If your soil needs

> If you're impatient for fruit, plant strawberries. With my system, you'll be able to start picking in only two months. Just cut off the runners instead of the flower buds. See "Strawberries in 60 Days" on page 258 for details.

lime, do not apply more than is recommended; too much lime reduces the size of both the plants and the fruit.

Start your patch with at least 25 strawberry plants. Set the plants about 3 feet apart. Plant them shallowly so their crowns are not submerged; the base of the crown should rest at ground level.

Matted-Row Planting

If you're willing to wait a season for your first crop of berries, you can get away with fewer plants to start with and less work every year by planting in matted rows. To develop a matted row, place plants 18 to 24 inches apart in rows spaced 3 or 4 feet apart. Pull off all the blossoms the first season, and runners will soon spread everywhere, filling in the spaces between the plants. The only runner removal you'll need to do is to keep paths clear.

Renovate your strawberry bed after harvest by mowing it with a lawn mower set on "high." Then leave the mother plants standing and dig or till the rest under. Clean up the cut leaves (compost them if they're not diseased), apply an inch of compost, and add fresh mulch. New runners will grow all summer to fill in the rows for next season.

Spaced-Row Planting

The intensive method is a bit more work than matted rows, but it will reward you with 50 percent more berries. Set plants 12 inches apart in rows spaced 30 inches apart. Pinch the blossoms and, as runners begin to form, cut off all but four from each plant. Train the remaining four runners to form a row on each side of the mother plant.

A spaced-row planting can be renovated in the same way as matted rows—by leaving a strip of strawberries standing in each block of plants and digging the rest under. Or you can dig under only the middle row of mother plants and train runners off the remaining rows.

CONTINUING CARE

Strawberries are shallow-rooted plants, with three-quarters of their root system in the

To grow strawberries in a matted row, set plants 18 to 24 inches apart in rows separated by 3 or 4 feet. Remove all the blossoms the first season, but let the runners grow. Just pull off enough runners to keep the aisles clear. Next season, you'll have strawberries to spare.

upper 3 inches of the soil. During periods of little or no rainfall, the plants will suffer unless you intervene. Make sure they get an inch of water every week to keep them growing. Mulch will also help keep the soil moist. See "Fall and Winter Care" on the opposite page for mulching tips.

Weed control is essential in the new strawberry patch. Cultivate the plants as often as necessary to control the unwanted invaders. Removing the weeds in their early stages prevents them from sapping soil nutrients and keeps their roots from becoming intertwined with the roots of the strawberry plants. If the weeds establish a foothold, it will be almost impossible to remove them without disturbing the strawberries' shallow root system.

Feed your strawberries with liquid seaweed sprays in spring until the buds open. In early summer, spray with compost tea, or apply 2 cups of compost tea per foot of row.

PEST AND DISEASE CONTROL

Aphids and spider mites have a fondness for strawberries. Both are hard to spot unless you check the plants carefully, especially the undersides of the leaves. Aphids themselves may not kill plants, but they can quickly spread viruses through your strawberry patch. Spider mite damage will show up as a slight bronzing of the leaves. The bugs seldom kill a plant but may reduce the yield. To control both aphids and mites, spray regularly with water or insecticidal soap; be sure to apply it on both sides of the leaves.

Strawberry root weevils, also called strawberry clippers, eat half-circle holes around the margins of leaves and clip off flower stems. Larvae can bore into the crowns and roots of plants, hollowing them out. Keep them off your plants by covering the crop with floating row covers. Rotenone will kill the adult weevils, while a soil

Strawberries in 60 Days

If you don't mind going to a little trouble, you won't have to wait a full year for your strawberry planting to start paying off. You can make plants give you fruit in eight weeks. The trick is to pamper them a bit. To get that early crop, you must make sure that the young plants aren't held back.

First, grow day-neutral strawberries in raised beds. Raised beds provide better drainage for the root zone, and that's crucial since strawberries are prone to a number of diseases when grown in waterlogged soil. Raised beds also improve air circulation and expose the plants to a maximum amount of sun.

The "pruning" technique is just the opposite of the normal method. Leave all of the blossoms, but cut off all the runners. Cutting runners helps the plants conserve their energy and stay productive longer. Make sure your plants are mulched, watered as needed, and fed with a compost topdressing. Then get ready to enjoy those berries!

drench of parasitic nematodes will knock out the larvae.

Birds are also fans of ripe strawberries. Netting or floating row covers will keep them off your fruit as long as you bury or weight the edges.

Buy certified disease-free plants to avoid bringing problems into your patch. Many cultivars are resistant to serious strawberry fungal diseases like red stele and Verticillium wilt. If your plants wilt for no apparent reason, dig and destroy them immediately. Plants with red stele have stunted gray or purplish leaves. If you dig one and cut open a root, it will have a red core. If these diseases strike, destroy infected patches immediately, and don't plant strawberries there for at least ten years. (Makes more sense just to start with disease-free stock, doesn't it?)

Gray mold, caused by airborne fungal spores, will quickly turn berries into fuzzy gray balls. It may affect only one berry on a plant or every berry. Remove the infected fruits as soon as you spot them (be careful not to spread the spores), then burn them, bury them in an out-of-the-way spot, or dispose of them with your household trash; don't put them in the compost pile. If powdery mildew is a problem in your garden, spray the plants with baking soda solution or sulfur from the time growth begins.

HARVESTING

When your strawberries have turned bright red, it's time for a taste test. Handle ripe berries carefully (if any are left when the "taste test" is over!) since they bruise easily, and bruised berries often fall prey to mold. Pick strawberries when they're dry; they'll keep longer.

FALL AND WINTER CARE

The care of your strawberry patch doesn't end with the end of summer. Although a light frost won't hurt the plants, they do need to be protected from temperatures below 20°F. So, in many parts of the country, you'll need to cover the plants with a light, fluffy mulch like straw. When applying the mulch, spread it uniformly over the entire planting. Four inches, when settled, should provide ample protection.

Not only will the mulch give the plants much-needed winter protection, it will also provide benefits the next year. When spring arrives and new growth starts, scratch off about half of the mulch (the plants will grow through a light covering) and throw the rest into the aisles. The recycled mulch will retard weed growth and conserve moisture. Best of all, the mulch will help keep sand and grit off the berries.

MAINTAINING THE PATCH

Given enough time and space, I'd love to be able to start a new bed of strawberries every spring. But with good care, a single bed can keep pumping out fat, luscious berries for three, four, or five years. All the original plants won't last that long, but they can be replaced by the daughter plants forming at the ends of the runners. Pull up weak, woody, or exhausted old plants, and fill the bare spaces with sturdy, well-rooted runners.

After three to five years, pests and diseases have usually sapped a bed's strength. Till your patch under and start over with new plants in a different location. If you start the new bed the year before you till in the old one, the strawberries will keep coming.

PROPAGATION

Strawberry plants will begin forming runners the first year. If the soil isn't especially fertile, three or four runners per mother plant are plenty. If you've enriched the soil with lots of organic matter and the plants are very vigorous, you could leave a few extra runners on each plant. The first runners are the strongest and most vigorous, so count on those for propagation. Snip off unneeded runners near the crown of the mother plant.

Usually, runners can root themselves right through a soft mulch. You can prompt them to root where you want them by putting a stone on the long stem and loosening the soil underneath. When the runners are well established, sever their tie to the mother plant.

CROW'S PICKS

As with most fruits, which strawberry cultivars you choose to grow will depend on where you live. My favorites for the North are 'Tribute', 'Tristar', and 'Sparkle'. Down South, you can also grow 'Tribute' and 'Tristar', but substitute 'Ozark Beauty' for 'Sparkle'. In the West, choose 'Douglas', 'Hood', and 'Ogallala'. Strawberries don't need pollinators, so you can plant as few or as many cultivars as you like.

Alpine Strawberries

Alpine strawberries are gourmet treats that can be grown in any region where standard strawberries grow. Alpines are miniatures, with small-scale leaves, little white flowers, and tiny, cone-shaped fruit. The plants set fruit from late spring through fall.

Start These from Seed

Alpine strawberries can be started from seed. For a good-size crop the first year, start seeds as early as possible, preferably indoors, in March. The seed is very fine, so sow it in sifted soil. Press it into the surface, then cover with damp newspapers. Provide even moisture. The seeds will germinate in three to four weeks.

Begin checking the seed flat about one week after sowing. As soon as a seedling is up and looks sturdy, transplant it into a 1½-inch pot filled with equal parts perlite, peat moss, and compost. Six to eight weeks later, put the young plants into larger containers, using the same mix, or plant them in a permanent spot.

Planting Alpines Outdoors

Soil for alpines should be loose, fertile, and full of organic matter. Like all strawberries, they must be transplanted carefully; be sure you don't cover up the center growth of little leaves that form the crown. Set seedlings 2 to 2½ feet apart, then mulch. Unmulched plants will be damaged or killed in midsummer by drought and in winter by freezing.

You can grow alpines in sun or shade. For a large, early June crop, grow them in an open, sunny area.

The only additional care alpines need is pruning each spring. Cut off old growth to make way for new leaves, flowers, and fruit.

PART V

Let's Grow Flowers, Trees, Shrubs, and Lawns

15

Let's Grow Flowers

Let's start this chapter with another of Crow's Rules of Great Gardening: No garden is complete without flowers. Don't try telling me that you don't have any room for flowers. The dedicated gardener can find a place for annuals, perennials, or roses in any landscape. I've found that the best results often come when flowers are combined—or even integrated—with vegetable and fruit plantings.

In many ways, growing flowers is similar to growing vegetables, but there are a few striking differences. Here's a look at a few key points, starting with the simplest of all flowers, annuals.

Annual Choices

There are so many species and cultivars of annual flowers, how do you even begin to choose which ones to grow? First, remember that the flowers won't look good unless they grow well, so choose species that do well in your part of the country. Take a cue from successful flower gardeners in your neighborhood and town. See what grows well for them, and don't be afraid to be a copycat. No matter where you live, I'm sure you'll find many species and cultivars that will suit your particular soil and climatic conditions.

Next, look at height. If you want to grow a whole bed or border of annuals, choose cultivars of different heights. Plant the taller ones in the back of the bed, the midsize ones in the middle, and the dwarf plants in the foreground. This arrangement will have a big impact and give you beautiful color throughout the summer.

Another great trick is to plant bushy annuals among your perennials to hide dying foliage. First, consider the

When planting annuals in a bed or border, consider their eventual heights carefully. Plant the lowest-growing annuals in front, the medium ones in the middle, and the tallest in back to create a step effect. That way, you can enjoy all your annuals since none will conceal the others.

height of the perennials you want to hide. Even if you have a bed of perennials that look good all summer, you can still surround it with a border of dwarf annuals to set it off. And, of course, you can plant annuals here and there in any perennial bed to provide extra color all season. But in this case, the annuals should be no taller than 18 to 20 inches so they won't dominate the bed.

Next, you must consider color. To my mind, annuals are meant to be mixed. If the predominant color of the perennials is yellow, don't use the same color annuals for filling in. Instead, use flowers with striking colors, such as bright red cockscomb or blue ageratum.

GROWING ANNUALS

There's more to growing great-looking annuals than simply determining the length of your growing season, the amount of your summer rainfall, and whether you have a sunny site for them. Healthy annuals also depend on fertile soil, good-quality seedlings and bedding plants, and good general care.

Any good, organically rich soil will grow beautiful annuals as long as it retains sufficient moisture and has good drainage. Too often, flower beds are made from subsoil taken when the basement of the house was dug. This kind of soil contains few, if any, plant nutrients, and it cakes hard in dry weather. If this sounds like your flower bed, rebuild the soil with organic matter like compost, shredded leaves, manure, or organic fertilizer. Spread on a 2-inch-thick layer of any of these materials and work it in thoroughly.

I think rotted poultry, rabbit, and goat manures are about the best soil conditioners and fertilizers for growing annuals. Not only are they full of valuable plant food, they also provide humus for the soil and release plant nutrients slowly so that the annuals grow and bloom steadily all season. If you'd rather not mess with manure, you can use cottonseed meal, bonemeal, kelp, or blended organic fertilizer. Before planting, broadcast these fertilizers at the rate recommended on the label. Ten to 20 pounds per 1,000 square feet (reduce the amounts proportionally for smaller beds) should be about right for average soils.

SOWING ANNUAL SEEDS

Sure, you can trot down to the garden center in spring, pick up some flats of annuals, and pop 'em in the garden. But—did you guess?—I like to start my annuals from seed. Not only do you save money, but you'll have the satisfaction of knowing you're giving your plants the best possible start. And think of how many more annuals there are to choose from in the catalogs than in the store!

When selecting annuals, keep in mind that there are two basic types: hardy and tender. Hardy annuals such as balsam, four-o'clocks, cornflowers, and larkspurs can survive a light frost. You can sow them directly in the garden in late fall after the weather turns cold. You can also plant them in spring, but fall planting gives them an earlier start. Freezing shouldn't harm the seeds. Hardy annuals will sprout in spring. Should a late frost hit, it won't damage the hardy foliage.

Tender plants such as ageratum, morning glories, China asters, zinnias, and marigolds can't withstand frost. They must be sown in a cold frame or hotbed, then transplanted in spring after all danger of freezing has passed.

Even though hardy annuals will survive if you sow them right in the garden, I've found that most annuals grow best when transplanted rather than direct-seeded. (Transplanting seems to create a better and larger root system.) So I start them in a cold frame, greenhouse, or

Tiny seeds like those of petunias and snapdragons can be a real challenge to plant. The trick is simply to sprinkle them on the soil surface, then rake them in lightly with a coarse comb.

hotbed. If your season is long, you can sow them thickly in a small section of the garden and transplant them later.

Here's Crow's simple rule of thumb for annual seeds: Sow them according to thickness. The smaller the seed, the more shallowly you should plant it. Tiny seeds, such as those of petunias and snapdragons, should be sprinkled on the surface and merely raked in with a coarse comb. Always water with a fine spray.

If you only need a few flowering plants and you don't have a cold frame, don't sweat it. You can start annuals indoors in pots or flats of rich garden loam mixed with peat moss, vermiculite, fine sand, and perlite. After sowing, put the pots in a sunny window. Or, even better, start the seeds under fluorescent lights hung just a few inches above the flats. You'll have to provide nitrogen by watering your pots or flats once every three weeks with a weak fish emulsion or liquid seaweed solution.

ANNUALS OUTDOORS

When the outside temperature regularly rises above freezing, you can begin to

Blooms among the Broccoli

Traditionally, the cutting garden is a sunny area located on a secluded part of the property where flowers and other ornamentals are grown specifically to be cut for use in the house. Although I don't have the time or the space to maintain a separate cutting garden, I still have plenty of flowers to cut in season because I plant them in among my vegetables.

As long as I give it a little thought, these flowers won't displace any vegetables. I don't interplant flowers with my short-season crops—that would wreck the subsequent successions. But when gaps appear in rows of beans or other direct-seeded vegetables due to uneven germination, I quickly pop in some annual flowers.

When interplanting flowers and vegetables closely this way, I've found that it's better to start with bedding plants rather than to seed the flowers directly in place. That way, I know I'll have plenty of flowers pronto!

Don't use flowers that will be taller than the vegetables at maturity. Dwarf marigolds are fine for planting between peppers; bushy 4-foot giant marigolds would be a mistake. Confine the taller flowers to rows of their own, or plant short-growing vegetables around any of the tall marigolds, zinnias, or cosmos. Put the vegetables at the flowers' feet on their sunny side.

At first glance, sunflowers might not seem to be a good candidate for intercropping. But I've found that the lower leaves of these tall plants often get mildew and drop off as summer advances. That leaves sunspace for annuals between the sunflowers.

Another Kind of Cutting Garden

If you're practicing intensive succession planting of vegetables, it's just not practical to interplant them with flowers. Instead, reserve a 5-foot-wide strip along the front of your garden for a combination planting of herbs and flowers for cutting. The 5-foot width makes for easy harvesting and maintenance because the center of the bed can be worked from both sides.

You can freely combine herbs and flowers in 4 × 4-foot blocks. Weeding isn't a problem once the plants grow together. Some of my favorite plants for this kind of garden are herbs like basil, thyme, summer savory, sweet marjoram, anise, and hyssop combined with flowers such as calendula, marigolds, annual phlox, petunias, celosia, and snapdragons.

Strawflowers are a good candidate for the vegetable garden. Their papery blooms are colorful and make great dried flowers, but the plants themselves are generally ugly and would detract from the display of a regular flower bed.

harden off your annual transplants, just as you would with vegetable plants. When the average daytime temperature is 50°F, set the plants in place in the garden.

I find that there's usually sufficient rainfall throughout the summer to satisfy the moisture needs of annuals. Most have long roots that reach far down into the soil

in search of moisture between rains. If you do need to water, do it in late afternoon—but early enough to give the plants time to dry off before dark. Mildew spores develop rapidly on damp foliage during warm nights.

If you grow a selection of annuals, you can enjoy beautiful and colorful flowers in your garden from May until frost. Look over the Annual Gallery on page 275 to see which ones appeal to you.

Perennial Power

Gardeners are catching on that herbaceous perennials are the best deal going. Although the seeds cost only a little more than annual seeds, perennials are like that famous little battery bunny: They keep going, and going, and going, continuing year after year with little or no attention. This means you are free to mulch the cukes, de-bug the cabbage, and tie up the tomatoes while your flower friends are blooming their heads off in a succession of vibrantly welcome colors.

However, perennials are not "care-free." Because they stay in one place for years, they require even better soil preparation than annuals. Be sure to spade the soil to a depth of at least 8 inches and work in plenty of organic matter to improve drainage.

Most perennials will bloom the first year if they're seeded early enough. Unlike annuals, many perennials require regular division. Divide your perennials when you notice that the flowers are either dwindling in size or outgrowing their space. To divide, chop down through the root mass and separate sections of the plant. Or dig up offsets or suckers that come up some distance from the mother plant. Sometimes the process rejuvenates the old plants, but in any event, it ensures that you'll never be without your favorites.

To divide a clump of a perennial plant like this iris, carefully dig it from the garden bed in late fall or early spring, retaining as much soil around the roots as possible. Place the clump on a flat surface, and try to pull apart sections of root and rhizome or crown with your hands. If this doesn't work, cut them apart with a sharp knife.

Perennials return each year like old friends who aren't demanding but are easy to get along with. As you enjoy their procession of color from spring through fall, it's reassuring to know that most of them will be there year after year to enjoy while you're busy in the garden with your herbs and vegetables. I've included a selection in "Perennial Favorites" on page 292.

Bulbs for Brightness

In the rush to plant annuals and perennials, please don't overlook bulbs. Both spring- and summer-flowering bulbs are among the easiest of all garden plants to grow. I enjoy the whole procession, from the earliest snowdrops, through the daffodils and tulips, to lilies-of-the-valley, glads, and cannas, and on to the delicate crocuses of fall. You, too, can have beautiful bulbs year after year if you follow my easy system. Here's what to do.

CUT OFF FLOWERS AFTER THEY FADE

Immediately after the plants bloom, remove all dead flowers. Food produced in the green leaves and stem is stored in the bulb. The more food that's produced, the larger the bulb and, consequently, the larger the plant and flower the following year. Seed production uses food that would otherwise be stored—cutting off spent flowers will prevent seeds from forming. I cut the flower off at the top of the stem, leaving the stem, which will also produce food for the bulb.

You may be tempted to remove the leaves and stems as soon as they become unsightly. Don't! They're producing food for next year's growth. There's no reason to look at a dying bulb, however—just plant something in front of it to mask the aging leaves. Baby's-breath is a good choice, with its delicate flowers and full, airy greenery.

MULCH WHEN THE FALL FREEZE ARRIVES

As soon as the ground has frozen, apply a thick mulch to keep the soil frozen until the true spring thaw. If you allow the ground to alternately freeze and thaw, heaving will occur, which in turn can expose and dry out the bulbs. The mulch for bulbs should be loose, with good air circulation and drainage—straw is my top choice.

FEED BULBS EARLY IN THE SPRING

The best time to fertilize bulbs is when the young leaves first push out of the ground. However, you can fertilize bulbs throughout their active growing period, until just before full bloom. After bloom, the bulbs store food for the following spring, then go dormant.

Bulbs need high levels of phosphorus and potassium. Phosphorus promotes strong stems and bright flowers, while potassium builds firm, healthy bulbs. Bonemeal is an excellent source of phosphorus. So is ground phosphate rock. Good sources of potassium include granite dust, wood ashes, greensand, potash rock, and seaweed. One pound of a half-and-half combination of phosphorus and potassium fertilizers should be adequate for 20 square feet of garden.

MOVING BULBS AROUND

If you want to transplant or divide bulbs, do it after the leaves have died back. Hyacinths and some daffodil cultivars need dividing more frequently than other bulbs—often every two or three years.

You can lift bulblets, carefully break them away from the mother bulb, and replant them. Don't force apart bulblets that are still joined to the mother bulb; the basal plate (the part at the bottom of the bulb) won't separate with the immature bulblets. Bulblets must include a portion of the basal plate to survive, since it is the root-producing part of the bulb.

Many people dig their tulips every year, then replant them in the spring. Professional gardeners do this to remove ugly, aging foliage from their beautifully tended beds. For the home gardener, a screen of bushy plants will disguise bulbs and end the chore of annual digging, curing, storing, and replanting.

A Run for the Roses

All right, roses are shrubs. But I think of them as flowers since that's what I grow them for. And I plant them with flowers—in the garden with my perennials and annuals. So here they are, in the flower chapter. But shrub or flower, I mean to tell you how to grow roses right.

Whether your tastes run to down-home rugosa roses, classy and finicky hybrid teas, bountifully blooming floribundas, or high-stepping climbers, the basic care program is just about the same. It's essential to follow certain practices to get the plants off to a good start.

The general rule is to locate roses so that they have full sunshine all day, though they do quite well in a warm climate with at least five to seven hours of sun. Also, one veteran rosarian after another points to having well-drained soil as a key to success. So get plenty of shredded leaves, compost, and other organic materials into the spot well in advance, if possible. Test the soil to see if water puddles for long periods or drains nicely. If it doesn't drain well, try somewhere else. Aim for soil that's slightly on the acid side, preferably with a pH of about 5.7 to 6.3.

Give your roses enough room. Space bush or shrub types 3 to 5 feet apart and climbers at 8 to 10 feet. Hybrid teas and their cousins, the floribundas and grandi-floras, should be spaced 2½ to 4 feet apart, or a little more where temperatures stay mild.

Where winter temperatures drop to no more than −10°F (Zones 6–10), it's safe to plant roses in spring or fall—basically, you can plant them any time the ground isn't frozen. In colder areas, plant in spring so your roses are well established by fall.

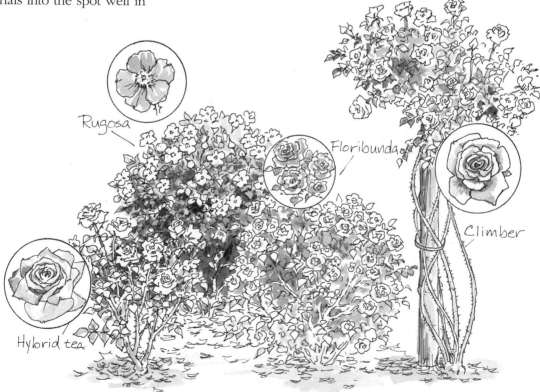

There are many types of garden roses, including hybrid teas, rugosas, floribundas, and climbers. Choose the ones that suit your tastes and needs—hybrid teas if you love cut flowers; rugosas for a sturdy, disease-free hedge or accent plant; floribundas for abundant bloom in the perennial border; or climbers to add color to a wall or fence.

FEEDING, MULCHING, AND WATERING ROSES

When it comes to feeding and mulching roses, you've got your choice of organic materials. Besides bonemeal and aged composted manure, some of my favorite fertilizers include cottonseed or soybean meal, ground potash, rock phosphate, blended organic fertilizer, blood meal, aged mushroom compost, and fish emulsion. I've even used human hair, a nitrogen source many gardeners say produces longer stems, larger buds, and deeper color tones.

Bonemeal rates as my number-one fertilizer choice at planting time. I usually throw in two or three handfuls and mix it into the soil for each plant.

Mulching also helps feed the soil. All the prize-winning rosarians agree that mulch is just about essential. You can use everything from shredded bark and wood chips to coffee grounds. For weed control as well as moisture conservation, a layer of organic matter like hay, shredded leaves, or well-rotted sawdust is very effective.

Apply the mulch in spring, about a month before the plants bloom. First, pull any weeds and rake the soil lightly. Then spread the material evenly around the plants to a depth of 2 to 3 inches or more. Some gardeners like mulches up to 4 or 5 inches deep, especially of loose, porous materials such as hay. They add more mulch as it decays into the topsoil.

Watering is important, too. Mulch is effective in conserving moisture, but most roses are heavy drinkers. They'll grow better if you keep the soil evenly moist until they establish a strong root system.

CONTROLLING ROSE PESTS AND DISEASES

As for pests and diseases, remember that healthy, vigorous plants are their own best defense. But if worse comes to worst, there are some very effective organic insect and disease controls.

Milky disease spores (Bacillus popilliae) are an effective long-term solution to Japanese beetles since they wipe out beetle grubs when applied to the lawn. And don't discount good old handpicking: In the early morning, when the adult beetles are sluggish, pick them off the foliage and drop them into a jar of soapy water.

Ladybugs will do a fast job of cleaning out aphids, mites, and scale insects. A strong jet from the hose will clear off aphids and mites; if they persist, douse them with insecticidal soap. Soap and alcohol (1 tablespoon of isopropyl alcohol in a pint of insecticidal soap spray), applied every three days for two weeks, will control the

❧ Tomato Leaf Tea

Tomato leaf tea is an Amish remedy that can be used to battle blackspot, the worst disease of roses. The tomato plant secretes solanine (a toxic substance found in several members of the nightshade family), which seems to inhibit the troublesome fungus disease.

To make up a solution to spray on your roses, grind up a handful of tomato leaves and mix them with 3 pints of water and 1 ounce of cornstarch. (A blender will do the best job of liquefying it.) Spray the "tea" on your roses, and store what's left in the refrigerator for later use.

🌹 Rugosa Rose Rules

The rugosa rose (*Rosa rugosa*) has inspired renewed interest in old roses among organic gardeners. The hardy rugosa makes a fine hedge plant, often growing as high as 6 feet and as wide as 4 feet. Plants bear plenty of single, semidouble, or double white, pink, rose, or red-purple flowers (depending on the cultivar) and attractive corduroy-like foliage. When rugosas bloom, their fragrance fills the air around them.

But not only is the rugosa a handsome bloom-filled bush, it produces something good to eat as well. The fat, showy red rose hips are an abundant, tangy source of vitamin C.

Rugosas are so tough, they're about the only roses that thrive in the salt air and sand of seashore areas. (Their high salt tolerance makes them great choices for roadside plantings, too.) They seldom have any insect or disease troubles, and they take both heat and extreme cold in stride—some are hardy all the way to Zone 2! What's more, they keep blossoming again and again all season.

Harvesting Rose Hips

For good production of hips, plant at least two cultivars to encourage cross-pollination. Good drainage is a big factor, too. Although rugosas will grow vigorously even in poor soil, like all plants they respond to better treatment with better growth and more blooms.

The hips, which are the fruits of the rose, form after the flower petals have fallen. So, for the largest crop, don't cut your rugosa flowers—enjoy them outdoors instead.

Harvest your rose hips in late fall, when they've reached full color and are richest in food value. If they're still orange, it's too early, but don't let them go beyond a deep apple red. Be ready to share some hips with the birds. (Pheasants are especially fond of them.)

Just like other fruits, different kinds of roses produce different kinds of hips. Those of the rugosa are large, often over 1 inch in diameter. Interestingly, rose hips grown in northern countries contain more vitamin C than those farther south—possibly nature's way of taking care of her creatures in colder climes.

scale if your ladybugs are taking a vacation.

Three fungal diseases can plague roses: blackspot, powdery mildew, and rust. The best defense is to plant resistant cultivars. You can also cut down on disease by pruning to keep plants open to air and sunlight, siting them where air circulates freely, and spacing them far enough apart to promote good air circulation. It's also a good idea to use soaker hoses or drip irrigation to keep water off the foliage and to water early in the morning.

If a fungus shows up, spray plants weekly with fungicidal soap or wettable sulfur to control the existing infection and prevent the damage from spreading. Antitranspirants and baking soda have also proved effective as fungus preventives, but note that word: preventive. To be effective, you need to apply these materials regularly and start the applications before you see any sign of fungus.

PRUNING ROSES

I'm a firm believer in rose pruning. That's because a rose bush must be kept young to retain its vigor and produce blooms of high quality. The way to rejuvenate your roses is to prune them each year so that the upper part of the plant is never older than two years, regardless of the age of the roots.

Rose bark is thin and becomes hard as it ages, causing the sap ducts under the bark to become constricted. In other words, a hardening of the arteries sets in. As a result, the foliage becomes small, improperly nourished, and an easy prey to disease. Also, as your roses get older, they'll develop a lot of puny little roses on stubby stems that are much too short for cutting. Pruning produces fewer but larger flowers on longer stems.

Pruning also keeps the bush to a useful and balanced size year after year and concentrates the energy of the roots into fewer shoots. This means that each shoot will be under pressure to start vigorous growth.

Keep in mind that plants breathe through their foliage. The roots inhale moisture from the soil around them and exhale it through their leaves. As soon as enough foliage grows to comfortably release the moisture obtained through the roots, growth slows down for a while and bloom buds appear. If the required amount of foliage is distributed among a large number of shoots on an unpruned plant, each shoot will grow but only produce a few leaves, resulting in short stems. Therefore, the fewer the shoots, the more leaves per shoot and the longer the stems. The closer to the crown you prune, the more vigorous the growth and the bigger and more perfect the blooms, though there will be fewer of them.

Pruning Hybrid Teas

Prune hybrid teas immediately after you've removed their winter protection. Cut back any wood that's been

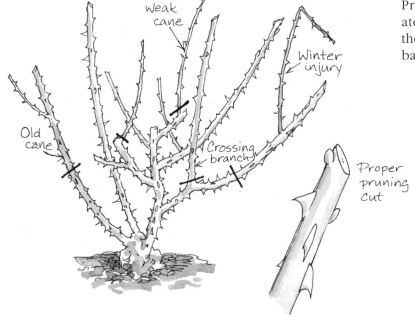

Weak cane

Winter injury

Old cane

Crossing branch

Proper pruning cut

Wait until spring to prune hybrid tea roses. That way, you'll have a good look at whatever damage the winter weather has done. First, cut back the injured wood to the nearest live bud. Then, cut back everything else to about 8 inches above the ground. Make your cuts just above a healthy bud, slanting away from it so water will run off, reducing the chance of disease.

injured during the winter to the nearest live leaf bud, and trim out any branches that look weak. Old stems that haven't been injured can be cut off about 8 inches from the ground.

Pruning Floribundas

Floribundas need the same surgery as hybrid teas, only you should leave the stems at least 12 inches long. If you want taller plants, prune to a maximum height of 15 inches.

Pruning Climbers

Both large-flowered and everblooming climbing roses bloom only on wood that's at least two years old. Therefore, you need to leave this wood on the plant when you prune. When everblooming climbers have finished their original bloom, only the flowers should be plucked off. Don't remove any foliage, as reblooming occurs from the top leaves immediately below the flower clusters.

There's a Sucker Born Every Minute

Or at least it feels that way when you have to prune them out. While you're pruning, keep a sharp lookout for suckers—shoots that start below the bud or graft joint. You should remove them as close to the

root as possible, especially on a grafted plant. That's because they're part of the rootstock (usually the unimproved seedling) rather than the desired cultivar grafted on it.

Summer Pruning

In addition to spring pruning, you may have to do some summer pruning, which mainly involves cutting off the spent flowers. When cutting roses, remove at least half the stem or, better still, cut above the second full set of leaves from the main cane or branch. By removing the foliage, you'll be impeding the breathing apparatus of the plant, which will immediately begin to replace the missing foliage. The result: long stems with good flowers. If the dead bloom is merely cut at the first leaf, eventually the top bud will grow an inferior bloom perched on a short, stubby stem.

WINTERIZING ROSES

When the golden shades of autumn begin to fade and that persistent nip in the air becomes an outright chill, it's time to weatherproof your roses. Exactly how much you have to do depends on the types of roses you have.

Roses differ in natural hardiness almost as much as

the months of the year differ in temperature. Don't assume your hybrid tea roses will make it through the winter unprotected just because your neighbor's shrub roses do. Hybrid teas are very tender and will need some protection.

Right after the first killing frost, while the soil can still be worked, is the ideal time to start digging. For hybrid teas, polyanthas, and grandifloras, mound up the soil around the base of the plant, and stake and tie all canes that could be blown around. A firm cushion of soil, even though frozen, will conduct heat from the deeper layers of warmer earth and keep temperatures above the killing point.

You'll find that if you cut your hybrid teas to about 9 inches from the ground, mounding will be simpler. However, don't assume that cutting to this height will eliminate spring pruning—it won't. Some of the wood may very well be damaged over the winter.

Pile the soil 9 to 11 inches high over the crowns of your plants. Make sure that you aren't busily uncovering roots that have stretched a little farther than you expected. Rather than risk exposing any rose roots, you can bring in soil from another part of the garden.

Even after your roses are mounded, keep a close eye on them. Check from time to time to make sure your soil isn't washed away before the ground freezes. If the temperature doesn't dip below 0°F, this is all the attention your roses will need to drowse contentedly through the bleak winter months.

If you're growing roses in an area where the mercury regularly drops below 0°F in winter (Zones 2–6), you'll need to provide additional protection. Cover the soil mound with a loose mulch of hay, straw, and straw manure. Don't use leaves or grass clippings since they hold too much moisture.

Contrary to what many people think, the roses' winter mulch is meant to prevent the ground from thawing, not to keep it from freezing. It's the constant thawing and freezing of the soil that damages plants. Frequently, rose cultivars that are winter-hardy in bitterly cold areas are damaged in a more southerly location. That's because in warmer areas, the temperature fluctuates more. This fluctuating temperature in winter is far harder on the plants than a consistently low one.

So wait until after

Don't apply winter mulch to roses until after the first killing frost of fall. Then mound up the soil to a depth of about 9 inches all around the plant. In severe climates, cut the plant back first so it is completely covered. Early in winter, you can add a blanket of straw mulch to the soil mound for extra insulation.

freezing weather arrives to put your straw mulch on. By this time, mice and other rodents will have been driven under cover elsewhere, so they won't take up residence in your rose bushes.

Winterizing Climbers

Climbing roses require a different sort of treatment. They need weatherproofing where temperatures plummet to 0°F and below (Zones 2–6). First, take the canes from their supports, place them on the ground, and hold them down with wire pins. Then heap several inches of soil over them.

Even when temperatures never become too severe, it's important to shelter roses from the winter sun and drying winds, particularly when they're growing in an exposed location. When your climbing roses are left on the trellis, be sure to securely tie all long canes that can be whipped about. Cover as much of the plant as you can with straw, binding it around the plants so it won't blow off.

Winterizing Tree Roses

Tree roses, also called standards, are the most vulnerable of all roses to winter injury. That's because they've been grafted at the top of a long rose "trunk," so the desirable cultivar forms a ball of growth at the top. To protect your tree rose over winter, wrap the head of the plant in straw and encase it in burlap.

Enjoying Your Flowers

You see, there are plenty of ways to include color, fragrance, and beauty in your landscape. It doesn't take a huge perennial bed to make an impact with flowers. Anywhere they go—in pots, baskets, among the green beans—flowers make a garden more interesting, not only to us, but to wildlife as well.

ANNUAL GALLERY

BLUEBONNETS

Bluebonnets (*Lupinus subcarnosus*) look like little lupines. Their fat spikes of blue pealike flowers rise 8 to 12 inches above green lupine foliage.

The bluebonnet isn't fragile or finicky, despite its ladylike name. I've seen whole fields of these flowers growing on otherwise unproductive land. They seem to defy drought and freezing spells, taking care of themselves quite satisfactorily with no outside help.

However, like most plants, bluebonnets will grow better if you give them center stage in the planting bed—they just don't like competition from other plants. And that's just as well because I think they're at their most beautiful when they're grown as a solid mass of blue.

A rich, well-drained soil will produce larger and more richly colored blooms than those that grow in meadows. So spread a generous layer (up to 2 inches thick) of decayed manure, compost, or both, over the bed and till it in deeply. Then water the bed and allow it to settle before you plant the seeds.

Sow the seed outdoors in early spring in a sunny site with good drainage, and cover lightly with soil. Plant bluebonnets in their permanent location—since their roots penetrate to surprising depths, they are difficult to transplant successfully.

Once the seedlings are up, they form a rosette of leaves, which does very little until the weather is warm. Then growth is quite rapid—bloom stalks appear, and the plants are on their way to becoming traffic-stoppers.

Bluebonnets don't need additional fertilizing since they have deeply penetrating roots and the nitrogen-fixing ability of legumes. Because of their deep roots, bluebonnets really don't need a mulch, either. However, mulching with whatever is available—hay, straw, leaves, or grass clippings—will prolong their bloom period.

When the blossoms fade and seeds are forming, the plants will appear somewhat untidy. If they're in a flower bed, you may be tempted to pull them out. That would be a mistake. Let the seeds form! You can allow the plants to self-sow, or collect seed to plant elsewhere. Since bluebonnets grow to a height of up to 12 inches and bloom early in the season, you can plant taller, later-blooming annuals in front to use as a screen until the seeds ripen.

When mature, the seedpods resemble those of sweet peas. They're about 1 inch long, buff-colored, and brittle. The pods pop open to fling the seeds far and wide. If you put them in a paper bag and leave them within earshot, they'll provide amusement for a week or more by making a clearly audible "Bang!" as each pod explodes. After collecting the seed, store it in sealed containers and keep it in the refrigerator until next planting season.

At that time, consider planting any surplus seed on an unproductive piece of land. Bluebonnets will enrich and open up the soil each year, spreading in thrifty colonies until, as Thoreau said, "The Earth is blued with it."

🐦 CROW'S TIPS

Nature has provided the bluebonnet seed with a hard, almost impervious coat to protect it during dormancy. This coating causes the seed to germinate erratically. Three years may pass before the coat has worn away enough for the seed to absorb moisture and sprout.

For this reason, you'll get a higher percentage of germination if you scarify (scratch) bluebonnet seeds before planting. It's not as hard as you might think. Just spread a handful of seeds on a concrete surface and rub them gently with a brick, taking care not to remove the seed coat completely. This procedure should help you obtain a good stand the first year. Afterward, your bluebonnets will self-sow and will be so prolific that you won't have to worry about germination.

CELOSIAS

Celosia *(Celosia cristata)* is one of the most versatile annuals. There are two distinct flower forms: crested and plumed. The crested types produce plush, velvety flower heads arranged in clusters called cockscombs. The plants usually bear one or more large cockscombs surrounded by several smaller flowers. Plumed celosias bear upright, feathery flower heads.

Although celosias are usually found in

brilliant colors of red, yellow, and orange, they have lately been bred in pastel colors like peach and primrose. Crested celosias are sometimes multicolored, with most of the flower being one color and the crested tips hightlighted with a second color.

Celosias reach 1 to 3 feet tall and bloom through summer and autumn. These tender annuals make excellent summer bedding plants, but they have many other uses, too. Dwarf cultivars are perfect for growing in window boxes or wooden tubs, or for edging a mixed flower border. They are also well suited to rock gardens and provide an excellent over-planting for spring bulbs.

Plant 2-foot-tall cultivars in the middle of a border, and use the taller cultivars toward the back. Medium and taller cultivars are especially effective in mass plantings, while the tallest cultivars can provide landscape accents. The tallest celosias can even be planted as a temporary hedge.

You can plant seeds in open ground during May, but this procedure won't provide much color until midsummer. For a longer blooming period, sow celosia indoors or in a hotbed six weeks before the frost-free date in your area. The seeds germinate in ten days. Celosia will bloom between 75 and 104 days from the time the seeds are planted.

Be sure to give your plants plenty of space—crowded conditions will slow growth and reduce the quality and size of the flower heads. Space them according to the height of the plants. Large plumed celosias may be planted as far as 2 feet apart, while 1 foot is enough for shorter cultivars.

For the largest flower heads, give celosia rich soil with lots of organic matter. The plants will tolerate poor soil and dry conditions, but they'll grow best with plenty of moisture. To prevent rot, be sure the bed is well drained.

Crow's Tips

Celosias make great cut flowers since they remain in perfect condition for a long time. They also dry well—just air dry by hanging them upside down. A single, large, crested type provides a dramatic accent to any indoor arrangement; the plumed celosia adds bright splashes of color.

COSMOS

A delight to see growing in any garden, cosmos is another one of those "old-fashioned" flowers that suddenly seem very up-to-date. Although they look feathery and delicate, they are actually robust annuals. The blossoms are large and flat, with silky, daisy-like petals surrounded by bright green foliage on slender stems. Their colors range from white, pink, and rose for garden cosmos

(*Cosmos bipinnatus*) to scarlet, yellow, and orange for yellow cosmos (*C. sulphureus*).

Cosmos plants tend to be tall—3 to 6 feet, depending on the cultivar—so they're usually used as background flowers for borders, against fences, or to screen an area. New homeowners who need quick-growing plants while their perennials and small woody ornamentals are getting established will find cosmos wonderful for filling in blank spaces.

Not only are cosmos decorative in the garden, but they make wonderful cut flowers, too. Just drop a bouquet of them into a vase, and they practically arrange themselves. The foliage is graceful and feathery, so the plant even makes good greenery for other arrangements.

You can sow cosmos in early spring or in the fall. If you've made up your mind where you want them, you can plant seed directly in your garden. If you decide to change their location, they won't mind, since they transplant very easily when they're young. They also reseed readily, so you'll probably have cosmos for years to come.

Unlike most plants, cosmos prefer a soil that's not too rich. (Rich soil usually promotes foliage instead of flowers.) These plants flourish in a rather poor, light soil. Broadcast the seed or plant it in rows, then cover it with about 1/4 inch of soil. When the plants are about 3 inches tall, thin them out to about 1 to 2 feet apart.

Cosmos plants are fairly cold hardy. They like full sun but will grow in partial shade. When the plants are about 2 feet tall, you can pinch out the tops to stimulate branching out and greater flower production. Cut off all dead flowers except at the end of the season, when you want seeds to form so the plants can self-sow. It's fine to cultivate around the base of the plants, just don't go so deep that you injure the roots.

Cosmos are sometimes subject to a stem blight. The infection, which eventually kills the plant, shows up as brown spots that gradually girdle the stem. The best control is to pull out affected plants as soon as infection occurs and destroy them. Keep your soil free of any plants that could carry the blight over the winter.

Crow's Picks

Most cultivars offered by seed companies start blooming in July and continue until frost. The most popular cultivars are 'Radiance' (deep rose flowers), 'Purity' (white), 'Pinkie' (pink), 'Fiesta' (orange striped with scarlet), and 'Dazzler' (deep crimson).

FOUR-O'CLOCKS

Four-o'clocks (*Mirabilis jalapa*) are more than just pretty faces. Sometimes called "marvel-of-Peru," these natives of tropical America get their common name from their habit of opening their many tubular, five-petaled flowers at about 4:00 in the afternoon. (But don't try to set your watch by them—depending on the intensity of the sun, they may open earlier or later.) When planted without shade, they'll grow fine but may not flower until evening.

Solid or candy-striped blossoms of deep maroon, rose, or yellow make four-o'clocks charming flower favorites. Because of these plants' dark green oval leaves and bushy, branching habit, they are also used as substitutes for shrubbery on new building sites or among young shrub plantings. They grow quickly from seed to a height of 2 to 3 feet. Although they have soft, succulent stems,

Four-o'-Clocks

they need staking only in windy spots or in areas with heavy foot traffic.

Four-o'clocks normally require several hours of sunlight. However, I've seen them bloom abundantly from early afternoon on when planted in a narrow space on the north side of the house.

Wait until the warm days and nights of late May to direct-seed four-o'clocks. They like a germinating temperature of 70° to 75°F, and the young plants are prone to injury from cool nights. Sow thinly over a bed prepared with fine soil and peat moss mixed together. Once your flowers are well established and blooming, you can keep them flowering longer by removing the spent blossoms occasionally.

Four-o'clocks are tender perennials that will overwinter in Zone 10. (If you're not familiar with plant hardiness zones, the whole country has been divided up into geograpical bands, called zones, based on average winter low temperatures. It's important to know what zone you live in since lots of perennial plants, including fruit trees, ornamental trees, and shrubs, as well as

flowers, are often described with their hardiness zone range. That's the number of zones where the plant can usually survive the winter. See the USDA Plant Hardiness Zone Map on page 366.)

Although they're not hardy in cooler climates, where they're usually treated as annuals, four-o'clocks self-sow and often come up year after year in the same place. Gather some of the large, ¼-inch, pellet-shaped seeds to give to gardening friends who may wish to start them early indoors or in a greenhouse.

CROW'S TIPS

To get a head start on plants or to preserve certain colors, you can dig the tuberous roots of the four-o'clocks after frost kills the tops in the fall. Expose them to the sun for several hours to dry them thoroughly. Then store them in dry sand or peat moss in the root cellar or a cool corner of the basement until the following May, when you can plant them outdoors.

GERANIUMS

Geraniums (*Pelargonium* spp.) are year-round flowers that grow outdoors from late spring to fall and indoors during the colder season. They live a straightforward existence, cheerfully demanding little food and almost no care in return for handsome foliage and lavish blooms. I like to plant geraniums on either side of the front walkway. Other plants often object to the heat thrown off by the cement, but geraniums can take it, providing cheerful, summer-long bloom in a problem place.

Scented geraniums have leaves that smell like rose, mint, nutmeg, lemon, chocolate, and many other fragrances. They're delightful to grow in the herb garden as well as in pots. You can grow these special geraniums without any trouble at all once you've accustomed yourself to raising the ordinary kind. It's true that some are a little shy to bloom, but the fragrance of the leaves when the sun strikes them makes up for hesitant flowering.

Geraniums

seaweed sprays are good, but bonemeal is one of the best all-around sources of phosphorus. I always put a little in the potting mix for geraniums, and I like to top-dress with it, too, once the plants are settled outside and blooming strongly.

Outdoors, geraniums make excellent bedding plants. Sink them into the ground in the pots they've been grown in. It's a busy time in the garden both when you take them outdoors in spring and again in the fall when you bring them back in—having them in pots simplifies both jobs. When you set them out, put a thin, flat rock under each pot to keep the roots from growing through the drainage holes.

Like four-o'clocks, geraniums are actually tender perennials. The plants are woody, but the shoots are tender and soft, making it exceptionally easy to get rooted cuttings from them. In fact, taking cuttings is the easiest way to propagate geraniums. Here's what to do:

Select a 3- to 4-inch-long branch with three sets of leaves. Cut straight across the stem with a sharp knife just below the joint from which the lowest leaves grow. Pull off all the leaves but two or three at the top—these remaining leaves will keep the cutting nourished while the roots are forming. Stick the cutting in a well-ventilated box filled with sand, vermiculite, or peat moss. Keep the box out of direct sun, and the cutting will just take off.

A very good potting mixture for geraniums is 7 parts rich garden soil, 1 part coarse sharp river sand, and 2 parts organic fertilizer. If your soil is inclined to be acid, add a little lime.

Although geraniums aren't very demanding, they need an ample supply of phosphate. They need it so badly that a deficiency is the first thing to suspect if your plants don't do well. Liquid fish emulsion or

Geraniums from Seed

Thanks to present-day plant breeders, there are hybrid geraniums that grow as easily from seed as zinnias or marigolds. Similar to the bedding geraniums, they are even better-branched for more bloom. They're also very vigorous and fast-growing, and they produce bright flower heads 4 inches or more across. By growing geraniums from seed, you'll have a wide color choice, including red, scarlet, salmon, pink, white, and bicolor.

Geranium seeds are fairly large and easy to handle. Sow them at least eight to ten weeks before the last expected frost. Use the same soil mixture as you would for starting other annuals. Or you can use a mix of 2 parts peat moss and 1 part sand, or 3 parts compost and 1 part sand.

To grow bedding geraniums, fill a 6-inch-deep flat with 4 inches of planting mix. Firm it down gently with a flat board. Sprinkle the soil with water until it is well moistened throughout. Spread a 1-inch-deep layer of dampened sterile sphagnum moss over the mix and firm it gently with the board.

Sprinkle the seeds thinly over the entire surface ($^1\!/_2$ inch between seeds is not too much) and cover them with $^1\!/_8$ inch of the same moistened sterile sphagnum used underneath. Firm gently with the board again to eliminate air pockets.

After sprinkling the seeds lightly with water, cover the entire flat with a large sheet of transparent plastic. This will eliminate the need for watering as the seeds germinate. Covering the flats with plastic also helps to maintain an even temperature and the moist conditions necessary for good germination.

At the first sign of green, remove the plastic covering so the growing plants will have good air circulation. Within 8 to 14 days, germination will be complete. Before long, the flat will be filled with sturdy geranium seedlings already showing the characteristic brown circle on their tiny green leaves.

When the seedlings reach $^1\!/_2$ inch tall, gradually introduce them to direct sunlight. Like most annuals, geraniums benefit from transplanting. If plants are crowded in the flat, transplant them as soon as they're large enough to handle. If they are well spaced, transplant them when they are about 2 inches tall. Since most will be used as bedding plants and for flower boxes, give the roots as much space as possible by transplanting directly into the soil in the greenhouse bench or hotbed.

Wait for a warm, cloudy day in spring to transplant the seedlings again, this time into a cold frame if you have one. To hasten the process, gently firm the loose soil, then make holes in the bed with a small peg,

spacing them 4 inches apart in all directions. Set one plant into each hole and firm the soil carefully around it with your fingertips.

After they are all planted, give them a thorough soaking with a micronutrient-rich foliar feed like sea kelp or fish emulsion to lessen transplant shock. Once the plants become accustomed to their new surroundings, they'll grow rapidly. In a matter of weeks, the cold frame will be a mass of green, filled with the heavenly scent of fresh, healthy geranium foliage.

When the weather settles, you can move the young plants to a permanent bed or box. To eliminate wilting caused by transplant shock, water them heavily, then transplant during a slight drizzle. By the time the weather clears, the plants will have settled in and will welcome the warm sun.

CROW'S TIPS

If your geraniums refuse to bloom in winter, there's probably either too much nitrogen in the soil, too little sunshine, or too little difference in the temperature between the day and the night. Refrain from overfertilizing, keep the plants cool at night, and give them all the sunshine you can. You'll have beautifully blooming plants all winter long.

IMPATIENS

If you're not a seed-starting nut like I am, you can buy impatiens (*Impatiens wallerana*) as bedding plants started at a greenhouse, which is what most gardeners do. In fact, impatiens are now the most popular bedding plants in America. That's because of their ability to cover themselves with cheery flowers even in the deepest shade.

Since impatiens grow about 7 to 12

inches tall, they make ideal bedding or border plants. Bright green leaves set off 1- to 2-inch-wide flowers in shades of white, pink, red, peach, and magenta; some are also striped. The nonstop display will go on in full sun if you keep the soil moist. But in the shade, there's nothing like impatiens for color.

Once you have impatiens, you can keep them going for as long as you like by taking slips and starting new plants. You can get many new plants from a single parent plant. Even the leaves will take root and grow.

Slips can be started any time, but I've found that February or March is the best time to start new plants for summer's flowers. Snip off about 2 inches of the new growth at the root of the plant, or snip small branches; leave three or four leaves on the slip. Use a sharp knife so you can make a clean cut.

Root the slip by placing the cut end in a glass or bottle of water or in moist sand. I've found a good way to get a lot of plants rooted in a small space. First, I cut off the rounded tops of gallon-size glass jugs with a glass cutter. Then, I put a couple of inches of sand in the jugs and add water until the water level is even with the top of the sand. Then, I stick lots of slips and leaves into this thoroughly saturated sand and cover the jugs with clear plastic bags.

I set the jugs on a table by a southeast window, adding water occasionally to keep it level with the sand. Before long, a mass of roots is growing out of the cut ends, and you have a bunch of new plants ready to transplant. The rooted slips are usually ready to move in about a month, de-

pending on how warm they have been kept. You can plant the rooted slips directly in the flower bed if there is no danger of frost.

To transplant, dig a hole for each plant, set the plant in the hole, and water generously. Mix a trowelful of compost with the soil from the hole, then pack it firmly around the roots so no air spaces are left. Space the plants about 15 inches apart and mulch them with a 1-inch-deep layer of rotted leaves to control weeds and conserve moisture.

Impatiens from Seed

If you're an experienced seed sower and have a greenhouse or a good set of grow lights, you may want to try starting impatiens from seed. That way, you'll have a much better choice of cultivars than you would at the local garden center.

Impatiens are slow to germinate and to grow, so start them at least eight weeks before your planting-out date. Sow the seeds

Impatiens

in flats in a mixture of equal parts of good garden loam and sand. Plant them ¼ inch deep, water, then cover the flats with plastic bags until the seedlings are up. In the spring, when you're absolutely sure there's no chance of a late frost striking, transplant them outside to a bed in a shady location.

🐦 CROW'S TIPS

Did you know that impatiens do well as houseplants? You can enjoy winter blooms from plants that have given you a delicate display all summer.

In fall, as soon as there is a hint of frost in the air, dig up a plant or two to brighten winter's cold and often dreary days. To dig the impatiens, first loosen the soil around the plant. Make sure the soil is damp enough so it will lift out in a solid clump and cling to the roots.

Put coarse gravel in the bottom of a pot so the plant will have good drainage. Then slip a trowel under the plant, lift it out, and set it into the pot.

NASTURTIUMS

Nasturtiums *(Tropaeolum majus)* seem right at home in the vegetable garden. In fact, these bright, extremely colorful flowers are often grown as a food crop, albeit a specialty one. The leaves lend a distinctive peppery flavor to salads, and they can be added to soups and sauces as well. The blossoms are often used to adorn upscale salads. The leaves, young seedpods, seeds, and even flowers can be pickled. Because of its use as food, this plant is sometimes called Indian cress.

Common nasturtiums have bright green shield-shaped leaves. (One cultivar, 'Alaska', has beautiful cream-splotched leaves.) Flowers come in cheerful, glowing colors of yellow, orange, scarlet, or dark reddish purple, or in combinations of these. The lower flower petals are often fringed. The flowers are wonderfully fragrant.

Some nasturtium cultivars have a climbing habit; others were bred to be bushy. Climbing cultivars grow up to 8 feet and are fine for covering trellises or climbing poles.

Garden nasturtiums are very attractive in borders and make excellent edgings for plantings of taller flowers. They also look good in boxes, tubs, pots, and hanging baskets. Nasturtium foliage and flowers make charming cut-flower bouquets.

Nasturtiums are easy to grow. They like a sunny location but also do well in partial shade. They bloom better in a rather poor, dry soil and will grow vigorously even in a gravelly or sandy soil. If the soil is too rich and moist, the plants will be luxuriant but produce few flowers.

Nasturtium seeds are large and easy to handle. In spring, after the weather and soil have warmed, sow them right where the plants are to grow. They germinate in about

ten days and the plants bloom quickly.

If you want to get a jump on the growing season, you can also start nasturtiums earlier in containers in a warm, sunny spot indoors. They'll begin to blossom in as little as four to six weeks, and they'll continue to bloom freely from late spring through autumn until frost.

Given conditions to their liking, nasturtiums will provide a season-long bounty of bloom, tangy leaves for eating, and pest protection for other plants. And all with very little care.

 ### CROW'S PICKS

When it comes to nasturtiums, I especially like the 'Gleam' series. These hybrid doubles come in a wide assortment of colors. They're well behaved and stay low when grown on the ground, providing a very attractive groundcover for a sloping bank such as the ones we have here at the farm. As trailers and climbers, they are equally wonderful for walls, low fences, and hanging baskets.

*I admit a partiality for climbing nasturtiums. Besides the climbing cultivars of garden nasturtium, there are several other climbing species. The best known of these is fancifully called the canary-bird vine or canary-bird flower (*Tropaeolum peregrinum*). An excellent plant for trellises and other supports, it grows to a height of 8 to 10 feet and bears pale yellow flowers. Canary-bird vines are good for growing on fences and are well suited for screens.*

*Another climber, the perennial flame-flowered nasturtium (*T. speciosum*), has finely divided foliage and small scarlet flowers. It looks great growing up an evergreen—the conifer looks like it has burst into bloom! This nasturtium will overwinter in Zones 7–9. In cooler climates, you can save its tuberous roots and plant them the following season or pot them up for indoor bloom through the winter.*

 ## Nasturtium Companions

Nasturtiums are always an important part of my vegetable garden, where they're a good companion for the food crops. From what I've seen, they seem to repel whiteflies and squash bugs. They keep away cucumber beetles, too.

Nasturtiums have the opposite effect on aphids, so they can serve as a trap crop. The plants contain mustard oil, which attracts aphids away from other vegetables in the mustard family, like cabbage, cauliflower, radishes, kohlrabi, Brussels sprouts, turnips, and collards.

SNAPDRAGONS

Snapdragons *(Antirrhinum majus)* are old standbys in my summer annual bed. They offer two huge advantages for the gardener who wants summer-long beauty without much fussing: They bloom right through the hottest days of the year without flagging, and they're non-fading in the scorching sun of midsummer. And their spikes of rich, velvety blooms—in shades of white, yellow, red, pink, purple, and apricot—glow like few other flowers. All snapdragons are ideal for cutting because they last and last in water.

You can fill a border or add a cheery touch to many corners of the garden with snapdragon cultivars of all sizes. I especially like the intermediate heights, which are about 2 feet tall and don't need staking. But don't forget the 3-foot giants for the back of the bed and the 6-inch miniatures for edging. You can also put a few of the

Snapdragons

half with sand and vermiculite; then moisten it thoroughly. Sow the tiny seeds on top of the moistened mix and slip the flat into a plastic bag.

Find a warm place for the flat where it won't be disturbed. Snaps germinate best at about 60° to 65°F. Check the moistness of the soil from time to time. Never let the seeds dry out, but don't allow them to germinate and grow in a soggy environment, either.

When the soft mat of green seedlings appears, put the flat in your sunniest window, preferably in an unheated room. Let the young plants grow until they reach 6 inches in height, then pinch off the tops. Stick the tops you pinched off into a box of sand with a plastic cover draped over it— they'll root in a matter of days in this warm, damp environment.

Pruning the young snaps makes the plants bush out, and they'll produce many more blooms in the long run. When your pinched-off tops are well rooted, remove the plastic cover and put the flat in a cool, bright window where the plants will grow strong.

Do you have a cold frame? If so, that's the perfect place to harden off your little plants for a week or two before setting them out. Otherwise, you can put them in a window in a cool garage, or even in a wooden box in the garden. (Be sure to cover the box with a sheet of glass if frost threatens.) Hardened off this way, your snap-dragons will take a light frost in their stride, and you can get them into their beds about the same time you set out pansies.

You can sow snaps directly in place in the garden, but you'll have to wait until late summer for blooms. Sow seed in rows or broadcast it. You can put ⅛ inch of soil over the seeds or merely water them in and tamp

trailing snapdragons in your rock garden. You'll love them not only for their unusual creeping habit but for their rich, uninhibited bloom, too.

Set snaps where their rich, glowing colors show off to best advantage. There are no blues among them, but just about every shade of snapdragon goes well with blue. Here's one of my favorite combinations: white lilies among rose-colored snaps with blue forget-me-nots at their feet. It's an unfor-gettable sight!

The blooming season of snapdragons is limited only by how early you plant the seeds. The end of January is a good time to start them indoors. Prepare a flat by filling it with compost and rich soil, mixed half and

(continued on page 288)

The Hanging Garden

You can make sure your favorite plants really get noticed if you grow them in a beautiful and unusual hanging garden. With hanging baskets, a drab, uninteresting porch or plain covered patio can be transformed into one of the loveliest sections of the entire garden, or it can serve as a complete garden in itself. Even a simple outside wind shelter with an open latticework ceiling becomes a place of beauty when you convert it into a hanging garden resplendent with colorful plants.

You'll get the most impact from hanging baskets if you mix the types and varieties of plants in them rather than using all one kind. You will probably want to include the traditional ivy and begonias in your hanging baskets, but there is no need to limit your choices to just these. Some of the loveliest gardens are made up of combinations of ordinary plants that are seldom used together. Consider nasturtiums, fuchsias, petunias, chrysanthemums, and shrimp plants when making your selection. More of my favorite choices include campanulas, ferns, dianthus, cinerarias, lobelia, lotus, black-eyed Susans, coleus, and the ever-popular geraniums.

'Tiny Tim' tomatoes and everbearing Alpine strawberries are just two of the window box crops that will yield delectable harvests in hanging containers.

Choosing a Container

You may want to use the readily available plastic hanging baskets. But I like to use a variety of clay pots, wire basket planters, and rot-resistant wooden boxes in interesting combinations. Clay pots retain more moisture than wire planters and are easier to handle. Wire planters, though they dry out more quickly, allow more planting space since you can plant flowers on the open sides as well as the top. And plain or decorated wooden boxes can add a nice touch to any area you'd like to spruce up.

If you want to try wire planters, line them before planting so they'll hold soil. Coarse sphagnum moss is easy to mold when damp to make a liner, but unfortunately, it soon turns brown. Most hanging-basket enthusiasts prefer sheet moss, which stays green indefinitely. Overlap the moss strips carefully so there are no tiny openings that soil can sift through. Moisten the sphagnum moss or sheet moss lining, then fill the basket container with soil.

I like to make my own hanging-basket soil mix, using 2 parts garden soil, 1 part coarse sand and bonemeal, and 1 part compost. (Use 1 teaspoonful of bonemeal for each pint of mix.) I pack the soil reasonably well as I set in the plants, filling each basket to within about an inch of the rim.

If I'm using a porous container like a wire basket or clay pot, I dip the whole basket in a pail of water for a few minutes and let the soil settle for a day or two before planting. You can add more soil to fill low spots.

Set the plants in place before you start planting them to make sure your combination really looks good. Remember to put trailing plants around the edges and upright or bushy kinds toward the middle. When your containers—filled with soil and plants—are ready to hang, keep in mind that they'll be heavy. You'll need to give them strong support, so hang them with heavy wire or chains.

Choose the site for your hanging garden carefully. Protect your baskets from the harmful effects of strong, drying winds by giving them a partially sheltered location. Most hanging gardens thrive in cool shade, but be sure they receive enough sunshine for growth during part of the day.

Care for Hanging Baskets

Once the containers are suspended and your hanging garden is beginning to develop, your plants will need watering often because of the drying effects of the sun and wind. Water the plants at least once a day. If the weather is particularly hot, you may find it necessary to water some of your delicate plants twice a day.

I use a small-nozzled watering can for my routine container watering. Once a week, I remove all the containers from their supports and give them a good soaking in a water-filled tub. Both these types of watering will avoid washing out the soil, especially in newly planted baskets where there is not yet enough root growth to hold the soil.

Hanging baskets require a little extra care to keep them in perfect condition. Be sure to pinch your plants back and pluck off dead petals and leaves immediately to ensure well-formed, healthy plants with lush foliage.

If you want more luxuriant growth, you can use a micronutrient foliar spray to supply the plants with some extra organic nutrients. Spray water on your plants occasionally to keep them fresh-looking and to help control pests. Hanging baskets in a window garden or on a porch should also be turned regularly so that different sides face the sun—this will help keep the growth balanced.

If you forget to water your hanging baskets one day and your garden looks limp and lifeless, don't despair. Take it to your watering tub right away and let it sit in there and soak until the soil is completely saturated. Then hang the basket up in a cool, shady spot for the rest of the day. By the next day, the plants should have recovered, and you can move the basket back to its normal spot.

very gently, if needed. If you sow outdoors where the sun is going to be hot, it's a good idea to protect beds or rows with cheesecloth for a week or two.

Prepare the beds carefully. Snapdragons like a full day of sunshine. They prefer, but don't insist on, perfect drainage, and they like their soil rich and a bit on the alkaline side. Add a light sprinkling of dolomitic lime if your soil tends to be acid.

Give snaps—even the short ones— plenty of elbow room. For best results, allow about 18 inches between plants for the giant cultivars, 10 inches for the intermediates, and about 6 inches for the tiny ones.

Snapdragons require a great deal of water. Of course, if you've mulched yours heavily, you won't need to water much. When you do water them, lay the hose down and let the water run right onto the roots.

Snapdragons bear so bountifully that it's a good idea to provide them with extra food. Feed them from the time the first bud appears until about the middle of August. Use a micronutrient-rich foliar feed—I like a mixture of sea kelp and fish emulsion.

CROW'S TIPS

If you hate to give up your snapdragons when winter comes, don't. Let the ground freeze, then cover the soil with a 3- or 4-inch layer of a good porous mulch. If necessary, hold the mulch in place with pine boughs. It's all but certain that early spring will find lusty little plants pushing through the mulch, raring to grow. The advantage to overwintering snaps this way is that you can preserve the colors in your border for the coming season.

If your winters aren't too bitter, you can also start some leftover snapdragon seeds in the cold frame in the fall. They'll grow slowly over the winter, making husky little plants for spring flowering.

STRAWFLOWERS

Maybe it's my Amish training, but even when growing flowers, I look for practicality. I like a plant that can do more than one thing. That's why one of my favorites is the strawflower *(Helichrysum bracteatum)*. Strawflowers look great in the garden, and I think they look even better after they're dried and arranged indoors.

Because annual strawflowers are compact (15 inches to 3 feet tall, depending on the cultivar), they're ideal for border plantings. They are also bothered by few insects. Pick your favorite color—red, yellow, pink, bronze, or white—or grow a mixture for drying. Dwarf cultivars have blooms up to $1\frac{1}{2}$ inches wide. Larger cultivars sport double blooms up to $2\frac{1}{2}$ inches across.

For the earliest flowers, start seeds indoors or in your greenhouse about mid-March. Press the seeds gently into a seed-starting mix in flats or pots. They must have light and a temperature of 70° to 75°F for good germination. You should see little seedlings peeking through the soil about a week after planting. Water moderately. Once a month, put a little fish emulsion or manure tea in the water.

When the seedlings have two true leaves, transplant them to a larger container and space them 3 to 4 inches apart, or put them in individual pots. Keep the soil moist.

While the seedlings are growing, prepare the planting bed outdoors. Choose an area in full sun. Mix organic matter, such as shredded leaves, well-rotted manure, or homemade garden compost, into the soil. When the weather has warmed up and all threat of frost has passed, harden off the plants and set them out in your garden. Space the transplants 12 to 15 inches apart.

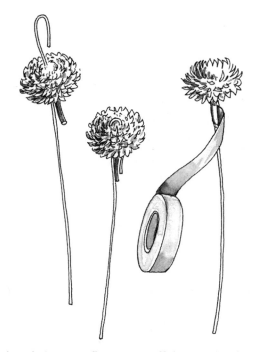

When drying strawflowers, cut off the stem just behind the flower head. Make a small hook at the end
of a 20-gauge florist's wire and insert it through the
flower head. Draw the wire down tightly so the
hook is concealed in the flower. Wrap the "stem"
with green florist's tape for a more natural look.

To extend the flowering season, sow seeds
directly in the garden at the same time.

Drying Strawflowers

To dry strawflowers, cut the blossoms just as
the first two rows of petals have opened. If
you let the flowers open more than that before picking them, they'll keep maturing as
they dry until the centers turn white and
fluffy, then go to seed. At that point, they are
not much good for use as dried flowers.

Remove the fragile stem and leaves at
the base of the flower head before the
flower dries. Replace the stem with a piece
of 20-gauge florist's wire cut to the stem
length you want. Insert one end of the wire
through the cut stem and into the head.
When the flower dries, the sap will act as

cement and the wire will become securely
attached to the head.

To hold the wire even more securely,
you can shape it into a small hook at one
end before pushing the straight end down
through the flower head so the petals will
cover the hook. Then gently pull the hook
into the flower head. However, if you aren't
careful, you may find that the hook is visible
after the bloom dries. You'll get the hang of it
after you've experimented on a few flowers.

You can also try leaving an inch or two
of the stem on the flower head. Once it's
dried, the stem will hug the wire snugly, and
you can display the blooms in arrangements
with the stems partly showing.

Once you've wired the strawflowers,
you need to hang them up to dry. (An alter-
native is to stand them upright in vases or
pint-size milk cartons.) Make small bunches
of each color, with six to eight flowers in
each bundle, depending on how large the
blossoms are. Wrap rubber bands tightly
around the stems to prevent the flowers from
falling out of the bundle as they dry and
shrink. Hang the bundles upside down in a
dry, dark, well-ventilated area, such as your
basement or attic. To promote good air circulation for complete drying, keep the bundles
an inch apart.

It will take from 10 to 14 days for the
stems to harden. The flowers are completely
dry when the stems snap instead of bending.
When the flowers are dry, layer them between tissue paper and store them in covered
boxes until you get an urge to make an
arrangement.

Keep in mind that these "everlasting"
flowers don't really look great forever. Once
you put them in an arrangement, sunlight and
dust will fade the colors. So enjoy them indoors while they last, then replace them annually with a fresh batch.

Everlasting Choices

If you'd like to add shades of blue and lavender to your dried arrangements, statice (*Limonium sinuatum*) is the plant to choose. The flowers of this annual are borne in sprays of white, rose, blue, yellow, or lavender, and they retain their natural shape and color quite well when dry.

Because statice is susceptible to fungal attack under damp conditions, it's especially important that you plant it in well-drained soil in full sun. Statice requires a long growing season, so start the seeds indoors eight to ten weeks before the last frost.

Blue salvia (*Salvia farinacea*) is one of the few flowers that dries to a true Wedgwood blue. The small blossoms grow in a tight spike, unlike the more commonly grown red salvia. Both types can be dried very easily.

Globe amaranth (*Gomphrena globosa*) has red, pink, salmon, purple, or white flowers resembling clover. Because it is heat- and drought-tolerant, globe amaranth is especially easy to grow. Sow the seed outdoors in late spring. This native of tropical America needs full sun and thrives in moist, well-drained soil supplemented with compost.

All dried flowers should be cut just before they're fully open. To prevent excessive wilting, cut the flowers in the afternoon after all the dew has dried, then take them inside quickly. Leaves don't normally dry effectively, so remove them from the stems.

Dried flowers are fun to grow, and the arrangements make fine gifts. So give a little thought to next year's long winter months when planning your flower garden, and add a selection of colorful everlastings. You'll be rewarded with hours of enjoyment and beautiful bouquets of dried flowers for home decoration.

SWEET PEAS

Here's a romantic old favorite that deserves to make a comeback. Sweet peas *(Lathyrus odoratus)* come in climbing cultivars, early-flowering bush types, dwarfs, knee-high lovelies, and heat-resistant floribundas. All come in an array of colors to rival any rainbow, and most are wonderfully scented.

The first thing to remember is that these flowers are members of the pea family, and just like their edible cousins, they do best in cool weather. Treat them accordingly, and plant as early as the climate will allow. As a rule of thumb, that's as soon as the soil has thawed to a depth of 8 inches.

To hasten germination, soak the seeds in tepid water for several hours. As soon as they begin to swell, they're ready to plant.

Like garden peas, sweet peas can manufacture their own nitrogen. But you'll give them a leg up if you inoculate the seeds with the same nitrogen-fixing bacteria you buy for your garden peas.

To avoid root rot and other diseases, choose a spot where this flower has never grown before (or at least not for several years). Sweet peas prefer very fertile, alka-

4 inches apart, then cover them with 2 inches of soil. As the plants grow, fill the trench with more earth until it's level with the area around it. Provide some sort of sturdy support for the plants to climb on, such as chicken wire, a trellis, pea brush, or even stakes and strings.

Thin the seedlings by pulling up every other plant. As much as this hurts, it's worth the sacrifice to have husky, healthy plants with a wealth of blooms. Gently water to soak the roots of the remaining plants, then apply a mulch of straw close to the plants on all sides. If you mulch before hot weather sets in, the straw will keep the roots cool and help protect the plants from the sun.

Besides rewarding you with colorful flowers, sweet peas are excellent soil conditioners. Through their roots, valuable nitrogen is drawn into the soil. So planting them in a different location each year not only prevents problems with disease, it also allows them to spread their good work over the entire garden.

line soil. If the soil has recently been under cultivation without having been limed, apply a slow-acting lime when preparing the bed—finely ground limestone is excellent for this purpose. Mix in generous amounts of well-rotted manure or compost.

Sweet peas are normally grown in a trench about 6 inches deep. Since they prefer firm ground, the best time to prepare the seedbed is late fall so that it can settle by spring. To give the soil an extra boost before planting, gather a few bottom leaves from the matted leaf carpet in the woods and mix them into the soil, or scatter them over the seedbed. Wait a week or so to give the soil time to settle, then plant.

Sow the seeds about 6 inches deep and

Sweet Pea Circle

Here's one of my favorite ways to grow flowers: I attach a circle of strings running up to a bird feeder and plant sweet peas beside the strings. The lavender, pink, and white blossoms of the sweet peas climbing up the feeder make a pretty addition to any garden and are a real compliment-getter. Not only will they attract birds to the feeder, but bees will buzz happily among them, pollinating away. My sweet peas provide a show all summer long.

CROW'S TIPS

Never allow sweet peas to run out of water or food. If you want to keep your young plants happy, try my "Tea for Sweet Peas" recipe: Fill a barrel about one-quarter full of manure. Then add water up to the halfway mark and stir thoroughly with an old paddle or shovel. When the cloudy mixture settles, the tea is ready to be served to the thirsty, hungry sweet peas. Apply the tea with a watering can to moisten the soil at the base of each plant.

If you do this extra work, you'll be rewarded with a constant supply of colorful flowers that must be gathered daily. Sweet peas enjoy being picked—if you ignore them, they soon lose their strength and fail to bloom, probably feeling unappreciated.

CROW'S PICKS

Baptisia (Baptisia australis), known to some as perennial sweet pea, blooms in late May and June. This member of the sweet pea family grows as a 2- to 4-foot bush with smooth, gray-green foliage that turns dark at the end of summer.

The dainty flowers of baptisia are clustered in showy spikes that are a lovely shade of indigo. This color gives baptisia its other common name, blue false indigo. The flowers form attractive dark gray seedpods that add interest to the garden in winter.

Unlike the sweet pea, baptisia prefers growing in full sun and in average to light well-drained soil. Once established, these hardy plants require almost no attention. Baptisia is hardy in Zones 3–9.

PERENNIAL FAVORITES

BASKET-OF-GOLD

Basket-of-gold (*Aurinia saxatilis*), or perennial alyssum, is one of the earliest-blooming, and therefore most welcome, perennials in my garden. As its name implies, it's literally covered with masses of cheerful yellow alyssum-like flowers in early spring. Plants grow only 10 to 12 inches tall and sport rosettes of fuzzy gray-green leaves. The cultivar 'Citrinum' has flowers with a softer yellow color than the species.

Basket-of-gold thrives in sunny spots and in soil that dries quickly. It's an ideal plant for rock gardens. Overly rich or moist soils will cause plants to flop and possibly even rot out in the center, so don't try to do this plant any favors with extra soil preparation. After flowering, cut plants back by one-third to encourage more compact growth. You can propagate it by division or cuttings. This perennial is hardy in Zones 3–7.

BLANKET FLOWERS

Blanket flower *(Gaillardia aristata)* begins blooming early in summer and is not even discouraged by the first light frosts of fall. With petals that combine red, orange, and yellow, it looks like a fringed daisy. It likes sun, laughs at drought, and—if you pull the seed heads off regularly—blooms heavily.

Blanket flower reaches 2 to 2½ feet tall and has long (10-inch) bright green leaves. It's a great plant for wildflower meadows, or for adding a little hot color to a well-drained sunny border. It's also perfect for seaside gardens, since it is heat- and drought-tolerant. In fact, the only place it grows poorly is in rich, moist soil, where it blooms less and produces lush, floppy growth. You can grow blanket flower from seed sown outdoors in fall. Divide plants every two or three years in early spring for best bloom and vigor. Blanket flower is hardy in Zones 2–10.

GARDEN CHRYSANTHEMUMS

There's a gardenful of difference in garden chrysanthemums *(Chrysanthemum × morifolium)*. They capture the blazing beauty of the autumn woodlands with colors that stretch from frosty white to soft yellow, from golden amber and burnt orange through mauve, pink, magenta, red, and lavender.

Chrysanthemums prefer life on the sunny side. They like to bask in the crisp, bright glow of Indian summer, shaking their shaggy heads in the early-fall breezes as the days become shorter.

Spring is the ideal time to plant chrysanthemums because the plants will have time to become established before blooming. Prepare the soil about ten days before you're ready to plant. Dig and loosen it to a depth of 8 inches. Work in peat moss and composted manure—the more organic matter, the better. You'll get the healthiest specimens from fertile, well-drained soil.

Next, dig a hole large enough to provide a spacious new home for your mums. Allow the roots to spread out—be careful not to jam them into a narrow hole where they'll be cramped. As you plant, press the soil firmly around the roots to avoid air pockets between the roots and the soil. Then water the plant. Usually, spring rains will supply chrysanthemums with enough water, but be careful that you never allow them to become parched. During dry spells, quench their thirst regularly with a deep, thorough drenching. Mulch heavily to protect the tender roots.

Chrysanthemums are undemanding, adaptable plants that don't need coddling, but that doesn't mean they don't need some attention. For example, it's important to pinch plants back at regular intervals to encourage branching. When they've reached a height of 6 to 8 inches, snip off the light green growing tips so the plants will produce strong side branches. If you don't clip these tips back, the plants will develop limp, spindly stems. Pinch all shoots every two weeks until mid-July. In autumn, the mature plants will be husky and bushy, with each branch producing clusters of freely blooming blossoms.

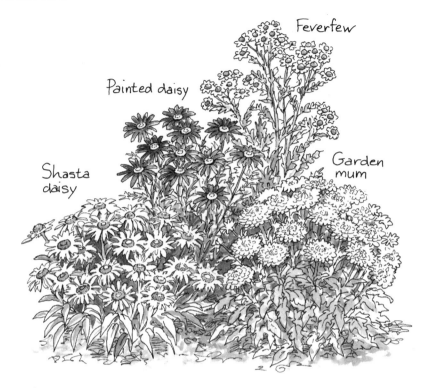

When in bloom, chrysanthemums command your attention simply because they're too striking to overlook. However, after blooming, they require a bit of care, too. After the plant tops die, cut them to the ground. Gather up fallen leaves and remove the mulch you applied in the spring. New shoots will start growing in late fall—spread a new mulch to protect them for the winter.

Mum Dos and Don'ts

Like many other garden favorites, chrysanthemums are prey to several disfiguring diseases. It's much easier to prevent these maladies than it is to cure them. So follow these mum dos and don'ts:

♣ **Don't** plant mums in wet, shady places.

♣ **Don't** crowd the plants. Free air circulation is vital for normal development.

♣ **Do** stake the plants. By keeping the branches off the ground, you won't be inviting pests.

♣ **Do** water early in the day so the leaves have a chance to dry before nightfall. Fungal diseases flourish on wet leaves.

These simple precautions can do much to guarantee a brilliant autumn display. Chrysanthemums are among the most versatile and dependable perennials. They create a harmony of color and design that will keep your garden blanketed with bloom right up until winter skies cast a shadow over the entire scene. Mums are hardy in Zones 4–9.

 CROW'S TIPS

To achieve mammoth exhibition blooms, you should disbud large-flowered mums. When plants are approximately 6 inches tall, pinch out the growing tip. New shoots will soon emerge along the

stem—break off all but three of these newcomers, and allow the remaining ones to grow into branches. When flower buds show, remove all but those on the top 3 inches of the branch.

As these top buds develop, examine the first or crown bud. When you're certain it's healthy, pinch off all other buds. Do this by carefully bending the stem of the bud downward and sideways with your thumb. The stem should snap off easily at the point where it joins the branch.

OTHER CHRYSANTHEMUMS

I love mums, but there are other perennials in the chrysanthemum genus that are just as rewarding. Try these:

Painted Daisies

Painted daisies (*Chrysanthemum coccineum*) bloom in early summer, with 3-inch single daisy flowers in pink and rose tints. If planted in a southern exposure, they fade more rapidly, so try to choose an eastern exposure. Although the bloom time is short at best, the flowers are so attractive I think they earn their keep in the garden. And the foliage helps compensate with its persistent ferny sprays. Plants reach 1½ to 2 feet tall and are hardy in Zones 3–7.

Painted daisy's other common name, pyrethrum, should ring a bell with organic gardeners. These plants are a natural source of pyrethrum, one of the most widely used organic insecticides. You can try making your own pyrethrum by drying and powdering the flower heads.

Shasta Daisies

I think Shasta daisies (*Chrysanthemum* × *superbum*) are among the most rewarding plants you can grow in a sunny bed. Their clusters of glossy, deep green leaves topped with long-lasting white daisies just look like summer to me. Shastas bloom for over a month each summer, giving cheerful white-and-yellow color to my garden. They make great cut flowers and add an oxeye daisy look to a meadow garden. Plants grow 1 to 3 feet tall, depending on the cultivar. They require only half a day of sun and are tolerant of almost any kind of soil. Shasta daisies are hardy in Zones 4–8.

Feverfew

This old-fashioned flower is one of my all-time favorites. The tiny, double white flowers of feverfew (*Chrysanthemum parthenium*) resemble garden mums, grow in sprays, and are in bloom all season. (Once the first blooms are gone, shear the plant back and, in no time at all, there are many more sprays of bloom.) Plants grow 2 to 3 feet tall and are bushy, with typical chrysanthemum foliage. Bugs steer clear of feverfew, and winter seems to have no effect on it. It's hardy in Zones 4–8.

DAYLILIES

Daylilies (*Hemerocallis* spp. and hybrids) are real workhorses in the garden. Their handsome clumps of 2- to 3-foot straplike leaves act as garden accents all season, while their cheerful trumpet flowers brighten beds, borders, fences, and even roadsides in spring and summer.

Daylilies are available in every color from near-white to purple—red, yellow, pink, peach, orange, and bicolors are all popular choices. Some cultivars are fragrant. Literally thousands of daylily cultivars are available through catalogs and garden centers. Keep in mind that catalog photos and descriptions are often misleading. If you want a particular

Daylilies

JOHNNY-JUMP-UPS

color, buy plants in bloom at a garden center so you know what you're getting.

The name daylily comes from the fact that each bloom is only open for a day. But each plant bears loads of buds, so these low-maintenance plants make a big landscape impact. (Did you know the buds are edible? Some folks stir-fry them, while others add them to salads.)

This uncomplaining, reliable perennial does best for me when its feet are in the shade and its head is in the sun. But don't plant daylilies near shrubs to get this effect; when the shrubs grow tall, they'll make too much shade and cause the plants to stop flowering. Plant daylilies in a spot where they get only morning sun, and they'll do fine.

Divide daylilies when the clumps get too big, or when you'd like more plants. Dig up the plants in late summer and separate the fleshy roots so you get a few good-size clumps.

Hybrid daylilies are hardy in Zones 4–9. Some species daylilies are hardy to Zone 2.

Johnny-jump-up *(Viola tricolor)* is a petite pansy relative that is often grown as an annual, but it's a short-lived perennial that reseeds readily. (Hence its name—you never know where it will "jump up!") The appealing little pansy faces in yellow, white, and purple add spots of bright color to the garden from spring through fall. (You can also buy cultivars with white, yellow, blue, or purple flowers, but I enjoy the multicolor display.) Plants grow 6 to 12 inches tall and bear bright green, narrow, succulent-looking leaves.

Johnny-jump-ups will grow in any exposure, but bear larger, deeper-colored flowers in partial shade. They thrive in moist, humus-rich soil, but they'll come up in the most surprising places—even between bricks in a walkway! By nipping off faded blooms, you will keep a succession of the mini-pansies coming along. They're hardy in Zones 3–8.

LUPINES

The lupines (*Lupinus* spp. and hybrids) are a lovely and diverse group of garden annuals and perennials, including the Russell hybrid lupines and the wild Texas bluebonnet. (See "Bluebonnets" on page 275 for the related annual bluebonnet.) Members of the genus have a wide color range, including pastels and bicolors.

Hybrid lupines—the kind most people grow because they're big and colorful— grow 2 to 3 feet tall, with thick, showy flower spikes and bright green fingered foliage. The plants bloom in late spring. Because they aren't heat-tolerant, they fare best in cool-summer areas.

Lupine seeds are easy to grow in well-drained soil. (Incidentally, in some parts of Europe, the seeds of the white lupine are used for food.) Pick the broad, hairy seedpods when they're turning brown, and hang the heads upside down in a cool, well-ventilated place. When the soil has warmed up in the spring, soak the seeds to soften the hard coats, then plant them in a sunny site in rich, well-drained soil. Sow seeds about 1/2 inch deep. Keep the seedlings well watered, but don't let the soil get soggy. Although lupines are fond of moisture, they dislike wet feet.

You can propagate lupines in the fall by digging up sideshoots. Don't despair if your clumps don't reappear after a couple of winters—lupines tend to be short-lived. Just keep propagating them from seeds and sideshoots so you have a good supply. Hybrid lupines are hardy in Zones 3–6.

ORIENTAL POPPIES

The oriental poppy (*Papaver orientale*) is a very hardy perennial that does well under adverse conditions with little care. It grows 2 to 3 feet tall and has large, fernlike leaves that go dormant in summer. Oriental poppies bear huge, cup-shaped, crinkled-paper flowers in bright shades ranging from white through apricot, pink, and scarlet to a red so deep it's almost black. They bloom in early summer.

I've found it doesn't pay to mess with starting poppies from seed. Instead, start plantings of oriental poppies from root divisions. That way, you can be sure you'll get a particular cultivar and color, plus quick bloom. If you aren't in a hurry, root cuttings will give the same results.

Plant poppies anywhere they will get a full day's sun, but keep them away from the base of shrubs or trees that will deplete the

Oriental poppy in bloom in early summer (left). Bare spot left by dormant poppy concealed with a spreading plant like baby's-breath (right).

soil's nutrient supply. Also, remember that poppies hate to be disturbed once they've become established. Until a substantial root system develops—about two years for root divisions—they flower very little. After that, their growth becomes lush and they increase in size and quantity of bloom as each year passes.

It's important to get new plants off to a good start. Oriental poppies are heavy feeders. The more organic food available to them, the thicker their foliage and the more flower buds they will set. Here at Spring Meadow, we prepare our poppy beds by replacing the subsoil with garden loam fortified with composted manure plus bonemeal, cottonseed meal, rock phosphate, and greensand.

Plant poppy divisions during spring or early fall. Set them toward the middle or back of the bed since their foliage browns after bloom and dies back by the middle of

August. Try locating them so that surrounding perennials that bloom after the poppies fade will preserve the beauty of your flowerbed.

Set one root division in each planting area or three in a triangle, spacing them 2 feet apart in all directions. The roots are rather long, so you'll need a deep hole to plant them. Keep the crown of each division 3 inches below ground level. Hold it in place with one hand while using the other to work soil firmly around the roots to eliminate air pockets. Then cover the crown with soil and press down gently with the heel of your hand to form a slight depression to catch rainwater.

Water each new planting deeply, unless rain is in sight, then cover with a 4-inch-deep coarse mulch such as straw. Mulching keeps the soil moist and cool until the topgrowth begins. When green shows beneath the mulch, move enough aside to enable the young shoots to absorb the sun's warmth.

Once established, oriental poppies have few demands. All they ask is a good top-dressing of organic fertilizer every spring. Work it into the topsoil in early spring right after raking out the perennial borders. In summer, remove all poppy seed heads after the petals fall so that the area will not be re-seeded with unwanted plants. Mulch cuts down on weeding during summer months and conserves moisture.

PEONIES

Of all the familiar perennials we grow, it would be hard to choose one more impressive than the peony (*Paeonia* spp.). For beauty, practicality, and easy culture, very few plants compare with this ancient oriental flower.

The peony bears beautiful, fragrant flowers in late spring and early summer. Blooms may be single, semidouble, or double and come in a range of old-fashioned colors, including pink, salmon, white, and red. The reds range from rouge to dark maroon, with scarlet, crimson, and cerise somewhere in between.

A double peony is many times larger than a rose. In fact, it can be so heavy that, unless it is staked, the whole stalk will bed down to the ground. (This often happens when rain adds to the flower's weight.) If you don't want to stake your peonies, try growing singles, semidoubles, or the smaller old-fashioned doubles rather than the huge new cultivars.

Peony foliage is handsome, too. From the time the reddish, asparagus-like shoots first appear in spring until the plants mature into 1½- to 3-foot-tall shrubs, they add interest to the garden. The glossy, dark green, deeply lobed foliage often turns a glowing wine red in fall.

Preparation is the key when it comes to

Peony in bloom—glory in the garden (left). Dormant peony ready to plant (right)—don't bury the eyes too deep or bloom will be delayed.

planting peonies. Take the time to search out a good site for the plants—they can live a hundred years in one place, so it's worth it to give them a choice spot. Peonies prefer a well-drained, sunny site. They don't like acid soil, so test your soil before planting. If the pH is below 6.5, sweeten up the selected piece of ground with a shovelful of wood ashes or a couple of handfuls of lime. As long as the pH is suitable, just about any good soil that's well-worked with a little manure or other organic matter will satisfy peonies.

You can plant peonies in spring or fall. Make sure the bed is made and ready to go when the roots arrive. Check the roots when you unpack them—each should have at least three buds (called "eyes"). Most companies will guarantee this number of buds, as three is the minimum required to ensure bloom the first year.

Dig each hole so that when planted, the buds will be from 1½ to 2 inches below the soil surface. Tamp around them carefully to press out pockets of air. After planting, aside from dressing the peony bed each year with a little manure, your work is forever done. You'll have lovely blossoms for a lifetime. Peonies are hardy in Zones 2–8.

CROW'S TIPS

Peony root was once so coveted by the ancient herbalists that in order to protect their supplies from pillage, they claimed that anyone who tried to dig it up would be driven mad by its hideous screams. They also told folks that the only safe way to take peony root from the ground was to harness a dog with a rope, hook the dog to the root, and make him pull it out. That way, the root couldn't blame a human for the deed.

I've dispensed with the dog and found that a spading fork works quite well. I gather the roots on any nice day in November, when I've taken care of all the other garden chores. You can lift and divide peony roots about every three years, but be sure the sections you replant contain at least three buds.

16

Let's Grow Trees and Shrubs

Trees and shrubs are some of the most versatile, permanent plants you can grow. And I've found that they can become the life of the garden. In fact, they do surprising things for both your front and backyard. Your job is to make sure all the surprises are pleasant since these plants can be very large and long-lived. To plan a successful planting, consider how to plant trees and shrubs so that they work to you and your garden's advantage.

Starting with Trees

Trees are the sturdiest of the plant kingdom's residents and the longest-living of all forms of life. So when growing these durable plants, it's a good idea to learn as much as you can beforehand.

The fundamentals of planting and caring for trees are basically the same, whatever type you choose.

As with many plants, transplanting is the most critical time in the life of a tree.

The key is to put the right plant in the right place at the right time.

I've planted trees in both early spring and early fall, and I've found that they're both good planting times. But "early" is the operative word here. It's important to purchase and plant early enough so that some new root growth occurs before the young tree endures a season of hardships—for example, the heat of summer or the cold of winter.

Two Types of Trees

There are two general classifications of trees—deciduous and evergreen.

The leaves of deciduous trees die with the approach of shorter days and colder weather, often turning brilliant shades of red, yellow, orange, and purple in the process.

Evergreen trees hold their leaves during the winter or until after one or two new leaf crops have grown, thus displaying an abundance of green foliage throughout the year. Often, these leaves take the form of slender needles or tight scales, as in the case of pines, firs, and cedars. These trees bear their seeds in cones and are therefore called conifers. But bear in mind that while all conifers are evergreen, not all evergreens are conifers. For example, magnolias, rhododendrons, and the many other broadleaved evergreens are not conifers.

SOIL WORK

Virtually all trees need a well-drained soil. So I always test the drainage where I plan to set out trees. Here's my favorite way to do it: I dig down about 2 feet, fill the hole with water, then allow it to stand. I walk away and come back in an hour or two. If the water is all gone, I know the soil drains well. But if there's still a fair amount of water in the hole, I know the drainage needs some improvement or I should find a new place to plant.

I know I can improve drainage and build up the soil by turning in compost or other rich organic matter. If I have time, I can grow a cover crop such as clover or winter rye to improve the soil's structure.

But simply loading up the planting hole with nice compost, manure, or soil won't do the trick. When soil amendments are added to improve drainage or fertility, problems often arise from making the planting hole too comfortable for the roots. The radical transition from the loose planting mix to the heavier native soil surrounding it can stop the roots in their tracks. This is known as the "flowerpot effect"—like the walls of a flowerpot, the surrounding soil acts as a barrier to root growth.

The heavier the soil, the fewer amendments required. To improve the fertility of heavy soils, use organic fertilizers that don't add bulk, such as rock phosphate, greensand, bonemeal, kelp meal, and gypsum. Be sure to incorporate them deeply and widely to put them in direct contact with the roots. Manures, blood meal, and leather meal can burn young roots and should be applied only in the second or third year and thereafter. Even then, you should sprinkle them on the soil surface and water them in so the nitrogen will leach into the root zone.

Sandy soils, on the other hand, can benefit from amendments that add both fertility and bulk. These soils can accommodate more amendments than clay soils can because new roots can easily make the transition from the planting hole to the loose surrounding soil. Compost, aged manure, and rich organic topsoil are ideal amendments in sandy soils. You can mix them at a rate of one part amendments to two parts soil and add them to the planting hole.

TIME TO PLANT

If you're planting bareroot stock, remember that the

wholesale grower leaves a large portion of the root system behind. So don't trim the roots except those that are broken or damaged. Soak the roots in a bucket of diluted liquid seaweed for 12 to 24 hours before planting. (This step is especially important if you purchased a mailorder tree.)

As the roots are soaking, gather up all the tools you'll need: shovel, spading fork, hose, cart, bucket of water, stakes, wire, shears, tree wrap, compost, and a balanced organic fertilizer.

Careful timing is required whether it's spring or fall. Dig when the soil is soft and slightly dry—a gentle whack on a lump of soil should cause it to crumble. If you have to really break up the clods, the soil is too wet or too dry.

Whenever I plant, I remember what Old Zeb used to say to me: "Better a 50-cent tree in a 5-dollar hole than a 5-dollar tree in a 50-cent hole." Dig the planting hole large enough to receive the roots when they're spread in a natural position. For balled-and-burlapped trees,

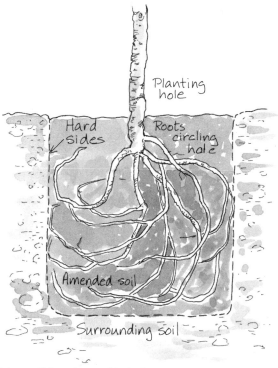

It's possible to be too kind when transplanting a tree. If you amend the soil in the planting hole too much and don't break up the soil on the sides of the hole, the roots will stay right there and won't try to penetrate the hard sides of the planting hole to get into the surrounding soil. This is called the flowerpot effect.

dig at least 2 feet wider than the root ball. Do the same for container-grown trees. Dig the hole deep enough so you can set the tree the same level at which it grew in the nursery. (You should be able to judge this by a visible soil line on the tree trunk.)

Unfortunately, the most common excavating techniques produce the flowerpot effect. Digging a planting hole with an auger or a spade slicks the walls of the hole,

smoothing the clay particles as if they were worked on a potter's wheel. The result resembles a clay pot in the ground. With a loose soil mix inside the augered hole, new roots won't venture into native soil. A garden shovel can produce the same smooth-walled effect in moist, clay soil. So use a spading fork to dig the hole for your tree. A spading fork is also handy for loosening the sides and bottom of the hole. Swing the fork's tines into the walls and twist. Then jab the fork into the bottom of the hole and rock it back and forth to heave the soil slightly. This fracturing makes it easier for roots to penetrate the surrounding soil.

Set the root ball in the hole with enough soil mix beneath it to bring the tree's base almost to ground level. Half-fill the hole with soil mix and tamp it down with your feet. Add a bucket or two of water and let it soak in. Complete filling in around the root ball with good soil, forming a slightly concave bed extending out as far from the

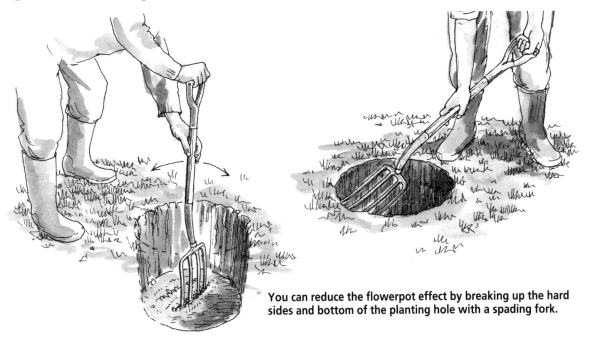

You can reduce the flowerpot effect by breaking up the hard sides and bottom of the planting hole with a spading fork.

trunk as you can manage. Try not to leave any air pockets.

Replace the soil from the hole with good topsoil or a mixture of soil and amendments. Put the sod and weeds in your compost pile—don't just dump them into the hole as backfill material. If you do, it could result in the formation of methane gas, which is toxic to young roots.

To discourage crown rot, mound a soil mixture 6 to 12 inches above the original soil surface over the entire area of the planting hole. The mound may settle to about half its original height, but the crown of the root system will still be elevated for good drainage.

The soil mixture for the mound should have a high percentage of amendments to encourage drainage. Adding compost, rotted horse manure, or shredded leaves will help provide some of the additional volume needed to build the mound. Mix one part of the amendment you've chosen with two parts soil. Since mounds dry out quickly, be sure to use mulch around the tree.

WRAP, STAKE, AND MULCH

After the tree is in place, settle the soil around the roots by watering thoroughly. It's also a good idea to wrap the trunk with tree wrap or burlap to prevent sunscald.

Transplanted trees may need support. Constant wind can tear out new root hairs almost as fast as they form. Drive a strong stake into the ground about 7 to 10 inches from the trunk. (Wood poles work well.) Next, put a wire through a piece of old garden hose and form a figure eight around the stake and trunk. If the tree trunk is over 3 inches in diameter, support it with three wires. Stake one to the ground in the direction of the prevailing wind and stretch the other two to form a triangle. Keep the tree securely staked through one full growing season.

Spread a straw mulch over the newly dug area

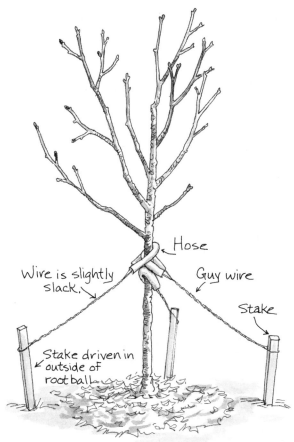

Hose

Wire is slightly slack.

Guy wire

Stake

Stake driven in outside of root ball

Young trees should be staked securely. Drive three strong stakes into the ground about 7 to 10 inches from the trunk. Place one stake in the ground in the direction of the prevailing wind, and place the other two to form a triangle. Tie the tree to the stakes securely with three wires wrapped in sections of old hose where they touch the trunk. Keep the tree securely staked through one full growing season.

around the base of the tree. This is especially important during the tree's first growing season. Not only does it conserve moisture, but it also keeps the soil cool under the hot summer sun—two conditions that are required for vigorous root growth.

Don't overwater your new tree. Too much water in the soil excludes oxygen and leads to root rot. To encourage fast development of root hairs, keep the soil moist, not soggy.

The Need to Feed

Trees in the forest ordinarily take good care of themselves. Many of the nutrients taken by the trees from the soil are returned when the leaves fall to the ground and break down. It's a simple cycle of rotating fertility. In this way, nature maintains the supply of available nutrients. Any small loss of nutrients is soon recovered by progressive weathering (which breaks rocks into minerals), rain (which carries dis-

solved nutrients), and other natural phenomena. So, we know we don't need to fertilize the trees in the forest. But what happens when you plant a young tree in your backyard or in your orchard? Shouldn't the tree still be able to take care of itself?

Forests develop according to the law of survival of the fittest. If a piece of land is suited to the growth of oaks and beeches, then oaks and beeches will crowd out any other seedlings that creep in. If an area is best adapted to the growth of pines or other conifers, then those trees will predominate. In a forest, the right type of tree is almost always growing in the right place. If it isn't, nature will soon replace it.

When you plant trees on your lawn, the natural selection of species is cast to the winds. You probably want several different types of trees that don't normally

Drip line

2' fertilizer band

Fertilize each spring by spreading a mix of organic fertilizers and compost in a 2- to 3-foot-wide band around the drip line of the tree.

they can be extremely important to the proper growth of trees on a lawn.

CROW'S FEEDING FORMULA

My simple, basic feeding formula for trees includes blood meal or fish meal for nitrogen, rock phosphate or bonemeal for phosphorus, granite dust or greensand for potash, and kelp meal for trace elements. Apply 1 pound of each ingredient for each year of the tree's age.

Fertilize in early spring. If the tree is small, broadcast the material evenly in a strip starting 6 inches from the trunk and extending to the end of the drip line (the outer edge around the tree's spread of branches). For larger trees, concentrate the applications in a 25- to 35-inch band around the tree at the drip line. To build up the organic matter content of the soil, work in about 3 inches of compost each spring.

Here's another recipe I've used on trees: Combine one part ground limestone, two parts rock phosphate, three parts greensand, three parts kelp meal, and five parts blended organic fertilizer. Apply the mix at the rate of 1 pound for each foot of drip line diameter. For example, if the tree measures 15 feet from tip to tip of its

grow in your area and aren't really suited to your soil or climate. And instead of a natural mulch of leaves around the roots, there will be a lawn, which will be trampled by children's feet and the constant passage of the mower. Maybe your lot has been bulldozed in the recent past, which means the trees may be growing in topsoil

mixed with subsoil. All of these factors make life difficult for trees.

You can make grass grow on a 1-inch layer of topsoil, but you can't expect trees to thrive in such a place when they don't have their customary mulch of leaves. So, while fertilizing and soil conditioning may be out of place in the forest,

opposite branches, then you would broadcast 15 pounds from the tree trunk to the drip line. To complete the annual treatment, apply a 4-inch mulch.

You can try both formulas and see which one works best for you. Regardless of which fertilizer mixture you choose, it's a good idea to work the material into the soil to encourage deeper root growth. You can do this by making holes in the soil with a bar or pipe, then placing the fertilizer in each of them. The holes should be about 1 foot apart, starting from the trunk and extending to the drip line.

Foliar feeding with a liquid fish and kelp solution works well, too, especially when your trees are under stress. It supplies minerals and growth regulators directly when they're not available from the soil and helps the trees grow to their optimum size.

Practical Pruning

Pruning is basically a commonsense practice that preserves a tree's health and appearance. It is not a cure-all to correct the problem of trees spaced too closely. But you *can* control and confine the shape and appearance with careful pruning.

There are a few general rules of pruning that I've found very useful. For example, you should start with the suckers, the small sprouts that shoot up from the soil line near the trunk. Prune them off completely, and your young tree will grow faster without the competition.

Remember that if you prune only the side branches and leave the leader (the central trunk of the tree) intact, a tree will continue to grow upward. But cutting off the leader forces the side branches to grow, so the tree becomes more dense and bushes out. And pruning the branch tips without cutting them back to the main trunk causes thicker growth of stems and leaves on the

Step 1: When pruning branches, remove just above an outward-facing bud. Make a slanting cut so water will run away from the bud rather than into it.

Bud

Step 2: Always remove the suckers at the base of a tree since they sap the tree's strength and ruin its form. Cut them off at or just below ground level.

Suckers

branch, especially if you cut ¼ to ½ inch above a bud or leaf joint.

Keep in mind that pruning is not meant to interrupt growth, but to increase the plant's vigor and to give it a neater appearance. The shape, size, and health of the growing plant is directly affected by how and when you prune. For example, shrubs pruned severely for a formal hedge sacrifice bloom for form. If pruned lightly, many hedges of flowering shrubs will reward you with more blooms. So before you begin pruning, it's important that you know how to do it the right way and at the right time.

Shrub-Pruning Scenarios

Never prune spring-blooming shrubs such as forsythias or lilacs until after they bloom—otherwise, you'll cut off all the flowers! Prune the late-summer-blooming shrubs only lightly in fall, winter, or early spring.

Forsythias will continue to bloom heavily if left unpruned, so it's wise to cut out only the dead and weak stems; prune the shrubs from ground level rather than shearing them back. Prune lilac, flowering quince, and flowering almond sparingly immediately after they bloom.

Roses are pruned by cutting back the hard wood to encourage abundant floral growth. As soon as the buds begin to swell in early spring, trim the shrubs back to three to five of their sturdiest canes, cutting out the weaker canes at ground level. Cut back the remaining canes to about four buds—usually 5 to 6 inches above ground level.

THE RIGHT WAY TO PRUNE

Always use a sharp, clean tool, whether you choose a pruning saw, shears, or loppers. Start at the top of the plant and work your way down, looking for misshapen or crossed branches as you go. To prevent the spread of decay, cut out all broken, dead, or diseased wood. If you must remove a larger branch, make a preliminary undercut so that you don't strip the bark when the branch snaps. (See the illustration on page 307 for the right way to make pruning cuts.)

To prune, make a diag-

onal cut ¼ inch above a bud facing out from the center of the tree or shrub. Make sure the cut slants away from the bud, or water will run into it and encourage disease. Cutting to an outward-facing bud promotes well-shaped growth. If you cut to an inward-facing bud, the tree will quickly become a congested tangle of branches.

When you cut a branch, make the cut right outside the branch collar (a slightly swollen area where the branch joins the trunk). Don't leave a stub, which will interfere with the normal growth of protective callus tissue.

WATCH OUT FOR WOUNDS

While you're pruning, keep an eye out for wounds that expose the wood beneath the bark. This type of shallow scrape has killed off many a good tree. It's an open invitation to bacteria, fungi, and many insects that normally leave healthy trees alone. Don't even *think* about covering such a wound with tree dressing—it's been proven that these substances do more harm than good. The tree itself will grow a normal callus to close the opening, but you can help by carefully trimming off loose, rough, or protruding chips or bits of torn wood.

Tree wounds may be the last thing you're thinking about while you're pruning, but they're even more important than the pruning cuts themselves. Ornamental shade trees such as dogwood, Japanese weeping cherry, and flowering crabapple can easily become malformed if wounds are ignored.

WHEN TO PRUNE

Most deciduous trees react best to dormant pruning during late winter, but there are exceptions. The maple tree is one. Maple trees should be pruned only in late spring, or in summer before September. Maple sap is "up" and flowing in the fall, winter, and early spring. Pruning during that period can cause severe "bleeding," which could result in the tree's death.

Pruning may seem intimidating or time-consuming, but it's well worth it. Just watching your pruned tree grow straight and true can give you a great feeling of accomplishment. The strengthened tree, the increased number and quality of flowers and fruits, and the greater abundance of colorful beauty in all seasons bring their own reward.

An Ounce of Prevention

You've gotten your tree off to a good start, but your job isn't over—not by a long shot. The kind of protection you give your tree in the years to come is just as important as the effort you put into planting it. The health of the tree—not to mention flower, fruit, and nut production—depends on how good a maintenance job you do.

Here are a few simple tricks that will really help your trees.

PROTECT TREES FROM SUNSCALD

I don't know what it is about them, but young nut trees seem particularly susceptible to sunscald. To protect a tree for the first few years until its bark has become tough enough to withstand the intense rays of the sun, use a stretchable 2-inch-wide paper tape made especially for wrapping trees. Whitewashing the trunk is also a time-honored way of protecting trees from sunscald.

Root-Prune before Transplanting

If you're planning to transplant small trees and shrubs, it might pay to do a little root pruning one season in advance. Pruning the roots encourages the development of lots of feeder roots close to the trunk, thus lessening the shock for the plant when it's moved. Here's what to do:

Using a sharp spade, dig to the depth of the spade straight down into the soil around the base of the tree or shrub. Picture how much of the root ball you're going to move, and slice at the outer edge.

Keep the spade straight down; don't cut into the root area at an angle. Step on the spade with steady pressure until it cuts through the side roots of the plant and you feel them break.

That's all there is to it. By the following year, the plant will have developed a healthy root system close to its trunk, where you can dig it all up.

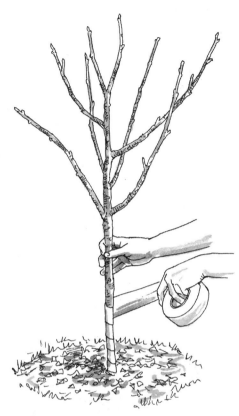

In sunny areas, young trees should be protected from the scalding sun. Put white tree wrap, a stretchy sun protector, around the trunk. Check it periodically to make sure it's not girdling the bark.

ELIMINATE INSECT HIDEAWAYS

These simple techniques can really cut down on pest problems: Scrape the bark of trees to kill overwintering larvae. Prune off split or injured branches where insects might hide or disease might start. Interrupt the insect breeding cycle by making sure wormy fruit is picked up. (You can either compost the fruit or feed it to the chickens.)

PROTECT TREES FROM THE WIND

Dwarf trees are especially likely to suffer wind damage. To protect trees from being uprooted by the wind, anchor them to the ground with stakes and wires that are padded with rubber where they touch the trunk or branches. (Turn to page 305 to see how to stake a tree.)

DON'T LET FROST NIP YOUR TREES

Frost may not harm hardy trees. In fact, many need a certain amount of cold weather in order to bloom or bear well. But frost *can* damage a beautiful spring flower display or a crop of fruit or nuts if it hits a tree in blossom. You can, however, take steps that will make a difference.

For instance, don't plant ornamental flowering trees or fruit and nut trees on a southern slope or in another sheltered place where they might bloom too early. And don't plant trees in low spots where frost will settle.

When the ground is frozen hard in midwinter, apply a heavy straw mulch to keep the soil from warming up quickly in the spring.

Another trick is to apply a liquid kelp foliar spray. It's been said to increase frost resistance in trees and shrubs by super-nourishing them with essential trace minerals. It can also save your fruit crop if frost occurs during bloom. Spray when the leaf buds begin to open and again when the flower buds start to show color. For fruit trees, spray a third time after the petals fall.

KEEP ANIMALS OFF!

Mice and rabbits may gnaw your trees' bark during the winter and can kill a tree by girdling the bark. Wrapping the trunk with a spiral plastic tree protector will fend off gnawing animals in addition to preventing sunscald.

PROTECT PLANTS FROM MISTAKES

Little lapses can cause big damage to trees. Forget to remove the tree's ID tag and it might eventually girdle the tree. Ignore the suckers that originate below the graft and sooner or later they'll take over, causing the tree's top to die off and the plant to revert to its rootstock variety. Put too much manure around fruiting or ornamental pear trees and the resulting lush growth will be subject to fire blight.

There's more to raising trees than digging holes and planting them. To plant a tree is to make a strong commitment to the land and to future generations.

My Favorite Tree—The Flowering Dogwood

There are a lot of trees to choose from, but I don't have any trouble naming my favorite: It's the flowering dogwood. And I'm not shy about singing its praises.

Tier after tier of white spring blossoms are followed by clusters of bright red berries and deep mahogany foliage in autumn. As an extra dividend, the pleasingly shaped branches are twigged in red and tipped with pearly gray buds in winter. The year-round beauty of this decorative tree is unsurpassed.

The flowering dogwood grows in a wide variety of climates and soils, and is hardy in Zones 5–9. Even if it is accidentally chopped down, this amazing plant will often rise again, sending up a beautiful new tree from the

old roots. In its native environment it reproduces easily, both from seed and from shoots springing up from the roots of established trees. An old tree subjected to repeated drought may look like it's dying, but after a rainy season it comes alive again, laden with waxen white blooms and lush red berries. It's enough to make you wonder if an old dogwood ever dies.

THE TROUBLE WITH DOGWOODS

I can almost hear your protest: "If a dogwood is all that tough and healthy, then what's happened to mine?"

You may think it's the most finicky, disappointing tree you've ever tried to grow. You may have trouble nursing it through the first year. You aren't alone. Despite the tree's many virtues, almost everyone has trouble growing dogwoods.

Why? The trouble starts with transplanting. When this lovely tree reluctantly leaves one home for another, it becomes the number-one problem child of the entire garden. It resists transplanting. Experts agree that dogwoods have trouble adapting to a garden setting unless you understand their special needs.

By nature, the dogwood is an understory tree in the woods. It seldom stands alone, especially when young. It has very shallow roots that grow sideways through the soil. It likes woodsy, humusy, acid soil. And it can't endure wet feet, so good drainage is a must.

DOGWOODS MY WAY

Don't despair. You *can* grow gorgeous dogwood trees successfully—if you follow my rules.

··· Don't Plant Deep
Plant shallowly, and don't allow the roots to dry out during the first two years. The reason for this rule is that dogwoods have no taproot. Their roots spread outward, growing just beneath the surface of the soil.

··· Protect Your Trees
Shield your dogwoods from hot sun, extreme heat, and cold. (See "An Ounce of Prevention" on page 309 for special tree-protection techniques.)

··· Give Your Trees Shelter
Plant your dogwoods in the partial shade of a house or hedge. Or, better still, plant them under a large tree such as an oak, sycamore, maple, or pine.

··· Add Organic Matter

Use plenty of shredded leaves, peat moss, compost, and other organic matter to enrich the soil. The more acidic types like oak leaves and peat are best.

··· Hold the Pruners

Don't prune your dogwood, except to correct initial defects when setting it out. Allow low-growing branches to cascade to the ground, which is nature's way of adding grace, protecting shallow roots, and preserving moisture.

··· Stake the Trees

Even a mild wind can sway a young tree enough to disturb the shallow roots. As a result, the roots can't establish themselves.

··· Keep the Roots Cool

If you plant in the spring, do so while the ground is still cool—dogwood roots cannot take hold in hot soil. To keep the roots cool in the summer and warm in the winter, mulch heavily with oak leaves, pine needles, or straw. After the third or fourth year, also apply a winter dressing of barnyard manure. This raises the temperature at the roots by several degrees and promotes growth.

··· Improve Drainage

Although frequent watering is necessary, wet feet are fatal. Heavy clay soils are no place for dogwoods. Improve such soils first with *lots* of organic matter.

··· Plant Late

Don't begin fall planting until there have been three hard frosts. From then on, plant when the ground isn't frozen.

Dogwoods are understory trees. They grow best when they're planted in the dappled shade of a large tree.

··· Transplant Carefully

If you're digging up young trees, rake the soil away gently and lift out the shallow roots from all directions, keeping as many of the hair-like feeder roots as possible. Cut off any damaged segments. If the weather is dry, soak the roots in water for 24 hours before planting.

··· Water Well

The reason for frequent watering is obvious: Dogwoods have shallow, wide-ranging roots and no taproot to draw up food or water. Once a dogwood's roots dry out completely, they are gone, dead. Nothing can revive them. To avoid losing the roots this way, be sure the soil is well drained, and add generous amounts of spongy organic matter.

··· Don't Mow the Trees Down

I'm always shocked when I see yet another dogwood that's been butchered by a lawn mower. It's as though people can't resist ramming the trunk on their way past, creating bulging, unsightly scars around the base of the tree in the process. But the initial damage is the least of the plant's troubles. An open wound like this—especially one that's repeatedly opened with every mowing—provides an open door for dogwood anthracnose, the disease that's attacking dogwoods all along the East Coast. Healthy, uninjured dogwoods are seldom bothered by anthracnose. But beat your tree up with the mower, and it won't take long to succumb.

Everlasting Evergreens

Anybody can buy an evergreen tree from the garden center. But for special gardening pleasure and satisfaction, why not try starting some conifers from seed? It's easier than you might think.

STARTING FROM SEED

To grow an evergreen from seed, first you have to find a seed donor. Spend some time scouting the local parks and forests. Take note of the most beautiful trees, then come back for cones when they're ripe. I like to harvest cones from mature trees—those that have attained their full vertical growth and are spreading out, with their top branches up in the sun. They should be in a grove of trees like them, not standing alone. Vigorous trees produce the best seed.

It's time to start collecting the cones when they turn from green to brown. They should be opening and about to release their seeds so that with just a little pressure, they fall into your hands. (If you dent a seed with your thumbnail and it releases a milky fluid, it's too early.) Watch the squirrels for the right date—when they start cutting down cones, you can be sure the seeds are ready for storage. Take seeds only from dead cones—that is, those that will float when dropped into water.

To make a cone release its seeds, warm it in the sun for a day or two. Then tap it sharply with a hammer and shake it in a paper bag until the seeds drop out. Store the seeds in brown jars with screw-on lids and leave them in the refrigerator over the winter months.

You'll notice that most conifer seeds are winged. That's nature's way of spreading them over a large area. Removing the wings increases their readiness to germinate, so store them with the wings on. Then, when you remove the seeds from storage in early spring, rub the wings off.

Dampen the seeds slightly by spraying them with warm water and rubbing them gently between your hands. Then pour the seeds into a bowl filled with warm water. The good ones will sink; the dead ones will float.

🌟 **Let's Get Growing**

START WITH A GOOD SEEDBED

Nothing will give your conifers a better start in life than a carefully prepared seedbed. Site the seedbed in partial shade since the seedlings don't like hot, dry conditions. Conifers do quite well in a variety of soils—all the way from acid to quite alkaline. However, the seeds germinate better in slightly acid soil.

Follow nature's lead and dig rich organic matter into the soil. A porous soil rich in peat moss, shredded leaves, or decayed pine needles and covered with a thick mulch is ideal.

To sow, broadcast the seeds. Don't bother to sow them neatly in rows—the tiny trees do better if they stand close together in a little thicket. Also, don't make the common mistake of planting the seeds too deep in the soil; it's better to err on the side of shallowness. Plant them no more than twice their depth. Water well, but avoid puddling.

Germination begins when the seed absorbs water from the soil. After about 30 days, you can start looking for tiny spears emerging from the soil. During this time, be sure the soil remains moist (but not sopping wet). The seedling tree roots will be tiny, hairlike, and close to the surface, and should not be allowed to dry out.

When all the little trees are up, carefully spread a light mulch of pine needles. Mulching will help cut down on weeding, preserve the soil moisture, and ensure an even root temperature. Add more mulch as the trees grow so that their tops show just above it.

After the seedlings have spent a year in the seedbed, or when they are at least 4 inches tall, line them out in the nursery bed. Be sure they have direct sun, a little richer soil, more water, and adequate drainage. Set them 5 inches apart in rows; allow 1 foot between the rows.

If you prefer, instead of transplanting the seedlings into rows, you can plant them in large pots or cans filled with humus-rich soil mixed with sand. (Make sure there are holes in the bottom for drainage.) You'll be able to place these trees in the best spot for their development, but they'll require more frequent watering than those planted in the ground.

After one year in the nursery bed or containers, transplant your trees to their permanent location. Once they're set out where you want them, all they'll require is good drainage, soil rich in organic matter, room to stretch out their great limbs, and a little relief from weeds in their early years.

Who knows? You may start a small stand of pines, a natural monument that lasts for years. Even in its silence, it will say much about the person who planted it.

Hedge Shears for Pruning

You can use power hedge shears to prune evergreens and hedges. They're faster and more effective than hand-pruning for formal shaping. But hand-pruning is better for stimulating the plant to fill certain spots or holes with new growth. Whichever technique you choose, cut near the junction or above a bud. That way, the pruned ends will be hidden by new foliage growth, and the plant will have less of a scalped or butchered appearance.

Pruning Conifers

After about two years, your conifers will be growing rapidly. From then on, you should prune them to maintain a desirable shape. Unlike deciduous trees and shrubs, which grow most of the summer, evergreens make only one fast spurt of growth during their growing season. Pruning should begin as soon as the new growth is an inch or two long. Since the growing season is short, in most cases one or two prunings are enough.

For quicker recovery, prune conifers while they are growing or just after the new growth stops for the year. If you have a variety of conifers, you can stretch out the pruning season since they don't all make their growth at the same time. Most evergreens—including spruces, yews, firs, and pines—grow in early summer, so the best time to prune them is May or early June. Hemlocks and arborvitae (white cedar) make their growth in late June or July, so prune in mid- to late summer.

Keep in mind that many yews and some junipers occasionally have a second growth flush later in the season, so

Most evergreens should be pruned in late spring to help them grow to their best shape. Just remove enough of the new growth to give them the form you like.

they may need another trimming in late summer.

In most areas, pruning after July 1 is almost certain to retard next year's growth. That's because you'll be removing new bud development on the tips.

HOW TO PRUNE

Prune yews, junipers, and hemlocks $1/4$ inch above a bud so that new growth from the bud can quickly hide the site of the cut. You may remove nearly all of the new growth of spruces, pines, and firs. But never cut into the older growth; it recovers poorly and remains stubby.

Besides keeping the tree small, early-summer pruning also encourages density. Cutting the end tips of the new growth stops all further growth upward and outward, and encourages lateral branching, which makes the plant attractively thick and bushy. A second pruning, about a week after the first, can reshape any stray branches that have developed.

Shearing early in summer also leaves no unsightly stubs. Any cutting of the soft, new growth heals quickly, and buds for next year's growth will form where the cut was made. By midsummer, there will be no sign that the tree was ever pruned.

Be sure to shear the sides as severely as the top. Sprawling conifers that are merely topped aren't any more attractive than tall, straggly ones. Just visualize how you want the tree to look, and cut accordingly. There's no need to worry about joints and buds, as with fruit trees. Branching on conifers will take place naturally.

Can all conifers be pruned as tightly as this? Apparently they can. Even the long-needled pines take on a completely different

The Zen of Pruning

Besides knowing why, how, and when, a certain mental attitude is necessary for good pruning. Don't let those studies of plants screaming in pain scare you. There's absolutely no evidence that an evergreen is in any way distressed by pruning. In fact, a well-pruned plant will usually outlive an unpruned one. It will be more disease- and insect-resistant, and will certainly be much more attractive where space is limited. Just tell yourself it's all for the good of the plant, and slash on. If you make a mistake, nature's new growth will cover it up.

appearance when sheared severely. Again, don't be afraid to be drastic, and do all the cutting when the trees are growing or just after new growth has stopped.

Winter Protection

More than most other plants, evergreens need winter protection. They can't protect themselves during the winter by dropping their leaves, so the water continues to evaporate through the leaves. Too much wind and winter sun can cause an excessive loss of moisture, which results in winter burn. You can prevent this severe drying by watering, mulching, and shielding your plants.

As summer draws to a close, take mental inventory of your evergreen stock.

Decide which of the winter foes you must guard the plants against—wind and drought are the most common problems. Before the frost is on the pumpkin, apply these simple methods of protection.

WIND SHIELDS

You can cover your evergreens with burlap or a screen. If you use burlap, stretch it on a wire frame over the entire plant. To make a screen, set up lath or burlap on the east and south sides of the plant. Both methods are recommended for the smaller conifers, especially if the trees are in an exposed position.

Slender evergreens with long, erect branches, such as the junipers, are often whip-

ping posts for winter gales. The dwarf evergreens used in foundation plantings also suffer. To protect these vulnerable plants, you can make windbreaks from slatted fencing held in place by steel posts.

If you live in an exposed area where the winds are heavy, try wrapping your conifers in burlap. Start at the bottom of the plant and tie a stout cord to one of the branches. Then walk around the plant, lifting each branch and holding it in place with the cord until you reach the top and the plant is hog-tied like a calf at a rodeo.

Next, apply 3-inch-wide strips of burlap, starting at the bottom. Fasten the end of one strip to the first round of cord with heavy safety pins. Then walk around the plant as before, winding the burlap upward and fastening each lap in several places with pins. If you like, you can cover the top with a square of burlap pinned in place or with any other cap that will shed the snow. Your conifer may look like a mummy, but it will probably still be there to greet the spring.

CORRECTING PLANTING MISTAKES

Some of us have given the north wind various unprintable names because it tilts our newly planted evergreens to one side. But it's not always the wind's fault. The tilting is often the result of faulty planting—that is, the soil may not have been properly packed around the roots and trunk at planting time.

You can remedy this problem by arranging three stakes in a triangle around the tree trunk and passing wires between the stakes and around the trunk. (Protect the bark from wire cuts by wrapping the wire with pieces of rubber hose.) I guarantee that this method will make the most oblique conifer perpendicular.

MULCH SAVES THE DAY

When freezing weather strikes, evergreens are better off if the soil is moist. Mulch applied in the fall holds in soil moisture and helps plants get through the winter the right way. It also serves to keep the soil evenly cool instead of alternately warm and cold, which can damage the roots.

Excellent materials for evergreen mulch are straw, salt hay, oak leaves, and peat moss. The mulch should be no deeper than 4 inches and should extend a little beyond the natural spread of the roots.

Shrubs for Every Landscape

There may be nothing in all the landscape as versatile as shrubs. They can soften angles and corners, hug the house, and provide an eye-pleasing sight overall. Shrubs can offer a succession of bloom during spring, summer, and fall, and those that are evergreen will carry color through the winter.

SHOPPING FOR SHRUBS

When shopping for flowering shrubs, keep the color of your house in mind. Select shrubs that will show flowers and foliage at their best against that color. For example, forsythia or yellow roses aren't as attractive in front of a yellow house as holly bushes or red roses. Use only low-growing shrubs under first-floor windows and dwarf to medium-size plants at the sides of steps or small entrances. Avoid planting too many deciduous shrubs next to the house—they shed all their leaves in fall and look dull in winter.

Most front yards benefit from one lone, eye-catching specimen shrub. It may have showstopping flowers, beautiful berries, or unusual foliage. Match the ultimate size of the shrub to the size of your front yard. Dwarf, semi-dwarf, or slow-growing types are usually best as specimen shrubs in small yards. Flowering quinces are good choices, as are cranberrybush viburnums, shrubby flowering crabapples, winterberry hollies, or, in a shady yard, rhododendrons or oakleaf hydrangeas. Whichever you choose, set it out on the lawn far enough to allow for growth without crowding sidewalks or paths.

For the backyard, try placing flowering shrubs here and there to add splashes of green or other hues to flat settings. Azaleas, lilacs, crape myrtles, and forsythia are all suitable for this purpose.

Use hardy shrubs like euonymus (burning bush) or rugosa roses for a fence that's more practical and attractive than wood or metal. They're also friendlier than a wall or fence along neighboring boundaries and patios. And they double as ecological aids to curb sound and improve the air quality. They even add a sweet or spicy fragrance to the scene.

SHRUBS FOR WILDLIFE

A thicket of shrubs provides a natural sanctuary for birds, toads, and other forms of wildlife that are delightful to

You can make your backyard a mini–wildlife sanctuary by planting shrubs and trees that produce berries and seeds for birds and other critters. Elderberries, raspberries, bush cherries, and currants all add color and flavor to this backyard.

watch and essential to your yard's environmental balance. Other than pesticide spraying, nothing discourages these benefactors more than whole yards, fields, or neighborhoods devoid of trees or any protective clump or screen of bushes.

Try to include evergreens as well as plenty of fruit- and nut-bearing plants for year-round shelter in your wildlife setting. Both evergreen and deciduous hollies are excellent choices, as are most viburnums, bayberries, serviceberries, and roses with large, edible hips like rugosas. Bramble fruits such as red and black raspberries, as well as blueberries, bush cherries, and currants, are all bird pleasers. I like 'em, too!

From Planting to Pruning

Now that you know what shrubs can do for the land-scape, how do you get them off to the best start?

First, make sure you plant them at the right time. Early-fall planting is best for bareroot and balled-and-burlapped shrubs. That's because plants set out in autumn usually make root growth during the fall and winter months, so they're able to become established before warm weather hits. You can transplant container-grown shrubs throughout the spring and summer, provided you water the plants regularly.

GETTING SHRUBS IN THE GROUND

I like to dig a big hole for shrubs, then amend the soil in the hole. This goes counter to the wisdom for planting trees, but since shrub roots don't travel as far as tree roots, the flowerpot effect poses less of a risk, especially in a big hole.

I dig the planting holes twice the width of the root ball and 1½ times as deep as its height. Then I add peat moss, compost, or shredded leaves to the excavated soil at the rate of one part organic matter to three parts soil. I mix it in thoroughly, then place enough of this mixture in the bottom of the planting hole so that the top of the root ball is at ground level when placed in the hole. (For azaleas, rhododendrons, and camellias, be sure to place the top of the ball 1 or 2 inches higher than ground level.)

If you're planting container-grown shrubs, here's what to do: First, remove the container. If you see a tangled mass of roots when you slide the plant from the container, make several vertical cuts with a knife to prevent the roots from continuing to grow in a circle. Treat balled-and-burlapped plants as though you were planting them container and all. Cut off any cords or wires and loosen the burlap at the top of the root ball. And make sure it *is* burlap! If it's plastic, peel or cut it off before planting.

When placing a bare-root plant in the hole, be sure to spread the roots out completely so they can take advantage of the moisture and

When planting container-grown trees or shrubs, check the root ball carefully. If the roots have grown into a circling, tangled mass, make some vertical cuts with a knife to loosen them up before planting. Make the planting hole 2 times as wide and 1½ times as deep as the root ball.

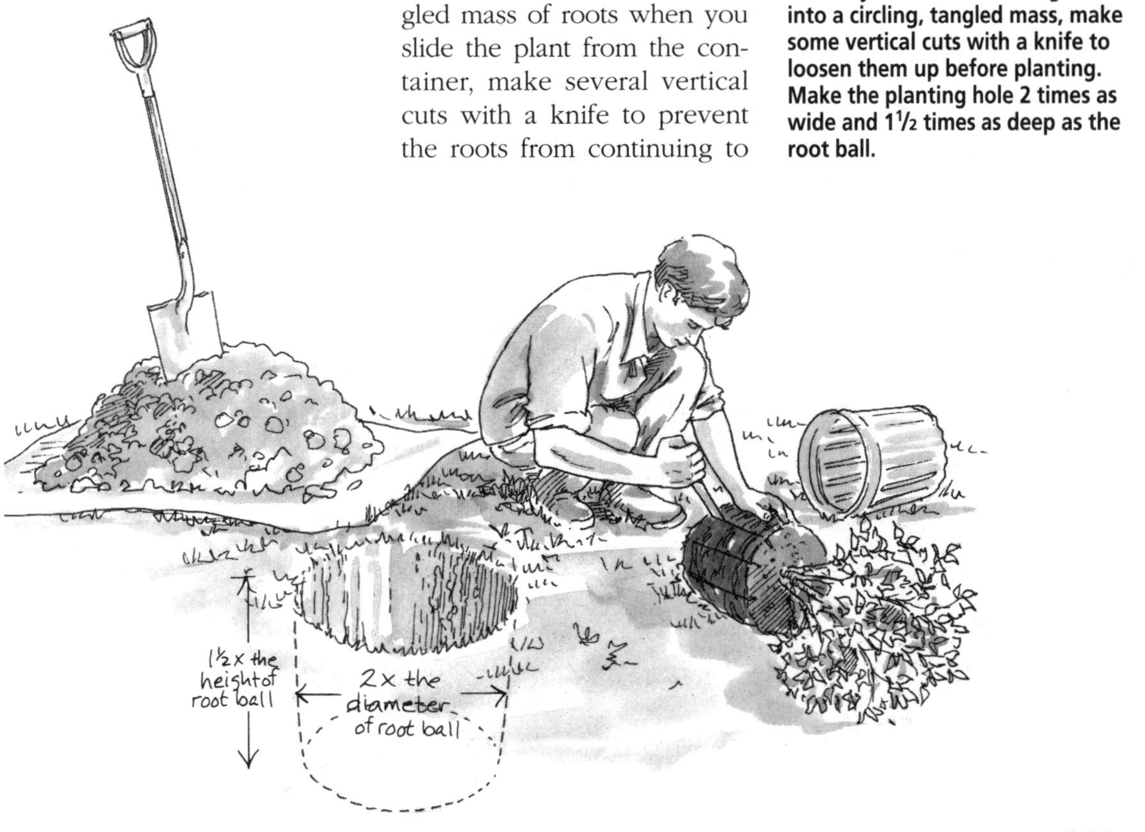

1½ x the height of root ball

2 x the diameter of root ball

compost. Often, hollies, aza-leas, boxwoods, and camel-lias are set too deeply for proper growth. When these plants are buried in the soil, they grow poorly and eventu-ally die. So make sure you set them no deeper than they were growing in the nursery.

Once your shrub is in place, refill around the sides of the root ball with your topsoil mixture. With the shovel handle, tamp the soil downward and under the ball to remove air pockets. Firm the remaining soil to-ward the ball. Then fill the hole with water and allow the soil to settle.

With the remaining mix-ture, refill the rest of the hole and firm again. The top of the ball should be slightly covered. Using the subsoil,

construct a water ring 2 or 3 inches high around the out-side of the planting hole. Then apply 2 inches of mulch from the water ring to the main trunk of the plant and water again. The ring acts as a saucer, funneling water down to the plant's roots.

PRUNING YOUR SHRUBS

There's no point in denying it: Most shrubs need some sort of pruning. Ornamental plants or woody shrubs can't go long without pruning if they are to serve their intended purpose in the landscape.

Pruning is done for five reasons:

1. To develop or main-tain a desired shape or size.

2. To remove older stems and encourage vig-orous young ones to take their place.

3. To remove diseased or injured parts.

4. To balance root and branch systems.

5. To remove dead wood.

Shrubs that flower after June, like rose-of-Sharon, hy-drangeas, and viburnums, usually do so on growth that's been made in the same year, so they have ample time to produce their flowering stems. This late-blooming type of shrub should be pruned in fall or winter, while it's dormant.

Evergreens such as holly and abelia are grown for fall and winter foliage

Rules for Watering Shrubs

I can't give you exact rules for wa-tering since your soil and the condition of your plants will ultimately determine when and how much you should water. (Remember the rule of observation!) But when watering, keep these general rules in mind:

🍃 Don't water until the plants show signs of wilting before noon.

🍃 Apply water slowly so it can soak into the soil. The rate of application should vary from ½ to 1 inch per hour according to the soil

type. (One inch of rainfall equals approximately 625 gallons per 1,000 square feet. Using a 50-foot hose, it would take at least three to four hours to add 625 gallons.) Wet the soil thor-oughly to a depth of 8 to 10 inches.

🍃 Never water by spraying only the surface of the soil. Light watering encourages shallow root development.

🍃 Avoid late-afternoon watering. The leaves don't have much time to dry before nightfall, and wet foliage invites many plant diseases.

More Plants from Cuttings

Nature has given plants a strong will to live. So propagating by taking cuttings from plants is a relatively foolproof process. It's simple if you take cuttings at the right time of the year for a particular plant.

Although most plants commonly reproduce from seed, cuttings are a faster way to go. In one season, you can produce a plant that's more than twice as big as a seedling started at the same time. And all you need are a knife and a rooting box—a flat or a long, narrow plastic or wooden box filled with moist soil.

Softwood and Hardwood Cuttings

Whether you make softwood or hardwood cuttings depends on the time of year. The first flush of growth in spring is soft. A few weeks later, the tissue matures and begins to harden. By fall, the plant has hard wood.

Thus, softwood cuttings are made in spring or early summer, semi-hardwood cuttings in summer and early fall, and hardwood cuttings from late fall to early spring.

There's a slight difference between softwood and semi-hardwood. In some plants, like camellias, it's easy to see the difference, since the softwood turns from greenish to a light red or brown when it changes to semi-hardwood.

Taking Softwood and Semi-Hardwood Cuttings

To make softwood or semi-hardwood cuttings, choose wood that hasn't grown too fast or too slow and is free of disease. Cut the stem from 4 to 6 inches long, and try to include three or more nodes with leaves attached.

Before sticking cuttings into the rooting box, remove the leaves from the bottom quarter of the stem. Place the box of cuttings in the shade. Keep the soil in the box moist.

Taking Hardwood Cuttings

There are two kinds of hardwood cuttings: the ones that you take from evergreen plants such as junipers, and the ones that you take from deciduous plants such as grapes. The hardwood cuttings of evergreen plants are treated in the same manner as semi-hardwood cuttings.

Take hardwood deciduous cuttings when they're completely dormant, from late fall to early spring. Ideally, they should be about 18 inches long. Place them in a long, shallow box and cover them with moist sand, sawdust, or peat moss. Then leave the box on the shady side of the house. Or store the cuttings in a plastic bag in the refrigerator. While in storage, each stem will form a callus. Once the weather warms, stick the cuttings into the soil to grow.

When it comes to dormant hardwood cuttings, the most important thing to remember is that shoots grow up and roots grow down (a phenomenon called polarity). The part of the stem that will eventually form the top must always be kept at the top. A simple way to avoid a mistake is to cut straight across the stem on the part that will be the top, and make a slanted cut on the end that will form the roots. When you're ready to place the cutting in the soil, merely push in the pointed end.

effect, so don't prune them in fall. Instead, prune these just before growth starts in the spring. You can prune azaleas while they're in flower—a great idea, since the blossoms can be used in home arrangements.

Pyracantha, nandina (heavenly bamboo), and Japanese quince produce berries and flowers on branches that are more than one year old. For this reason, don't prune these shrubs unless absolutely necessary.

Two Favorite Shrubs

Once again, it's time for me to play favorites, to make a

Mist Propagation

How do you start 100 new plants from cuttings in a space no larger than 2 × 3 feet? With mist propagation.

Euonymus, chrysanthemums, geraniums, roses—in fact, almost every kind of flowering plant or decorative evergreen—can be successfully started this way. Any softwood cutting seems to root easily with mist propagation.

You can make an inexpensive mist house from scrap lumber. Begin with a 2 × 3-foot wooden floor. Attach 4-inch-high sideboards all the way around the base. Using this tray as a base, frame a kennel-like house with 2-foot-high sides topped by a gabled roof. Cover the entire framework with 8-mil poly to allow sunlight to penetrate easily. Hinge one side to permit easy access to the interior.

Install a mist nozzle, complete with a garden hose fitting, 2 feet above the floor, with the nozzle directed upward into the gabled roof. Attach a garden hose to the nozzle and lead it out of the box through a hole in the floor. The box is now ready to be filled.

Fill the bottom tray with vermiculite, and use 3-inch peat pots to hold the cuttings. Fill each peat pot two-thirds full of vermiculite; fill the top third with tightly packed soil so there is enough firmness in the potting medium to support the cuttings in an upright position.

Take 4- to 6-inch softwood cuttings and remove the bottom set of leaves. Thrust each stem into a filled peat pot. Label the pots, then place them in the mist box and twist the pots into the vermiculite so they won't fall over.

A box like the one described above holds 100 cuttings. When the water is turned on, the interior becomes filled with a foglike mist. Turn the water on at sunup and off at sundown. Water consumption should be of no concern, since the nozzle in use permits the passage of only a half-gallon per hour.

After two weeks, the roots should start breaking through the sides of the peat pots and spreading into the vermiculite in the tray. In three weeks, a good root system will have formed and the new plants will be ready to move into a permanent location. To minimize root disturbance, transplant peat pots and all.

Plants that are moved from the high humidity of the mist house into direct midsummer sunlight will have a tendency to wilt. So shade them with floating row covers and spray them with water at regular intervals for the first two or three days. After that, the plants should grow well on their own.

sales pitch for two flowering shrubs that I wouldn't be without: azaleas and lilacs.

AZALEAS

You can grow azaleas successfully only if you cater to their taste for a humusy soil. Each year, thousands of gardeners try to grow them without a sense of humus: The results aren't funny!

Azaleas' requirements are simple, but rigid: an acid soil that's rich in organic matter, a heavy mulch, constant moisture, good drainage, filtered sunlight, and absolutely no cultivation.

The most common symptom of an ailing azalea plant is chlorosis, a yellowing of the leaves. This is not a disease; it simply means that the soil is not sufficiently acid.

The importance of mulching azaleas can't be overemphasized. The roots are extremely shallow—most of them spread out within 3 or 4 inches of the soil surface. They must be kept moist at all times and protected from the heat of summer and the cold of winter. And they must never be disturbed by cultivation.

Other than the fertility provided by the decaying

Azaleas can be left to grow naturally, but you may want to prune them for shape, size, or heavier flowering. Cut just below the faded flower right after it has finished blooming.

mulch, azaleas require only a feeding of cottonseed meal once a year to keep them in good condition. Apply it immediately after the blooming season at a rate of $2^{1}/_{2}$ pounds per 100 square feet. If your azaleas seem to be lacking vigor, you can apply a second feeding of cottonseed meal three weeks later, but never after June. Later feedings will encourage new growth that won't be hardened against winter cold.

Siting Azaleas

Azaleas need some sun to bloom well, but the direct rays of the summer sun are usually harmful. The buds for the coming spring form during the summer and fall, and the plants need plenty of moisture during that time. That's why azaleas thrive on the edge of woods where they get filtered sunlight, or in sheltered locations where they receive partial sun.

Plants grown in dense shade or those that are overfed or fed late don't withstand the cold well. Azaleas will survive severe cold if they're protected, but the flower buds may be injured, especially if they're showing color.

Azalea Pruning Tactics

You may prune azaleas to keep them at the desired size and to make them produce more flowers. Ideally, the plants should be dense and well branched, since a flower forms at the tip of each branch. Prune immediately after the plants bloom so that the new flower buds can form during the summer.

Choosing the Right Azalea

Azalea colors range from white to pink, lavender, salmon, orange, and red, as well as bicolors. There are so many cultivars, it's hard to choose. Plants can be anywhere from 2 to 8 feet tall, and are hardy in Zones 5–9, depending on the cultivar. So the first step is to choose a cultivar that's hardy in your area and a height that's right for your site.

Once you've chosen a type of azalea that will suit you, you need to consider color. Here are some tricks I've developed to narrow the color choices: In small gardens a single color is most effective, especially when combined with plants of the same color that are in bloom at the same time. For instance, try white azaleas under dogwood or pink azaleas near redbud. You can also echo the colors of azaleas later in the season with summer-blooming impatiens, which thrive under similar conditions.

LET THE LILACS BLOOM

Some shrubs can get by on their foliage alone, but anyone who has sniffed the aroma of lilacs on a warm, dampish evening in spring knows that lilacs are grown for flowers. The incredible bloom tresses on these 4- to 8-foot shrubs just knock me out! Of course, not all lilac flowers are lilac—they range from white to deep purple.

Unlike azaleas, lilacs

aren't at all hard to please and are adept at taking care of themselves when necessary. They can take the cold winters of New England or the warm summers of the Mid-Atlantic states. Lilacs are hardy in Zones 3–8, depending on the species.

Although they prefer a slightly alkaline soil, lilacs do well planted close to acid-loving shrubs such as azaleas—just work a little dolomitic limestone or wood ashes into the soil around them each spring. Give lilacs a summer mulch of composted horse manure and shredded leaves, and the roots will be protected from the blistering sun while your soil is being enriched.

Bringing on Bloom

Lilacs are only finicky in one respect: Sometimes they just won't bloom. What can you do about that? You have several choices. The first option couldn't be easier: Don't do anything. Just wait. You need to have a little patience with lilacs. Don't expect them to flower until they're at least 4 feet high.

Lilacs are sun lovers and won't perform where they're overshadowed. If that's the case, a change of scene may inspire your shrub to blossom. You can move them in either spring or fall, and

can even transplant large lilacs as long as you leave a big ball of soil around the roots and prune the branches back by one-third.

Root pruning will also encourage lilacs to bloom. In spring, dig a 2-foot trench slightly within the outside limit of the branches. Then place a generous layer of aged manure in the bottom of the trench before you refill it with soil.

Pruning Lilacs

If your plants are old enough to bloom but just won't, you may be pruning them improperly. The time to prune a lilac is right after it flowers. Next year's flower buds begin to form immediately after the blooming period; if you delay pruning a month or two, you'll be chopping off next year's blossoms.

Unless your lilac is hopelessly overgrown, don't cut it back too severely. A gradual reshaping is best. First, cut off any branches that crowd or cross each other. Prune just enough to keep the center open, cut out dead or diseased wood, take out suckers, and remove dead flowerstalks.

Unkempt, neglected lilacs respond best to gradual rejuvenation. Try cutting one-third of the branches each year over a three-year

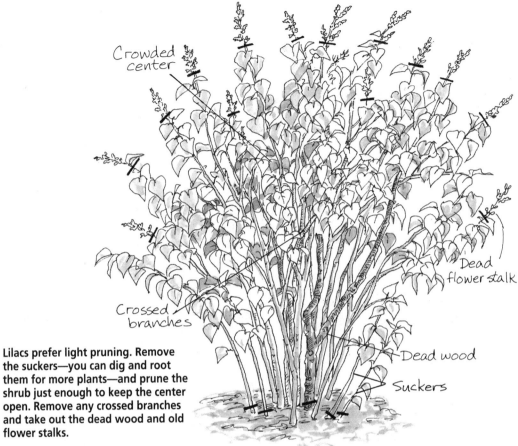

Crowded center

Crossed branches

Dead flower stalk

Dead wood

Suckers

Lilacs prefer light pruning. Remove the suckers—you can dig and root them for more plants—and prune the shrub just enough to keep the center open. Remove any crossed branches and take out the dead wood and old flower stalks.

period. If your shrub is extremely ungainly and beyond the help of moderate pruning, trim the branches to within 1 foot of the ground. Don't expect bloom for anywhere from two to four years because the new growth will be too young to set flower buds.

What about Mildew?

I know, I know. Your lilacs bloom beautifully, but they get powdery mildew. The leaves get a white, fuzzy coating, and the plants look about as appealing as a mealybug. But they don't have to. If you give your lilacs a sunny site with good air circulation, prune to keep them open so air can move within the branches, and resist the urge to water the foliage, you'll greatly reduce the chance of mildew attack.

Some lilacs are less prone to mildew than others, too. 'Miss Kim' Manchurian lilac (*Syringa patula* 'Miss Kim') and the Meyer lilac (*S. meyeri*) are both renowned for mildew resistance. But if only the old-fashioned lilacs will do for you, you can also prevent mildew by spraying regularly with antitranspirants or a baking soda solution. At the first sign of mildew, apply an organic soap-based fungicide or a sulfur spray.

17

Let's Grow a Lawn

People make too much of lawns. They're always out there feeding, scalping, and poisoning their lawns with bags of chemicals. What a waste of time and money! And what a crime against the environment! In this chapter, I'm going to show you a better way.

Growing a good lawn shouldn't be a puzzle. You can take some of the mystery out of it if you learn a little bit about what grass seeds need to grow well.

Most types of grass grow from a seed so small that it takes millions of them to make a pound. Once in con-tact with wet soil, the seed absorbs moisture, the embryo starts to grow, and in a week or two, a root tip breaks through the seed coat and pushes down into the soil.

At about the same time, a bud shoot breaks out and starts up toward the sunlight. This is a critical time for the tiny plant. The soil surface must be kept moist or the embryo may not survive.

Lawn Care Basics

You don't have to be an ex-pert to grow a fine lawn. But you do have to stick to sen-sible practices.

In most of the country, the best time to start a new lawn is between late August and late October. Most grasses get off to a good start in au-tumn and become well estab-lished by spring. The rainfall and cool nights of fall en-courage the development of extensive root systems—and good root systems are better able to withstand the hot, dry weather of summer. There's also less competition from weeds or pests in autumn.

Like other plants, healthy lawn grass needs a sturdy foundation: a loose, porous soil into which air, water, and roots can penetrate, and an adequate supply of rich, natural food. Although good types of grass can overcome many obstacles, they can't grow in a lifeless soil or an environment that remains unfavorable.

The soil under sod should be loose enough to drain well and allow airflow. If you have tight, heavy clay, you'll need to loosen it with organic supplements: Aerate with a spike-toothed tool, then spread compost before seeding.

When you are fertilizing your lawn, keep in mind that a successful lawn needs a balance of nutrients to spur healthy growth. You can turn to one of the many balanced organic lawn fertilizers now on the market, which are both safe and easy to use.

So whether you're planting a new lawn this year or rejuvenating one, get down to brass tacks. Do the job right from the start for an organic lawn you can really live with.

PLANNING TO PLANT

Choose grass seed carefully. No one grass type or mixture is ideal everywhere. The cultivar or blend that will do the best job for you depends on many factors: where you live, the type of soil you have, and how much sun or shade your lawn will receive.

Once you've chosen the grass that's best for your situation, you can't just run out and scatter seed around. Take the time to do some preparation first. Believe me, it pays. Here's my seven-step lawn-prep program:

1. Till the soil to a depth of 6 or 7 inches. Don't work the soil too deeply. A good stand of grass can be established even in 2 or 3 inches of good soil if drainage is good.

2. Have a soil test done to determine pH and fertilizer needs.

3. Smooth and grade the seedbed until it's uniform.

4. Sow the seed carefully. Spread half the seed in one direction and the remainder in the opposite direction to ensure even coverage.

5. Apply a mulch of finely screened compost or peat moss. Use about $1\frac{1}{2}$ pounds per 1,000 square feet for bluegrass, and 2 pounds per 1,000 square feet for fescues.

6. Firm the soil by rolling or raking lightly.

7. Keep the soil moist, but not soaked, until the grass is up. This may mean watering twice a day when rainfall is sparse. At first, sprinkle lightly each day, using a mist sprayer so you don't wash out the seeds. But be sure to apply enough water each time so that it penetrates the subsoil.

A Winning Combination

If you think a lawn ought to look more natural than a putting green, you can grow my favorite type—a mix of bluegrass and white clover. White clover is a legume, so it draws nitrogen from the air and stores it in the soil, where the bluegrass can use it for fertilizer.

Louis Bromfield, the noted author, farmer, and conservationist, was one of the first to describe how this grass and legume partnership works. He observed that in renovating poor pastures, he only had to apply lime to get a transformation. The lime made the white clover grow vigorously. As it grew, it stored nitrogen in the soil. When the soil was rich enough, the bluegrass responded to the nitrogen and it also grew vigorously, dominating the white clover until the nitrogen was used up. Then the clover came back strong, built up the nitrogen reserves, and the cycle started all over again.

SEEDING CLOVER AND BLUEGRASS

To seed white clover, use 1 pound per 1,000 square feet.

There are seven simple steps to establishing a lawn:

Step 1: Till the soil to a depth of 6 or 7 inches.

Step 2: Have the soil tested and add necessary nutrients.

Step 3: Grade the area evenly with a garden rake.

Step 4: Carefully sow a grass that's right for your area.

Step 5: Cover the lawn lightly with screened compost or peat moss.

Step 6: Rake again or roll to firm the soil.

Step 7: Keep the area evenly moist with a mist sprayer until the grass is well established.

White clover was once an important part of a fine grass seed mix. It fixes nitrogen and adds to the fertility of the soil—and the beauty of the lawn. Clover makes a fine mix with Kentucky bluegrass or other grasses.

Broadcast it on bare land or right over the top of your lawn. The best time is in late winter or very early in spring, when the ground is frozen. The tiny seeds will fall into the pitted, frozen surface, and when the ground thaws, the soil will cover the seed.

If bluegrass is in short supply on your lawn, sow in early autumn. The seed will usually germinate if you throw it on bare ground, but you'll get a better stand by covering the seed and firming the soil over it.

CARING FOR THE CLOVER-BLUEGRASS LAWN

The bluegrass–white clover love affair works best when the soil pH is between 6.5 and 7.0. Apply about 2 pounds of lime per 100 square feet every three years—if you overdo it, you'll get too much white clover and not enough bluegrass.

When you mow, don't remove all the clippings, especially if your soil is on the poor side—they'll eventually break down and release nitrogen to feed your grass. A mulching mower does a great job of chopping clippings so they break down fast.

LEARNING TO LOVE CLOVER

Unfortunately, too many people still believe that white clover is a weed, but this legume has many merits in the lawn. The low, sweet-smelling, white blossoms have a beauty all their own.

What's more, clover can store well over $100 worth of nitrogen in an acre of lawn every year without any expenditures of money or fossil fuel energy. And that's beautiful, too!

Try the Tough Turf: Zoysia

No doubt about it, bluegrass makes a great-looking lawn. But it's not the toughest turf going. There's another surprising sort of lawn grass that overcomes the shortcomings of bluegrass. It's zoysia.

This amazing warm-season grass thrives on midsummer heat and sunshine and completely ignores drought. It grows so thick and sturdy that it squelches crabgrass and never gives any other common weeds a chance to get started. It beats bugs and grass ailments, too.

Zoysia will grow in sandy soil and on steep slopes. It can withstand hot, dry weather and is even shade-tolerant. The only place it won't thrive is deep shade—it should have at least three to four hours of sun each day.

This tough grass grows best in a soil with a pH of

Growing Good Grasses

The first step in growing a great lawn is starting with the right grass. If you're sowing a new lawn or just overseeding a ragged old one, take some time to pick the type that's best for your area and needs.

New cultivars are disease-tolerant. Some even resist insects. Many can withstand a fair amount of shade. Some stand up to heavy foot traffic. Others require less frequent mowing.

Here's a short list of groundskeepers' favorites to get you started in the right direction.

Northeast and Upper Midwest

Fine Fescue
'Atlanta', 'Reliant', 'Spartan'
Kentucky Bluegrass
'America', 'Blacksburg', 'Liberty', 'Midnight'
Perennial Ryegrass
'Palmer', 'Pennfine', 'Repell', 'Yorktown II'
Tall Fescue
'Mustang', 'Olympic', 'Rebel II', 'Silverado'
Zoysia
'Midwestern'

Humid South

Bahia Grass
'Argentine', 'Paraguay', 'Pensacola'
Bermuda Grass
'Tifgreen', 'Tifway', 'Vamont'
Centipede Grass
'Oaklawn', 'Tennessee Hardy'
Fine Fescue
'Aurora', 'Reliant', 'Spartan'
St. Augustine Grass
'Better Blue', 'Floratine', 'Roselawn'
Zoysia
'Emerald', 'Meyer'

Plains

Bermuda Grass
'Tifgreen', 'Tifway'
Buffalo Grass
'Prairie', 'Sharp's Improved', 'Texoka'
Fine Fescue
'Aurora', 'Reliant'

Kentucky Bluegrass
'America', 'Dawn', 'Harmony'
Perennial Ryegrass
'Blazer', 'Palmer', 'Yorktown II'
Tall Fescue
'Apache', 'Clemfine', 'Rebel'

Southwest

Bermuda Grass
'Midirion', 'Tifgreen', 'Tifway II'
Buffalo Grass
'Prairie', 'Sharp's Improved', 'Texoka'
Fine Fescue
'Scaldis', 'Waldina'
Kentucky Bluegrass
'Classic', 'Glade', 'Trenton'
Perennial Ryegrass
'Citation II', 'Palmer', 'Tara'
Tall Fescue
'Apache', 'Arid', 'Mustang'
Zoysia
'Flawn'

Northwest

Fine Fescue
'Enjoy', 'Reliant', 'Scaldis'
Kentucky Bluegrass
'Blacksburg', 'Challenger', 'Midnight'
Perennial Ryegrass
'Manhattan II', 'Palmer', 'Repell'
Tall Fescue
'Falcon', 'Houndog', 'Mustang'

about 6.5. If your soil is more acid than this, use lime to reduce the acidity. The lime will also make other nutrient elements more available to the plants.

PLANTING ZOYSIA

You can't produce zoysia from seed. Instead, you must propagate it vegetatively, either by plugs or by root runners obtained by tearing up pieces of established sod.

Zoysia is usually planted as plugs. 'Meyer Z 52' is the best cultivar. It adapts to a wide range of climates and can be used on almost any soil type. It has dark green leaves that closely resemble 'Merion' Kentucky bluegrass in color and texture.

To establish a new lawn, plant plugs on 8- to 12-inch centers. Plugging is done with a simple tool that makes a 1-, 2-, or 3-inch-diameter hole in the soil.

Plant plugs between May and August. That way, the new planting can take maximum advantage of favorable summer growing conditions. Water immediately after planting and as often as needed thereafter to keep the soil from drying out. Keep the soil moist (not saturated) until you can see new growth.

Plug plantings usually require 6 to 18 months to produce a complete cover. Under ideal conditions, they may spread 6 to 8 inches in one summer. Zoysia generally needs two seasons to become thoroughly established, and the plugs can take two to three years to totally cover the ground, unless they're thickly planted.

ZOYSIA CARE TIPS

Although zoysia roots spread rapidly, topgrowth is quite slow, so much less mowing is necessary. Most grasses require mowing at least once a week during the summer, but zoysia needs to be mowed only once a month. (More frequent clipping—especially with a reel mower—will help control weeds until the zoysia is established.) For best appearance, cut it to about 1½ inches. Zoysia has a fluffy, thatched look if it's allowed to get tall.

Thatch—the accumulation of grass roots and creeping stems above the soil—is one of the most common problems with zoysia. Remove thatch as often as needed. (See "Thatch in the Grass" on page 338 for more on coping with thatch.)

Zoysia is usually started from plugs, or small tufts of sod. It takes a while to spread, so the closer you plant the plugs, the less weeding you'll have to do.

The Groundcover Alternative

There are some places in a landscape where a lawn just doesn't belong. Anyone with problem spots on a lawn, in a corner of a garden, or on a steep bank should consider planting groundcovers instead. These low-growing plants have good strong roots, plus the ability to spread and hold down the soil. They usually don't need mowing and will often grow in shady, steep, or poor-soil spots.

You're probably familiar with the common, reliable groundcovers such as vinca (*Vinca minor*, also called myrtle), pachysandra (*Pachysandra terminalis*), and English ivy (*Hedera helix*). They all make tight mats within a few years after planting. (And vinca has pleasant, 1-inch-wide blue flowers that rise above its dark, shiny oval leaves in the spring.) All three flourish in the shade. Vinca is hardy in Zones 4–8, pachysandra in Zones 5–7, and English ivy in Zones 5–9.

Vinca, pachysandra, and English ivy are very easy to propagate. All you have to do is lift and divide them, so you need only a moderate number of plants to get started. Once established, groundcovers like these can take the place of grass in shady areas where lawns struggle or won't grow.

Some herbs are also used as groundcovers. Mother-of-thyme (*Thymus serpyllum*, also called creeping thyme) spreads well, grows only 1 inch tall, and bears small purple flowers that bloom all summer. It will thrive in sun and dry soil, lives a long time once it's established, and is easily propagated by division. It's a good choice to grow among stepping-stones. Mother-of-thyme is hardy in Zones 4–9.

Creeping speedwell (*Veronica repens*) grows to about 4 inches tall and forms a mossy, prostrate mat. Its blue flowers come and go in May, and it can be very attractive when planted with spring bulbs. Like mother-of-thyme, it's suitable for growing among stepping-stones. This little veronica thrives in sunny places. It will self-sow, or you can propagate it by division. Creeping speedwell is hardy in Zones 5–8.

If you're into edible landscaping, there are a few plants you can use for groundcovers *and* good eating. If your soil is acid, try lowbush blueberries (*Vaccinium angustifolium*) or black huckleberries (*Gaylussacia baccata*). They're both small shrubs (about 3 feet tall) with good red fall color and delicious fruit. They can take partial shade (but you'll get more fruit in full sun) and are hardy in Zones 3–7.

For a tall groundcover suitable for steep banks and along roadsides, I like daylilies (*Hemerocallis* spp. and cultivars). Their handsome foliage clumps look good even when the plants aren't in bloom, and they grow well in full sun or partial shade. Daylilies are hardy in Zones 2–9, depending on which ones you grow. Believe it or not, the shoots are tender and tasty, and the buds and flowers make great Sunday morning fritters at our house.

MAKE A ZOYSIA LAWN

If you want to establish zoysia in your old lawn, first remove a plug of old sod the same size as the one you'll be planting. Next, put a small amount (½ teaspoon) of organic fertilizer in the hole that you just made. Insert the new plug carefully.

Plugs planted in existing turf can take two to

five years to produce a complete cover. Mowing and fertilizing are the most important factors in determining the rate of spread. Close mowing and summer fertilization will encourage zoysia to grow more rapidly; high mowing and fall fertilization will speed up the growth of bluegrass and fescue.

WHAT'S THE CATCH?

So what's the catch with this wonder grass? For one thing, zoysia doesn't survive temperatures of 0°F and below, so you can't grow it if you live outside Zones 7 to 10.

There's another hitch for fans of fields of green: Zoysia turns straw-colored earlier than other grasses—in fact, right after the first killing frost. That's how I pick out the zoysia lawns every fall. But

How to Propagate Groundcovers

Nothing is simpler than dividing groundcovers. Take a sharp-edged trowel or spade and thrust it down to sever the rooted shoots, suckers, or offshoots of the mother plant. It's rarely necessary to slice through the main plant, as you do when dividing perennial clumps. Since the little plantlets are very sensitive to shock, plant them as soon as possible in well-prepared soil. The best time to do this is in early spring. You can also divide groundcovers in the fall, provided the soil is moist enough and there's enough growing time before frost for the transplant to reestablish itself.

I also find it easy to take cuttings of groundcovers. Plants such as English ivy (*Hedera helix*) or moneywort (*Lysimachia nummularia*) can be cut somewhere between the top two and four nodes of the mother plant. Insert the cuttings in a good rooting medium such as sand or perlite, or a mix of equal parts sand, peat moss, and garden loam.

Keep an eye on the young cuttings. Give them a light pull every once in a while. As soon as you feel the tug of roots when you try to pull out the cutting, it's time to transplant to a richer growing mixture with more garden soil, or to put the new plant out in the garden.

Many groundcovers are easy to propagate from cuttings:
1. Cut pieces two to four nodes long from the mother plant. (The nodes are where the leaves come out of the stem.)
2. Stick the cuttings into a sterile, moist medium like sand or perlite and wait for them to root.

it's still smoothly dense and attractive. It's just a nice, uniform beige rather than green.

Spring Lawn Care

One of my first (and most pleasurable) tasks of spring is to take my annual walk across the lawn to check on its health. I want to get a good look at how it survived the winter. Just strolling across the awakening greenery gives me a good sense of how *I* survived the winter as well.

Then it's time to start the spring lawn care program. I start it as soon as the frost is out of the ground and the sod is dry enough to walk on.

I begin by rolling the turf with a 100-pound roller to correct soil heaving and to bring the topsoil and subsoil together again. Two passes at right angles—east-west and north-south—are plenty. Too much rolling can cause soil compaction and make it more difficult for air and water to penetrate.

Next, I rake the lawn with a bamboo or spring rake to remove debris left by the winter. Raking also helps open the turf to the air and light.

A SIMPLE SOIL TEST

It's also a good idea to have the soil tested and see what's

One of your first jobs in the spring should be to rake your lawn to remove debris left from winter. I like to use a bamboo rake to avoid injuring the grass.

going on at the root level. Take soil plugs about 6 inches deep from four or five widely separated places. If the samples show good soil structure and root growth at the 6-inch mark and the soil crumbles readily, then I know I have no compaction problems.

But if the roots are few and scanty and the soil is hard and lumpy, then I might aerate the turf. It's surprising how quickly aeration can add new life to an old lawn.

AERATING YOUR LAWN

I use a garden fork, thrust into the affected area at a 40-degree angle, to loosen the soil and admit light and air.

Special hand aeration forks work the same way and also remove cores of earth to speed up the job.

If you have an extra-large lawn with a history of fungal or insect problems, consider renting a self-propelled power rake, renovator, or spike-tooth roller. They'll really give the lawn a good going-over.

FILLING IN LOW SPOTS

Not only do low spots in the lawn spoil its appearance, but they can also be sources of fungal infection since they tend to be damp. I don't try to roll them level. Instead, I fill them with a mix of weed-free soil and compost, which

I spread in the depressions and smooth with the back of a rake.

If I find any deep "sink-holes," I cut the sod and lift it. Then I fill the hole with soil and replace the sod on top of it. I water generously to settle loose soil and eliminate large air pockets around the grass roots.

RESEEDING BARE SPOTS

Bare patches on the lawn are signs of underlying problems, such as thatch, compacted soil, improper mowing or watering, or planting the wrong seed mixtures.

If your lawn is scraggly but still consists of at least 50 percent grass, you can coax it

back to a lush green by simply reseeding the worn areas. You might be tempted to just throw up your hands and start all over again, but patching can save you up to half the time and energy it would take to rebuild an entire lawn.

Do your repairs in late spring or early fall, when the

Reseeding bare spots is like starting a mini-lawn:

Step 1: Dig up the area to 5 inches deep with a spading fork and remove any weeds, stones, or roots.

Step 2: Rake the area smooth.

Step 3: Spread an inch or two of organic matter like compost and work it in.

Step 4: Sow an improved grass seed by broadcasting it over the bare spot.

soil is not too wet. First, dig into those worn spots with a spading fork. Sink the fork about 5 inches with your foot and, as you lift out the soil, flip it over and let it drop with a force that will break up large lumps. Then rake the area smooth and remove any roots and stones that the digging might have unearthed.

Spread an inch or two of compost over each area, and work it into the soil as deeply as you can. The more compost you can work in, the better—it will pay off during the summer by helping the soil to retain much-needed moisture. Finally, rake the area smooth, leveling it so it's even with the surrounding lawn.

Once you've prepared the soil in the bare spots, feed your entire lawn with a blended organic lawn fertilizer. Use a spreader, and make sure the fertilizer is dispensed over the worn areas as well as the existing lawn.

Now it's seeding time. Be sure to use a good lawn seed mixture to repair the worn areas. (Use a grass mix that matches your existing lawn; see "Growing Good Grasses" on page 330 for the best grasses for your region.) If the bare spots are very large, sow with your spreader. Otherwise, broadcast the seed by hand

at the rate recommended on the package.

Rake the seeds into the soil lightly. Then tamp the soil firmly using the soles of your shoes, a roller, or the back of your rake. To protect your seeded areas, cover them with a light straw mulch.

Watering is the next step, and it's one of the most important in encouraging your seeds to sprout. Use a fine spray, and water at least once a day. Never allow the seeded area to dry out. If you do, your seeds won't germinate and all your efforts will have been in vain.

The grass will require daily watering until it becomes strong and lush. In about ten days, green fuzz will appear. In time, it will match your established lawn. If your old grass requires mowing before your new spots are ready, set up stakes around the young grass to remind you to stay away.

As you repair your lawn, take samples of the soil from the four corners as well as the center. Put them in a box, shake the box to mix them, then bring or mail the sample to a soil-testing laboratory. If the results indicate that your soil needs lime, you can spread it on your entire lawn after your worn spots have become reestablished.

All-Season Care

In most of the country, watering the lawn is an overrated practice. A lawn that is well established in good, rich, organic soil only needs watering in times of drought.

During droughts, you should water your lawn infrequently but heavily—enough to soak the soil thoroughly to a depth of 8 to 12 inches. Frequent, light watering will encourage the development of shallow root systems, which can't withstand dry spells.

Watering in the morning is preferable to evening soaking. That's because grass that's damp overnight is susceptible to fungal infection. (See "Dealing with Disease" on page 339 for more on when to water.)

MOW-TIVATION

When it comes to lawn care, mowing takes up the most time. But the best mower in the world won't give you a healthy lawn unless you follow these three sound mowing practices:

1. Mow high—2½ to 3 inches.
2. Mow regularly, as often as grass growth requires.
3. Never cut more than ⅓ of the total length of the grass blade at one cutting.

Why Mow High?

Cutting the grass high helps keep weeds and crabgrass out by robbing them of sunlight and air. Also, the growth rate and health of your grass depend on the food manufactured in the blades, not in the roots. Most folks aren't really aware that grass, like all green plants, lives and grows principally on food made in its leaves or blades.

The grass blade, just like the leaf on a tree, gets its raw materials to make the plant food from both the soil and the air. Since the food factory is above ground, the shorter you mow, the less leaf area is left, and the less food the plant is able to manufacture through photosynthesis.

Mow your lawn under 2½ inches, and you're slowing down food production too much: You're endangering the vigor and even the life of the grass plants.

All too often, homeowners are led to believe that they can mow the grass as close as possible without injuring it, as long as they dump more and more toxic chemicals on their lawns. Nothing could be further from the truth.

Don't forget that repeated close mowing causes a corresponding reduction in the depth of the roots. It's

simple: A small topgrowth just can't sustain a large and vigorous root system. In turn, a stunted root system can't withstand a severe drought or put on healthy blade growth.

So, set your blade at 2½ to 3 inches. You'll also find that high mowing won't spoil the appearance of your lawn. A well-mowed lawn, 2½ inches or more high, will make just as fine and handsome a green carpet as the closely shaved turf of the putting green. It's the evenness of the surface that

creates the beauty of a lawn, not the closeness of the cut.

Remember, too, that for the best-looking, healthiest lawn, you should keep your cutting blade sharp. It should be sharp enough to cut cleanly without tearing or ripping the grass.

DIET FOR A SMALL PLANT

I believe in feeding my lawn, but I don't believe in dumping on bags of chemical fertilizers. Why use organic fertilizers?

First, organic fertilizers

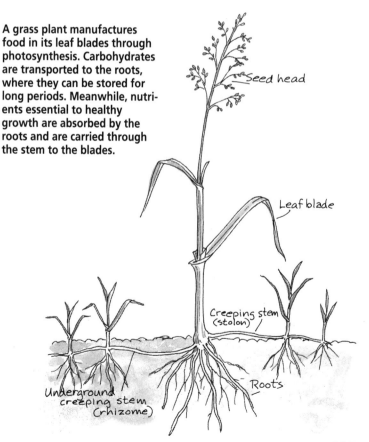

A grass plant manufactures food in its leaf blades through photosynthesis. Carbohydrates are transported to the roots, where they can be stored for long periods. Meanwhile, nutrients essential to healthy growth are absorbed by the roots and are carried through the stem to the blades.

Seed head

Leaf blade

Creeping stem (stolon)

Roots

Underground creeping stem (rhizome)

accelerate the growth of soil microorganisms that are essential to rich, productive soil, which in turn produces thicker, greener grass. Second, they speed up seed germination, thereby giving the lawn a fast start. Third, turf grown with organic fertilizer has been shown to actually resist plant diseases. Fourth, when you use an organic fertilizer, grass develops a large root system, which helps prevent weeds from getting established.

There are other advantages, too. Fertilizers that are high in organic matter build humus in the soil, thus helping lawns resist drought conditions and erosion. They create a "soil bank" effect that allows the soil to store up elements not used the first year following their application. These elements don't burn out—they remain in the soil and provide continuing nourishment for the lawn from year to year.

Of course, an organic fertilizer will never burn a lawn. Some manufacturers claim chemical fertilizers won't burn. However, that's qualified by a big "if": They won't burn *if* they're used exactly as directed, which means keeping the lawn moist and using the chemicals in small, carefully controlled amounts.

Last, but not least, or-ganic fertilizers save you a lot of money because they're slow release and long lasting. They'll give you a healthy, trouble-free lawn at low cost. I'd say it's time to make them a regular ingredient in your lawn care program.

What to Use

If you have it, compost makes a great all-purpose lawn fertilizer. Top-dress with a thin layer of finely screened compost in spring and fall.

The best organic nitrogen sources are composted sewage sludge (such as Milorganite), cottonseed meal, soybean meal, liquid manure, and composted manure. You can use any of these at approximately 15 to 20 pounds per 1,000 square feet. Dried blood and blood meal are also excellent since they have a high (8 to 14 percent) nitrogen content; apply 10 pounds per 1,000 square feet.

Use ground rock phosphate or bonemeal to supply your lawn with phosphorus, and greensand or granite dust for potassium. Apply 2 to 3 pounds of ground phosphate, 5 pounds of bonemeal, and 15 to 25 pounds of greensand or granite dust per 1,000 square feet.

When to Spread It On

Spread organic fertilizers over your lawn in both spring and fall to encourage the lush growth of your lawn.

The Lawn Health Care Plan

No one needs trouble, especially with their lawn. Yet troubles do occasionally come in the form of diseases, insects, and weeds. Why?

Weather extremes may be one reason. Insect or disease cycles may be another. Airborne weed invasions can also cause trouble for lawns. Whatever the cause, there are natural remedies that can minimize the damage and help you cope with any of the problems facing you as a lawn keeper.

THATCH IN THE GRASS

Thatch isn't a disease, weed, or pest. But people tend to be afraid of thatch in their lawns. In fact, many people spend a lot of money getting rid of thatch. But just what are they getting rid of?

Thatch is an accumulation of grass roots and creeping stems that are tough and tend to break down slowly. If you overwater, have poor and compacted soil, or soak your lawn with chemicals, the thatch may not break down at all. That's because the earthworms and other soil organisms that normally break thatch down have been killed off.

If you can see a mat of thatch beneath your grass, follow this program:

1. Cut back on watering.
2. Aerate your lawn. (See "Aerating Your Lawn" on page 334 to find out how.)
3. If you have acid soil, add lime to bring the pH to 6.5 to 7.5.
4. Top-dress your lawn with compost. (See "Diet for a Small Plant" on page 337 for details.)

These four simple steps will encourage soil organisms to recolonize your lawn. Soon, deep thatch will be a thing of the past. (A little thatch isn't a problem, and remember—grass clippings *aren't* thatch!)

DEALING WITH DISEASE

A lot of folks seem to worry about lawn diseases, too. Many will spend good money to have someone spray poison all over their yard just to make sure that a disease doesn't occur.

That's incomprehensible to me, especially when it's so easy to prevent lawn diseases through proper cultural control.

The trick is to make

your lawn as strong and self-sufficient as possible from the start. Don't pamper it with extra watering or with super-high nitrogen fertilizers that make it too easy for the grass to get its food. Both practices keep the grass from developing strong, deep roots that must reach down into the soil for nutrients.

Almost all midsummer fungal lawn diseases—brown patch, leaf spot, pythium, and others—are caused by too much water. The grass needs more oxygen during the hot summer days. But in midsummer the air is humid, and the grass is covered much of the night and part of the day with clinging droplets of moisture. The soil itself can be clogged with water, which can suffocate the roots by depriving them of air.

You can build a healthy lawn by improving soil drainage and maintaining adequate soil aeration, since both measures will encourage stronger roots and topgrowth. Keep in mind that watering late in the evening may be good for your schedule, but it's bad for the lawn. That's because the grass stays wet all night, which invites molds and other fungi.

Low mowing also encourages disease. A close shave weakens the grass and stimulates more succu

lent and tender leaf growth, which is more vulnerable to fungi. Many diseases attack the lower leaves first, but on lawns cut at 2½ to 3 inches, new leaves can grow quickly enough to replace the lower infected ones; that means that no permanent damage will occur.

In addition, short blades mean short roots. About 95 percent of all the food taken in by grass is absorbed by the blades through the process of photosynthesis. When you shave your turf down to the soil line, food production virtually ceases and the plant's root system is weakened.

Applying fertilizer to speed summer growth is another practice that can lead to lawn trouble. During the summer, the tender young leaf blades are particularly vulnerable to fungal diseases because the prevailing temperatures and moisture conditions favor their enemies. If you stimulate succulent grass growth then, they're easy prey for diseases. But fertilizing in early spring or fall encourages growth when diseases pose less of a danger.

I can't stress enough how much liming can help prevent lawn diseases. Turf that is grown on strongly acid soil is much more susceptible to diseases than a lawn established on a neutral soil.

One effective way to keep turf diseases down is to plant a mixture of grasses. Different diseases attack different types of grasses—for example, brown patch strikes the bent grasses, while leaf spot hits the bluegrasses. But in a mixed lawn, the disease organisms soon reach a species that is resistant, and their progress is slowed or halted.

Top Five Diseases

Five of the most frequently encountered grass diseases include fairy rings, dollar spot, melting-out, snow mold, and slime molds.

The fungi that cause **fairy rings** grow outward in a circle. When conditions are favorable for them, mushrooms emerge from the underlying fungal growth and form the characteristic rings or parts of circles. You can easily control them if you treat them early: Aerate the ring with a spading fork, making holes 2 inches apart and as deep as possible. Begin about 2 feet outside the ring and work toward the center.

Dollar spot is characterized by small, nearly white, round areas about 2 inches in diameter. It strikes during periods of moderate temperatures (60° to 80°F)

and excess moisture, or when too much thatch has built up. Turf that is deficient in nitrogen tends to develop more dollar spot. To control this fungus, keep thatch to a minimum, water your lawn only as needed, mow high, and rake vigorously. Also, apply adequate nitrogen. (See "Diet for a Small Plant" on page 337 for nitrogen sources.)

Melting-out (also called fading-out) attacks bent grasses, fescues, and Kentucky bluegrass, and occurs in all parts of the country. It's most destructive during hot, humid weather from May to October.

Diseased areas appear yellowed or dappled green, as though the grass were suffering from iron deficiency or low fertility. When the disease is uncontrolled, the grass "melts out," leaving dead, reddish brown patches.

Moist conditions favor melting-out, which first appears on shaded plants and is most severe on closely clipped turf. To combat this fungal disease, reduce shade in the yard and improve soil aeration and water drainage.

Snow mold attacks grass in winter, either under snow cover or during cold winter rains. The disease shows up in the spring as irregular spots of nearly white, dead grass. To

avoid snow mold, eliminate fall fertilizing with commercial nitrogen fertilizers, which cause the grass to become succulent. Use a good organic lawn fertilizer instead.

Slime molds appear as small white, gray, or yellow slimy round masses growing over grass blades. Although they're most common in spring, slime molds can occur in midsummer or fall following heavy rains and disappear as soon as dry weather arrives. The mold inhabits the soil, feeding on decaying organic matter. You can remove slime molds by sweeping infected areas with a broom or spraying them forcefully with a garden hose.

A COUPLE OF BAD BUGS

With two exceptions, pests aren't usually a big problem in lawns. However, some grasses are more subject to attacks by certain insects than others. Avoid planting susceptible grasses in areas where pests are common. For example, sod webworms and cutworms often attack dichondra in southern lawns, but Bermuda grass and zoysia are almost immune to these worms.

Let's take a closer look at the two most common pests in our lawns:

··· Chinch Bugs

Chinch bugs are serious lawn pests. It's the immature bugs, or nymphs, that cause the damage. They're about ¼ inch long, and black with a white spot on their back, between their wings.

These insects prefer hot, sunny lawns. Irrigation will help reduce chinch bug populations. Or you can control them by spreading sabadilla dust on your lawn.

··· Japanese Beetles

The Japanese beetle may be one of the most destructive of all lawn pests. The larvae, which are 1-inch-long white grubs with brown heads, eat grass roots, causing the grass to die off in patches.

The best-known method for safely controlling Japanese beetles is milky disease. Developed in 1933, this bacterial organism (*Bacillus popilliae*) produces a fatal disease in the grub. To use, simply apply the powder to your lawn. However, it may take a year or more before you see its effects. And it doesn't work well in cold climates.

Other options include applying parasitic nematodes to the lawn and walking over the turf with special spiked sandals in late spring and fall

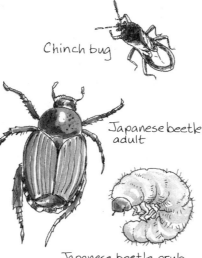

Chinch bug

Japanese beetle adult

Japanese beetle grub

The chinch bug is often a problem on hot, dry, sunny lawns. Adults are just ¼ inch long and are orange-brown to black. They'll show up first in the driest areas, such as along a sidewalk. Japanese beetle grubs feed on grass roots, killing off patches of sod in no time at all. The adults are ½-inch-long, metallic blue-green beetles with coppery wings, while the grubs are 1-inch-long, C-shaped white larvae with brown heads.

to kill the grubs and aerate the lawn at the same time. (These sadistic-looking sandals are available from garden supply catalogs and garden centers.)

You can try to control the adult beetles by handpicking them and dropping them into jars of soapy water. The best time to handpick is in the early morning, when the beetles are groggy. Look for them on your roses, hollyhocks, and other flowers and shrubs, not on the lawn. (They're ½ inch long and metallic blue-green, with coppery wings.) You can also spray the adults with ryania or rotenone.

WHIPPING WICKED WEEDS

Undoubtedly, weeds are problems, but they're also symptoms of other problems. For example, weedy lawns can indicate soil conditions that are unsuitable for growing healthy grass, such as low fertility, extreme acidity, or poor soil structure. Low mowing or a bad choice of lawn seed mixtures can also cause weeds to proliferate.

Building up the soil organically is one of the best ways to lick the weed problem. (See "Diet for a Small Plant" on page 337 to find out how.)

Another way to control weeds is to interplant white clover with grasses. The clover will eventually choke out the weeds.

Mowing is a more effective method of keeping weeds in check than most people realize because it allows grass to crowd out the weeds. As I've said, the best mowing height is generally 2½ to 3 inches.

Crabgrass Control

The real secret of crabgrass control is contained in one simple formula: Crabgrass and good lawn grasses thrive under different growing conditions. You can encourage or discourage the weed by altering its environment.

Good lawn grasses need a fertile topsoil and regular mowing at the height that suits them best. For example, perennial ryegrass, one of the most common good grasses, grows 2 feet high in its normal habitat. If it's kept trimmed to 1 or 1½ inches, it's going to have a difficult time. So, during the hot summer months when weeds take hold, it helps to let the grass get as high as 3 or 4 inches.

Crabgrass has a slightly different set of preferences. It doesn't grow as strongly on good soil as good lawn grasses do. It can't stand the competition from ryegrass and bluegrass when they have a good soil to back them up.

Crabgrass likes to grow low to the ground, so it's not stunted by low mowing. Quite the contrary, low mowing gives it the room it needs to spread out and grow strongly.

So, my crabgrass control program is simple: Just work to make your yard a better place for the good lawn grasses to grow.

First, and most important, create a good soil structure by adding plenty of compost or other organic matter into your lawn soil.

Of course, it would be better to treat your lawn soil with organic material before the grass is planted, since that way you could work it in deeply. But if you're curing a weed problem on a lawn that's already established, you can still improve the structure by regularly spreading organic materials on top of your lawn.

Spread liberal amounts of phosphate rock, potash rock, and lime on your soil, if needed. For an average soil, apply 10 pounds each of phosphate, potash rock, and lime per 100 square feet. Other organic fertilizing materials that can really boost lawn growth include dried blood, cottonseed meal, and soybean meal. These three are especially rich in growth-promoting nitrogen.

Aerate your soil as much as possible. Don't be afraid to really shake up your soil—air and moisture are needed below the surface to encourage thick grass roots.

And if you have a lawn sweeper, use it to pick up crabgrass seeds and dump them in the compost heap.

Crabgrass is a prostrate, spreading annual weed that needs light to thrive. If you keep your lawn mowed high, less light will penetrate to the ground, and crabgrass won't be so eager to grow there.

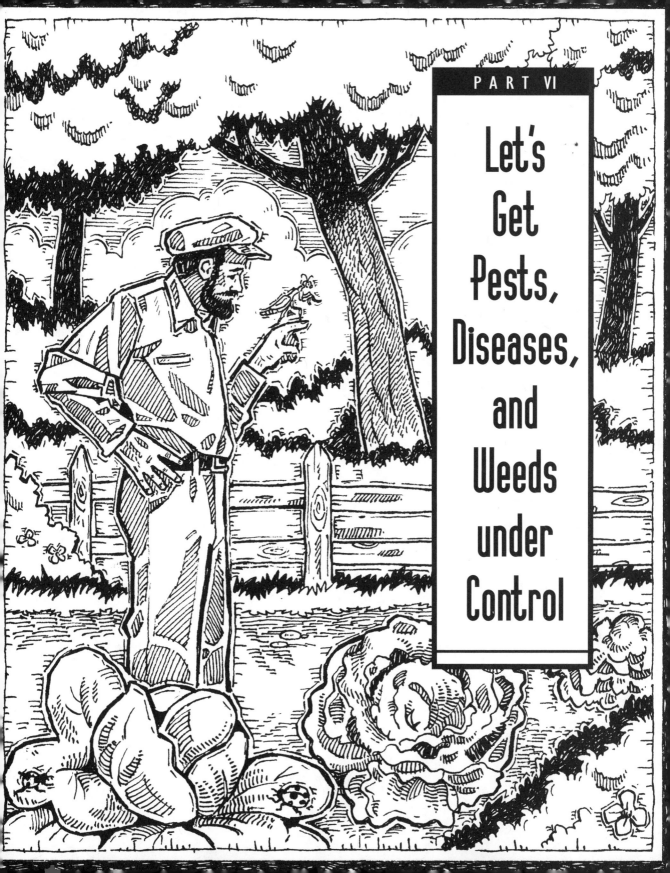

PART VI

Let's Get Pests, Diseases, and Weeds under Control

18

Let's Control Pests and Diseases

I don't like seeing pests and diseases on my plants any more than the next gardener. But I resist the urge to grab a spray can every time I see a bug. In this chapter, I'll tell you how to cope with your plants' problems *without* resorting to the can.

Natural Systems

Diversity and stability are the secrets to a healthy garden, and intercropping is the key. I believe that mixed cropping patterns are essential in the garden. A diverse planting design allows for a richer and healthier relationship between plants and the environment.

Year after year, I've found that as long as I maintain diversity by planting in patches and blocks rather than planting long rows of monocrops, I don't have any major pest problems. Planting patterns like these encourage beneficial interactions between insect and plant life.

To get the most out of diversity, you should plant intensively. I plant most rows 6 inches apart, with in-row spacing even closer. This means that plants will barely touch each other when fully grown. If you alternate the rows with fast- and slow-

maturing crops, the fast ones will be gone by the time the slow ones need room.

To improve the ecological stability of your garden, try experimenting with some of the following techniques:

♣ Grow flowers in your vegetable beds to serve as food for natural enemies of pests. The flowers of certain plants like yarrow and Queen-Anne's-lace provide pollen and nectar for various beneficial insects.

♣ Grow aromatic plants. They interrupt the feeding behavior and other biological activities of pests

When a garden is designed with diversity in mind, it's generally healthier because growing many different types of plants attracts beneficial insects that feed on destructive ones. A diverse planting also makes it harder for pests and diseases to find vulnerable crops.

by masking the odor of the host plant.

♣ Use trap plants to lure pests away from the main crop. You can control the pests on the trap crops or save them for the beneficial insects.

♣ Choose resistant cultivars. Many plants have been specially bred to resist the attacks of particular pests and diseases.

♣ Plant hedgerows and shelter belts to provide a refuge for natural pest enemies. These plants can give alternate food sources for beneficial insects and predators.

Nontoxic Techniques

Nothing succeeds like success. As soon as you start letting a few simple nontoxic techniques go to work against insects, other steps will fall right in line and pest problems will dwindle.

If you're using chemical pesticides, the first thing to do is to stop, cold turkey. Without these poisons permeating your air, soil, water, and plants, some of nature's

intended protection has a fighting chance to work. Helpful insects can go back on the job.

Plants themselves respond to the advantages of a natural and balanced environment as well. They develop stronger root systems, and they regain their inherent resistance to pests that healthy plants have. Even birds come back on the garden scene to lend a hand and an appetite.

WHO'S A PEST?

The first step in learning to distinguish the predator insects from the injurious insects is to redefine the term "pest." Contrary to the chemical industry's misguided philosophy that "the only good bug is a dead bug," most crawling things are simply that—crawling things. In fact, many are actually extremely useful in the garden.

So you must realize that a garden should *not* be insect-free. On the contrary—if you want to achieve successful biological control in your garden, it must be *filled* with insects. And some of these insects should be so-called pests.

In fact, what the chemical industry labels as "pests" are, in reality, a valuable food source for the beneficial insects. It's necessary to have small populations of some of the less destructive pest insects in the garden to serve as food for the beneficial insects.

Just don't panic if you see injurious insects in your garden. This doesn't necessarily mean your garden is in

danger. It may even be a sign that it's strong and healthy. You may find this hard to believe, but sometimes insects that chew or suck on plants don't cause damage.

Also, keep in mind that there is much insect activity in your garden that you can't even see. Many parasites are so tiny that you don't realize they're at work.

The *Trichogramma* wasp is a good example. It's almost microscopic, yet it often achieves a high degree of insect control in the garden. In many cases, this predator is so effective, you don't even realize that pests were present in the first place.

THE ROTATION EQUATION

Like beneficial insects, crop rotation is an effective bug-stopping tool. Planting the same vegetable in the same place every year just allows certain insect pests and diseases to build up.

Crop rotation can play a very important part in ridding the soil of pests like the white grub (the larva of the June beetle). Because of its restricted feeding habits, the grub can feed only on the roots of plants in the grass family. It will destroy forage grasses or grain crops grown on land that had been in sod.

If you've converted a patch of lawn into a garden plot, you should first plant it in a legume such as peas, beans, or clover. Since grubs won't feed on the roots of legumes, the pests will soon perish, leaving the soil safe for vegetable planting.

Cover crops help, too.

In a good rotation, the garden is divided into four quadrants, with related plants all planted in the same bed. Each year, the plants in each quadrant are moved a quarter turn to a new bed.

Good Companions

You can't talk about natural control without mentioning companion planting. The main purpose of companion planting is to use mixed plantings to repel insect attack. It's a controversial topic, but I've found through trial and error that certain plants do have fewer problems when placed near plants of a different species.

Plants that repel insects can serve the gardener in remarkable ways. Even when plant species are mixed by chance, there are fewer insect problems.

I've found that beans and potatoes make good garden mates. The beans confuse Colorado potato beetles, while the potatoes protect the beans from Mexican bean beetles. Other good combinations include soybeans planted near corn (to protect against chinch bugs and Japanese beetles), and tomatoes near asparagus (to repel the asparagus beetle).

It seems to me that pests simply avoid strong-smelling, strong-tasting leaves. So I always grow marigolds and nasturtiums between rows of vegetables and between fruit trees to repel aphids. I interplant chives or garlic with lettuce to keep the aphids away from that crop. And I plant basil near my tomatoes, eggplant, and peppers in the hope that it will repel flea beetles. I also plant mustard near cabbage and cauliflower to act as a trap crop.

Some of my other favorite combinations are asparagus with parsley, carrots with cucumbers, and beets with kohlrabi and spinach. And I always plant onions in my carrot bed to try to baffle the carrot rust fly. Garlic and marigolds are among my favorite all-purpose insect-repelling plants, but the list keeps expanding as more gardeners try companion planting and share their results.

Planting clover before seeding corn cuts down on grubs. Repeated cover cropping with alfalfa gradually reduces wireworms, and other legumes minimize soil nematodes.

By the same token, don't plant crops together that are attacked by the same enemies. Keep tomatoes away from corn, since both are victims of the corn earworm. Potatoes and tomatoes are both troubled by flea beetles, so don't plant them near each other, and don't plant one after the other in the same bed.

Added up, these techniques give the organic gardener an expanding arsenal of safe and effective ways to keep pests to a minimum. And they allow you to maintain a healthy interrelationship between soil, plants, and insects. But they're only the first steps in the pest control program.

Natural Insect Controls

A solid backyard pest control program should be a step-by-step approach. It should minimize the damage to life systems and encourage the natural controls that already prowl your garden path.

Plant diseases and heavy insect attacks can be due to some imbalance of environmental factors, such as soil nutrients. So it's important to encourage soil health. Healthy soil will give you healthy plants, and healthy plants resist insects and diseases.

To build healthy soil, use compost, manures, and organic amendments such as blood meal, bonemeal, and greensand. Grow green manures and apply mulch, natural rock powder fertilizers, and trace minerals. For more information on these topics, see Chapters 1 through 5.

BRING ON THE BENEFICIALS

For the organic gardener, bug-killing compounds and repellent sprays are a last resort. The focus should be on allowing a healthy mix of both good and harmful insects in the garden so that nature can set up her own delicate, yet effective system of checks and balances.

Sometimes a pest population will explode and threaten your plants with intolerable damage. You may want to try botanical insecticides or homemade sprays, but before you do, give biological controls a try.

You should add beneficial bugs to the garden to counteract an explosion of pests, but you shouldn't add them when the wolf is already at the door and the pest is already at your vegetables. This means that you must time the release of the beneficials so that they're ready when the pests start multiplying.

Natural insect controls available from insectaries include ladybugs, green lacewings, praying mantids, and *Trichogramma* wasps. These can be purchased through mail-order catalogs and garden supply centers. Beneficials should be released in late May or early June in order to meet the burgeoning pest population.

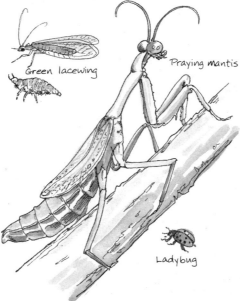

Green lacewing

Praying mantis

Ladybug

Ladybugs, green lacewings, and praying mantids are all good predators in the garden. They eat such pests as aphids and whiteflies.

MORE NATURAL METHODS

Once you put away the pesticides, there are many insect control methods you can use. For example, cultivation is a simple but very effective way to control soilborne insects.

Many species of insects lay their eggs in late summer, depositing them in shallow burrows in the soil. Some of these insects spend six to eight months as eggs in the upper 3 inches of soil. Then, in early spring, they emerge as adults. Tilling the soil in autumn will destroy these burrows and thus prevent the hatched insects from coming up in the spring.

Cutworm Cutoff

A very destructive insect that can be easily controlled by thorough tillage is the cutworm. These worms hatch in early spring and feed greedily on newly sprouted plants. They can survive for some time without food early in the season. But once they've feasted, they die quickly if their food supply is suddenly cut off.

The secret to controlling cutworms, then, is to starve them. Allow them to feed for a short time in spring, then destroy all vegetation by tilling it under. Keep the planting area free of all sprouting vegetation for at least three weeks. After that, the soil will be safe for planting vegetables.

Clean It Up

Good sanitation is another key to pest control. It's important to keep your garden as clean as possible, since a clean garden discourages most insects.

If piles of decaying crop refuse are left around, sow bugs and earwigs will soon find them and use them as

breeding places. And during the winter, pests retreat into plant refuse. To prevent a buildup of pests in spring, till under or compost surplus plant residue.

KNOW THY ENEMY

Last, but not least, to control insect pests organically, you must know them and learn their habits. Just knowing what a certain insect likes to eat and where the adult female lays her eggs goes a long way in helping you to rid your crops of that enemy.

Likewise, if you know the correct planting time for each crop, you can prevent serious damage by insects that feed on just one type of plant. And by knowing insect life cycles, you can time your plantings so that the crops mature before or after the insects hatch.

Take the Mexican bean beetle, for example. It feeds on nothing but bean-family members. If you plant your beans as early as possible, they'll mature before the beetles appear. To control these pests once they appear, pick them by hand and drop them into kerosene. Destroy all egg masses that you find on the plants.

Pest-Repellent Plants

To my mind, the safest and simplest tool to keep pests to a minimum is pest-repellent plants. It seems that most of the pest-repellent plants are herbs: strong-tasting and strong-smelling. You might hear scientists pooh-poohing the idea, but I believe that many of these herbs protect vulnerable crops in their close vicinity. And, if you liquefy the herbs, you can spray them on your crops to keep injurious insects away.

Although I can't really prove their power, here's my

One of the best pest control techniques is a thorough fall cleanup. Gathering up weeds and crop residue, composting them, and tilling the plot destroys the overwintering places of pests.

Marvelous Marigolds

Marigolds are a natural nematicide. That means they rid the soil of nematodes, those minute worms that feed on the roots of many plants, causing stunted growth. (If a plant is ailing for no apparent reason, you can usually suspect nematodes.) Crops liable to be damaged include tomatoes, eggplants, peppers, strawberries, and beans.

Marigolds work best if you plant them as a cover crop and then plow them under before planting a vegetable. Two species of marigolds are extremely effective: *Tagetes minuta,* a South American species, and French marigold (*T. patula*). Cultivars of these species, including 'Crackerjack' and 'Sparky', have been shown to have very strong nematicidal properties.

I especially like to grow marigolds where tomatoes and eggplant will be planted the following year. In the fall, I dig the plant residue into the bed or leave it on as a mulch over the winter.

To grow marigolds, scatter seeds thinly and barely cover them with fine soil. Then dampen the bed with a fine spray of water. (Marigold seeds are tiny and practically weightless, so even a moderate force of water will wash them right out of the ground.) Germination takes place in about eight days. Make sure the soil surface doesn't dry out before the seedlings are well established. To help condition the soil and keep it moist, spread a small amount of rotted manure, compost, or dry grass clippings over the bed after seeding.

Thin the young plants from time to time until they stand 10 to 12 inches apart. Transplant the surplus to your vegetable rows.

The results of interplanting marigolds may not show the first year since the substance that kills the nematodes is produced slowly in the roots of the plants, then gradually released into the soil. The nematicidal effect lasts several years, but keep on planting marigolds. As with garlic, you can never plant too many.

---

list of most valuable plants, with their reputed insecticidal power. Try them in your garden, and see if they work for you as well as they do for me:

··· Basil

Basil protects tomatoes—the plants work best as a border enclosing the tomato patch. Basil is famous as a fly repellent, too. You can pot it up for the house or terrace or grow it near an outdoor picnic, deck, or patio area.

··· Savory

Savory, especially the annual summer savory, protects beans of all kinds.

··· Sage and Mint

Sage and mint, two more aromatic herbs, protect cabbages and their relatives, including broccoli, cauliflower, kohlrabi, and Brussels sprouts.

··· Tansy and Yarrow

Tansy and yarrow are both valuable in keeping pests from your crops.

Tansy is much coarser than yarrow in looks and in growth. The plants grow 4 to 5 feet tall in rich soil and spread vigorously. They belong alongside permanent crops like raspberries or grapes. Tansy is also an excellent herb for the apple orchard.

Each fall, pull up surplus tansy and break it up, woody stalks and all. Then mix it with leaves as a mulch for your brambles and grapes. The tansy smell will still be strong the next season, and Japanese beetles—a scourge of those crops—will soon be gone.

Yarrow plants are easily controlled. Though 3 to 4 feet high, they seem appropriate in a border or in clumps here and there throughout the beds.

· · · Coriander and Anise

Coriander and anise also have a good reputation for repelling a variety of insects.

· · · Horseradish

Horseradish, a vigorous herb, has been used to repel potato bugs and other flying insects.

· · · Rue

Rue repels flies and vermin from the compost pile and discourages slugs in heavily mulched areas. In the kitchen, a branch of rue hung on the wall keeps out flies. Dried rue scattered in the cellar or attic banishes all loathsome bugs.

· · · Wormwood

Wormwood keeps woodchucks, rabbits, raccoons, porcupines, and other animals away from the garden.

· · · Feverfew

Feverfew seems absolutely bugproof. Grow it in a border near roses or near the vegetable beds. It can also be used as an herbal spray.

· · · Calendulas and Dahlias

Calendulas and dahlias seem to repel nematodes.

· · · Nasturtiums

Nasturtiums protect vine crops from their insect enemies.

Trap Plants

There's another, completely different way that plants can be used to control insects: as traps. The method is simple and effective. I do it by growing a limited number of "decoy plants" in the garden. These decoys have greater appeal to insect pests than the main crops do.

FOOLING POTATO BEETLES

Here's an example of one of my favorite trap crops: The greatest insect problem for potatoes here on Long Island is the Colorado potato beetle. Its tremendous appetite for potato plant leaves has driven more than one local potato grower out of business.

But don't let its name fool you. If given a choice, the potato beetle actually prefers eggplant. So I always plant a few eggplants to lure the beetles away from the potato patch. Once the beetles are congregated in large numbers on the eggplant, I pick them off and drop them into a container of kerosene or diesel fuel and water.

IN A PICKLE

The pickleworm, a real pest of cantaloupes and cucumbers, can be trapped by planting bush squash nearby. Planting a few bush squash over a period of several weeks usually gives effective results.

CORNY TOMATOES

Here's something I bet you didn't know: The corn earworm and tomato fruitworm are actually the same insect, *Helicoverpa zea*. So if it's tomatoes that you're most concerned about, intermingle sweet corn to act as a plant trap.

When given a choice, this pest has a preference for corn. By making a few small plantings of sweet corn, staggered over a period of several weeks, you can increase the effectiveness of the trap.

BYE-BYE, HARLEY

The harlequin bug is a very destructive pest, especially in the summer. If this colorful

You can use an insect's weaknesses against it. For example, by planting a few sacrificial eggplants, you can attract Colorado potato beetles, distracting them from your potato crop. Check the plants daily; pick and destroy the pests.

Dill will lure the tomato hornworm away. Plant it in the general vicinity of your tomato plants.

Maggots injure germinating corn as well as cabbage seedlings. Plant radish strips nearby to attract the maggots away from these crops.

I've found that by using plant traps along with cultural controls, such as companion planting and crop rotation, I get the most pest control advantages. If you rotate your crops annually, you can improve the productivity of your soil, and that in itself is a great help in controlling many insect pests.

Organic Sprays and Dusts

When push comes to shove in the battle against insects, organic sprays are an important ally. Properly used, they can control a legion of marauding garden pests without hurting the environment. Choose your product with care; some work specifically against certain insects, while

insect is prevalent in your area and you're growing cabbage, use a trap crop. Thin strips of radish, turnip, or mustard planted around the perimeter of the patch should lure it away from your cabbage.

BEETLE BAIT

You probably know the Japanese beetle, a voracious pest with an indiscriminate appetite. It feeds on countless vegetable plants, flowers, trees, shrubs, and deciduous fruits. Fortunately, there are a few that it favors—I use them as beetle traps.

Protect corn by planting small strips of soybeans, which the beetles prefer. White roses are one of the most effective decoys you can use to trap these insects. Zinnias also work well.

MORE TRAP PLANTS

Hyssop, a fine garden herb with many uses, makes an excellent trap plant. Grow it to divert cabbage butterflies away from cabbage, Brussels sprouts, kale, and kohlrabi.

others can affect a whole range of plant and animal life.

The most important thing to remember about plant-derived insecticides like rotenone, pyrethrin, ryania, and sabadilla is that even though they're natural, they aren't completely harmless to humans or the ecosystem. That means it's better to start with a less toxic control like insecticidal soap, BT, or diatomaceous earth first, then use a botanical spray if the first remedy fails.

DIATOMACEOUS EARTH

Diatomaceous earth is a natural product that kills insects mechanically. Its microscopic particles pierce the waxy coating that covers an insect's external skeleton, a thin, hard frame that's the only thing keeping vital fluids inside. The insect gradually loses moisture and dies. It takes diatomaceous earth about 12 hours to work.

Although diatomaceous earth isn't a cure-all for garden pest problems, it's very effective against slugs, Colorado potato beetles, squash and cucumber beetles, root maggots, aphids, bean beetles, cabbage loopers, tomato hornworms, various fruit tree flies and worms, Japanese beetles, pink boll weevils, lygus bugs, thrips, mites, earwigs, cockroaches, termites, snails, slugs, ants, and corn earworms.

Diatomaceous earth works best when applied as a 2- to 3-inch barrier on the soil around plants. Replenish the barrier when the soil has dried after each rain. You can also use it as a foliar dust. Generally safe to humans in its pure form, diatomaceous earth dust can still irritate your lungs, so it's best to wear a protective dust mask when applying it.

MILKY DISEASE AND BT

We know that insects can be beneficial in the garden, but can the same thing be said for diseases? Yes it can, if that disease is either milky disease or BT.

Milky disease, often called milky spore, is a powder made from grubs inoculated with the bacteria *Bacillus popilliae*. It's most often used to control Japanese beetle larvae. Milky disease gets its name from the fact that the normally clear blood of the beetle becomes milky white when it's infected with the disease.

Since a Japanese beetle spends ten months of every year as a grub in lawns at the root level of grasses, inoculating your lawn with milky disease is the best way to halt its development into an adult bug. You can apply milky disease dust any time the soil isn't frozen. The grubs contact the spores and move through the ground. As each infected grub dies, the disease spores multiply and spread.

It can take up to three

☀ My Home Brew

I like to make nonpoisonous sprays from plants to use as insect repellents. My favorite brew is a solution of chopped-up onions and feverfew, which I find effective for ridding roses of aphids.

I'll try any strong-smelling plant or any plant that's pest-resistant. Some of my concoctions have included elderberry leaves, as well as parsnip foliage and roots. By using herbs and flowers, rather than toxic chemicals, to keep insects to a minimum, I've succeeded in keeping my garden healthy and preserving the balance of nature.

years for milky disease to become established in most of your yard. But once established, the disease remains effective for 20 years because the spores stay in the soil.

If leaf-chewing caterpillars are a problem in your garden, another bacterial bug killer, BT (*Bacillus thuringiensis*) is the answer. BT attacks tomato hornworms, cabbageworms, loopers, and cankerworms. It also stops insects that pass through a caterpillar stage, such as gypsy moths and tent caterpillars, by disrupting their cellular functions and paralyzing their guts. It works a few hours after being ingested.

Observe your plants closely, and spray or dust only when you see insects beginning to feed. BT is available in different varieties; the one that kills caterpillars is called BTK (*Bacillus thuringiensis* var. *kurstaki*). Applications of BT are most effective in the spring and again in the summer, when larval feeding activity is the greatest.

What's great about BT is that you can apply it right up to the day of harvest. Treated vegetables may be picked and eaten any time thereafter. Why doesn't it hurt humans, if it's so effective against caterpillars? Because, luckily for us, the human stomach is too acidic for these bacteria.

Good Old Garlic

Most pests seem to avoid members of the onion family, such as chives, garlic, and onions. I consider garlic to be the most valuable pest-repellent plant.

I plant garlic cloves near roses, fruit trees, cabbages, and other susceptible crops to keep aphids away. Sometimes I make a garlic and tansy spray to chase Japanese beetles away from red raspberries.

INSECTICIDAL SOAP

Insecticidal soaps can be store-bought or made at home. To make your own, mix 3 teaspoons of liquid dish soap (like Ivory) with a gallon of water. You can spray insecticidal soap on your plants to control aphids, whiteflies, scale, thrips, leafhoppers, and many other pests.

Insecticidal soap works by coating the pest and penetrating its shell, eventually causing dehydration. It's nontoxic to people and pets. However, it is toxic to beneficial insects. Also, beans and cucumbers are adversely affected by soap sprays, so use another control if pests are attacking them.

ROTENONE

In the gardener's organic arsenal, rotenone is one of the toughest weapons. An extract of tropical plants, rotenone is a broad-spectrum organic bug killer. That means it kills many kinds of insects on many kinds of crops and ornamentals.

Rotenone is a contact and stomach poison that quickly kills Mexican bean beetles and cabbageworms. It's also effective against other beetles and various weevils, thrips, and European corn borers. Apply it as a dust or wettable powder spray.

Unfortunately, rotenone is also toxic to fish, so it should not be sprayed near any body of water. It can also kill birds and beneficial insects. If you're buying rotenone, read the label carefully to be sure that it hasn't been fortified with chemical toxins.

PYRETHRIN

Pyrethrin is a well-known organic bug killer derived from

pyrethrum daisies, which are close relatives of chrysanthemums. The dried flower heads have been used in insecticidal sprays and dusts for over 100 years.

Pyrethrin is a contact insecticide used to control dozens of fruit and vegetable pests. It paralyzes and kills aphids, leafhoppers, cabbage loopers, whiteflies, corn earworms, and thrips. It's especially useful as an orchard spray and is nontoxic to bees, ladybugs, and warm-blooded animals, although there have been cases of human allergic reactions.

Pyrethrin is a very potent pesticide and, although it is organic, should be used only when absolutely necessary. Whatever you do, don't confuse pyrethrin with pyrethroid insecticides. The latter belong to a group of synthetic pesticides that have a residual effect and are dangerous to bees, fish, and humans.

RYANIA

Ryania is a mildly alkaline pesticide made by grinding up the roots of a South American shrub. It is used to control corn borers, codling moths, oriental fruit flies, cotton bollworms, and other pests.

SABADILLA

Sabadilla, an extract made from *Schoenocaulon officinale* seeds, is used as a dust or wettable powder spray to control many insects, including grasshoppers, European corn borers, codling moth larvae, armyworms, webworms, silkworms, aphids, cabbage loopers, melon worms, squash bugs, harlequin bugs, and numerous household pests.

Sabadilla has been used as a natural control since the sixteenth century. Marketed under the trade name Red Devil Dust, it can irritate mucous membranes if used without a protective dust mask. Sabadilla can also harm pets if they come in contact with it, and it's toxic to honeybees.

SUPERIOR OIL SPRAYS

Organic gardeners have another potent, yet safe organic insecticide in their arsenal: superior or horticultural oil. It's actually a refined petroleum oil.

When sprayed on trees in the spring, just before the buds open, this oil is effective against a host of sucking and

Superior or horticultural oil is an excellent control for scale, aphids, and other insect pests. One of the best times to apply this oil is while trees and shrubs are dormant, during late winter and early spring. Take care to apply it evenly over the whole plant. It will suffocate overwintering pests.

chewing insects such as aphids, thrips, mealybugs, whiteflies, pear psylla, and various forms of scale and red spider mites. It also kills the eggs of codling moths, oriental fruit moths, leafrollers, and cankerworms.

Superior oil works by encasing trees in an envelope of oil, thus suffocating the pests. The older oils were so heavy they could only be applied while the trees were dormant (and were therefore called "dormant oils"). However, the improved formulas are lighter, so you can even spray them in summer, when the trees are fully leafed out.

Applying Oil

The best time to apply oil to dormant trees and shrubs is in late winter or very early spring. As spring approaches, the shells of insect eggs and the covering of scale insects become softer and more porous. At that time, the spray can penetrate more effectively.

Some experts advise spraying twice for best control. The first spray can be applied in late fall or during the first warm spell in earliest spring. The most important time, however, is just before the buds open, which can vary from February to May, depending on the location.

It's better to be too early than too late. You should never spray oil while the flowers are open since it can interfere with pollination and fruit set. If you didn't spray in time, wait until later, when the fruits have formed.

To spray, pick as calm a day as you can. Spray all around each tree for even coverage; any excess will just drain off. Concentrate on the trunk, large branches, and crotches. But get out to the edges, too, since insect eggs are often laid on branch tips.

You can use oil sprays on all trees, shrubs, and evergreens except blue spruce. That's because spraying blue spruces can make them turn green!

The Reason for Diseases

Disease and insect infestations are part of nature's crucial process of keeping life in balance. But many of us have trouble seeing disease and insect problems in their true ecological perspective.

Too often, we view our gardens as factories for the production of food. Any intruders—be they diseases, insects, or foraging birds—are automatically classified as "enemies" to be wiped out with toxic sprays.

Step one in acquiring the right attitude toward diseases is to avoid hysteria. You must realize that these bad parts of life are just as natural as the good parts, and they

☀ Sulfur Sprays

Fungal diseases can be as serious as insect pests, but many can be handled organically. Ground sulfur rock has been used for hundreds of years to control brown rot on stone fruits, scab on pears and apples, rust on snapdragons and carnations, and blackspot and powdery mildew on roses, phlox, zinnias, sweet peas, and lilacs. It's easy to mix and it spreads well, sticking to both sides of the leaves.

You can apply sulfur with a duster or dilute it with water and spray it. Sulfur works best if you apply it early in the year. In summer, it's not as effective and can actually harm the plants if it's spread when the thermometer hits 85°F. It can also damage fruit trees when sprayed within two weeks of an application of a dormant oil spray.

may even be able to teach us something.

Diseases can be signals that indicate underlying problems. When disease strikes your garden, don't ask, "Why me?" Instead, ask, "What am I doing that's out of step with nature?"

AN OUNCE OF PREVENTION

Our plants are besieged by a host of organisms that can cause diseases. Some of these disease organisms may be present in the soil before we even start our gardens. Others may originate from plants or soil brought in from other sources. Let's take a look at a few of the ways you can keep your garden free of disease without turning to toxic chemicals:

Choose the Right Site

Many diseases, especially those caused by fungi, are encouraged by low, damp ground. When selecting a garden site, look for both good soil drainage and good air circulation.

Build the Soil

Organic matter keeps diseases at bay in two ways: First, it improves drainage. Thus, water won't sit at the base of the plants, where it could cause rots, slimes, and other fungal infections. And second, a humus-rich soil builds healthy plants that resist all sorts of insects and diseases.

Mulch the Garden

Mulches help to maintain an even supply of moisture and prevent your soil from drying out. They also help keep soilborne diseases from splashing on foliage and spreading disease spores. Mulch is often all you need to keep septoria blight from wiping out your tomato plants.

Feed Your Crops

Fertilizing to encourage fast growth will keep plants healthy and thus less liable to succumb to disease. The nitrogen in well-rotted manures will spur rapid growth, while its phosphorus content will increase both bloom and fruit set.

Rotate Your Vegetables

Moving vegetables around from year to year can keep soil diseases to a minimum. Corn smut, downy mildew, and wilts may all be prevented by rotation. You can also control clubroot of cabbage by practicing rotation.

Plant Resistant Cultivars

Find out which vegetable diseases are prevalent in your region. Then, when you shop for seeds or plants, look for cultivars that will resist or tolerate those diseases. Catalogs and plant tags will tell you which diseases each cultivar resists.

Disease-Stopping Systems

There are many steps you can take to forestall diseases, including following my prevention program. Once you've taken the basic precautions, though, you'll also need to know how to cope with the occasional disease outbreak. You'll find information on specific diseases affecting certain crops in Chapter 10. But here are descriptions of a few basic problems, along with some recommended "cures."

BEASTLY BACTERIA

Bacteria can cause wilts, blights, spots, galls, and other repulsive diseases like slime flux. You can't really cure most bacterial infections, though you can contain their damage by removing infected parts. The best tactic is to plant resistant cultivars whenever possible.

To prevent bacterial infection, keep your plants as healthy as you can by using good growing techniques. Try to avoid injuring your plants. Copper and streptomycin

· DISTRESS SIGNALS ·

A plant will always let you know if it's in trouble. If you interpret the problem correctly and treat it promptly, you have a good chance of saving the plant. Here are some symptoms of plant distress and their possible causes. Note how many of them are simple cultural problems rather than diseases.

SYMPTOM	CAUSE(S)
Leaves curling inward or downward	Overfertilization
Yellowing and dropping lower leaves	Overfeeding Magnesium deficiency
Leggy plants with long, weak stems and large spaces between leaves	Insufficient light Excessively high temperatures Crowded plants
Bud drop	Dry air
Skimpy root growth	Poor drainage Low soil fertility Temperatures too low Insufficient air spaces in soil
Leaf discoloration	Nutrient deficiency
Pale leaves	Nitrogen deficiency
Leaves reddish purple on undersides	Phosphorus deficiency
Bronzing or browning of leaf edges	Potassium deficiency
Discolored roots	Overfeeding
Mold on soil surface	Poor drainage Insufficient soil aeration Lack of air circulation
Green algae on soil surface	Too much water Lack of air circulation
Failure of seeds to sprout	Temperature too low or too high Soil allowed to dry out Seeds planted too deeply Old seeds, poorly stored Insufficient contact between seed and soil Damping-off disease

sprays can control some bacterial diseases like bacterial spot. If you can't control the disease promptly, destroy the infected plants. To avoid bacteria buildup in the soil, rotate your crops.

Fight Fire Blight

One of the most devastating bacterial diseases is fire blight, which attacks apples, pears, and other rose-family plants. It causes infected flowers, leaves, and shoots to shrivel and look blackened and scorched.

To fight this disease, plant fire blight–resistant cultivars. Prune out infected growth (cut 6 to 12 inches below the visible signs of infection), then burn it. Spray plants with copper sulfate or bordeaux mix while they're dormant, and apply streptomycin while they're in bloom.

FRIGHTENING FUNGI

The best way to control fungal diseases is to keep your garden clean. Dispose of all crop residues—don't till them back into the soil. This step is critical because, in the fall, fungi like rust can form overwintering spores that will germinate the following spring.

Don't work with your plants when the foliage is wet. If you do, it's easy to spread fungal diseases from one plant to the next.

Keep a sharp eye out for leaf spots and other signs of fungal infection. Pick off the infected leaves and remove them from the garden.

Don't forget to rotate your crops. Rotation helps discourage fungi by depriving them of their food and breeding sites.

Mildew No More

Two of the most common fungal diseases are powdery mildew and downy mildew, which cover infected leaves with white or gray powdery or furry growth. Mildew can be a major problem, especially in wet weather. The best protection against these diseases is to buy resistant cultivars and use good cultural practices.

Proper spacing helps to keep mildew in check. If your plants are severely infected, pull out every other plant to provide maximum sunlight and air circulation.

Another way to prevent these diseases is to avoid wetting the foliage when you water since damp leaves are prone to mildew attack. (This is where a soaker hose really comes in handy.)

To keep mildew at bay, you can also spray your plants with sulfur according to package directions. Or, mix 1 teaspoon of baking soda and 1 quart of warm water and spray it on the foliage. Spraying both sides of the leaves with compost tea will also check mildew.

VILE VIRUSES

There's no cure for a virus. If your plants are infected, the only recourse is to pull them up and destroy them before the disease spreads to surrounding plants. That means that prevention is critical—nobody wants to lose a crop (or even a plant) without a fight. The simplest and best prevention is to buy resistant cultivars—just look for this information as you page through the catalogs.

If you aren't growing a resistant cultivar and your plants look stunted with patchy, mottled coloration on the leaves, they've probably contracted a virus. Besides mottling foliage, mosaic virus sometimes causes fruits to be misshapen. That's because infected plants have insufficient foliage to supply food and to cover the fruits.

Aphids are the primary virus carrier. To make sure they don't infect your plants, control them with insecticidal soap from the time they're just little seedlings. Floating row covers will also keep these pests off your crops—if

Darn Damping-Off

Damping-off fungus is a complex microorganism that often attacks and kills small seedlings. When it strikes, you'll find bunches of seedlings that have dropped in their tracks. It's too late to stop it by then—the damage is done. You need to concentrate on prevention. Here's how to keep damping-off in check:

- ❧ Maintain good air circulation around seedlings
- ❧ Keep soil level high in flats
- ❧ Thin seedlings to avoid overcrowding
- ❧ Avoid overwatering

you get the covers on before the aphids find your plants.

Besides controlling aphids, there are other tricks for discouraging mosaic and other viral diseases. Don't grow susceptible crops near one another (muskmelons near squash, for example). And keep areas bordering the garden free of weeds, which can host both viruses and aphids.

Just Say No to Drugs

For the past few decades, the use of toxic chemicals has skyrocketed. At the same time, the quality of our food, water, and soil has been deteriorating. With the increasing dangers from chemical use in our gardens, we can see why there's a need for further study and understanding of the crop ecosystem.

Chemical methods of disease prevention or cure are based primarily on neutralizing the agent germ. But as organic gardeners, we seek balance and wholeness and a proper—not an exclusive—place for ourselves, our plants, and our animals in nature.

Now, more than ever, is the time to study and understand garden biology and ecology. The relationship between plants and the environment is critical. Our own survival, as well as our crops', is at stake.

CHAPTER

19

Let's Work on Weeds

The life of a weed is a horror story that none of us gardeners wants to view. First, those tender little tips of green spring up between our garden rows. Then, unless we can counter that ever-present urge to relax during summer growing weather, the baby weeds turn into vigorous monsters that literally smother all those fine plants we've worked so hard to establish.

No, weeds are no good at all. Ninety-nine out of 100 gardeners would agree. But I'm the one contrary thinker who'll tell you to wait a minute before condemning weeds so heartily. Think about it: Could weeds actually be a blessing in disguise?

Working Weeds

Weed control is, and always will be, necessary in the garden. However, the benefits these wild plants can provide organic gardeners can't be denied. Take a new look at how useful weeds can be, and put all that lush growth to work in your garden.

Weeds are great additions to the compost heap. After you've composted them, they'll add organic matter to lighten clay soils, build up sandy soils, and enrich all your flowers and vegetables. And the 160°F heat of a well-made compost pile destroys practically all weed seeds, so there's no danger of spreading trouble.

Weeds are also valuable mulch material. They conserve moisture, regulate the soil temperature, and reduce your cultivating chores. Ironically, they also keep down other weeds.

Weeds add important nutrients to the soil, too. In the annual cycle of birth and death, weeds decay, releasing many mineral elements that the roots have brought up from deep in the soil.

Where the soil is left un-planted, weeds can retain soil nitrogen, which otherwise would leach away. Weeds also serve as free green ma-nure crops; plow them under or disc-mulch them before they go to seed.

Weeding Right

You don't want to allow weeds to overrun your garden just because they have a few desirable qualities. After all, a weed's goal is the same as any other plant's—to procreate and take over the world. Weeds aim to survive, and they make as much seed as they can.

WHEN SHOULD YOU WEED?

It's important to get out the hoe early. Start three or four days after sowing. Use a tined tool or a hoe and stir the soil 2 inches deep. The seedbed will be soft and the work will go quickly.

Even if no seedlings are up, the weed seeds are ger-minating, and they'll dry out and die in the stirred soil. The next crop of weeds has to wait for rain or push up through 2 inches of soil.

ANNUAL WEEDS

Late weeding controls winter annuals—the weeds that ger-minate in the fall, overwinter as small plants, and go to seed in mud-time. They're easy to overlook in fall and hard to reach in spring.

A cover crop will smother most winter annuals. If you're growing crops that overwinter, like strawberries, asparagus, or parsley, be sure to keep on weeding late in the fall. A few weeds can sprout even after frost.

EASY WEEDING

Season-long weeding is an easier job in some gardens than in others. Beds planted closely and evenly are less work than the same-size planting set out in rows. Planting crops in rows ex-poses a lot of soil, and weeds sprout all season long.

But no matter how you garden, you'll be repaid for season-long weeding with better yields this year and fewer weeds next year.

SHALLOW TILLING

My favorite weed control technique is shallow tilling, which means cultivating only the top 3 or 4 inches of soil. This isn't a new idea. Farmers and horticulturists have been talking about it since the turn of the century as a way of systematically ridding the top layer of soil of weed seeds.

Here's how to do it: In spring, get out your rotary tiller and set it at the most shallow setting. Use it to culti-vate the top 3 or 4 inches of soil—and I mean *only* the top 3 or 4 inches.

Stirring up this layer will cause most of the weed seeds there to germinate but won't disturb the bulk of the weed seeds, which are buried deeper. Those seeds that do sprout can be quickly dis-patched with a little hoeing or hand pulling. Eventually, over three to five years, the weed seeds in the top layer of soil will be down to a manageable number.

Shallow tilling works best in a raised bed system. As the soil in raised beds is washed down, new weed seeds are exposed and even-tually germinate. As seedlings emerge, you can cut them down. The idea is to germinate as many weeds as possible through repeated tillings.

If you shallow till an or-dinary garden where the soil is walked on, compaction can occur. And without deep tillage to break it up, the compacted layer could slow your plants' root growth.

Checking Compaction

In heavy soils, shallow rotary tilling can also compact the soil. Use a spading fork to

What Weeds Say

Put your weeds to work! Certain weeds are accurate indicators of soil quality. By reading weeds, a canny gardener can tell a lot about the garden's conditions. Here's how:

🍃 Ferns, horsetail, sedge, rush, cattail, buttercup, and pennywort indicate a wet soil and possibly a drainage problem.

🍃 Sorrel, dock, wild strawberry, and brambles point to an overly acid soil.

🍃 Devil's paintbrush and spurge grow in poor, dry soil.

🍃 Knotweed is a sure sign of a tight, compressed soil that needs to be broken up or supplemented with lots of compost.

🍃 Self-heal and wild onion indicate a deep clay that needs both compost and sand.

🍃 Chicory and teasel love limestone soils. If you have these weeds, test the pH and, if necessary, incorporate quantities of oak leaves, peat moss, or other acidic materials.

🍃 If your soil has lots of nitrogen, you'll find plants such as mayweed and barnyard grass.

🍃 Sandburs and sheep sorrel usually indicate that the soil is both acidic and nitrogen-deficient.

🍃 Weak, impoverished soil will produce such telltale weeds as crabgrass and hawkweed.

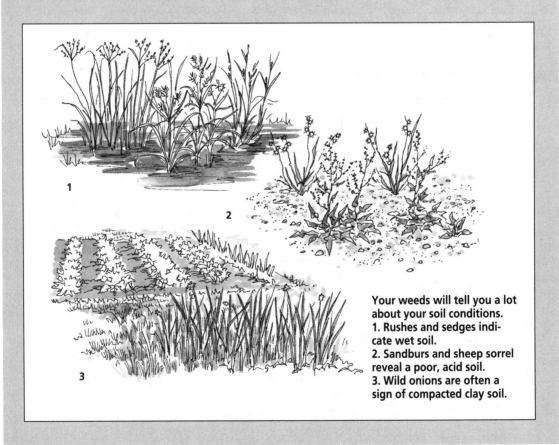

Your weeds will tell you a lot about your soil conditions.
1. Rushes and sedges indicate wet soil.
2. Sandburs and sheep sorrel reveal a poor, acid soil.
3. Wild onions are often a sign of compacted clay soil.

check for a compacted layer. If you find compaction, you can use the fork to pierce and break up the soil, too.

Hold That Mulch

When you're using the shallow tilling method, don't mulch right away. Wait until after a second or third spring tilling. That way, the weeds will have had several chances to germinate.

Locking Out Weeds

Obviously, if you want the shallow-till method to work, you'll have to make sure no new seeds infiltrate the garden while you're getting rid of those that are already there. There are several ways to lock weeds right out of your garden.

CUTTING DOWN ON WEED SEEDS

The best way to keep your weed problems from multiplying is to watch your garden closely and make sure that no weeds go to seed. Repeat: *Don't let weeds set seed.* Cut them off, pull them up, hoe them down—torch them, if you have to. But get them before they get you. You should weed every seven to ten days if you want to interrupt the weed-to-seed cycle.

CHANGE THE PROGRAM

Many weeds thrive when the same crop is grown year after year, so rotate heavy-feeding crops such as corn, tomatoes, and cabbage with light feeders like pole and bush beans, carrots, and beets.

MADE IN THE SHADE

Garden crops themselves can help control weeds by crowding and shading. A dense planting of buckwheat, for example, can crowd out weeds. Once corn grows tall enough to shade the rows, new weeds cease to grow vigorously and may disappear altogether. Unstaked tomatoes grown next to asparagus will shade out weeds in the asparagus row in midsummer. (And, according to companion gardening lore, the two plants are beneficial to each other.)

Shade is key to this kind of weed control. It's the most effective herbicide you can use on sun-loving weeds.

THE MIRACLE OF MULCH

Mulching with any kind of organic matter, such as grass clippings, hay, or shredded leaves, keeps light from reaching weed seeds. So the seeds that need light to germinate can't sprout.

Mulch not only suppresses weeds, it keeps the soil moist and cool on hot, dry days. And weeds that can germinate in the dark—and manage to push their way up through the mulch—are easier to pull from soft, moist soil.

Mulch is an easy way to control weeds. And keeping the soil moist is a benefit for your crops. So are the nutrients that mulch releases into the soil as it breaks down.

SOLARIZE YOUR SOIL

Another way to lock out weeds is called "soil solarization." To solarize the soil, start with a tilled, raked garden bed, and water it well. The next day, cover the entire bed with clear 3- to 6-mil plastic, then bury the edges so it can't blow off. As the sun strikes the dark, wet soil through the clear plastic, it will warm it, encouraging rapid germination of weed seeds. But when the tender seedlings come up, they'll "cook" in the hot, steamy atmosphere under the plastic.

To make sure you kill *all* the weed seeds, you have to leave the plastic on for an entire summer. (Avoid deep-tilling your solarized soil or you'll bring up a new weed generation and have to start all over.)

USDA Plant Hardiness Zone Map

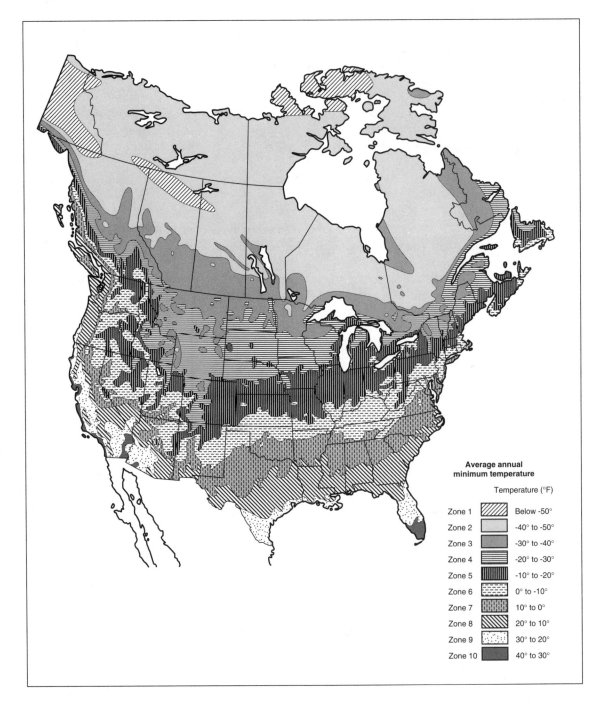

**Average annual
minimum temperature**

Temperature (°F)

Zone 1		Below -50°
Zone 2		-40° to -50°
Zone 3		-30° to -40°
Zone 4		-20° to -30°
Zone 5		-10° to -20°
Zone 6		0° to -10°
Zone 7		10° to 0°
Zone 8		20° to 10°
Zone 9		30° to 20°
Zone 10		40° to 30°

Sources

SEEDS AND PLANTS

Adams County Nursery, Inc.
P.O. Box 108
Aspers, PA 17304
Fruit trees

Bear Creek Nursery
P.O. Box 411
Northport, WA 99157
Fruit trees: scionwood, bud wood, budded trees, and rootstocks

W. Atlee Burpee & Co.
300 Park Avenue
Warminster, PA 18974

The Cook's Garden
P.O. Box 535
Londonderry, VT 05148

Edible Landscaping
P.O. Box 77
Afton, VA 22920
Specializes in fruits

Hastings
P.O. Box 115535
Atlanta, GA 30302
Specializes in plants for southern climates

Ed Hume Seeds, Inc.
P.O. Box 1450
Kent, WA 98035
Specializes in untreated vegetable seeds

Johnny's Selected Seeds
2580 Foss Hill Road
Albion, ME 04910
Vegetable and herb seeds

Native Seeds/SEARCH
2509 North Campbell Avenue #325
Tucson, AZ 85719
Southwestern native and heirloom vegetable and herb seeds

New York State Fruit Testing Cooperative Assoc., Inc.
P.O. Box 462
Geneva, NY 14456
Annual membership fee; new and time-tested fruit cultivars

Park Seed Co.
P.O. Box 31
Greenwood, SC 29647

Pinetree Garden Seeds
Route 100
New Gloucester, ME 04260
Inexpensive, small seed packets

Raintree Nursery
391 Butts Road
Morton, WA 98356
Specializes in fruits, nuts, and edible plants

St. Lawrence Nurseries
R.R. 5, Box 324
Potsdam, NY 13676
Specializes in hardy fruits and nuts

Sandy Mush Herb Nursery
Route 2, Surrett Cove Road
Leicester, NC 28748
Specializes in rare and unusual plants

Seed Savers Exchange
3076 North Winn Road
Decorah, IA 52101
Annual membership fee; heirloom fruits and vegetables

Seeds Trust High Altitude Gardens
P.O. Box 4619
Ketchum, ID 83340
Specializes in seeds for high altitudes and cold climates

Shepherd's Garden Seeds
6116 Highway 9
Felton, CA 95018

Southern Exposure Seed Exchange
P.O. Box 158
North Garden, VA 22959

Stark Bro's Nurseries & Orchards Co.
Highway 54
Louisiana, MO 63353
Fruits

Stokes Seeds, Inc.
Box 548
Buffalo, NY 14240

Territorial Seed Co.
P.O. Box 157
Cottage Grove, OR 97424
Vegetable seeds for the maritime climates of the Pacific Northwest

Wayside Gardens
1 Garden Lane
Hodges, SC 29695
Perennials, bulbs, and roses

White Flower Farm
Litchfield, CT 06759
Perennials and bulbs

GARDENING EQUIPMENT AND SUPPLIES

Bountiful Gardens
19550 Walker Road
Willits, CA 95490
Also offers organically grown herb and vegetable seeds

Gardener's Supply Co.
128 Intervale Road
Burlington, VT 05401

Gardens Alive!
5100 Schenley Place
Lawrenceburg, IN 47025

Harmony Farm Supply
P.O. Box 460
Graton, CA 95444

Necessary Trading Co.
P.O. Box 305
422 Salem Avenue
New Castle, VA 24127
Soil amendments and organic pest controls; large quantities only

Peaceful Valley Farm Supply Co.
P.O. Box 2209
Grass Valley, CA 95945

Smith & Hawken
25 Corte Madera
Mill Valley, CA 94941

The Urban Farmer Store
2833 Vicente Street
San Francisco, CA 94116
Water-conserving irrigation systems and other supplies

SOIL-TESTING FACILITIES

A & L Agricultural Labs
7621 White Pine Road
Richmond, VA 23237

Biosystem Consultants
P.O. Box 43
Lorane, OR 97451

The Spring Meadow School of Organic Farming and Gardening
441 North Country Road
St. James, NY 11780

Timberleaf
5569 State Street
Albany, OH 45710

Wallace Labs
365 Coral Circle
El Segundo, CA 90245

RECOMMENDED READING

Adams, William D., and Thomas R. Leroy. *Growing Fruits and Nuts in the South.* Dallas, Tx.: Taylor Publishing Company, 1992.

Appleton, Bonnie Lee, and Alfred F. Scheider. *Rodale's Successful Organic Gardening: Trees, Shrubs, and Vines.* Emmaus, Pa.: Rodale Press, 1993.

Ball, Jeff. *Rodale's Garden Problem Solver: Vegetables, Fruits, and Herbs.* Emmaus, Pa.: Rodale Press, 1988.

Ball, Jeff, and Liz Ball. *Rodale's Flower Garden Problem Solver.* Emmaus, Pa.: Rodale Press, 1990.

Ball, Jeff, and Liz Ball. *Rodale's Landscape Problem Solver.* Emmaus, Pa.: Rodale Press, 1989.

Barton, Barbara J. *Gardening by Mail: A Source Book.* 4th ed. Boston: Houghton Mifflin Co., 1994.

Benjamin, Joan, and Barbara W. Ellis, eds. *Rodale's No-Fail Flower Garden.* Emmaus, Pa.: Rodale Press, 1994.

Bradley, Fern Marshall, and Barbara W. Ellis, eds. *Rodale's All-New Encyclopedia of Organic Gardening.* Emmaus, Pa.: Rodale Press, 1992.

Brickell, Christopher. *Pruning.* New York: Simon and Schuster, 1988.

Carr, Anna, et al. *Rodale's Illustrated Encyclopedia of Herbs.* Edited by Claire Kowalchik and William H. Hylton. Emmaus, Pa.: Rodale Press, 1987.

Childers, Norman F. *Modern Fruit Science: Orchard and Small Fruit Culture.* Gainesville, Fla.: Norman F. Childers, Publisher, 1983 (available from Horticultural Publications, 3906 NW 31st Place, Gainesville, FL 32606).

Coleman, Eliot. *Four-Season Harvest: How to Harvest Fresh, Organic Vegetables from Your Home Garden All Year Long.* Post Mills, Vt.: Chelsea Green Publishing Co., 1992.

Creasy, Rosalind. *The Complete Book of Edible Landscaping.* San Francisco: Sierra Club Books, 1982.

Ellis, Barbara W., ed. *Rodale's Illustrated Encyclopedia of Gardening and Landscaping Techniques.* Emmaus, Pa.: Rodale Press, 1990.

Ellis, Barbara W., and Fern Marshall Bradley, eds. *The Organic Gardener's Handbook of Natural Insect and Disease Control.* Emmaus, Pa.: Rodale Press, 1992.

Gershuny, Grace. *Start with the Soil.* Emmaus, Pa.: Rodale Press, 1993.

Halpin, Anne Moyer, and the Editors of Rodale Press. *Foolproof Planting: How to Successfully Start and Propagate More Than 250 Vegetables, Flowers, Trees, and Shrubs.* Emmaus, Pa.: Rodale Press, 1990.

Hupping, Carol, et al. *Stocking Up III.* Emmaus, Pa.: Rodale Press, 1986.

Hynes, Erin. *Rodale's Successful Organic Gardening: Improving the Soil.* Emmaus, Pa.: Rodale Press, 1994.

Hynes, Erin, and Susan McClure. *Rodale's Successful Organic Gardening: Low-Maintenance Landscaping.* Emmaus, Pa.: Rodale Press, 1994.

Jeavons, John. *How to Grow More Vegetables Than You Ever Thought Possible on Less Land Than You Can Imagine.* Rev. ed. Berkeley, Calif.: Ten Speed Press, 1991.

Kourik, Robert. *Drip Irrigation for Every Landscape and All Climates.* Santa Rosa, Calif.: Metamorphic Press, 1992.

Martin, Deborah L., and Grace Gershuny, eds. *The Rodale Book of Composting.* Emmaus, Pa.: Rodale Press, 1992.

McClure, Susan, and C. Colston Burrell. *Rodale's Successful Organic Gardening: Perennials.* Emmaus, Pa.: Rodale Press, 1993.

McClure, Susan, and Sally Roth. *Rodale's Successful Organic Gardening: Companion Planting.* Emmaus, Pa.: Rodale Press, 1994.

Michalak, Patricia S. *Rodale's Successful Organic Gardening: Herbs.* Emmaus, Pa.: Rodale Press, 1993.

Michalak, Patricia S., and Linda A. Gilkeson. *Rodale's Successful Organic Gardening: Controlling Pests and Diseases.* Emmaus, Pa.: Rodale Press, 1994.

Michalak, Patricia S., and Cass Peterson. *Rodale's Successful Organic Gardening: Vegetables.* Emmaus, Pa.: Rodale Press, 1993.

Nick, Jean M. A., and Fern Marshall Bradley, eds. *Growing Fruits and Vegetables Organically.* Emmaus, Pa.: Rodale Press, 1994.

Phillips, Ellen, and C. Colston Burrell. *Rodale's Illustrated Encyclopedia of Perennials.* Emmaus, Pa.: Rodale Press, 1993.

Pleasant, Barbara. *Warm-Climate Gardening.* Pownal, Vt.: Storey Communications, 1993.

Schultz, Warren. *The Chemical-Free Lawn: The Newest Varieties and Techniques to Grow Lush, Hardy Grass.* Emmaus, Pa.: Rodale Press, 1989.

Smith, Miranda. *Backyard Fruits and Berries.* Emmaus, Pa.: Rodale Press, 1994.

Smith, Miranda, and Anna Carr. *Rodale's Garden Insect, Disease & Weed Identification Guide.* Emmaus, Pa.: Rodale Press, 1988.

Whealy, Kent, and Steve Demuth, eds. *Fruit, Berry and Nut Inventory.* 2nd ed. Decorah, Iowa: Seed Saver Publications, 1993 (available from Seed Savers Exchange, 3076 North Winn Road, Decorah, IA 52101).

Whealy, Kent, ed. *Garden Seed Inventory.* 3rd ed. Decorah, Iowa: Seed Saver Publications, 1992 (available from Seed Savers Exchange, 3076 North Winn Road, Decorah, IA 52101).

INDEX

Note: Page references in **boldface** indicate illustrations. *Italicized* references indicate tables.

A

Achillea millefolium, 196–97, **197**
Acid rain, 33–34
Aeration of lawns, 334
Alfalfa, as cover crop, 40
Allium schoenoprasum (chives), 183, **183,** 194
Allium tuberosum, 183, **183**
Aluminum, in soil, 33
Alyssum, perennial, 292
Anethum graveolens (dill), 189, **189,** 194
Animal manures, 24–27
Animal meals, 27–28
Anise, pests repelled by, 352
Annuals
        choices, 263–64
        gallery, 275–291
        growing, 264–65, **264**
        outdoors, 265–67
        sowing seeds, 265, **265**
Antirrhinum majus, 284–85, **285,** 288
Aphids, as virus carriers, 360–61
Apples, 217–20, **218**
        cultivars, 206
        planting seeds, 208
        pollination, 212–13
Apple scab, 204, **205**
Apricots, 221–22
Artemisia abrotanum, 195–96, **195**
Asparagus, 82, 96–98, **96**
Aurinia saxatilis, 292, **292**
Autumn. *See* Fall
Azaleas, 323–24, **323**

B

Bacillus thuringiensis (BT), 105, 113, 205, 355
Bacteria
        disease, 358, 360
        in soil, 6
Baptisia, 292
Basil
        pests repelled by, 351
        sweet, 186–87, **186**
Basket-of-gold, 292, **292**

Beans
        dry, 98–99, **98**
        lima, 99–100, **100**
        snap, 100–102, **101**
Bee balm, 192, **192**
Bees, pollination by, 212, 213
Beets, 102–4, **103**
        as fall crop, 81
        planted with kohlrabi, 69
Belgian endive, 117
Beneficial insects and animals, 53–54, **53,** 349, **349**
Berries, 240–60
        bushes, 201–2
        propagating, 212
Biodynamic/French Intensive planting, 74–75
Birds
        shrubs and, 317–318, **318**
Blackberries, 82, 241–44, **241, 242, 243**
Blackspot, 270
Blanket flower, 293, **293**
Blood meal, in compost, 16–17
Blueberries, 202, 244–48, **244, 248**
        lowbush, 246, 332
        softwood cuttings, 212
Bluebonnets, 275–76, **275**
Bluegrass, white clover and, 327–29, **329**
Bonemeal, 16–17, 270, 338
Borage, 192–93, **192,** 194
Bordeaux mix, 204
Boron deficiency, **36,** 37
Brambles, 240
        blackberries, 241–44
        propagation, 212
        raspberries, 252–55
        transplanted in fall, 82
Broccoli, 104–5, **104**
Brussels sprouts, 81, 106–7, **106**
BT, 105, 113, 205, 355
Budding, 209–10, **210**
Bulbs, 267–68
Bush beans, 100–102, **101**
Butterhead lettuce, 137

C

Cabbage, 107–9, **107**
        Chinese, 118–19
        as trap crop, 353

Cabbage butterflies, 353
Calcium
        deficiency, **36,** 37
        in soil, 33
Calendulas, pests repelled by, 352
Cantaloupe (muskmelon), 138–40
Caraway, 188, **188**
Carrots, 109–12, **109**
        as fall crop, 81
        with onions, parsnips, and leeks, 110–11
        with radishes and onions, 69
Carum carvi, 188, **188**
Catalogs, ordering from, 49–52, **50,** 54, *54*
Caterpillars, 355
Catnip, 190, **190**
Cauliflower, 112–13, **112**
Celery, 81, 114–15, **114**
Cell packs, 89
Celosias, 276–77, **276**
Chamomile, German, 191, **191**
Cherries, 223–24
Chicons, 117
Chicory, 115–17, **116**
Chinch bugs, 341, **341**
Chinese cabbage, 81, 118–19, **118**
Chives, 183, **183,** 194
Chrysanthemum coccineum (painted daisies), **294,** 295
Chrysanthemum morifolium, 293–95, **294**
Chrysanthemum parthenium (feverfew), **294,** 295
Chrysanthemum × *superbum* (Shasta daisies), **294,** 295
Chrysanthemums, garden, 293–95, **294**
Clary, 186
Clay soil, 3, **3, 4,** 5, *35*
Climbing roses, **269,** 273
Cold frames, **86,** 86–87, **87,** 136
Colorado potato beetles, 352, **353**
Companion planting, 69, 348. *See also* Interplanting
Compost(ing), 14–23
        advantages of hot compost, 22–23
        greenhouses and, 89, 90
        ingredients, 14–17, **15,** 20
        leaves, 16, 20–22, **21**

Compost(ing) *(continued)*
    making and working piles, 17–19
    as mulch, 43
    in seedling mix, 57
    sheet or trench, 18, **18**
    soil compaction from, 10
    spreading, 20
    time for, 19–20
Compost bins, 17, **17**
Conifers, 302. *See also* Evergreen trees
Coriander, 189, **189,** 352
Corn, 119–21, **120,** 352
Corn earworms, 352
Cosmos, 277–78, **277**
Cover crops, 38–40, **39**
    benefits, 41
    for pest control, 348
    sowing, **40,** 41
Crabapples, 212–13
Crabgrass, 342, **342**
Crop rotation, 73
    for disease control, 358
    for pest control, 347–48, **347**
Crown rot, 304
Cucumbers, 121–23, **121**
Cultivars
    descriptions in catalogs, 50, **50**
    pest- and disease-resistant, 52
Cultivation of soil, 8
Cutting garden, 266
Cuttings
    fruit from, 210–12, **211**
    from shrubs, 321
Cutworms, 349–50

D

Dahlias, pests repelled by, 352
Damping-off fungus, 361
Daylilies, 295–96, **296,** 332
Days to maturity, 50, *51*
Deciduous trees, 302
Diatomaceous earth, 354
Dill, 189, **189,** 194, 353
Disease. *See also specific plants*
    catalog abbreviations, *54*
    control, 357–61
        bacteria, 358, 360
        fungi, 360, 361
        for lawns, 339–40
        for orchard, 204–5
        prevention, 358
        resistant cultivars, 52
        viruses, 360–61
    symptoms and causes, *359*

Diversity in garden, 53–54, 345–46, **346**
Dogwood, 311–13, **312**
Dollar spot, 340
Dormant oil, 205
Double digging, 12, 74–75, **75,** 76
Downy mildew, 360
Drainage for trees, 302
Drip irrigation, 64
Dry beans, 98–99
Dry-weather planting, 78, 79–80
Dust mulch, 10
Dwarf fruit trees, 201, 205–7, **206,** 215

E

Earthworms, 5, 6, **7,** 43
Eggplant, 123–24, **123,** 352, **353**
Elderberries, 248–49
Endive, 124–26, **125**
    Belgian, 117
    curly, as fall crop, 81
Equipment and supply sources, 367
Evergreen trees, 302
    pruning, 314–16, **315**
    seedbed, 314
    starting from seed, 313
    winter protection, 316–17

F

Fading-out, 340
Fairy rings, 340
Fall
    greenhouses and, 92
    growing season (*see* Season extension)
    planting schedule, 181
Feeding formulas, 96
Fennel, 190, **190**
Fertilizers. *See* Organic fertilizers
Feverfew, **294,** 295, 352
Fire blight, 360
Fish emulsion, 30
Floating row covers, **65**
Floribundas, **269,** 273
Flowerpot effect, 302, 303, **303, 304**
Flowers, 263–300
    annuals, 263–67, 275–85, 288–92
    bulbs, 267–68
    dried, 290
    hanging garden, 286–87
    perennials, 267, 292–300
    roses, 268–75
    among vegetables or herbs, 266
Foeniculum vulgare, 190, **190**
Foliar feeding, 30–31, **30,** 307

Forsythias, pruning, 308
Four-o'clocks, 278–79, **279**
French Intensive planting, 74–75
Frost
    fruit trees and, 213
    plant vulnerability to, 84
    protection from, 83–86
    transplants and, 65
    tree protection from, 310
Fruits, growing specific, 217–39
Fruit trees and bushes, 201–15
    dwarf trees, 201, 205–7, **206,** 215
    feeding, 207
    making room for, 201–2, **203**
    natural orchard, 202–5
    pest and disease control, 204–5, **205**
    planting and care, 206–7, **207**
    pollination, 206, 212–13
    propagation, 208
        cuttings, 210–12, **211**
        grafting, 208–10, **210**
        layering, 212
        suckering, 212
    pruning, 204, 207
    rootstocks for sale, 209
    starting from seeds and stones, 208
    thinning, 213–15, **214**
    tree sizes, 205
Fungal disease, 204, 360
    of lawns, 339, 340
    sulfur sprays for, 357

G

Gaillardia aristata, 293, **293**
Gardening equipment and supply sources, 367
Garden planning, 47–55
Garlic, 126–27, **127,** 355
Garlic chives, 183, **183**
Gaylussacia baccata, 332
Geraniums, 279–81, **280**
Germination
    of seeds, 59–61
    succession planting and, 72
    temperatures, 52
Globe amaranth, 290
Gomphrena globosa, 290
Gooseberries, 250–52, **250, 251**
Gourds, 127–29, **128**
Grafting, for fruit trees, 208–10, **210**
Granite dust, 28
Grapes, 82, 225–30, **226, 228, 229**

Grass clippings, 15, 43
Grasses. *See* Lawns
Greenhouses, 89–92, **91**
Green lacewings, 349, **349**
Green manures. *See* Cover crops
Greensand, 28, 338
Groundcovers, 332, **333**

H

Hanging garden, 286–87
Hardening off
    cold frames and, 86–87, **86**
    transplants, 61, 63–64
Hardiness zones, 217, **366**
Hardpan, 11, 13, **13**
Hardwood cuttings, 211, **211**, 321
Harlequin bugs, 352–53
Hay, as mulch, 43
Heat, for germination, 60, **60**
Hedera helix (English ivy), 332, 333
Heirloom seed, saving, 55
Helichrysum bracteatum
    (strawflowers), 266, 288–89, **289**
Helicoverpa zea, 352
Hemerocallis spp., 295–96, **296**, 332
Herbs, 182–98
    aromatic, for bees, 192–93
    with edible seeds, 188–90
    flavorful, 183–188
    flowers planted among, 266
    perennial, fall transplant, 82
    pungent landscape, 194–97
    for tea, 190–91
    volunteer, 194
    winter protection, 198
Horseradish, 129–30, **129**, 352
Horticultural oil sprays, 356–57, **356**
Hotbeds, 88–89, **88**
Huckleberries, black, 332
Humic acids, 23
Humus, 5–6
Hybrid tea roses, **269**, 272–73, **272**
Hyssop, as trap plant, 353

I

Ice, for frost protection, 83–84
Impatiens, 281–83, **282**
Indoor growing period, 52
Insecticides, organic sprays and dusts,
    353–57
Insects. *See also* Pest control
    beneficial, 53–54, **53**, 349, **349**
    screen tent for, **79,** 80
    tree protection from, 310

Intensive planting, 74–75
Interplanting, 69–72, **71**
    incompatible plants, 72
    succession planting and, 66–67,
    68
Iron, in soil, 33
Ivy, English, 332, 333

J

Japanese beetles, 341, **341**, 353, 354
Jerusalem artichokes, 130–31, **130**
Johnny-jump-ups, 296, **296**

K

Kale, 81, 131–32, **131**
Kitchen waste, in compost, 15–16
Kohlrabi, 132–33, **132**
    as fall crop, 81, 83
    planted with beets, 69

L

Ladybugs, 349, **349**
Lathyrus odoratus, 290–92
Lavandula spp., 194–95, **194**
Lavender, 194–95, **194**
Lawns, 326–42
    all-season care, 336–38
    bluegrass and white clover,
        327–29, **329**
    choosing grasses, 330
    crabgrass control, 342, **342**
    pest and disease control, 338–41
    spring care, 334–36, **334, 335**
    starting and caring for, 326–27,
        328
    zoysia, 329, 331–34, **331**
Layering, 212, 230
Leaf bud cuttings, 211
Leaf mold, making, 22
Leaves
    in compost, 16, 20–22
    as mulch, 43
    plant spacing and, 67
    shredding, 21, **21**
Leeks, 110–11, 133–34, **134**
Lemon balm, 193, **193**
Lemon thyme, 187
Lemon verbena, 198
Lettuce, 134–38, **134**
    as fall crop, 81, 83
    types, 137
Lighting. *See also* Sunlight
    supplemental, in greenhouses, 90
Lilacs, 324–25, **325**

Lima beans, 99–100, **100**
Lime, amount to raise soil pH, *35*
Limonium sinuatum, 290
Loam soil, 3, **4**, 35
Lupines, 297, **297**
Lupinus subcarnosus, 275–76, **275**
Lysimachia nummularia, 333

M

Maggots, 353
Magnesium deficiency, **36**, 37
Manganese, in soil, 33
Manure, 24–27, **27**
    in compost, 16
    fertilizing program, 28
    green (*see* Cover crops)
    as mulch, 25
    nutrient composition, *25*
    phosphorus and, 28
    poultry, 26, 28
    storing, 26
Manure tea, 27
Maple trees, pruning, 309
Map
    of garden, 49
    USDA plant hardiness zones,
    366
Marigolds, 351
Matricaria recutita, 191, **191**
Matrix planting, **69**
Melissa officinalis, 193, **193**
Melting-out, 340
Mentha spp., 191, **191**
Mentha pulegium, 193, **193**
Mexican bean beetle, 350
Microorganisms
    compost and, 15, 18, 23
    in soil, 6, **7**
Mildew, 325, 360
Milky disease/spore, 341, 354–55
Minerals for plants, 28–29
Mint, 191, **191**, 351
Mirabilis jalapa, 278–79, **279**
Mist propagation for cuttings, 322
Monarda didyma, 192, **192**
Moneywort, 333
Mosaic virus, 360–61
Mother of thyme (creeping thyme),
    187, 198, 332
Mounding, 245
Mowing lawns, 336–37, 339, 341
Mulch(ing), 8, 42–44. *See also* Organic
    matter
        asparagus and, 97

Mulch(ing) *(continued)*
 benefits, 42–43, 44
 for bulbs, 268
 for disease control, 358
 laying on, 43–44, **43**
 manure as, 25
 materials, 43–44
 for orchard, 202
 for roses, 270, 274, **274**
 for shading soil, 79
 soil compaction and, 11, 12
 transplants and, 64
 for trees, 304–5, 317
 for warm-season crops, 44
 for weed control, 365
Mums, 293–95, **294**
Muskmelons, 138–40, **139**
Mustard greens, as fall crop, 83
Myrtle (vinca), 332

Ｎ

Nasturtiums, 283–84, **283,** 352
Nectarines, 231–34, **232**
Nematodes, 341, 351
Nepeta cataria, 190, **190**
Nitrogen
 alfalfa and, 40
 in compost, 16, 17, 21–22
 deficiency, 35–36, **36,** 44
 for lawns, 327, 338
 in manure, 25, *25,* 26
 in organic fertilizers, *29*
 in rock powders, *29*
NPK analysis
 of manure, *25, 26*
 of organic fertilizers, *29*
 of rock powders, *29*
Nutrients. *See also* NPK analysis; *specific nutrients*
 closely spaced plants and, 74
 for fruit trees, 207
 for trees, 305, 306–7

Ｏ

Ocimum basilicum, 186–87, **186**
Oil sprays, 356–57, **356**
Okra, 140–41, **140**
One-crop bedding, 66, **68**
Onions, 141–43, **142**
 with carrots and radishes, 69
 with carrots, parsnips, and leeks,
  110–11
 perennial, fall transplant, 82
 Spanish, 144, **144**

Open-pollinated crops, 55
Orchards, 202–5
Oregano, 183–84, **183**
Organic fertilizers
 animal and vegetable meals,
  27–28
 animal manures, 24–27
 commercial granular, 29
 for disease control, 358
 foliar feeding, 30–31
 for fruit trees, 207
 green manures, 38–41
 for lawns, 337–38, 339
 minerals for plants, 28–29
 soil compaction and, 12
 for trees, 302, 306–7, **306**
Organic matter, 5–9
 soil compaction and, 10
 for soil fertility, 74–75
Oriental poppy, 297–99, **298**
Origanum vulgare, 183–84, **183**
Oyster plant, 159

Ｐ

Pachysandra, 332
Paeonia, 299–300, **299**
Painted daisies, **294,** 295
Papaver orientale, 297–99, **298**
Parsley, 184–85, **184**
Parsnips, 110–11, 145–46, **145**
Peaches, 231–34, **232**
Peanuts, 146–47, **146**
Pears, 234–37
Pear trees, dwarf, 206
Peas, 80, 147–49, **148**
Pelargonium spp., 279–81, **280**
Pennyroyal, 193, **193**
Peonies, 299–300, **299**
Peppers, 71, **71,** 149–51, **150**
Perennials, 267, **267,** 292–300
Perlite in potting mix, 57, 58
Pest control, 345–57. *See also* Insects;
 specific plants
 for lawns, 340–41
 natural and nontoxic methods,
  345–50, **346, 349, 350, 353**
 for orchard, 204–5
 organic sprays and dusts,
  353–57, **356**
 with plants, 350–53
 resistant cultivars, 52
 wood ashes for, 33
Petroselinum crispum, 184–85, **184**
Petunias, planting seeds, **265**

pH of soil, 31–35, *35*
Phosphate
 in compost, 16
 for lawns, 338
 rock, 16, 28
Phosphorus
 for bulbs, 268
 in compost, 16
 deficiency, 36, **36**
 in manure, *25*
 in organic fertilizers, *29*
 in rock powders, *29*
 in soil, 33
Photosynthesis, 337, **337**
Pickleworms, 352
Pineapple sage, 186
Pine needles, as mulch, 43
Planning the plot, 47–55
Planting, 66–76
 double digging, 74–75, **75**
 French Intensive method, 74–75
 interplanting, 69–72
 raised bed gardening, 66–67, **68**
 saving space, 67, 69, *70*
 small-space benefits, 75–76
 succession, 72–74, **73**
Plant sources, 367
Plastic bags, for germination, 60, **60**
Plowpan (hardpan), 11, 13, **13**
Plums, 237–39, **238**
Pole beans, 100–102, **101**
Pollination, 55
 of fruit trees, 206, 212–13
 of squash, 168, **168**
Poppy, oriental, 297–99, **298**
Potash, 28–29
Potassium, 28–29
 for bulbs, 268
 deficiency, 36–37, **36**
 for lawns, 338
 in manure, *25*
 in organic fertilizers, *29*
 in rock powders, *29*
 in seaweed, 31
 in soil, 33
Potato beetles, 352, **353**
Potatoes, 151–54, **152**
Potting soil, 56–58
Powdery mildew, 360
Praying mantids, 349, **349**
Propagation mats, 60, **60**
Pruning
 conifers, 314–16, **315**
 fruit trees, 204, 207

shrubs, 308, 320, 322, 323, 324–25
trees, 307–9, **307**
Pumpkins, 154–55, **155**
Pyrethrin, 355–56

R

Radishes, 156–57, **156**
with carrots and onions, 69
as fall crop, 83
as trap plant, 353
Raised bed gardening, 66–76, **68**
Raking lawns, 334, **334**
Raspberries, 252–55, **253, 254**
fall transplant, 82
propagating, 212
Record keeping, 47–49, **48**
Repotting, 61
Rhubarb, 82, 157–58, **157**
Rock phosphate, 16, 28
Rock powders, 29, *29*
Rolling for lawns, 334
Rootbound plants, rescuing, 58
Root growth of seedlings, 58–59
Roots, plant spacing and, 67
Rosa spp. *See* Roses
Rosemary, 185, **185,** 198
Roses
feeding, mulching, and watering,
270, **274**
growing, 268–69
pests and diseases, 270–71
pruning, 272–73, **272,** 308
tomato leaf tea and, 270
types of garden roses, **269**
winterizing, 273–75, **274**
Rosmarinus officinalis (rosemary), 185,
185, 198
Rotation of crops. *See* Crop rotation
Rotenone, 355
Row covers, floating, **65**
Rows in the bed, 67, **68**
Rue, pests repelled by, 352
Rugosa rose, **269,** 271
Rutabagas, as fall crop, 83
Ryania, 356
Ryegrass, winter, 40

S

Sabadilla, 356
Sage, 185–86, **186,** 351
Salsify, 158–59, **158**
Salt hay, as mulch, 43
Salvia, 290
Salvia elegans, 186

Salvia farinacea, 290
Salvia officinalis, 185–86, **186**
Salvia sclarea, 186
Sandy soil, 3, **3, 4,** 5
lime and sulfur added to, *35*
for trees, 302
Sanitation, for pest control, 350
Savory, pests repelled by, 351
Sawdust, as mulch, 44
Screen tent for bugs, **79,** 80
Season extension, 77–92
cold frames, **86,** 86–87, **87**
dry-weather planting, 79–80
fall crops, 81–83
frost protection, 83–86
hotbeds, 88–89, **88**
planning fall garden, 80–81
shade in summer garden, 79
solar greenhouse, 89–92
for spinach, 164
tender fall crops, 80
Seaweed, 30, 31, 43
Seaweed spray, 205
Seed(s)
heirloom cultivars, saving, 55
quick start in hot weather, **78**
soil temperatures for planting, *52*
sources, 367
starting indoors (*see* Starting seed
indoors)
tiny, planting, **265**
Seed catalogs, ordering from, 49–52,
50, 54, *54*
Seedling mix, 57–58
Self-pollinated crops, 55
Shade
for seedlings, 64
in summer garden, 79
weed control and, 365
Shallots, 159–60, **160**
Shallow tilling, 363, 365
Shasta daisies, **294,** 295
Shrubs, 316–25
azaleas, 323–24, **323**
cuttings, 321
lilacs, 324–25, **325**
mist propagation, 322
planting, 318–20, **319**
pruning, 308, 320, 322, 323,
324–25
roses, 268–75
shopping for, 317
watering, 320
for wildlife, 317–18, **318**

Shungiku, 160–61, **161**
Silt soil, 3, **3, 4**
Site
for disease control, 358
for orchard, 202
Slime molds, 340
Snap beans, 100
Snapdragons, **265,** 284–85, **285,** 288
Snow mold, 340
Soaps, insecticidal, 355
Softwood cuttings, 212, 321
Soil
baked (sterilized), 57
basic information and care, 1–13
chemicals and, 9
color, 2–3
compaction, 9–10, **11**
determining and correcting
problems, 11–13
prevention, 10–11
shallow tilling and, 363, 365
in compost, 16
deficiencies, 35–37
disease control and, 358
for lawns, 334, 339–40
microorganisms in, 6, **7**
moisture, transplants and, 61, 64
for orchard, 202
organic fertilizers for, 24–31
organic matter and, 5–9
particle size and texture, 3, **3, 4,** 5
pH, 31–35, *35*
potting, 56–58
solarization, 365
testing, 34
for trees, 302, 303, **303**
weeds and, 364, **364**
Soil sampling tube, **11**
Soil-testing facilities, 367
Solar greenhouses, 89–92
Southernwood, 195–96, **195**
Soybeans, 161–62, **162**
Spacing for planting, 51, 67, 69, *70,*
75–76
Spanish onions, 144
Speedwell, creeping, 332
Spinach, 163–65, **163**
as fall crop, 83
Malabar and New Zealand,
165–67, **166**
Spring, greenhouses and, 92
Spring Meadow Farm
manure fertilizing program, 28
organic matter management, 8

Squash
summer, 167–69, **167, 168**
as trap crop, 352
winter, 170–71, **170**
Starting seed indoors, 56–65
germination, 59–61, **60**
hardening off, 61, 63–64
potting soil mix, 56–58
root system growth, 58–59
setting out seedlings, 61, 63,
64–65
seven steps, 60–61, **62,** 63
supplies for, **59**
Statice, 290
Straw, as mulch, 43
Strawberries, 256–60, **256, 257**
alpine, 260
fall transplant, 82
suckering, 212
Strawflowers, 266, 288–89, **289**
Succession planting, 72–74, **73**
interplanting and, 66–67, **68**
Suckering, 212
Sulfur
amount to raise soil pH, *35*
deficiency, 37
sprays, 357
Summer squash, 167–69, **167, 168**
Sunflowers, 266
Sunlight
blocking, 79
in greenhouses, 88–92
for seed starting, 61, 63, 64
Sunscald, 309–10, **310**
Superior oil sprays, 356–57, **356**
Sweet basil, 186–87, **186**
Sweet peas, 290–92, **291**
Swiss chard, 171–73, **172**

T

Tagetes minuta, 351
Tagetes patula, 351
Tanacetum crispum, 196, **196**
Tansy, 196, **196,** 351–52
T-bud grafting, 209–10, **210**
Temperature
for germination, 52
for hardening off, 63
of soil, for planting seeds, 52
Tender fall crops, 80
Thatch, 331, 338–39
Thinning fruit trees, 213–15, **214**

Thyme, 187–88, **187**
creeping (mother–of–thyme),
187, 198, 332
Thymus ✕ *citriodorus,* 187
Thymus praecox subsp. *arcticus*
(creeping thyme), 187, 198, 332
Thymus serpyllum, 332
Thymus vulgaris, 187, **187**
Tilling
manure, 26–27, **27**
shallow, 363, 365
soil compaction from, 9, 10
Tomato blossom drop, 174–75
Tomatoes, 173–77, **173**
Tomato fruitworms, 352
Tomato hornworms, 353
Tomato leaf tea, 270
Topsoil, organic matter in, 8
Transplanting, 61–65
in fall, 82
nutrient dip and, 105
Trap plants, 352–53
Tree roses, 275
Trees, 301–16
evergreens, 313–17, **315**
feeding formula, 306–7
flowering dogwood, 311–13,
312
fruit (*see* Fruit trees and bushes)
nutrients and growth, 305–6, **306**
protection, 309–11, **310**
pruning, 307–9, **307**
soil work, 302, 303, **303**
time to plant, 302–4
types, 302
wounds, 308–9
wrapping, staking, and
mulching, 304–5, **305**
Trellis
for cucumbers, **121,** 122
for grapes, 225–26, **226**
for peas, **148,** 149
Trichogramma wasp, 347, 349
Tropaeolum majus, 283–84, **283**
Turnips, 83, 177–79, **178**

U

USDA plant hardiness zone map, **366**

V

Vaccinium angustifolium, 332
Vegetable meals, 27–28

Vegetables
flowers planted among, 266
growing specific crops, 95–180
Vermiculite in potting mix, 57, 58
Veronica repens, 332
Vinca, 332
Viola tricolor, 296, **296**
Viruses, 360–61

W

Warm-weather crops, mulch and, 44
Water
in compost, 18–19, 22
for lawns, 335, 339
for roses, 270
for seed starting, 61
for shrubs, 320, 322
Watermelons, 179–80, **179**
Weeds
benefits, 362–63
in compost, 16, 20, 23, 362
control, 341, 362–65
crabgrass, 342
prevention, 365
shallow tilling, 363, 365
winter annuals, 363
indicating garden condition, 364,
364
mulch and, 43
White clover, bluegrass and, 327–29,
329
Wind
transplants and, 64
tree protection from, 310, 316
Winter
greenhouses and, 92
herbs and, 198
roses and, 273–75
trees and, 316–17
Winter ryegrass, as cover crop, 40
Winter squash, 170–71
Wood ashes, 32, 33–34
Wood chips, as mulch, 44
Wormwood, pests repelled by, 352

Y

Yarrow, 196–97, **197,** 351–52

Z

Zinc, in seaweed, 31
Zone map, USDA plant hardiness, **366**
Zoysia, 329, 331–34, **331**